Accounting theor

Volume 1

A textbook for colleges and schools of business administration

Roy B. Kester

Alpha Editions

This edition published in 2024

ISBN : 9789362991324

Design and Setting By
Alpha Editions
www.alphaedis.com
Email - info@alphaedis.com

As per information held with us this book is in Public Domain.
This book is a reproduction of an important historical work. Alpha Editions uses the best technology to reproduce historical work in the same manner it was first published to preserve its original nature. Any marks or number seen are left intentionally to preserve its true form.

VOLUME 1

PREFACE

The basic soundness of the method of instruction in Accounting developed in this book has received substantial demonstration throughout five years of test. The Introduction to the first edition contained the following statement regarding the development of the subject:

"The method of approach as given in this volume is perhaps not orthodox but it has seemed that the student, given an understanding of the purpose which the accounting records are to serve, will be able to make that record with real intelligence instead of by rule-of-thumb. Accordingly, the balance sheet and the profit and loss statement are presented first, as the goal towards which all record-keeping looks. The student is taught to analyze business facts and conditions from the very beginning. He is then led, step by step, through the use of non-technical terms, into the ledger, where he sees the way in which the data which he has been using are summarized. The books of original entry are next explained, and the method by which the information is classified as it is brought onto the books. Finally, the business papers and documents which constitute the source of all entries are described."

To quote again from the original Introduction: "The subject is developed in such a way that the student knowing something of bookkeeping has little or no advantage over the one without such knowledge. This book has been written for the use of students in our colleges and universities desiring a first course in accounting. It gives the scope of the work in accounting offered in the first year of the School of Business of Columbia University."

The method then advocated and used in a few institutions has become quite generally accepted. It has justified itself by the ease and extent to which students without any previous training in accounting have grasped the essentials of the subject. Experience with the book in the classroom, however, and changing ideas with regard to manner of presentation and sequence of material, have shown as desirable a rearrangement of some parts and an addition of new material in places. Accordingly, a systematic revision has been made.

The arrangement of the subject matter of the first portion of the book has been altered but slightly. The use and function of the balance sheet and profit and loss statement have been somewhat amplified. The working sheet has been introduced earlier than in the first edition to afford an easy summary of the period's results. It should later on be made a part of the regular work of summarization. The controlling account is also explained earlier so as to afford more practice in its use. The accounting features of the partnership and of the corporation are given continuous treatment. Here a new chapter has been added, which discusses certain features of the corporation not treated in the original book such as the issue and sale of treasury stock and of bonds, bond interest as related to premium and discount, sinking fund, sinking fund reserve, redemption of bonds, etc.

The material presented in the last quarter of the book deals with the interrelations of accounting, financial management, buying, and marketing. Thus the chapters dealing with the handling of cash, notes receivable and payable, cash discounts, and balance sheet valuation, treat of the relations between accounting and financial management. Several chapters at the end treat of some special methods of accounting practice and of the basic principles of single entry. In this portion of the book new chapters on balance sheet valuation and on buying have been added.

Entirely new problem material has been furnished, carefully graded and related so far as possible to the subject matter of the chapters of the text. For the convenience of the student this material is separated from the text, and grouped in three appendices. A few of the problems have been drawn from the examinations of various state boards and the regents of the University of the State of New York, and from other miscellaneous sources, to all of which acknowledgment is due. The author is indebted to Mr. George B. Kelley for assistance in building up a large part of the practice material. It need hardly be said that a fundamentally sound knowledge of accounting cannot be gained without ample practice work. Theory can never be sure of itself until put to the test of practice.

The author desires to acknowledge again his debt to the many friends whose counsel and aid counted so largely in the first writing of this book. In the revision he finds himself still further indebted to many instructors in all sections of the country for criticism and suggestion. He desires especially to express his appreciation of the active co-operation of his associates on the Columbia staff of instructors in First Year Accounting, in particular Miss Nina Miller and Messrs. Ralph T. Bickell and E. Gaylord Davis. In the actual work of revision Messrs. Eskholme Wade, John Jaffee, and Raymond Gatchell have given valuable assistance.

ROY B. KESTER

Columbia University,
New York City,
   July 22, 1922

CHAPTER I
BASIC RELATIONSHIPS—PROPRIETORSHIP

Records and Their Functions.—As far back as our knowledge reaches, records of some sort have been kept and used and they have frequently formed the basis on which our knowledge rests. In a broad sense a record may be defined as a written memorial, a register or history of events, a testimony. Even though the desire to make and hand on to the future a record of achievement is a deep-seated characteristic, record-making has seldom been an end in itself. Knowledge of what has been done has always been a starting point and a guide for future achievement. The longhand or narrative record is indispensable in some fields of knowledge; the shorthand or statistical record is equally necessary in others. The statistical method and accounting are, without question, most potent agencies for the advancement of human knowledge and for the control of human relationships. They provide the basis in fact on which judgments must largely rest. This book, therefore, may begin by sketching the relation of accounting to some of the larger fields of human endeavor—the economic organization of society and the law—to point out its place in the business unit and briefly state the basic function it performs therein.

The Business Unit.—To carry on its various activities, economic society has organized itself into numberless separate units or business organizations. These units are the means through which society operates, their ultimate purpose being the easy and efficient satisfaction of human economic wants. Individual business units, conducted as they are by members of society, are under the broad general supervision of society as a whole. This is evidenced everywhere by the laws, licenses, and regulations by which society attempts to regulate the activities of the individual for the larger interest of society as a whole. As business is conducted in most parts of the world, it is highly individualized rather than communized. There is a growing tendency, however, for society to exercise a larger control and supervision over all types of individual activity, particularly with a view to conserving the welfare of its members. The business unit is thus the medium through which society works to satisfy its economic wants.

Internal Organization of the Business Unit.—Society early found that only by means of a highly specialized division of its activities was it possible to satisfy without waste its rapidly increasing economic wants. Individual business units are thus organized for the purpose of carrying on some one or more of these greatly subdivided activities. Within itself the business unit is organized into departments or divisions for the efficient and thrifty handling of its work. The two large divisions in any business undertaking have to do with what the economist calls the production and exchange of wealth, that is, commodities, services, and so forth. In carrying on these activities of production and exchange it has usually been found desirable to segregate into separate departments certain major functions which are common both to production and to exchange. What the major departments may be depends very largely upon the size of the business unit, its relative complexity of organization, and to some extent on the individual ideas of its managers. Throughout the business world one notes, however, a quite general departmentization under the following heads:

- 1. Finance
- 2. Procurement or production
- 3. Marketing or distribution
- 4. Personnel
- 5. General administration

There are two main activities under the control of the finance division of a business: (a) the problem of original investment, including that of location and acquisition of a plant suitable for the conduct of a contemplated business; and (b) the problem of operating finance, that is, of providing the business with a fund of working capital for its efficient operation. The financing of purchases, sales, credits, operating expenses, and so forth, comprises a large part of the work of finance of an operating or going concern.

In the second of the major departments, that of procurement or production, one finds these activities: (a) the purchasing of the stock-in-trade to be dealt in, if the concern is a trading business; or (b) the manufacture of the stock-in-trade, if the concern is a manufacturing business.

In the department of marketing or distribution, the following activities center: (a) those having for their purpose the creation of a market or demand for the commodity dealt in—the sales organization, the advertising activities, and so forth; (b) the actual selling of the commodity; and (c) the transportation and delivery of the product.

In the personnel department are included the human relations between employer and employee. The hiring and training of the employee, his classification and rating, his welfare and promotion, are the major activities here.

The function of the department of general administration is in the main that of supervision and management of the business as a whole. The general manager must have a view of all of the activities of the business. He must see that the various departments through which its activities are carried on are properly correlated, that it is so organized that its departments function smoothly and efficiently in the performance of their several duties. A consideration of the means employed by the general manager for the proper performance of his duty indicates the place of accounting in the business unit.

Place of Accounting in Business.—In a small business where the owner and manager is in close and intimate contact with these several departments, or perhaps where he focuses all of them within himself, he has no need of special means of keeping himself informed concerning the activities of his assistants, nor does he require an elaborate system of records to indicate the condition and state of the business at any time. In large businesses, however, where the volume and complexity of the commercial activities make it impossible for the executive, on whom rest the responsibilities for the successful conduct of the business, to have an intimate personal knowledge of all phases of the business, it is very necessary that some means be employed for supplying him with this vital information. Two types of information are necessary to him: (1) information about the business unit itself, its activities and condition; and (2) information about general economic conditions in the country, and particularly about other businesses in the same line of activity as his own. It is the function of accounting to supply information of the first type; it is the chief purpose of statistics to supply information of the second type. The accounting department, therefore, deals largely with the internal activities of the business, while the statistical department provides knowledge of the external relations of the business. A proper control and management of business affairs cannot be exercised without the information supplied by both departments. In the accomplishment of its function to supply the internal information, the accounting department reaches out into all of the main departments indicated above for data from which to make its record of the various activities of the business unit.

Purpose of Accounts.—Accounts record the business history of a concern. Their main purpose is to secure information concerning the results of business activity and endeavor. The record required for this purpose can be condensed and made very brief, although the full history of every business comprises a multitude of transactions with a great mass of details. The whole scheme and method of account-keeping is designed chiefly to collect the detail and use it mainly for building up a summary which shall give in rapid review the entire record for the fiscal period.

Account-keeping is to the bookkeeper what shorthand is to the stenographer—an abbreviated method of making the record. The uses to which the records are put, however, differ radically. Stenography abbreviates the writing of the spoken word with a view to its transcription into longhand;

accounting records business transactions in abbreviated form with a view to summarizing them further so as to secure a bird's-eye view of the operations of the business as a whole and to use it in the formulation of administrative judgments and policies.

In a large business there are executive duties within each of the five main departments. Accounting must supply the information on which each departmental executive will base his judgments and policies. The student will see, therefore, that the accounting department brings together a record of the activities of each of the main departments of a business. He will see, too, how the final output or product of the accounting department must be a summarization and interpretation of these departmental activities in order to provide a basis for the various executives on which to formulate their judgments and business policies. Accounting is, therefore, a handmaiden of the executives in the conduct and management of the business. It is the purpose of this volume to develop the technique of the bookkeeping and accounting record and to indicate some of its uses in the management of business.

Relation of Accountancy to Economics.—Economics is sometimes defined as the science of wealth, by which is meant a body of classified knowledge relating to wealth in the aggregate. Under the present-day political and social system, the ownership of wealth is very largely private. Furthermore, the division of labor, as industry is now organized, has been carried to a very high degree. Because of these facts the present elaborate organizations for producing wealth have given rise to an urgent need for some effective means of keeping record of their activities.

The effort of every individual engaged in industry is to increase wealth. He labors to extract the raw materials from nature, to shape and mould them so as to supply the wants of his fellowmen. He then distributes them by means of markets and exchanges so as to secure the greatest possible returns for his effort. As competition becomes keener and the margin of return per unit of product becomes smaller, he has to increase his volume of business to secure the same amount of profit as when he did a lesser volume of business.

To produce goods it is necessary to use the saved wealth of former periods to pay the expenses of materials, labor, management, etc., of the present period. One must consume wealth to produce wealth. After his product is made, he must seek the best market for its exchange or sale. This necessitates the use of a complex system of transportation and communication. Finally, during the whole process of production and exchange the estimated returns from the article must be distributed among the several parties engaged in their creation. To make this distribution on the basis of estimated returns, gives rise to the need—the absolute necessity—of an accurate record of the costs of the activities and processes all along the line. The record, then, of the value of the rights and properties of the various parties to the production and distribution of wealth, as society is now organized for its economic well being, is the special field assigned to Accountancy as related to Economics.

Relation of Accountancy to Law.—The determination of the rights of the several parties to the creation, exchange, and ultimate consumption of a product is the field of Law, more particularly Business Law. The determination by means of its records of the value and extent of these rights is the province of Accountancy as related to Law. Accountancy is thus seen to be the handmaiden of both Economics and Law. None of them can progress far without the help of the other two. All being related to, and arising out of manifold human endeavors, their progress and development is dependent upon, and limited only by, the progress of these endeavors.

The Fundamental Problem of Accountancy.—The aim of all private businesses being the increase of wealth, the first problem of accountancy is to determine how much wealth is invested in a given enterprise and what ownership or proprietorship exists at given periods, so that by comparison the increases and decreases in the proprietorship may be known. When accurate information is obtained, an intelligent plan of action can be adopted to remedy such ills of the business as are shown and to increase any profitable line of activity. Accordingly, proprietorship and its changing values are the basic problems of accountancy as well as of business.

Definition of Terms.—Before proceeding to a definition or determination of proprietorship, it is necessary to understand what is meant by the terms "assets" and "liabilities." The root idea of the word "assets" is "sufficiency." Specifically, assets are the "entire property of all sorts, of a person, association, or corporation applicable or subject to the payment of debts." Similarly, the liabilities of a person, firm, or corporation are his or its pecuniary obligations or debts. Proprietorship is the difference between the value of the assets and the amount of the liabilities, and is defined and measured by the equation:

$$\text{Assets - Liabilities = Proprietorship}$$

This proprietorship equation is a basic formula. It is also written:

$$\text{Assets = Liabilities + Proprietorship}$$

It will thus be seen that proprietorship represents the equity of the owners of an enterprise in its assets. The assets are first applied in paying the claims of creditors of the business, and whatever of them remains belongs to the owners of the business.

Development of the Proprietorship Equation—The Balance Sheet.— To indicate the basis of the standard form of the proprietorship equation, several illustrations will be given. The equation is in its simplest form when it indicates proprietorship in a new business immediately after the owner has invested cash to provide the business with capital. For example, assume that on January 1, 19—, James T. Runyon starts business by investing $5,000 cash capital in the enterprise.

Here the proprietorship equation is:

$$\text{Assets (cash \$5,000)} = \text{Proprietorship (\$5,000)}$$

As yet there are no liabilities. However, in order to carry on his business, Runyon must purchase a stock of merchandise and equipment for his store. Accordingly, he purchases store furniture and fixtures from Lowell Brothers for $500, of which he pays $250 in cash, and owes the balance. He also buys a stock of groceries for $2,500 from Reid Murdock & Co. on 10 days' time. He now has more assets than the original $5,000 cash, but he has become indebted for the additional amount, so that the amount of his proprietorship has not changed—as is shown by the following equation, somewhat more complex than the first:

ASSETS		- LIABILITIES		= PROPRIETORSHIP
Cash	$4,750	Lowell Bros. Claim	$ 250	
Furniture	500			
Merchandise	2,500	Reid Murdock Claim	2,500	
	$7,750	-	$2,750	=$5,000

Runyon now begins operations and after six months finds that his activities have comprised the purchase of delivery equipment for $300 cash; sale of goods amounting to $6,000; the payment of $1,000 cash for rent, clerk hire, and advertising; and sundry purchases of stock-in-trade and other items as needed. As a result he now has $1,000 cash on hand; customers owe him $3,000; his stock of goods still on hand is worth $2,100; he owes creditors $1,000 for goods bought and his clerks $50 for services rendered.

It is readily seen that as the number of assets and liabilities increases, the method of showing them that was used above becomes awkward and cumbersome; therefore, still using the equation, we make the following vertical tabulation to determine and show proprietorship:

Assets

Cash	$1,000.00
Customers	3,000.00
Merchandise	2,100.00
Furniture	500.00
Delivery Equipment	300.00
Total Assets	$6,900.00

Liabilities

Creditors for Merchandise	$1,000.00
Clerks for Services	50.00
Total Liabilities	1,050.00

Proprietorship

Capital	$5,850.00

This method of expressing the proprietorship equation is called a "Balance Sheet," or "Financial Statement."

Further analysis of the above information discloses the amount of Runyon's purchases and of his payments to creditors. Taking the transactions involving cash, we find that he had $5,000 to start with and received $3,000 from sales, or $8,000 in all. He bought furniture and delivery equipment for $800, and paid expenses of $1,000, in all $1,800. There is therefore a balance of $6,200 to be accounted for. $1,000 cash is still on hand, so that he must have paid creditors $5,200. Since he still owes creditors $1,000 for goods bought, his purchases must have been in all $6,200.

The ability to make accounting statements and to analyze accounting data for various purposes constitutes a very important part of the equipment of the accountant.

CHAPTER II
ASSETS, LIABILITIES, AND CAPITAL

Before discussing the form and content of the balance sheet and some of its major uses, the chief classes of assets, liabilities, and proprietorship or capital will be explained so that the student will have an intelligent notion of what is meant by each asset, liability, and capital item.

Kinds of Assets.—Accounting terms are not wholly standard. An account title is often used in one business to include items not mentioned under that title in another business. One finds also terms and titles peculiar to particular businesses. However, there is a tendency towards a standardization of the terms used in balance sheets. It is the purpose here to present and explain those which are common to practically all businesses. These include the asset titles Cash, Notes Receivable, Accounts Receivable, Merchandise, Investments, Deferred Charges or Expense Assets, Furniture and Fixtures, Delivery Equipment, Buildings, and Land.

CASH. Cash includes all kinds of money and usually whatever serves as a medium of exchange, which is in the possession or control of the business—deposits in banks, moneys in the safe and cash drawers, and sometimes funds in the possession of agents. Checks received in the regular course of business and not yet deposited in the bank are usually classified as cash.

NOTES RECEIVABLE. The formal promises to pay, made by others for debts owed the business, are classified under the general title Notes Receivable. Time drafts drawn on the debtors of the business and accepted by them may be included under this title, although they are sometimes shown under a separate title, such as Acceptances Receivable. This is particularly true when the acceptances are trade acceptances. It will be seen later that the promissory note has a somewhat different legal status from the open account claim against a debtor, and should therefore be classified under such title as will indicate the exact nature of the item.

ACCOUNTS RECEIVABLE. These usually represent the claims of the business against its trade customers for goods sold on open account and not paid for. The term is, however, broader than this, being sometimes used—although the practice is to be deplored—to include all claims against debtors except those which are in the form of notes.

MERCHANDISE. This asset represents the stock-in-trade in which the business deals. It is of course a sort of revolving asset, that is, merchandise is purchased and sold continuously, so that the stock-in-trade is constantly being turned over. The rate of turnover is very important, as will later be seen.

INVESTMENTS. This asset represents the stocks and bonds of other companies, municipalities, school districts, and so forth, owned by the business. As a usual thing there are seasons of the year when the cash funds of a business are built up and lie idle in the bank unless they are invested in securities of some sort. These securities can be reconverted into cash when the business requires a larger fund of cash.

DEFERRED CHARGES. Certain types of expenditure are necessary in every business to secure operating supplies. Fuel must be purchased for heating and power purposes; brooms, oil, waste, and other similar supplies are needed for cleaning and maintaining the business plant; stationery, stamps, wrapping paper, twine, cartons, packing materials, and so forth must always be on hand; insurance policies giving protection against fire are usually purchased for from one to three years and so are seldom completely used up at any given date. All items of this sort, necessary for the operation of the business but not dealt in as stock-in-trade, are called "expense assets." The portions of these assets on hand at a given time, the use of which will be deferred to a later period, are classified as "deferred charges."

FURNITURE AND FIXTURES. A business plant must be equipped with furniture and fixtures suitable for the display of the stock-in-trade, for the accommodation of customers, for the care and protection of the necessary records of the business, for the efficient performance of duties by the employees, and for other similar purposes. Assets of this type which are not a permanent part of the business plant but are removable should the business desire to change location, are listed under the title of Furniture and Fixtures. This may be subdivided to suit conditions. Sometimes several titles—Store Furniture and Fixtures, Office Furniture and Fixtures, Factory Furniture and Fixtures, Machinery and Tools—are used.

DELIVERY EQUIPMENT. If a business delivers its commodities it will usually have its own delivery equipment. This may comprise horses, wagons, harness, automobile trucks, and so forth. The delivery equipment may be used for both inbound and outbound deliveries.

BUILDINGS. All buildings owned by the business, whether used for business purposes or not, will usually be classified under the asset title Buildings. Store, office, factory, warehouses, residences owned and rented to employees—all assets of this type are to be listed here.

LAND. This item represents land—city lots, plant sites, and so forth—owned in fee simple or subject to mortgage. Sometimes when a plot of land is leased for a term of years and a lump sum payment made at the beginning of the lease, the asset may be included either under the title Land, or under the broader title Land and Leaseholds.

Kinds of Liabilities.—Just as with assets, there is not entire uniformity in terminology for the various classes of liabilities. The more common types of items met with are: Notes Payable, Accounts Payable, Accrued Expenses, Mortgages Payable, Bonds Payable, and so forth.

NOTES PAYABLE. These represent the formal promises to pay, signed by the business or its owners. They represent the formal claims of others, that is, creditors, against the business. Just as with notes receivable, it is sometimes desirable to make a more distinct classification of notes payable. In such cases the titles Acceptances Payable, Trade Acceptances Payable, Long-Term Notes Payable, etc., are used.

ACCOUNTS PAYABLE. Under this title are listed the liabilities to creditors on open account, as distinguished from those formally acknowledged by a written promise to pay. These include obligations to trade creditors for merchandise, supplies, equipment, and property of almost any kind purchased for use by the business. In a broad sense an account payable includes any item for which the business is liable.

ACCRUED EXPENSES. Accrued Expenses represent usually the accumulating but unpaid claims against the business for service rendered it, as distinguished from the Accounts Payable, which usually represent purchases of an asset of one kind or another. Thus the amounts due at a given time to employees for work done since the last date of payment of their wages, salaries, or commissions, to the landowner for the rent of leased premises, to lenders for interest on moneys borrowed, are items properly to be listed under this title.

MORTGAGES PAYABLE. These represent the claims of creditors against particular properties owned by the business but against which the creditors have been given a lien or preferred claim as security for the borrowed or unpaid amount. Mortgages are evidenced by a formal legal document and are usually recorded in the county clerk's office.

BONDS PAYABLE. These are a type of long-term mortgage which is split into lots of more or less standard amount and so made available to a larger number of holders than is usually the case with the ordinary mortgage payable. This type of liability is limited almost exclusively to corporations.

The student should realize that usually the owner or owners of a business enterprise have both assets and liabilities other than those employed in the business. These personal properties and obligations of the owners are not to be taken into account when showing the proprietorship of a business unit or enterprise. They are to be considered only in showing the total proprietorship of any individual owner, when of course all of his properties, both inside and outside of the business, must be listed.

Kinds of Proprietorship.—Proprietorship, called also Net Worth, is shown under such titles as Capital, Investment, Capital Stock, Surplus, Undivided Profits, Reserves, and so forth. The title used depends largely on the type of organization under which the business is operated.

CAPITAL. Under this title is shown the amount of the investment of each owner in a single proprietorship or partnership business. To show each owner's share in the ownership the title Capital is preceded by his name. Illustration of this is given on pages 19 and 20.

INVESTMENT. This title usually is synonymous with capital. Sometimes it is used to indicate the amount of original investment in the business as distinguished from the present investment.

CAPITAL STOCK. Under this title is indicated the sum total of the portions of net worth owned by the shareholders as evidenced by stock certificates and subject to their individual control. On page 20 is given an explanation of the way in which the proprietorship or net worth of a corporation may be composed of two (or more) parts: (1) the capital paid in by the owners; and (2) the capital, representing profits made but not distributed to the owners. While capital stock usually represents the capital contributed by the owners, it sometimes arises from other sources, such as the distribution of a stock dividend; but the portion of the net worth owned and controlled individually by the owners is the capital stock.

SURPLUS. In a corporation this represents the second portion of the net worth, as indicated in the preceding section. Surplus is sometimes defined as the excess of the net worth over the capital stock. In other words, it is the difference between the assets and the sum of the liabilities and the capital stock.

UNDIVIDED PROFITS. This is a term used chiefly in financial institutions to indicate the portion of the net profits concerning the disposal of which no action has been taken.

RESERVES. Under this title are included whatever portions of the surplus are set aside or reserved for specific purposes.

Where Surplus, Undivided Profits, and Reserves appear as parts of Net Worth, they together represent the difference between Net Worth and Capital Stock. The reason for the careful segregation of these items from the Capital Stock is given in the explanation of the corporate form of organization, on page 20.

Types of Business Organization.—Before proceeding with a discussion of proprietorship as it appears on the balance sheet, the three general types of business organization will be treated briefly, because the manner of indicating proprietorship is dependent to a certain extent on the type of organization. These types are: (1) the single or sole proprietorship, (2) the partnership, and (3) the corporation.

The Single Proprietorship.—The simplest form of business enterprise is that conducted by a single proprietor. This form is well adapted to businesses where the capital necessary for efficient production is small, where the processes are simple and capable of being handled by the average individual, and where the risks are slight. Very few legal obstacles are placed in the way of the individual desiring to go into business for himself, nor is a great deal required of him. In some cases registration and a license are necessary. The observance of the general laws, concerning the payment of taxes and of local regulations concerning disease and fire is all that is usually expected. Subject to the general restrictions which ordinary business acumen and foresight impose, one can enter practically any field of enterprise, as a single proprietor, have entire freedom and privacy in the conduct of his business, and share with none the results of his endeavor.

On the other hand, these conditions oftentimes prove to be decided disadvantages. As industry is at present organized, many fields of activity demanding large capital and many kinds of technical knowledge, are closed to the single proprietor. Freedom of action carries with it sole responsibility, and oftentimes the counsel and advice of others would prevent the disasters which sometimes overtake the single owner of a business.

The Partnership.—A partnership is "a contract of two or more legally competent persons to combine their money, property, skill, and labor, or some or all of them, for the prosecution of some lawful business and to divide the profits and bear the losses in certain proportions." There are different kinds of partnerships, as will later be shown, but the essence of each from the point of view of a working organization is mutual agency, each partner being the agent of the others, and, within the limitations of the partnership agreement, capable of acting as a principal for the firm. The partnership is subject to practically as few restrictions as the individual. In some localities, to secure the right to sue and be sued in the firm name, it is necessary to file in a public office a brief statement of the firm name and the names of its members.

The chief advantages of the partnership are larger capital and therefore access to fields closed to the individual; the combining of the business wisdom, skill, and knowledge of several individuals; the subdivision of duties and therefore the opportunity for specialization. While in the view of the business community the partnership is an entity or a business unit, it is not so in the sight of the law, each member of the firm being held liable to creditors for the entire debts of the partnership as if it were his sole business.

If any one member has to pay the firm debts, he has a claim against his copartners for contribution.

Some of the disadvantages of this type of organization are the possibility of friction among the partners and consequent delay of action; the extension to the firm of credit based not on the firm property but rather on the total property of the members, and the consequent liability of each partner and his entire private fortune for the debts of the firm.

It is important to note that the partnership agreement should be very carefully drawn to cover in detail the relations of the partners, their duties and their rights, particularly as to their shares in the profits or losses of the firm.

The Corporation.—The corporate type of business organization is distinguished from the other types discussed:

1. By the freedom of each owner from the personal liability for the debts of the business to any greater extent than his stock interest in the business, though frequently in financial corporations, and in a few states for all corporations, his liability is double that stated.

2. By each share of ownership being evidenced by a formal document called a certificate of stock.

3. By each owner being allowed a voice in the affairs of the business only to the extent of his stock ownership therein.

4. By the necessity of securing from the proper authorities permission to do business.

5. By the necessity of complying strictly with the terms of this permit and submitting to certain requirements such as the filing of annual reports, payment of special taxes, and the like.

The owners of a corporation, or its stockholders as they are called, conduct the business through a board of directors which they elect for that purpose and they review its management periodically, usually annually. In this way they exercise indirect supervision over the business. This remoteness of personal interest and supervision has been somewhat overcome by electing to the board only those largely interested in the business, and by retaining on the board those whose ability as managers has been tried and proved. The board usually hires and delegates to others the active management of affairs.

The advantages of the corporate form of organization are: (1) it limits the liability of its owners; (2) it lends itself well to accumulation of the large funds of capital necessary for the promotion of large-scale enterprises; and (3) it secures through its board of directors a convenient and effective means of centralized control and management.

Showing the Proprietorship of These Types.—The methods of showing in the balance sheet the proprietorship for these three types of organization differ somewhat. The title under which proprietorship is listed is Capital. In a single proprietorship such title is preceded by the proprietor's name, as shown in the following illustration:

Assets

Cash	$2,000.00	
Accounts Receivable	5,000.00	
Merchandise	3,000.00	
Furniture and Fixtures	500.00	
Total Assets		$10,500.00

Liabilities

Accounts Payable	$4,450.00	
Due Clerk	50.00	
Total Liabilities		4,500.00

Proprietorship

James Runyon, Capital	$ 6,000.00

In a partnership the capital is not shown in one item, each partner's interest being stated separately, thus:

Assets

Cash	$ 2,500.00	
Accounts Receivable	10,250.00	
Merchandise	8,750.00	
Furniture and Fixtures	625.00	
Total Assets		$ 22,125.00

Liabilities

Notes Payable	$ 1,660.00

Accounts Payable	5,465.00	
Total Liabilities		7,125.00

Proprietorship

Represented by:

James Runyon, Capital	$ 8,000.00	
Philip Adams, Capital	7,000.00	$ 15,000.00

In a corporation, proprietorship is shown by the aggregate of the outstanding shares of stock, which are valued at a fixed par, or cost, under the single title Capital Stock, and if the proprietorship is greater than that indicated under this title, the excess is listed separately under the title Surplus or some of the other proprietorship titles already explained. This method of showing proprietorship is prescribed by law and is an effort to inform creditors, or those who may become creditors, that the corporation has observed the legal requirement not to distribute to stockholders any of its original capital. Hence, the capital stock of the corporation must be listed separately from the other items of proprietorship. Any changes in proprietorship during the life of the corporation are taken care of under these other titles, somewhat as illustrated below.

Assets

Cash	$ 1,850.48	
Notes Receivable	1,645.65	
Accounts Receivable	15,285.35	
Merchandise	10,045.94	
Supplies	1,145.37	
Furniture and Fixtures	1,636.97	
Delivery Equipment	1,427.50	
Buildings	8,000.00	
Land	2,000.00	
Total Assets		$ 43,037.26

Liabilities

Accounts Payable	$ 5,762.26

Notes Payable	4,250.00	
Salaries Due but Unpaid	25.00	
Mortgage on Land and Buildings	3,000.00	
Total Liabilities		13,037.26

Proprietorship

  Represented by:

Capital Stock	$ 25,000.00	
Surplus	5,000.00	$ 30,000.00

CHAPTER III
THE BALANCE SHEET

Purpose and Use.—The balance sheet of a business is designed to show its financial condition at a given time. As previously illustrated, it marshals the assets in one list or schedule, and the liabilities in another. The difference between the totals of the two schedules gives the present or net worth of the business. In compiling a balance sheet it is not sufficient to give simply the figures of proprietorship or net worth; schedules of assets and liabilities must be drawn up to show the items making up that net worth. From the viewpoint of a prospective investor or purchaser, a banker to whom the business has applied for a loan, or a concern considering the advisability of extending it credit on a bill of goods, it makes all the difference in the world to know that with a net value of $10,000 the business has assets of $15,000 and liabilities of $5,000; or to know that its assets are $260,000 and its liabilities $250,000.

The ratio of total assets to total liabilities is almost as important information to an investor, purchaser, banker, or creditor as is the character of the assets and liabilities. If the assets are in properties for which there is not a ready market and the liabilities are claims which mature soon and will have to be met, the situation is unfavorable. If there are large values invested in easily salable assets; if there is a large balance of cash on hand after meeting current claims and providing for those which will soon mature; if other liabilities are of a more permanent nature, such as mortgages or long-time notes not requiring immediate attention—the situation may show evidence of too large a capital, or of inefficient management as indicated by the failure to invest a part of the surplus cash in properties from which some return might be secured.

Form and Content.—Questions of the kind raised above are not usually capable of definite answer from the information contained on the balance sheet alone. Oftentimes information as to the volume of business done, future plans for expansion or contraction of business operations, and so forth, is needed in addition to that supplied by the balance sheet. Of immediate interest to us, however, is the information contained in the balance sheet. Here two main problems are met: that relating to the form of the balance sheet, and that concerned with the content of the balance sheet.

By form of the balance sheet is meant its physical appearance—the arrangement and classification of its items. The form is not standard. In this country there are few legal regulations governing the way in which the records of a business are to be kept or its reports are to be made. Some efforts have been made, however, to establish a more or less standard form of balance sheet and to secure the use of standard titles in the balance sheet so that wherever found those titles can be relied upon to mean one and only one thing. Because balance sheets are not always drawn up for similar purposes, such regulations should not be too inflexible. The form of any business statement or report should always have regard to the purposes it is to serve. Standardization of form is desirable within this limitation.

By content of the balance sheet is meant the items that are admitted to it and the basis of their valuation.

These two problems of the balance sheet—form and content—are fundamental and will be briefly considered here.

Titles—Main and Group.—Instead of "Balance Sheet," other terms are used as names for the statement itself, such as "Financial Statement," "Statement of Resources and Liabilities," "Statement of Assets and Liabilities." Within the statement, Resources is an alternative title for Assets; and Net Worth, Present Worth, and Net Assets, for Proprietorship. For the present, use of the terminology previously employed will be continued, with the substitution, however, of the term Net Worth for Proprietorship.

The title of a statement should be full; it should include the name of the business enterprise and date, and should appear somewhat as follows:

SHONGOOD & GOODWELL
BALANCE SHEET
December 31, 19—

As stated, this should be followed by the schedules of Assets, Liabilities, and Net Worth. Since the statement is a formal one, due regard should be had for its general appearance, which should be neat and attractive. Further consideration will be given to some of these features in Chapters XXVI and XXVII.

Classification and Arrangement.—As indicated above, the balance sheet is used to picture the financial condition of a business at a given time. Some of the questions which arise in determining the financial condition of a business have already been mentioned. The chief use to which a balance sheet is put is the determination of the solvency of the business for purposes of getting credit extensions. By solvency is meant the ability of the business to pay its debts when due. Regardless of how great the excess of assets over liabilities is, if it is tied up in assets which cannot be used for the payment of debts, the creditors of the business will become impatient and may ask a court to take the control of the business away from its owners and place it in the hands of a representative of the court and the creditors, who will conduct the business for the purpose of converting assets into cash to a sufficient extent to pay all debts.

A balance sheet should therefore be so arranged that the condition of the business, viewed from the standpoint of its ability to pay its debts, will be clearly and easily determinable. Cash is usually the only medium used for the payment of debts. In the regular course of business, debts are incurred which come due at different dates. Hence it is not necessary to have on hand at a given time cash sufficient to pay all of the debts of the business. Certain classes of debts will not wait. The sums owed employees for services must usually be paid when due. The debt to the government for taxes, to the public service company for heat, light, and power, to the landlord for rent, to the bank for money borrowed—all these debts must usually be paid immediately as they come due.

The cycle of business operation includes the purchase of merchandise, the payment of operating expenses, and the conversion of merchandise into cash through sale, either directly, as when the sale is for cash, or indirectly as when credit is extended a customer and cash is later collected from him. This cycle or turnover of merchandise recurs constantly in the management of the financial affairs of a business. It is necessary so to order the buying and selling of goods and the collection of accounts from customers that there will be on hand at all times sufficient cash to pay the expenses of operating the business and the debts contracted in the purchase of merchandise. This is the vital and fundamental problem of the business executive. In the solution of that problem it may sometimes be necessary to borrow funds from the bank. Before lending money, the banker assures himself that the business will be in a position to repay the borrowed money when due.

The balance sheet, accordingly, should be so arranged that the condition of the business as related to its ability to pay its debts will be apparent. This requires a classification or marshaling of the assets which are concerned in the trading cycle on the one side, and the liabilities which must be assumed in conducting the business during the trading cycle, on the other.

At the head of the list of assets is the item Cash, the most liquid of all, as it can be used directly for the payment of debts. Following Cash come in order Notes Receivable, which, with proper indorsement, can be sold to the banker and converted into cash almost immediately; Accounts Receivable, which represent the claims against customers for merchandise sold and which are collectible within the term of credit extended to the customer; and finally, the Merchandise on Hand, which must be sold either for cash or on credit and then converted into cash by the collection of the outstanding accounts. Sometimes, also, there is included in this group the asset Investments, representing stocks and bonds of other companies which can be converted into cash by sale on a stock exchange. On such securities, and also on the notes receivable, there is usually at the date of the balance sheet some interest which has accrued and may not yet be collectible. It is customary to include the amount of this interest receivable in the same group with the assets from which it arises.

This group of assets, comprising Cash, Notes and Accounts Receivable, Merchandise, and so forth, is called the group of Current Assets. Asset items are classified as current if conversion into cash is expected within three to six months. These are the assets to which the current creditors of the business will have to look for the payment of their claims.

The claims of current creditors are usually included under the titles Notes Payable, Accounts Payable, and Accrued or Unpaid Expenses. The classification of a creditor in the current liability group is usually determined on a time basis. Thus, all debts that will have to be met within six months' or one year's time from the date of the balance sheet are usually classed as Current Liabilities.

The excess of current assets over current liabilities is called the working capital of the business; that is, an amount of the current assets equal to the current liabilities will have to be used for the payment of these debts, leaving the excess or difference free for use within the business. While it is not possible to determine, without considering all the circumstances in a given case, how large this working capital should be, the standard rule-of-thumb is that it should equal the amount of the current liabilities. It will thus be seen that the standard ratio of current assets to current liabilities is two to one. The solvency of a given business is always judged by a comparison of the current asset group with the current liability group.

The next main group of assets is given the title Deferred Charges. The content of this item was explained on page 12. Thus, if a management has paid some of its expense bills in advance—rent for January paid during December, for example—when showing its financial condition as at the end of December it is proper and necessary, in order to make an accurate showing, that all such prepaid expenses be listed as assets; for, had the payment not been made until the service which it purchased had been used up, the asset cash would have been larger by the amount of the prepaid expenses.

Similarly, with regard to the Accrued Expenses mentioned on page 14, whatever expenses have been incurred that properly belong to the past period, such as wages due but unpaid, are liabilities; for the cash would be smaller by the amount of such postponed or accrued items had the claims been met during the period. The close relationship of both deferred charges and accrued expenses to cash is thus apparent—the one as an indirect addition to the cash, the other as an indirect deduction from or claim against cash. Accordingly, deferred charges are shown on the balance sheet immediately following the group of current assets, whereas accrued expenses are listed with the current liabilities as noted above.

The next group of assets is called Fixed Assets. Under this title are listed those assets which are used for carrying on the business but are not bought for the purpose of being resold. A certain amount of capital must be invested in the physical business plant. Furniture and fixtures, delivery equipment, buildings, land, machinery and tools, and so forth, must be purchased before the business can commence operating. It is assets of this type that comprise the class of fixed assets. There is a corresponding group among the liabilities which are known as Fixed or Long-Term Liabilities. All debts maturing a year or more after the date of the balance sheet are classed as fixed liabilities. As examples of this class, we have long-term notes payable, mortgages payable, bonds payable, and so forth.

The difference between the fixed assets and the fixed liabilities indicates the amount of owner's capital which has been invested in the business plant.

The final group of assets is called simply Other Assets, and includes all assets which cannot be classified in any other groups, such as good-will, patents, trade-marks, accounts and notes receivable having a credit term longer than six months, and other similar items. If there are any liabilities not capable of classification in the two groups of liabilities given above, they may be put in a group called Other Liabilities.

For the purpose of an easy showing of these various groups and their titles, it is customary to list the amounts of the several detailed items of each group in an inner money column, and to extend the total into the adjoining money column on the line of the last item in the group. A similar arrangement is made of the groups of liabilities so that not only the items in the various groups but the group totals as well are available. The totals of the various groups give the grand totals for the assets and the liabilities respectively.

The balance sheet as now classified and arranged provides first a formal title, giving the name of the business and the date of the balance sheet; then the assets, under which appear the groups Current Assets, Deferred Charges, Fixed Assets, and Other Assets; under the liabilities appear the groups Current Liabilities, Fixed Liabilities, and Other Liabilities. The showing of Proprietorship or Net Worth under the three different kinds of ownership has already been set forth. The illustration on page 31 shows a typical form of classified balance sheet. This should be studied carefully, as it is the type which will be used hereafter.

The Problem of Content.—The form of the balance sheet serves the purpose of making easily available the information contained in the balance sheet. Form is of little value unless the content is accurate. What a balance sheet contains is, after all, far more important than its form. The problem of content comprises a consideration of two points: (1) the proper inclusion of all items, both assets and liabilities, belonging in the balance sheet; and (2) the correct valuation of the items so included.

With regard to the first, it may be said briefly that care must be exercised to see that all assets belonging to the business and having value, and that all claims against the business of whatever nature, are included.

Assuming that a given balance sheet contains a list of *all* the assets and *all* the liabilities, the further problem of the proper valuation of these items must be considered. A balance sheet in which the title Cash includes counterfeit bills, N. G. (that is, uncollectible) checks and other similar items, would not be considered a reliable balance sheet. Similarly, the basis for the valuation of each of the asset items must be investigated and determined correct before the balance sheet may be considered to represent the true financial condition of the business. It is the experience of every business that it cannot collect all of the credits extended to customers. Regardless of how carefully credit is granted, it will be found that some customers do not pay their debts. Accounts and notes receivable must, accordingly, be valued with a proper consideration for the estimated amount of the uncollectible portion. The stock of merchandise on hand must be valued according to the standard formula, at cost or market, whichever is the lower. The deferred charges group of assets will show the value of the unconsumed portions of the assets purchased, with due regard to the time element. Thus, a three-year insurance policy purchased at the beginning of the year will at the close of the year be valued at two-thirds of its original cost. The fixed asset group will be valued at cost less depreciation, which represents the amount of the loss in value of the assets due to wear and tear, lapse of time, and obsolescence.

In determining liabilities, providing they have all been included, there is not the danger of an understatement, because their amount is subject to verification on the basis of the creditors' claims. For obvious reasons the liabilities are seldom overstated.

General Principles Governing Form and Content.—In drawing up a balance sheet, the form must be flexible enough to meet whatever requirements for information may be placed upon it. Thus, a balance sheet to be presented to the banker as the basis of a loan should be carefully classified so as to show clearly the financial condition, and sufficient detail should be given to indicate the basis used in valuing the various items. A balance sheet drawn up for publication may, on the other hand, contain less detailed information and less attention need be given to its form. A balance sheet drawn up for use within the business itself may well contain very full information and its form should be such as will accurately portray the status of affairs. A balance sheet which shows on its face that cognizance is taken of uncollectible accounts and of the loss in fixed assets due to depreciation, is much more valuable as a financial statement than one lacking that information, provided of course it is to be used to indicate that consideration has been taken of those elements. Excepting for the general remark that regard must always be had to the purpose for which the balance sheet is drawn up, no hard-and-fast rule can be laid down in the matter of the relative fullness of detail with which it should be made.

Illustration. To illustrate the features of the balance sheet discussed in this chapter, the following statement showing the financial condition of the partnership of Jackson & Edwards is given:

JACKSON & EDWARDS
BALANCE SHEET JUNE 30, 19—

Assets

Current Assets:			
Cash		$ 2,365.00	
Accounts Receivable	$8,500.00		
Less—Reserve for Doubtful Accounts	170.00	8,330.00	
Merchandise		10,425.00	$21,120.00
Deferred Charges:			
License Fees Paid in Advance		$ 175.00	
Unexpired Insurance		75.00	
Supplies		80.00	330.00
Fixed Assets:			
Furniture and Fixtures	$ 750.00		
Less—Reserve for Depreciation	75.00	$ 675.00	
Buildings	$9,680.00		
Less—Reserve for Depreciation	242.00	9,438.00	
Land		2,500.00	12,613.00
Total Assets			$34,063.00

Liabilities

Current Liabilities:

Notes Payable	$2,500.00	
Accounts Payable	6,750.00	
Wages Accrued	250.00	
Interest Accrued	75.00	$ 9,575.00

Fixed Liabilities:

Mortgage on Land and Buildings	2,500.00	
Total Liabilities		12,075.00

Net Worth

Represented by:

S. J. Jackson, Capital	$10,267.00	
P. R. Edwards, Capital	11,721.00	$21,988.00

CHAPTER IV
THE COMPARATIVE BALANCE SHEET

Comparison of Net Worths.—The aim of every business enterprise is to increase its net worth. If James Runyon at the beginning of the year is worth $5,000 and at its close $7,500, it is evident that he has increased his wealth by $2,500. Very little information is given him or anyone else as to the manner in which the increase took place, except that it came about in the ordinary course of business. No criterion is given by which to compare effort with result. An increase of $2,500 may or may not be commensurate with the labor expended in effecting it. However, since a business is not likely to remain stationary, there is a degree of satisfaction in knowing merely the extent of the change in its net worth. The taking of an inventory, the appraising of the value of the assets from time to time, and the setting of the liabilities for the same dates over against them, is the method of determining the corresponding net worths. A comparison of these net worths shows their increase or decrease during the period. A further analysis of the individual items may be made. A comparison of each asset at the beginning of the period with its value at the end of the period, shows the increase or decrease in that item. A similar comparison of each liability item brings out the increase or decrease during the period.

How a Gain or Loss May Be Evidenced.—During a period a gain or increase in net worth may come about in one of four ways:

1. The assets may remain the same and the liabilities may decrease.

2. The liabilities may remain the same and the assets may increase.

3. The assets may decrease but the liabilities suffer a greater decrease.

4. The assets may increase but the liabilities undergo a smaller increase.

Provided no more money has been invested in the business, and none has been withdrawn, there has been in all the above instances an increase in net worth, that is, a profit has resulted. If the reverse of the above relationships obtains, there has been a decrease in net worth, or a loss.

The following statements illustrate the points discussed above.

AARON CONNERS
BALANCE SHEET,
June 30, 1921

Assets

Cash $ 1,000.00

Notes Receivable	250.00
Accounts Receivable	5,250.00
Merchandise	8,500.00
Store Fixtures	525.00
Total Assets	$ 15,525.00

Liabilities

Accounts Payable	$ 5,365.00
Notes Payable	1,250.00
Total Liabilities	6,615.00

Net Worth

Aaron Conners, Capital	$ 8,910.00

One year later Conners' financial condition is shown to be:

AARON CONNERS
BALANCE SHEET,
June 30, 1922

Assets

Cash	$ 850.00
Notes Receivable	100.00
Accounts Receivable	6,425.00
Merchandise	10,260.00
Store Fixtures	472.50
Delivery Equipment	350.00
Total Assets	$ 18,457.50

Liabilities

Accounts Payable	$ 6,192.75
Notes Payable	950.00
Accrued Salaries	50.50

Total Liabilities   7,193.25

Net Worth

Aaron Conners, Capital $ 11,264.25

The various types of information essential to judging the financial condition as disclosed by the above balance sheets will now be discussed.

Comparison of Balance Sheets.—A comparison of balance sheets gives more information than merely the amount of profit for the year. It indicates trends in the business. Thus a comparison of the notes and accounts receivable for the two years may give some indication of the vigor with which collections are pressed. If the volume of business done, that is, the amount of sales made, was about the same during the two years, and if there are more uncollected accounts at the close of the second year than at the close of the first, it would tend to show that collections were less satisfactory during the second year. Investigation may show that this is due to general conditions of business in the country rather than to failure to push collections vigorously. If there is any marked change in the amount of the stock of merchandise on hand it would invite inquiry. If the stock is much larger at the end of the second year than at the end of the first, it might indicate that the business man is speculating in merchandise, that he considers the buyer's market during the year particularly favorable and has laid in an abnormally large stock. A banker with large experience in similar businesses can formulate a fairly accurate judgment of how much working capital a concern should have invested in merchandise. With that as a criterion he can tell the normal amount of merchandise the business should carry.

A comparison of current liabilities for the two periods will indicate the extent to which borrowed working capital is being used. Thus, an unusual increase in stock-in-trade may be offset by an equally large increase in current liabilities, and so would indicate that the merchant has done his buying on credit or has used borrowed working capital to increase his stock. The danger of this is apparent in a fluctuating merchandise market, particularly if the swing is generally downward. A comparison of the working capital for the two periods gives useful information. A decrease in the amount of working capital may indicate an investment of it in fixed plant which, if continued, will lead to trouble with current creditors. An increase in working capital may point to the advisability of greater sales effort.

A comparison of fixed assets for the two periods will show the increase or decrease in the plant investment. If this has been offset by a corresponding increase or decrease in fixed liabilities, no additional capital of the owners has become tied up in fixed plant, while the reverse is true if there is not that correspondence between fixed assets and fixed liabilities. Where the ratio between current liabilities and fixed liabilities has increased, it may point to the desirability of funding some of the current debt. Short-term liabilities have apparently been incurred for the purpose of extending the fixed plant. It is usually desirable to convert, that is, fund these current liabilities into long-term liabilities in order to conserve working capital to pay current debts.

Thus it is seen that a proper understanding of the items in the two balance sheets and of their various interrelationships will oftentimes give very valuable information. Banks and business houses which are called upon to extend credit, maintain regular files of credit information, including periodic balance sheets, concerning their present and prospective customers, so that they can judge fairly accurately the condition of the businesses.

The Comparative Balance Sheet—Its Content and Form.—A comparison of the above balance sheets shows an increase of net worth of $2,354.25 during the year. It shows also that this profit is accounted for by an increase of $2,932.50 in the assets, which is offset by an increase of $578.25 in the liabilities, leaving a net increase of $2,354.25.

The two statements thus separated do not lend themselves easily to a comparison of individual items. Accordingly, a method of showing the comparison known as the "Comparative Balance Sheet" form is used. This brings all the data into juxtaposition and so makes comparison easy. The balance sheet for the current year is shown first, followed by that for the preceding year. The increase and decrease column uses the current year as a basis for comparison with the preceding year.

AARON CONNERS
COMPARATIVE BALANCE SHEET,
June 30, 1922 and June 30, 1921

Assets	1922	1921	Increase and Decrease
Current Assets:			
Cash	$ 850.00	$ 1,000.00 −	$ 150.00
Notes Receivable	100.00	250.00 −	150.00
Accounts Receivable	6,425.00	5,250.00 +	1,175.00
Merchandise	10,260.00	8,500.00 +	1,760.00
	$17,635.00	$15,000.00 +	$ 2,635.00

Fixed Assets:

Store Fixtures	$ 472.50	$ 525.00	-	$ 52.50
Delivery Equipment	350.00		+	350.00
	$ 822.50	$ 525.00	+	$ 297.50
Total Assets	$18,457.50	$15,525.00	+	$2,932.50

Liabilities

Current Liabilities:

Accounts Payable	$ 6,192.75	$ 5,365.00	+	$ 827.75
Notes Payable	950.00	1,250.00	-	300.00
Accrued Salaries	50.50		+	50.50
Total Liabilities	$ 7,193.25	$ 6,615.00	+	$ 578.25

Net Worth

Aaron Conners, Capital	$ 11,264.25	$ 8,910.00	+	$2,354.25

While it is true that a great deal of valuable information can be secured from a comparative balance sheet, and that this form of balance sheet locates definitely the changes in the asset and liability items, summarizes those changes, and shows the net profit, it nevertheless fails to disclose the forces within the business organization which have brought about the changes—it sets forth effect or result but not cause. A supplementary or rather a complementary statement is needed to show the reasons for the changes. This is discussed in the following two chapters.

CHAPTER V
THE ECONOMIC OR PROFIT AND LOSS
ELEMENTS OF A BUSINESS

Fuller Information Needed.—As indicated in Chapter IV, in the summarization of the business transacted during a given period, it is not usually sufficient to know how much net worth has changed; nor is the whole story told when it is known exactly what items are responsible for the change, that is, which of the properties are worth more and which are worth less at the end than at the beginning of the period. Additional information is necessary to account for the changes shown by the comparative balance sheet.

The proprietor who knows simply that his cash is $1,000 less now than it was at the corresponding time in the last fiscal period, has not the kind of control over his business that his competitor has who knows that the $1,000 was expended for an increased stock of goods, or that an outstanding liability of that amount has been settled, or that his expenses for the period have been larger by $1,000 than for the former period. His competitor may be worse off but he at least has the advantage of knowing the reason for his being so. He has made a correct diagnosis of the pulse beat of his business. If he cannot heal its ills or secure aid for it, he can at least have the satisfaction of giving it a respectable burial, and the autopsy will then disclose that he failed to take advantage of his information until it was too late.

However, the point should be clearly held in mind that the proprietor who knows exactly what is happening in his business is in a position to exercise a definite and sure control over it. Hence, the accounting department, to justify its existence, should aim to give full information as to what is taking place within the business and what eventually will be the result in its financial life. Only in this way can the department serve as a means of control.

Kinds of Records.—A business must have assets and usually must incur liabilities; a plant must be used, stock-in-trade must be bought, and sold, and usually sufficient capital must be provided for the extension of credit to customers. Capital for the payment of the operating expenses of the business, the maintenance of the plant, the payment of salaries and wages of employees, and so forth must at all times be provided. While it is true that the balance sheet shows the financial condition of the business, it gives little information as to the volume of business operations. It indicates the net worth and may even indicate the increase or decrease in net worth if the comparative balance sheet is used. Yet as to how that increase or decrease in net worth came about, little or no information is given. The balance sheet, in other words, is static; it indicates a quiescent state. It is a snapshot, showing the wheels of business momentarily stopped.

To give a full survey of the operations during a given period, a motion picture of the events between the dates of the balance sheets must be shown. Such a picture is dynamic. It gives a realization of the whirl and bustle of business being carried on. It pictures volume, content, and extent, whereas the balance sheet indicates the state arrived at as of a given moment. For purposes of management, which must control all the phases of business activity, a balance sheet is insufficient. A review of the factors producing results up to a given time must be had. Accordingly, the accounting department must supply not only information as to the present state of the assets and liabilities, but also information which indicates how the changes in assets and liabilities since the last fiscal period were brought about—what volume of transactions occurred, what expenditures of assets and energy were necessary to accomplish the results attained. This information, for purposes of internal management, is more vital than that concerning simply the present status of assets and liabilities. It is complementary to that obtained by a comparison of net worths and it is therefore explanatory of the changes in net worth.

The Net Worth Section Expanded.—In its operation of buying and selling goods, a business executes many different types of transactions. As was indicated in Chapter I, in the development of the proprietorship equation, some types of transactions have no effect on proprietorship, that is, they involve neither a profit nor a loss; while other types of transaction—the really vital types, because it is for these that the business is carried on—involve a change in proprietorship, either increasing or decreasing it. Goods are bought for one price and sold at a price sufficiently higher to pay for all the expenses of operating the business and leave a reasonable margin of profit. For example, goods may be bought for $1,000 and sold for $1,800, bringing about an increase of $800 in the sum total of the assets. This $800 may represent temporarily an increase in proprietorship but the increase must be used first to meet the expenses of operating the business during the period in which the sale is made, after which the net result represents the real or permanent increase in proprietorship. The temporary increase of $800 is offset by a temporary decrease of, say, $600 for operating expenses. It is vital to business management to have information not only concerning the net increase in proprietorship but also concerning these temporary increases and decreases. To give this information the net worth section of the balance sheet might be expanded as in the illustration given below.

Edwin Markham
Balance Sheet, December 31, 19—

Assets

Cash	$ 5,000.00
Accounts Receivable	75,000.00
Merchandise	20,000.00
Plant	50,000.00
Total Assets	$150,000.00

Liabilities

Accounts Payable	$30,000.00
Accrued Expenses	5,000.00
Mortgage on Plant	30,000.00
Total Liabilities	65,000.00

Net Worth

Edwin Markham:

Capital at the beginning of the year		$70,000.00
Profits during the year:		
Sales	$200,000.00	
Cost of Goods Sold	140,000.00	
Temporary Increase in Proprietorship	$ 60,000.00	
Operating Expenses	45,000.00	
Net Increase in Proprietorship	15,000.00	
Capital at the end of the year		$ 85,000.00

In the net worth section of this balance sheet, the capital with which the owner started operations for the year is given first. To this is appended a summary of the operations for the year resulting in a net increase in proprietorship which, added to the beginning capital, gives the capital in the business at the end of the year. This method of setting up the information concerning the operations of the business is not used to any extent because the information is of such vital importance that it deserves more display. Accordingly, a separate statement, known as the "Statement of Profit and Loss," or "Statement of Business Operations," is drawn up to explain the balance sheet net worth item, Net Increase in Proprietorship for the year, which shows just the amount of the net profit. The detail of this item is given in this complementary statement. The above illustration is given merely for the purpose of pointing out the relationship between the statement of operations and the balance sheet. From this it will be seen that the statement of profit and loss is really a part of the net worth section of the balance sheet.

TEMPORARY PROPRIETORSHIP RECORDS.—The proprietorship records, indicating as they do the sources of changes in net worth, are kept day by day as transactions take place, are summarized at the close of the period, and the net result is determined. They are called temporary because, as is seen, they do not at the time of record have regard for the final change in proprietorship. At the end of the regular periods, to determine the total or final change, the temporary proprietorship records are closed or transferred to the summarized record called the "Profit and Loss Summary."

Referring to the case of Aaron Conners discussed in Chapter IV, assume that the accounting department furnishes the following additional information from its records:

During the year from July 1, 1921 to June 30, 1922, Conners bought $22,362.50 worth of goods; his sales amounted to $28,465.20; he paid for help $3,050.50; his other expenses were $2,405.45; and he estimated the wear and tear on furniture at 10%, or $52.50. As shown in his statement for 1922, he had $10,260 worth of merchandise on hand on June 30, 1922.

The analysis of this information explains the changes in his net worth during the year. The goods he started with plus those purchased during the year are the total goods to be accounted for, which amounted to $30,862.50 ($8,500 + $22,362.50 = $30,862.50). These goods were accounted for by his sales during the year and the amount on hand. Knowing how much was on hand June 30, 1922, viz., $10,260, he determined that the goods sold must have been the difference or $20,602.50 ($30,862.50 - $10,260 = $20,602.50). The price which he received for these goods sold was $28,465.20; hence, his profits from sales were $7,862.70, the difference between selling price and cost.

We find, also, that the expenses he incurred in selling his goods and conducting his business generally were $3,050.50 for clerk hire, office help, delivery boys, etc.; and other expenses, such as rent, taxes, repairs, delivery upkeep, supplies, heat, light, and the like, amounted to $2,405.45. He estimated that his store fixtures depreciated in value $52.50. All these items, representing costs of doing business, amounted to $5,508.45 ($3,050.50 +

$2,405.45 + $52.50 = $5,508.45), which subtracted from his profits from sales, $7,862.70, gives him a net gain of $2,354.25 ($7,862.70 - $5,508.45 = $2,354.25). This gain tallies with the increased proprietorship of that amount shown by the balance sheet of June 30, 1922.

Without regard to a form which would be technically correct, the data of the preceding paragraphs may be shown as follows:

Goods on hand at the beginning, July 1, 1921	$ 8,500.00
Goods bought during the year	22,362.50
Total goods to be accounted for	$30,862.50
Goods accounted for, now on hand	10,260.00
Goods accounted for, by being sold	$20,602.50
Selling price of goods sold	$28,465.20
Cost price of goods sold, as above	20,602.50
Profit from sales	$ 7,862.70
Expenses of doing business:	
Clerk hire	$3,050.50
Other expenses	2,405.45
Depreciation	52.50
Total expenses	5,508.45
Net profit, or increase in net worth	$ 2,354.25

The technical form of the summary of the temporary proprietorship elements will be presented in the next chapter.

CHAPTER VI
THE PROFIT AND LOSS SUMMARY

Type of Information Needed.—The need and purpose of the information to be furnished by the temporary proprietorship records was pointed out in Chapter V. Without information of this sort, proper control of business operations cannot be exercised. These records supply a summarized picture of the activities of the business during a definite period, which have as their goal the increase in proprietorship—the making of a profit. In attaining this goal, two main types of activities or operations are entered into, usually classified under the heads of: (1) income or earnings, by which is meant those activities which immediately and directly increase proprietorship; and (2) expenses or outgo, comprising those activities which decrease proprietorship. Expenses are the costs incurred in securing income, and are therefore deductions from it. A fuller explanation of these terms will now be given.

Income.—Income is usually of two types: operating and non-operating. These terms are always relative; that is, what is an operating income in one business may be a non-operating income in another business. The term "operating income" is used to indicate the main sources of income in a given business. It is always the duty of the accounting department to indicate the sources of income. Thus in a trading or mercantile business, the selling of goods to customers is the main source of income. In a professional business, the selling of services, often titled "professional fees," is the main source; in a brokerage or commission business, commissions earned; in institutions, tuition and other fees; in a financial business, interest earnings; in a society, membership fees. These are typical titles for indicating the main source of income in the several kinds of undertakings mentioned.

While sales are the major source of income in a trading concern, there may be supplementary sources. It may own stocks and bonds from which income may be derived. In a manufacturing or mining enterprise the company may own dwelling houses and rent them to its employees. Conditions of travel and communication may also force it to provide stores, places of amusement, and so forth for its workers. From all these supplementary activities it will derive income. As it was not organized primarily for these purposes, but chiefly to manufacture, or mine a commodity, the income from these collateral activities is classed as non-operating income.

The distinction, then, between operating and non-operating income is, as mentioned above, always a relative one and will be determined in any given instance on the basis of major activities and supplementary or minor activities. Some of the titles under which income is recorded will now be explained:

SALES. Under this title is recorded the amount of sales of the stock-in-trade in a merchandising or manufacturing concern. The two elements included here, namely, the decrease of the asset merchandise and the increase of proprietorship—the true income element—will be discussed later.

SALES RETURNS. This title does not represent income but, as its name indicates, shows the amount of the goods sold which have been returned because of dissatisfaction with the quality or condition of the goods or some error in sending the wrong kind.

SALES ALLOWANCES. These are similar to sales returns in that they indicate a deduction from the sales income for the allowances made to the purchasers who for one reason or another have just cause to be dissatisfied with the goods but agree to retain them providing an allowance from the original selling price is made.

INTEREST INCOME. Under this title is recorded the income from money loaned or credit extended. Notes receivable and bonds are the usual sources. Sometimes open accounts receivable also bring interest.

RENTAL INCOME. Under this title is recorded income received from the lease of premises, lands, or buildings.

PROFESSIONAL FEES. Under this title is recorded the income from charges made for professional services.

COMMISSIONS EARNED. Included under this title is the income received from services rendered in the selling of commodities for a principal.

PURCHASE DISCOUNT. This represents the deduction allowed from the original charge for paying a debt in advance of the date named in the purchase contract.

Expenses.—Expenses are also of two types: operating and non-operating. The same distinction is made here as with income. Those expenses incurred in securing operating income are operating expenses, while those incurred in securing non-operating income or for other purposes are called non-operating expenses.

To secure control over the operating and non-operating types of activities, it is necessary to compare operating income with operating expenses, and non-operating income with non-operating expenses, in order to measure the return by the effort expended in securing that return. Some of the more common titles under which the record of expenses is made are as follows:

SALARIES (WAGES). Under this title is included the cost of the services rendered by employees. This may be classified in accordance with the department in which the service is rendered; for example, factory wages, salesmen's salaries, office salaries, and so forth.

TRAVELING EXPENSES. The costs of railroad fare, entertainment, and so forth, when traveling in the interests of the business.

ADVERTISING. The cost of publicity in making known the commodities offered for sale by the business.

BUYING EXPENSE. The costs incurred in making purchases for the business. These may comprise the salaries of buyers and all expenses in connection with maintaining a purchasing department.

RENT. The cost for the use of premises not owned.

PLANT MAINTENANCE. The cost of upkeep, repairs, and so forth, on the plant used by the business. The cost, by purchase or manufacture, of light, heat, and power is included here.

DEPRECIATION. The decrease in value of a fixed asset due to wear and tear, lapse of time, obsolescence, etc.

BAD DEBTS. The amount of outstanding accounts receivable which have proven or are judged to be uncollectible.

SALES DISCOUNTS. The cost incurred because of the financial policy of charging a customer a smaller amount than the amount of the bill, provided he pays by a given date.

TELEPHONE, TELEGRAPH, STATIONERY, POSTAGE, INTEREST COST, COMMISSIONS PAID, AND SO FORTH. These all indicate by their titles the nature of the expense or cost items.

The student should understand that expenses may be set up in very much greater detail than that indicated by the above titles. Usually the title under which record of an expense is made will indicate with sufficient clearness its character.

The Profit and Loss Summary.—As indicated in [Chapter V](), the profit and loss summary shows the manner in which the net worth of the business has been changed as the result of operations of the business, as distinguished from changes brought about through withdrawal or investment of capital. Although it is really a part of the balance sheet, which shows financial condition, because of its importance it is, however, set up as a separate statement. It amplifies and fills out the record shown by the balance sheet. It is a supplementary record because it gives additional information, and is complementary to the balance sheet because it rounds out and completes the story of business life there recorded.

Just as with the balance sheet, the main problems of the profit and loss summary relate to: (1) its form; and (2) its content. After an explanation of some of the terms used in connection with the summary, these two problems will be discussed.

The Fiscal Period.—Because of the work involved and the frequent incompleteness of the records at the close of each day, a daily statement of condition is very seldom made up. The business experience of a particular enterprise determines the frequency of preparation of these statements. Whatever the period may be between statements, be it a month, three months, a half-year, or a year, it is called the fiscal period, i.e., it is the period at the end of which records are summarized for the purpose of ascertaining the profit or loss for the period. For purposes of comparison with preceding and following fiscal periods, under similar conditions, the fiscal period should be, and usually is a period of regular length—a half-year or year being perhaps the most common, though in many enterprises it is customary to draw up supplementary monthly statements.

Need for the Physical Inventory.—Again, because of the work involved, especially where the product dealt in is small in value and sales are numerous—as in stores dealing in clothing, food, and the like—no record of the cost of each article is kept as it is sold, only the sale price being recorded. It is not possible, therefore, to determine from the records as usually kept, the cost of the goods on hand at a given time. The records are kept in this way, not because systems of accounting cannot be devised to make both records, but because the results obtained by such systems are not justified by their cost when other and less expensive means can be used with almost as satisfactory results.

The customary method of finding the cost of goods sold was indicated in Chapter V. Summarized, it requires that from the sum of goods on hand at the beginning and those purchased since, there be subtracted the goods on hand and unsold at the close of the period. This last item, the goods on hand and unsold, is secured by making an actual count and valuation of such goods at the close of the fiscal period. The expedient of physical inventory-taking is therefore brought in as an aid to the accounting records, but only in the interests of economy.

Form of Profit and Loss Summary

GENERAL PRINCIPLES GOVERNING MAKE-UP. The profit and loss statement, as the complement of the balance sheet, is just as formal in character and the same general considerations govern as the make-up of the balance sheet, viz.: (1) the general purpose it is to serve; (2) the likelihood of obscuring essential facts through too great detail; and (3) the general appearance is to legibility, clearness of form and expression, and arrangement on the page.

TITLE. The heading of the summary must show the name of the business, followed by the title of the summary and the statement of the exact period covered by it. It was noted in <u>Chapter V</u> that whereas the balance sheet is a statement of financial condition as at a given date, the profit and loss summary is a statement of operations which have taken place during a given period. Hence, it is not sufficient merely to state the date of the close of the period. If, as is usually the case, the fiscal periods are of uniform length in a given business, the phraseology "For the Period Ending ..." will be sufficient for use within that business. It is better, however, for all statements of operation to indicate the length of the period covered. A typical heading for the profit and loss summary is indicated below:

JAMES R. ROBINSON & COMPANY
STATEMENT OF PROFIT AND LOSS FOR THE SIX MONTHS' PERIOD
ENDING DECEMBER 31, 19—

ARRANGEMENT. The arrangement of the summary has already been indicated. The income from operations, that is, the operating income, is shown firsthand, and is followed by the operating expense, and then by the amount of the difference or the net result of operation. Next is shown the non-operating income, followed by the non-operating expense. The net result of this combined with the net result from operations gives the net result for the period, which is the figure shown on the balance sheet, the detail of which is explained by the profit and loss summary.

Content of Profit and Loss Summary.—The content of the profit and loss summary is determined by the need of information for purposes of management. A profit and loss summary which is sufficient for a small business, where the proprietor is in intimate contact with all phases of the business, would not give sufficient information for the proper control of a large business, where the managing executives are dependent for their information as to the various phases of business activity on reports made to them. There is, however, a fairly standard outline or skeleton in accordance with which this summary is usually drawn up. It is the purpose here to explain that outline.

The first section of the statement has for its purpose the separation of the sales item into its two elements, referred to above: (1) the Cost of Goods Sold, which indicates the amount by which the asset merchandise has been decreased through sale of goods; and (2) the Gross Profit or the excess of selling price ever cost, out of which must be met the costs of operating the business before the net change in proprietorship can be determined. This section is usually spoken of as the "trading" section of the statement. The set-up of this section shows, accordingly: (1) the Sales item, from which is shown deducted the amounts of sales returns and sales rebates and allowances in order to arrive at the figure of net sales; and (2) the Cost of Goods Sold, under which is listed the cost of goods sold as explained in Chapter V. This cost requires the showing of the initial inventory, the purchases for the period, the inward costs of laying down the merchandise at the place of business, such as insurance on goods in transit, freight and cartage costs, and so forth. From the sum of these items will be shown deducted the returned purchases and the amount of the final inventory, the difference indicating the cost price of goods disposed of by sale. With the "inward" cost of goods is sometimes included the sum total of all buying expenses. In other cases, particularly where a complete purchasing department is maintained, a separate buying expense section is set up to summarize these costs.

Following this trading section comes the formal statement of operating expenses which are usually classified for purposes of information into the groups: Selling Expenses, General Administrative Expenses, and Financial Management Expenses. Under each one of these groups should be listed the detailed items. Thus, under the selling expense group should be shown such items as salaries to salesmen; the traveling expenses incurred by them; the cost of publicity, advertising, and so forth; the sales management expense; and the delivery expenses, although these expenses are sometimes set up in a group by themselves.

The student will note that under the head of selling expenses are grouped all of the direct costs incurred in making sales.

Under the general administrative expenses should be shown such items as office salaries, stationery and supplies, postage, telephone and telegraph, light, heat, insurance, depreciation, and all other items which cannot be charged to definite departments of the business but must be borne by the business as a whole.

Under financial management expense should be listed the various items of expense which represent the financial activity of the business as related to its major purposes and which are operating financial expense items. Here will be shown such items as interest on money borrowed for operating the business; sales discounts granted customers in order to secure cash payments from them at an earlier date than the limit of the normal credit period allowed them; collection costs, and so forth.

A final section of the *operating* portion of the profit and loss statement lists the items of income arising out of the management of the working capital finances of the business. Interest received on customers' notes and on cash balances in the bank, and purchase discounts, are usually the only items of income under this head.

The difference between gross profit on sales and the sum of these operating expenses minus the financial income, is the operating profit of the business, sometimes called Net Operating Profit.

The section following this is devoted to the marshaling of the items of Non-operating Income and Expense. Whichever of these two groups is the larger is set up first, and from its total is deducted the total of the other group. The net amount is then shown extended under the item of net operating profit, to which it is added if it is a net income item and from which it is subtracted if it is a net expense item. The resulting figure is the Net Profit for the period.

Occasionally there are extraordinary items of profit or loss not to be classified under any of the above heads, which have to be shown in additional sections of the profit and loss statement. These are matters which will be taken up later.

It should be noted that the above paragraphs outline a simple statement of profit and loss for a commercial or trading business as distinguished from an industrial or manufacturing enterprise, the statement for which is somewhat more complex even in its general outlines.

Algebraic Content of the Profit and Loss Statement.—An algebraic presentation of the profit and loss statement is oftentimes valuable. The cost-of-goods-sold portion becomes:

- (1) Initial Inventory + Purchases
-    - Final Inventory = Cost of Goods Sold
- (2) Sales - Cost of Goods Sold = Gross Trading Profit

The rest of the statement is covered by the following equation:

- (3) Gross Trading Profit
- - (Selling Expenses
- + General Administrative Expenses
- + Financial Management Expense
- - Financial Management Income)
- ± (Non-operating Income - Non-operating Expense)
-

- = Net Profit

The Disposition of the Net Profit.—The net profit for the period belongs to the proprietor and constitutes an increase in his proprietorship or investment, unless he has already drawn out some of these profits as they accrued. In this case, his drawings must be subtracted from the net profit indicated before showing the increment to his net worth. Accordingly, a final section of the profit and loss statement may give the disposition of the net profit and its appropriation or addition to the previous net worth or proprietorship item. This section, when used, is known as the appropriation section. If the business is a partnership, this section should show in detail the distribution of net profit among the several partners according to the agreement among them as to the proportions in which they are to share gains or losses. If a corporation, it should give the disposition made of the net profit in the way of dividends to the stockholders, and any other appropriation made of these profits, including transfer to surplus.

Two illustrations—one very simple, the other more complex—typical of profit and loss summaries are given for the guidance of the student.

Illustration 1

AARON CONNERS
STATEMENT OF PROFIT AND LOSS FOR THE YEAR ENDING JUNE 30, 1922

Sales for the year			$28,465.20
Goods on Hand July 1, 1921	$ 8,500.00		
Purchases during the year	22,362.50	$30,862.50	
Goods on Hand June 30, 1922		10,260.00	
Cost of Goods Sold			20,602.50
Gross Trading Profit			$ 7,862.70
Clerk Hire		$3,050.50	
General Expenses	$2,405.45		
Depreciation	52.50	2,457.95	5,508.45
Net Profit for the year			$2,354.25

Illustration 2

KIMBALL AND MOREY
STATEMENT OF PROFIT AND LOSS FOR THE YEAR ENDING JUNE 30, 19—

Sales		$525,600.00	
Less:			
Sales Returns	$ 5,000.00		
Sales Rebates and Allowances	600.00	5,600.00	
Net Sales			$520,000.00
Cost of Goods Sold:			
Inventory, July 1, 19—	$ 96,670.00		
Purchases during the year	350,000.00		
Freight-In	1,000.00		
Insurance (Goods in Transit)	750.00	$448,420.00	
Less:			
Purchase Returns	$ 1,750.00		
Final Inventory, June 30, 19—	105,000.00	106,750.00	
Cost of Goods Sold			341,670.00
Gross Profit			$178,330.00
Selling Expenses:			
Salesmen's Salaries	$ 20,000.00		
Advertising	25,000.00		

- 47 -

Delivery Expense		5,000.00	$ 50,000.00
General Administrative Expenses:			
Office Salaries		$ 10,000.00	
Stationery and Supplies		1,500.00	
Postage		250.00	
Telephone and Telegraph		750.00	
Light and Heat		1,750.00	
Insurance (Stock and Fixtures)		1,500.00	
Depreciation:			
Furniture and Fixtures	$2,000.00		
Buildings	1,500.00	3,500.00	
Miscellaneous Expenses		750.00	20,000.00
Financial Management Expenses:			
Interest Paid		$ 250.00	
Sales Discounts		5,000.00	
Bad Debts		1,000.00	
Collection Costs		250.00	6,500.00
Total Operating Expenses			$ 76,500.00
Financial Management Income:			

Interest Received	$ 1,350.00	
Purchase Discounts	3,500.00	4,850.00
Net Operating Expense		71,650.00
Net Operating Profit		$106,680.00
Non-Operating Expense and Income:		
Income—Interest on Liberty Bonds	$ 2,000.00	
Expense—Loss on Stocks Sold	900.00	1,100.00
Net Profit for the year		$107,780.00
Appropriation of Net Profit:		
J. H. S. Kimball, ⅖ share	$ 43,112.00	
H. F. C. Morey, ⅗ share	64,668.00	$107,780.00

The Two Methods of Determining Net Profit.—It is particularly important to note that the profit shown by the profit and loss statement must be the same as that developed by the comparative balance sheet, since both cover the same period and constitute merely two ways of developing the same result. For this reason they are valuable in proving the correctness of results, acting as checks against each other. The student must bear in mind, however, that the increase or decrease in net worth as shown by the comparative balance sheet must always be adjusted by taking account of additional investments or withdrawals of capital before the net profit for the period can be determined, and therefore before this figure can be used as a check against the amount of net profit shown by the statement of profit and loss.

The accounting department keeps both classes of records, viz., the asset and liability records and the temporary proprietorship or income and expense records, not because both are needed to develop the amount of net profit—either class would do this—but because both are needed for the additional information which they give and which is valuable and necessary for the intelligent management of the business.

CHAPTER VII
INTERRELATION BETWEEN THE ECONOMIC AND THE FINANCIAL ELEMENTS OF A BUSINESS, AND SOME INTER-RATIOS

Various Aspects of the Temporary Proprietorship Records.—The profit and loss statement has been explained as a summary of the temporary proprietorship records kept for the purpose of registering the changes in net worth as they occur from day-to-day, and also for the purpose of noting the source or cause of many of the changes in assets and liabilities. The temporary proprietorship records may be regarded as the chronicle or history of the economic life of the business. The efforts of the business to produce income with the least possible outgo in the form of costs or expenses, may be viewed as the work of forces or agencies striving towards that end. Every effort is offset by the cost of that endeavor, and unless the result of the effort be more than its cost, its aim, viz., the increase of net worth, is not accomplished.

Relation between Profit and Loss and Financial Elements.—These income-producing efforts are the agencies that bring about the changes in the values of assets and liabilities. Expenses and costs are incurred for the purpose of securing income. Every expense or cost that is settled causes a diminution of business assets, usually of the asset cash. If not settled, it causes an increase in the liabilities, usually the accounts payable, for the business becomes bound by or liable for it. Both of these conditions result in a decrease in the net worth.

On the other hand, every item of income, as when a sale of goods is made, is reflected in an increase of assets or a decrease of liabilities. The result of every sale is usually an increase in the cash or in the claims against persons, the accounts receivable. The sale may sometimes result in a lessening of liabilities through a cancellation of the claims of creditors by means of the claims against customers arising out of the sale. This would be true when goods are bought from, and sold to, the same person. Thus there is constantly a direct interrelation between the financial and the profit and loss elements of every business.

Exchanges within the Asset and Liability Groups.—All changes in individual assets and liabilities, however, are not always the result of business or economic forces. There may be an even exchange of one asset for another asset, as when delivery equipment is purchased for cash. The asset Delivery Equipment is increased by the same amount as the asset Cash is diminished. Or if a bill of goods is purchased on credit, an increase of assets is exactly offset by an increase in liabilities. These changes are illustrated in the second example in Chapter I, showing Runyon's proprietorship.

It is seen, therefore, that the changes in individual assets and liabilities are not so certain an index of changes in proprietorship as those registered by the temporary proprietorship records. The vital history of a business is its profit and loss record, the story of its economic life. As a means of control this is of first importance because it chronicles the causes of most changes in financial condition. The statement of financial condition may be looked upon as a picture of the framework, the skeleton of the business personality, upon which is superimposed its economic structure. When both the financial framework and the profit and loss summary are given, it is possible with reasonable accuracy to tell the whole history of the business activities for the period covered.

Confusion between Profit and Loss and Balance Sheet Items.—The beginner frequently has trouble in making a proper classification of income items and sometimes of expense items. Take Interest Income as an example. The asset Cash Received is confused with the title Interest Income, which denotes the source of the cash received. The accounting department maintains both types of records. The receipt of cash arising out of interest income would be classified and recorded under two heads: (1) the asset Cash, to indicate the increase in that asset; and (2) the temporary proprietorship record Interest Income, to give the profit and loss information necessary for purposes of management.

Similarly, the beginner oftentimes confuses the sales income record with the cash record of a cash sale transaction. Also, when cash is disbursed for expense purposes, the decrease in the asset is often confused with the expense record. When an expense is incurred it brings about either a decrease in assets, usually cash if the transaction is settled at once; or an increase in liabilities, usually an accrued expense item if the transaction is not immediately settled. Accordingly, in making the record the accounting department must show the decrease in the asset or the increase in the liability in the balance sheet group of records and the source of that decrease or increase under some expense title in the profit and loss group of records. Familiarity with the titles appearing in the profit and loss statement should prevent this confusion.

Illustration.—To show the interactions between the balance sheet and the profit and loss groups of records, the following illustration is given. There is shown first a comparative balance sheet, indicating the condition of a business at the beginning and the end of a period. This comparative balance sheet, it will be noted, shows a net profit of $33,250. There is also given a statement of profit and loss, showing the sources of the income and the expenses of the business. The statement indicates a net profit of $33,250 for the period. By starting with the financial condition as indicated by the balance sheet at the beginning of the period and working into it the operations for the year as shown by the statement of profit and loss, and by using the balance sheet at the end of the period as a goal, we can trace the probable interaction of the two types of records for the period.

JACKSON L. GORDON
COMPARATIVE BALANCE SHEET
December 31, 1922 and December 31, 1921

Assets	1922	1921	Increase and Decrease
Cash	$ 10,000.00	$ 15,000.00	- $ 5,000.00
Accounts Receivable	100,000.00	119,000.00	- 19,000.00
Merchandise	70,000.00	65,000.00	+ 5,000.00
Unexpired Insurance	1,000.00	250.00	+ 750.00
Plant and Equipment	350,000.00	325,000.00	+ 25,000.00
Total Assets	$531,000.00	$524,250.00	+ $ 6,750.00
Liabilities			
Notes Payable	$ 30,000.00	$ 35,000.00	- $ 5,000.00
Accounts Payable	50,000.00	40,000.00	+ 10,000.00
Accrued Sales Salaries	2,500.00	1,500.00	+ 1,000.00
Mortgage Payable	150,000.00	200,000.00	- 50,000.00
Depreciation Reserve Plant and Equipment[1]	50,000.00	32,500.00	+ 17,500.00
Total Liabilities	$282,500.00	$309,000.00	- $26,500.00
Net Worth			
Jackson L. Gordon, Capital	$248,500.00	$215,250.00	+ $33,250.00

Jackson L. Gordon
Statement of Profit and Loss For the Year Ending December 31, 1922

Sales		$470,000.00	
Sales Returns		20,000.00	
Net Sales			$450,000.00
Cost of Goods Sold:			
Merchandise on Hand December 31, 1921	$ 65,000.00		
Purchases	305,000.00		
Inward Freight and Cartage	15,000.00	$385,000.00	
Deduct—Merchandise on Hand December 31, 1922		70,000.00	
Cost of Goods Sold			315,000.00
Gross Profit			$135,000.00
Selling Expenses:			
Sales Salaries	$ 20,000.00		
Advertising	30,000.00		
Sundry Sales Expense	10,000.00	$ 60,000.00	
General Administrative Expenses:			
Office Salaries	$ 10,500.00		
Insurance	3,000.00		
Sundry Office Expense	2,000.00		
Depreciation	17,500.00	33,000.00	

Financial Management Expenses:

Interest Cost	$10,000.00		
Sales Discounts	7,000.00	17,000.00	
Total Operating Expenses		$110,000.00	
Financial Management Income:			
Interest Income	$ 250.00		
Purchase Discounts	8,000.00	8,250.00	
Net Operating Expenses			101,750.00
Net Profit for the year			$ 33,250.00

INTERRELATION BETWEEN SALES INCOME, ACCOUNTS RECEIVABLE, AND CASH. In these two statements, if to the outstanding accounts at the beginning of the period we add the net sales for the period as shown in the profit and loss summary, and if from their sum we deduct the sales discounts allowed customers and the accounts outstanding at the close of the period, as shown by the comparative balance sheet, we arrive at the amount of cash received from customers during the year. This is shown by the following statement:

Accounts Receivable, December 31, 1921	$119,000.00	
Net Sales for the year	450,000.00	$569,000.00
Deduct:		
Sales Discounts	$ 7,000.00	
Accounts Receivable, December 31, 1922	100,000.00	107,000.00
Cash Received from Customers during year		$462,000.00

INTERRELATION BETWEEN PURCHASES, ACCOUNTS PAYABLE, AND CASH. The amount of cash paid for merchandise during the year may be arrived at similarly, as indicated by the following statement:

Accounts Payable, December 31, 1921 $ 40,000.00

Purchases during the year	305,000.00	$ 345,000.00
Deduct:		
Purchase Discounts	$ 8,000.00	
Accounts Payable, December 31, 1922	50,000.00	58,000.00
Cash Paid for Merchandise during year		$287,000.00

INTERRELATION BETWEEN CASH AND OTHER BALANCE SHEET AND PROFIT AND LOSS ITEMS. If to the amount of cash on hand at the beginning of the period we add the cash received from customers, as determined above, and that received from interest income, as indicated by the profit and loss statement, we arrive at the total cash available for use during the period.

Cash expenditures have been made for the following purposes:

1. Payments to creditors for merchandise of $287,000 as above.

2. Inward freight and cartage $15,000, as shown by the profit and loss statement.

3. Sales salaries $19,000. (This amount is determined by considering the expense of $20,000, as shown by the profit and loss statement, in conjunction with the unpaid sales salaries, as shown by the comparative balance sheet. Thus, if to the unpaid sales salaries amounting to $1,500 at the beginning of the period, we add the sales salary expense of $20,000 incurred during the period and from their sum we subtract the amount of unpaid salaries, $2,500, at the end of the period, we arrive at the amount of $19,000 spent for salaries during the period.)

4. Advertising $30,000.

5. Sundry selling expense $10,000.

6. Office salaries $10,500.

7. Insurance $3,750. (This amount is also determined by considering the amount of unexpired insurance as shown by the comparative balance sheet in conjunction with the cost of insurance used during the current period, as shown by the profit and loss statement. It will be noted that $250 worth of insurance was in force at the beginning of the period, that $3,000 worth of insurance was used during the period—hence it must have been necessary to buy additional insurance amounting to $2,750 during the period. When we find, however, that there is unexpired insurance at the end of the period amounting to $1,000, it will be seen that there must have been purchased during the period $3,750 worth of insurance.)

8. Sundry office expense $2,000.

9. Interest cost $10,000.

10. Plant and equipment $25,000. (It will be noted from the comparative balance sheet that there has been a net increase of only $7,500 in plant and equipment. While $25,000 was added to the plant and equipment asset during the year, there was a decrease in value due to depreciation, amounting to $17,500, as shown by the profit and loss statement. This depreciation expense is reflected as a decrease in the value of the asset Plant and Equipment and does not therefore decrease the asset Cash.)

11. Notes payable $5,000—the decrease being shown by the comparative balance sheet.

12. Mortgage payable $50,000—also shown on the comparative balance sheet.

If from the total cash available for use there is deducted the cash expended, as indicated above, the difference should indicate the amount of cash on hand at the close of the period. This balance of $10,000, as indicated by the tabulated statement below, is the amount shown by the comparative balance sheet as being on hand.

Cash Receipts:

Balance on Hand December 31, 1921		$ 15,000.00
From Customers, as above		462,000.00
Interest Income		250.00
Total Cash available for use		$477,250.00

Cash Expenditures:

For Purchases as above	$ 287,000.00	
Inward Freight and Cartage	15,000.00	
Sales Salaries	19,000.00	
Advertising	30,000.00	
Sundry Selling Expense	10,000.00	
Office Salaries	10,500.00	
Insurance	3,750.00	

Sundry Office Expense	2,000.00	
Interest Cost	10,000.00	
Plant and Equipment	25,000.00	
Notes Payable	5,000.00	
Mortgage Payable	50,000.00	467,250.00
Balance of Cash on Hand December 31, 1922, per Balance Sheet.		$ 10,000.00

By a careful study of the interrelations between various items as explained above, the student will see that the interactions between all of the transactions for the year as set forth in the comparative balance sheet and the profit and loss statement, have been indicated and proved. The proof is secured in the tie-up between the figure of cash as shown by the cash statement, and that shown in the comparative balance sheet statement as cash on hand at the end of the period.

Inter-Ratios and Their Uses.—Before leaving the study of the balance sheet and profit and loss statement and their interrelations, it is desirable to explain certain ratios between items found on both statements. These are ratios which are watched very carefully in judging the financial condition of a business. Their significance is apparent.

1. MERCHANDISE TURNOVER. By merchandise turnover is meant the rate at which the merchandise stock is moved or turned over by sale during the fiscal period. The ratio expressing the rate of turnover is found by dividing the cost of goods sold, as shown in the profit and loss statement, by the average inventory carried for the year. Where there are available only the figures of opening and closing inventory, the amount of the average inventory is taken as one-half of the sum of these two inventories. The rate of turnover varies in different businesses, ranging as high as 15 or 20 in some and as low as 1 or 2 in others. The value of a rapid turnover is apparent. One dollar invested in merchandise where the rate of turnover is 10 is equivalent to $10 invested where the rate is only 1. The more work a dollar does, the greater the profit possibilities.

2. WORKING CAPITAL TURNOVER. The amount of sales as indicated by the profit and loss statement, divided by the working capital—the excess of current assets over current liabilities—as determined from the balance sheet, is called the "working capital turnover." This indicates the rate at which the working capital is used in securing sales. Where the amount of working capital on hand varies markedly at different periods of the year, the average should be used as the basis for estimating the rate of turnover.

3. ACCOUNTS RECEIVABLE TO SALES. The fraction represented by dividing the amount of outstanding accounts at the end of the year by the volume of sales during the year, indicates the portion of sales which has not yet been collected in cash. If this fraction is multiplied by the length of the fiscal period, expressed in months, and the result compared with the normal credit term allowed customers, it will indicate the trend of collections. For example, if the outstanding accounts at the close of the period are $150,000, the sales for the year are $1,200,000, and the normal credit period is 30 days, it will be seen that by the above ratios the $150,000 of outstanding accounts represents on the average the sales for approximately 1½ months

$$\left\{ \frac{150,000}{1,200,000} \times 12 \text{ months} = 1\tfrac{1}{2} \text{ months.} \right\}$$

Since the credit term is only 30 days, the indication is that collections are slow and should be pushed more vigorously. It must be understood that this ratio indicates merely a trend and must be judged in the light of other significant facts in the business.

4. PROFITS TO NET WORTH. The net profit for the period divided by the net worth at the beginning of the period is used to indicate the per cent of earnings on the capital invested.

Other Ratios.—For the purpose of watching the progress of business operations, it is customary to develop the following ratios:

- 1. Cost of goods sold to net sales.
- 2. Gross profit to net sales.
- 3. Selling expenses to net sales.
- 4. General administrative expenses to net sales.
- 5. Net financial management expenses to net sales.
- 6. Net profit to net sales.

These ratios, set up each fiscal period and compared with similar ratios for previous periods, indicate very definitely the trend of income and expenses and are useful in the determination of business policies.

CHAPTER VIII
THE ACCOUNT

The Goal of Account-Keeping.—Throughout the preceding chapters constant reference has been made to records or data of the business furnished by the accounting department. Knowing the use made of these data in the compilation of financial and profit and loss summaries, we shall trace the process of gathering that information in exactly reverse order; first, through the ledger, where it is grouped and summarized in accounts and made ready for the preparation of statements; then into the books of original entry, where the information is first sorted and classified for posting to the proper ledger accounts, with a view always to fit it ultimately into the final statements of financial and business condition; and finally, to the business papers arising out of the transactions, which are the basis or first source of all accounting records.

The Ledger and Its Content.—The ledger may be defined as the book of accounts. In it are collected most of the data needed for the final statements showing the financial condition of the business. By means of its account titles, it makes an analytical record of all transactions, according to the information desired, and through the mechanism of the account it groups and summarizes all data affecting each particular account, thus furnishing the proprietor with totals instead of items. In the ledger, therefore, must be kept two main classes of accounts, viz., those used for making up the balance sheet and those used for making up the profit and loss statement. The one group shows assets and liabilities, and the other temporary proprietorship increases and decreases brought about by the receipt of income and the payment of expenses. The ultimate or net proprietorship is determined by the summarization of all temporary accounts in the way shown in preceding chapters.

THE LEDGER ACCOUNT DEFINED.—An account may be defined as a record of one or more items, either similar or dissimilar, relating to the same person or thing, kept under an appropriate heading or title. The record is kept in such a way as to make easy the addition of similar items and the subtraction of dissimilar items. Accounts are kept both with persons, as the accounts receivable and payable already mentioned, and with things, such as land, buildings, machinery, merchandise, cash, and the like. Some asset accounts and some accounts kept with persons are usually composed of both similar and dissimilar items. For example, the cash account is composed of both cash received and cash paid out items; the accounts receivable record both the items for which the person is in debt to the business and those which show the cancellation or settlement of the debt, in part or in full; and the accounts payable record the items for which the business is in debt to the person and those which show cancellation of the debt or settlement by the business. Accounts which record income and expenses usually comprise only similar items, as where all sales of merchandise are recorded under one head or account and all purchases under another.

THE ACCOUNT TITLE.—The title given to an account is important. It should indicate clearly the content of the account. Accuracy is a basic necessity in accounting. Correct titles are therefore essential. A title which does not clearly and truthfully indicate the nature of the account, or one which is so chosen that under it may be recorded items of various and doubtful kinds, gives prima facie evidence of an imperfect knowledge of accounting principles or of a desire to hide data which will not bear close scrutiny. Therefore, care should be exercised in the selection of titles.

The Two Sections of the Account.—To separate similar from dissimilar items, the account is divided into two sections, a left and a right section, as we shall call them for the present, which are shown in the standard form given in Form 1.

The account head or title is placed in the center over the division line. At the extreme left of each section are the date columns—year, month, and day. Note particularly where the "year" is shown. The space following is for explanatory matter; the next column, left blank in the illustration, is a reference column whose use will be explained later; and the last column in each section is the money column, where the dollar subsection column is further divided into columns for each digit of the amount. Care must be exercised to observe such rulings when writing in the amounts. The account with Cash in the illustration shows on the left a receipt of $150.25 from J. B. Givens, and on the right, the payment of $5.50 for stationery. These two items are entirely dissimilar. Another receipt of $72.69 on January 3 from cash sales is shown on the same side of the account as the record of the previous receipt and directly under it. Note that the name of the month is not repeated.

The Mechanism of the Account.—Thus the mechanism of the account is designed not only to give a brief history of each item entered therein, but primarily to bring together all items of the same kind relating to that account, so that they may be summarized. It should be thoroughly understood that all items on each side of the account are similar items, though the two sides themselves are of exactly opposite kinds. Where the account has entries on both sides, i.e., is composed of dissimilar items, a comparison of the totals of each group shows the condition of the account. In the Cash account given, the total of the left side, $222.94, showing receipts, compared with the total of the right, $5.50, showing disbursements, indicates that there is $217.44 cash now on hand. It is evident, therefore, that the account is a mathematical device for holding on one side all items to be added and on the other all items to be subtracted. Only in this way can addition and subtraction be performed within the account.

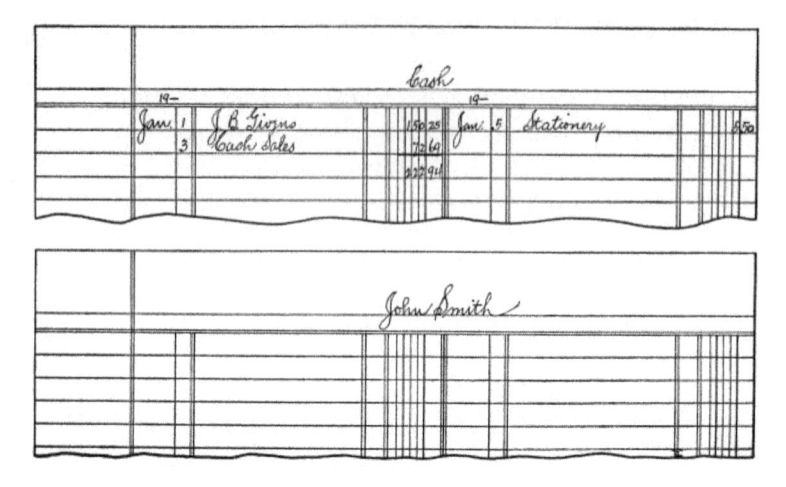

Form 1. Form of Ledger Accounts

The Number of Accounts.—The number of accounts to be kept in the ledger is determined by the minuteness of detail desired for the guidance of the management of a business. The financial and profit and loss statements usually lack detail and for this reason the items appearing thereon are frequently subdivided in the ledger into numerous accounts.

CHAPTER IX
THE ACCOUNT
(Continued)

The Balance of the Account.—As stated in Chapter VIII, the account is divided into two sections, a left and a right, for the purpose of separating items relating to the same account which are dissimilar, and thus affording a comparison between the totals of these dissimilar groups. An account containing dissimilar items may have the same total on both sides, in which case it is said to balance, i.e., the class of items on one side exactly balances or cancels those on the opposite side; or one side of the account may be larger than the other, in which case the amount of the excess is called the "balance" in the account, or of the account. An account takes its nature or classification from the larger side, on which the balance appears. The account balances are shown in summarized form on the balance sheet or the profit and loss statement.

The Account Title Indicative of Its Classification.—The account title or name should be so plain as easily to indicate its main classification. The two main classes of accounts are, as stated above, those relating to assets and liabilities, or property—things owned and things owed; and those relating to proprietorship—those showing the increases or decreases in net worth. The title of an account should clearly indicate whether the account belongs to the asset or liability class, or to the proprietorship class.

The accounts called Cash, Accounts Receivable, Mortgages Payable, Accrued Wages, clearly show assets and liabilities; while those entitled Sales, Rent Income, Wages, Expenses, indicate factors affecting proprietorship.

The Meaning of Account Balances.—In the asset accounts the larger side, and therefore the balance of the account, is normally on the left, i.e., the balance of Cash, Land, Buildings, Furniture and Fixtures, Notes Receivable, and the like are normally left-side balances. It follows, therefore, that all entries showing the acquisition or increase of assets are made on the left side of their accounts, and all entries showing the disposal or decrease of assets are made on the right side of the accounts. Very seldom are the cancellations listed on the right side in excess of the assets listed on the left.

In the liability accounts the balance is normally on the right side because liabilities are subtraction items from the assets and should, therefore, normally be on the opposite side of the account. Notes Payable, Accounts Payable, Mortgages Payable, Interest Payable, Rent Payable, and the like, have normally right-side balances. It follows, therefore, that all entries showing the assumption of liabilities are made to the right side of the account, and all entries showing the cancellation of these liabilities are made on the left side. Rarely are liability cancellations in excess of the liabilities owed.

As will be explained in Chapter XII, in the group of accounts indicating decreases in proprietorship, the balance, or larger side, is normally on the left; in the group showing increases in proprietorship the balance is normally on the right. The balances of the accounts, Wages, Salaries, Rent Expense, and all other expenses, are normally left-side balances. It follows, therefore, that entries showing the cost of such expenses to the business are made on the left side of suitably named expense accounts, and entries showing a reduction in the expenses are made on the right side. Items for wages, for example, are shown on the left side of the Wages account, and any subtractions because of overpayment or for other reasons, are shown on the right side of the account.

The balances of the accounts Sales, Rent Income, Interest Income, and other kinds of income, are normally right-side balances. From this it follows that entries showing income are made on the right side of a suitable account, and entries indicating a reduction or subtraction from the income shown are made on the left side of the account. For example, income from sales is shown on the right side of the Sales account, while any reduction of that income, as when goods are returned by customers, is shown on the left side.

Knowing, therefore, to what main class each account belongs—asset, liability, expense, or income—one always knows on which side the balance is normally, and also that the items on the opposite side are subtraction items. Subtraction can be shown in the account only by thus separating dissimilar items.

Relation of the Account to the Financial Statements.—The equation of the balance sheet is the equation of the ledger. The fundamental proprietorship equation is written in two ways:

- (1) Assets - Liabilities = Proprietorship
- (2) Assets = Liabilities + Proprietorship

The ledger (that is, the accounts in the ledger) is constructed in accordance with the second form of the proprietorship equation. In it are found all the accounts of the business, which are included under the classes Assets, Liabilities, and Proprietorship. Under Proprietorship are the subgroups: (a) Net Worth, or capital at the beginning of the period, and (b) Current Profit or Loss. The Current Profit or Loss is in turn shown by the two groups of accounts: (1) Income, and (2) Expense. This classification of the accounts and their relation to the balance sheet are illustrated graphically in the chart shown in Form 2.

The asset accounts have net left-side balances, as previously explained. Hence, if all the detailed accounts which record assets are brought together, the sum total of the left-side balances of these accounts will represent the total assets of the business. Liability accounts have right-side balances, as also explained. Therefore, if all the accounts that record the liabilities of the business are brought together, the sum total of their right-side balances will represent the total liabilities of the business. The proprietorship accounts have right-side and left-side balances. The *net total* of all the proprietorship accounts will be a right-side balance, however, and will show the present net worth of the business.

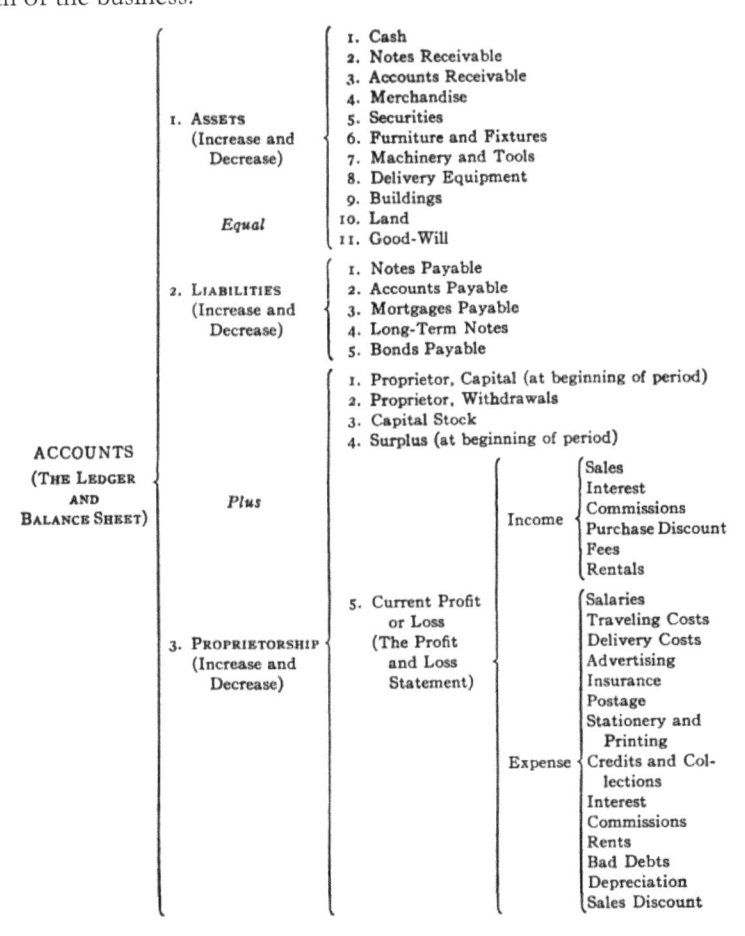

ACCOUNTS (THE LEDGER AND BALANCE SHEET)

1. ASSETS (Increase and Decrease)
   1. Cash
   2. Notes Receivable
   3. Accounts Receivable
   4. Merchandise
   5. Securities
   6. Furniture and Fixtures
   7. Machinery and Tools
   8. Delivery Equipment
   9. Buildings
   10. Land
   11. Good-Will

Equal

2. LIABILITIES (Increase and Decrease)
   1. Notes Payable
   2. Accounts Payable
   3. Mortgages Payable
   4. Long-Term Notes
   5. Bonds Payable

Plus

3. PROPRIETORSHIP (Increase and Decrease)
   1. Proprietor, Capital (at beginning of period)
   2. Proprietor, Withdrawals
   3. Capital Stock
   4. Surplus (at beginning of period)
   5. Current Profit or Loss (The Profit and Loss Statement)
      - Income: Sales, Interest, Commissions, Purchase Discount, Fees, Rentals
      - Expense: Salaries, Traveling Costs, Delivery Costs, Advertising, Insurance, Postage, Stationery and Printing, Credits and Collections, Interest, Commissions, Rents, Bad Debts, Depreciation, Sales Discount

Form 2. Chart of Accounts

Accordingly, when one views the accounts in the ledger in their fundamental groupings—namely, assets, liabilities, and proprietorship—it is seen that the equation of the balance sheet is also the equation of the ledger. The account is thus seen to be an integral part of the balance sheet. It is so arranged, however, as to sort and handle additions and subtractions and to furnish a net result for use in the balance sheet.

The asset portion of the proprietorship equation is in the ledger broken up into the various kinds of assets, record of which is desirable and necessary for purposes of adequate control of the business. In keeping the record, all the transactions affecting—that is, either adding to or subtracting from—a given asset are recorded in the account kept with that asset. In this way each account brings about a sorting of the transactions affecting it. It separates these transactions into two kinds, those which add to and those which subtract from its value, and by means of its net balance at any given time it summarizes the numberless transactions which have affected it during a period and gives a net result showing its present status.

In much the same way the liability item of the proprietorship equation is broken up in the ledger for purposes of detailed information, into a large number of individual liability accounts. The sum total of the balance of these accounts is the liability item of the proprietorship equation.

The proprietorship section of the equation is a little more complex when split up, as it is in the ledger. In accordance with the chart given in Form 2, it will be seen that proprietorship is classified in the two main groups: (1) capital at the beginning of the period, and (2) changes of capital during the period. It is this latter group of accounts which, as they are carried in the ledger, have both right-side and left-side balances. The income accounts, which tend to increase capital and which, when merged with the capital accounts at the beginning of the period, add to that capital, have right-side balances. The accounts which tend to decrease capital, that is, the expense accounts, because they are subtraction items, have left-side balances. The net increase (or decrease) in capital for the period is the excess (or deficit) of the total income accounts over the total expense accounts. The summarized result therefore of current changes in capital added to the capital at the beginning of the period, gives the proprietorship of the business at any given time.

At the beginning of a business enterprise the accounts in the ledger will be an opening balance sheet of the business. Day by day by day as transactions take place, there will be a constant change in the values of the assets, liabilities, and the proprietorship account which will thus express the changing financial condition of the business. Some assets will be increased while others will be decreased; liabilities will also change; and with these changes there will be brought about a change in proprietorship—an increase or a decrease. The ledger must record these changing values as they take place, so that the condition of the business can be determined practically at any time.

The ledger is thus seen to contain and comprise the balance sheet of the business at all times. Certain groupings, summarizations, and adjustments may be necessary before a balance sheet technically correct as to form and content can be taken from the ledger, but the fundamental balance sheet equation is always contained in the ledger. This is pictured graphically in the chart shown in Form 2. A further consideration of the relationships between assets, liabilities, and proprietorship leads us to an explanation of the principles or philosophy of debit and credit, a matter which will be taken up in the next chapter.

CHAPTER X
THE PHILOSOPHY OF DEBIT AND CREDIT

Double-Entry Bookkeeping.—Several systems or methods of keeping business records have at various times been in use. The method which at the present time is used by all businesses, excepting those of the simplest sort, is called "double-entry bookkeeping" and is the method which is being set forth here. It is based on the proprietorship equation expressed in the form: Assets = Liabilities + Proprietorship. It is possible to make a balance sheet if only asset and liability records are kept, because proprietorship is always the difference between them. Such a system of record-keeping would fail completely in giving the information as to the current increases and decreases in proprietorship and the causes of such changes. As was indicated in an earlier chapter, such a system would have the disadvantages which the comparative balance sheet has as a means of managing and controlling a business enterprise. The information which is given by the profit and loss records of the business would be entirely lacking.

Double-entry bookkeeping, accordingly, keeps a record not only of assets and liabilities, but also of proprietorship and its constantly changing value. The advantages of such a system were discussed when the need for the information furnished by the profit and loss statement was pointed out (see page 39). Not only does double-entry bookkeeping give this full and complete information, but it ties this information into a system whose mathematical accuracy and correctness can be proved. It is an invention or device whose purpose is definitely to give the desired information and to demonstrate the mathematical correctness of that information.

As already stated, the system of double-entry bookkeeping is based on the proprietorship equation. An equation is an expressed equality. The ledger kept by double-entry bookkeeping always maintains this equality. The sum total of the entries on the left side of all the accounts must equal the sum total of the entries on the right side of the accounts. The way in which the ledger becomes an expanded or detailed balance sheet was explained fully in the previous chapter. There it was shown that the sum of the net balances of all asset accounts, as carried in the ledger as left-side balances, at all times equals the sum of the net balances of the liability and the proprietorship accounts carried in the ledger as right-side balances.

It is evident that, if in place of the net balances of each group of accounts, the gross left- and right-side totals are substituted, the equation would still be maintained, inasmuch as the net balance in each instance is secured by subtracting the same amount, namely, the lesser total, from both sides of the account.

Under double entry, therefore, the equality of the left side of the ledger, that is, the total of the left-side amounts of all of the accounts, is constantly maintained with the right side of the ledger, that is, the total of the right-side amounts of all the accounts. The vertical division of the ledger separating an account into its left and right sides, may with little stretch of the imagination be considered an equality sign, which thus makes one big equation out of all the accounts in the ledger. Under double-entry bookkeeping, therefore, the principles of entry in the ledger are based on no logic or philosophy other than that which attaches to the fundamental proprietorship equation of the balance sheet. Double entry is an invention, a device, and its use requires adherence to the principles of entry necessary to maintain its equation. What these principles are will now be explained.

The Business Transaction Defined.—Reference has constantly been made to business transactions. It may be well to show the idea at the bottom of such transactions. We may define a business transaction as an exchange of values. It may be between persons, as when a sale is made, or it may be between accounts within the business itself, as when a transfer is made between accounts, i.e., when an item is taken from one account and transferred to another for the sake of more clearly showing its nature. Some authors further analyze transactions as *complete* when the bargain is fully consummated between the parties, as when delivery is made and the money is paid in cash; or *incomplete* as where something still remains to be done by either or both parties to the transaction. In this latter case, claims or rights of action at law arise to protect the parties until the transaction is consummated. But, since from the accounting standpoint a claim or right is one kind of property or asset, there is little need of this finer analysis.

Analyzing the Transaction as to Its Accounting Record.—When a transaction occurs in a business, it must first be classified before proper record can be made of it under the account title which groups transactions of a like nature. Its elements must be analyzed, its effect on assets and liabilities, or on expenses and income, must be determined. Has the transaction increased or decreased assets or liabilities, or has it increased or decreased proprietorship, or has it resulted in simply a transfer between accounts—these are the first questions to be determined. The basis of all fundamental classifications is the effect of the transaction upon the balance sheet and profit and loss statements. They are the goal towards which all records look, but the principle which determines the subdivisions in the main classes of accounts and the titles to be given to the accounts which are to be carried in the records, is the amount and kind of information desired by the management throughout the fiscal period. After the transaction has been properly classified, it is merely a matter of recording it according to the standards or forms of good accounting, which is merely a device for abbreviating the work of recording, i.e., the transaction is translated into correct accounting language.

The Use of Debit and Credit.—To show the side of the account affected by a transaction, the words "debit" and "credit" are used, indicating left and right respectively. The use of these words had its origin with transactions between persons and the accounts kept with them. The person owing was charged or debited, while the person to whom the business owed a debt was credited. Through use the terms have come to have the meaning stated first above, though still retaining their original connotation when applied to persons.

Fundamental Principle of Debit and Credit.—As stated in [Chapter V](), every transaction is recorded from two viewpoints, viz., its effect on the assets and liabilities and its effect on the proprietorship or net worth. Sometimes, however, the transaction may require merely a transfer entry, i.e., a transfer of an amount from one account to another without affecting the fundamental classes, as was shown above when defining the transaction as an exchange of values. If it is remembered that from long-continued custom asset accounts are debit accounts, i.e., normally have debit or left-side balances, and liability accounts are credit accounts; that expense accounts are debit and income accounts are credit, the fundamental principles for determining the debit and credit involved in every transaction become pretty well established in one's mind.

Starting, therefore, with the original investment, whatever form it may have, the transaction is reducible to the fundamental equation:

$$\text{Assets} = \text{Liabilities} + \text{Proprietorship}$$

in which "liabilities" may or may not be a "zero" quantity, depending on the nature of the investment. All transactions thereafter must be viewed according to their effects on the three terms of the equation above. We may summarize the effects produced by the various transactions of the business as:

Increase or decrease of assets
     "   "   "   " liabilities
     "   "   "   " proprietorship

with this qualification: that some transactions result in transfers only without affecting the totals of any of the three groups above, as when an asset is transferred from one account to another for purposes of more accurate classification.

The Debit and Credit Schedule.—Bearing in mind the customary distinction between debit and credit, and the fact that entry of a transaction is always made from a double viewpoint—that of cause and effect—every transaction may have its debit and credit determined by the following schedule:

Debit:

(1) Increase of Assets

(2) Decrease of Liabilities

(3) Decrease of Proprietorship

Credit:

(a) Decrease of Assets

(b) Increase of Liabilities

(c) Increase of Proprietorship

Debit and Credit Determination Illustrated.—Examples illustrating the various classes of transactions and the manner of determining their debit and credit will now be given. The student should strive to understand the double point of view necessary in determining debit and credit. It is perhaps well to call attention to the fact that the illustrations are entirely unrelated, i.e., do not constitute a sequence of events in any business. It should also be kept in mind that transactions are recorded always from the standpoint of the business whose records are being kept.

1. The purchase of merchandise for cash. The result is an increase of the asset Merchandise caused by the decrease of the asset Cash. Accordingly, the debit and credit of the entry for the transaction are shown by the above schedule under (1) and (a), i.e., debit Merchandise and credit Cash. The transaction is also an illustration of the transfer entry, in which there is no increase or decrease of total assets, liabilities, or proprietorship.

2. The purchase of merchandise on account. This results in an increase of assets caused by the increase of liabilities. The schedule above shows under (1) and (b) a debit to Merchandise and a credit to the personal account payable, indicated by the name of the creditor.

3. The receipt of cash for services performed, as when a broker receives the amount of his commission in cash. The result here is an increase of the asset Cash, caused by the increase of proprietorship, as the performance of services is the chief source of the broker's income. The schedule shows under (1) and (c) a debit to Cash and a credit to some temporary proprietorship account by name, as Commissions Earned.

4. The payment of a note payable in cash. This results in a decrease of the liability, Notes Payable, caused by the decrease of the asset Cash. Accordingly, debit Notes Payable and credit Cash, (2) and (a).

5. The settlement of a personal account payable by giving a note payable. The effect here is simply a cancellation of one kind of liability with another kind; it is a transfer entry. Debit the personal account payable; credit Notes Payable, (2) and (b).

6. The rendering of a business service to a creditor, thereby canceling an indebtedness to him; as when a physician renders medical aid to his creditor from whom he has purchased supplies. The effect is a decrease in liabilities and an increase in proprietorship. Debit the personal account payable, by name, and credit some temporary proprietorship account, by name, as Fees or Services, (2) and (c).

7. A workman is paid his wages in cash. The result is a decrease in proprietorship and a decrease in the asset Cash. Wages are a cost of doing business and therefore decrease Proprietorship. They are a service rendered to the business instead of by it—an expense as distinguished from an income. Debit the temporary proprietorship account, Wages, and credit Cash, (3) and (a).

8. The account of a lawyer is credited for the amount of his fee. A decrease of proprietorship, for the service rendered the business, and an increase in liabilities. Debit Legal Expense and credit the personal account payable, (3) and (b).

9. Transfer the net gain shown by the Profit and Loss account to the Surplus account. The result is a simple transfer, causing a decrease in proprietorship as shown in the Profit and Loss account and an increase in proprietorship as shown in the Surplus account. Debit Profit and Loss and credit Surplus, (3) and (c).

In a similar manner, all transactions may be analyzed and their entry in the accounts determined.

Necessary Equilibrium of Debits and Credits.—Before passing to more detailed rules for debit and credit, the necessary equality of debits and credits should again be pointed out. Starting with the proprietorship equation expressed in this form:

$$\text{Assets} = \text{Liabilities} + \text{Proprietorship},$$

of which the left side is represented in the accounts by debits and the right side by credits, the equality of the debit balances and the credit balances of the accounts in the ledger is readily seen. If, now, for all succeeding transactions an entry is made having an equal debit and credit, evidently the equilibrium of the total debits and credits in the accounts is maintained and the two sides of the ledger are in agreement. The making of an equal debit and credit for every entry is fundamental and must be strictly observed.

CHAPTER XI
DEBIT AND CREDIT AS APPLIED TO ASSET AND LIABILITY ACCOUNTS

Student's Use of Working Rules.—In order to indicate the more usual types of transactions which affect the asset, liability, and proprietorship accounts, a set-up of the various groups of accounts will be given, under which will be shown transactions recorded as debits and those recorded as credits. Accounts will be shown in the order in which they appear in the balance sheet. The accounts under each group will, of course, bear their own individual titles and not the title of the group. Only such entries as are more frequently met with will be given. Since in the group accounts given as guides only those entries appear which affect these group accounts, it is deemed impracticable to attempt to show the contra, or other side of each entry arising out of the transactions. However, the student should always supply mentally the contra of each entry shown in the group reference account. For the sake of clarity, the personal pronouns "we" and "us" will be used instead of the impersonal name.

Accounts with Cash and Notes Receivable.—Entries to the Cash and Notes Receivable accounts are comparatively simple and are shown in the following schedule:

(NAME OF ACCOUNT)

Debit:

(1) For all receipts or incoming items.

Credit:

(a) For all disbursements or outgoing items.

Transactions with cash are self-explanatory.

The accounts representing transactions with notes require some explanation. When, in the course of business, we receive a note, Notes Receivable is debited and the person who gives it is credited, because our asset Notes Receivable is increased and the claim against the open account of the person giving the note is decreased. Similarly, when that note is disbursed by us, i.e., goes out of our possession, the asset is diminished and therefore Notes Receivable is credited.

A note receivable can be disposed of in several ways:

1. Through its release on payment by the maker,

2. Through its transfer by us to another person in settlement of a claim against us, or

3. Through its sale to the bank.

In all of these cases the credit goes to Notes Receivable. In cases 1 and 3, the asset increased, viz., Cash, is debited; and in case 2 the liability canceled or decreased is debited. It may be stated, however, that in cases 2 and 3, instead of making the credit direct to the asset account Notes Receivable, it is better carried to a supplementary account, Notes Receivable Discounted, in order to show the liability arising from the fact that, through our indorsement, we guarantee to pay the note at its maturity in case the maker fails to do so. This is later explained in detail.

Accounts with Customers

(Name of Customer)

Debit:	*Credit*:
(1) For amount he owes us at beginning.	(a) For money he pays us on account.
(2) For goods we sell him on account.	(b) For notes he gives us us on account.
	(c) For goods he returns to us.
	(d) For discounts we give him.
	(e) For claims we allow him.

The balance owing us by a customer is an asset, and therefore a debit item.

Goods sold on account are charged to the customer because our claim against him constitutes an asset; at the same time the income account, Sales, is credited.

When a customer pays us on account, his account is credited and Cash is debited, showing an increase of the asset Cash and a decrease of the asset Accounts Receivable. Such an entry is simply a transfer from one account to another, an increase of one asset offset by a decrease of another asset.

When a customer gives us his note, his account is credited and Notes Receivable is debited, usually, with the face of the note.

When a customer returns goods to us, he is credited to decrease the original charge to his account and Sales or Returned Sales is debited to reduce the income originally credited to Sales. It is not necessary to make any other record of the returned goods, because, as was explained in Chapter VI, no day-to-day record is kept to show the decrease of the asset Merchandise through Sales. So, when goods are returned by a customer, the increase of the asset Merchandise will be shown at the end of the fiscal period when the merchandise inventory is taken, and no other record than that indicated is necessary.

When a customer is allowed a discount for the early payment of his bill, he is credited to reduce the original charge by the amount of the discount, and some temporary proprietorship account, as Discount on Sales, is debited to show the decrease in proprietorship resulting from the allowance of the discount.

When a customer is allowed a claim for reduction in his bill on account of damaged goods or the like, the entry is similar to the one next above—debit Claims and Allowances and credit the customer.

The Merchandise Account

(MERCHANDISE)

Debit:	*Credit*:
(1) For merchandise on hand at the beginning.	(a) For sales of merchandise.
(2) For purchases of merchandise.	(b) For returns of merchandise purchased.
(3) For all costs necessary to bring the merchandise from its place of purchase to its place of sale.	
(4) For goods returned by customers.	

Entries in the Merchandise account require no explanation excepting the debit entry (3). The value of the asset Merchandise is not the price paid for it at the point where purchased, for it is of no value to the business until it is placed on the shelves ready for sale. Accordingly, the value of the asset Merchandise is not determined merely by the price paid the vendor, but by this price plus all of the costs necessary to bring the merchandise to the store. Inasmuch as the merchandise is sold normally for more than it cost, the credit entry in the Merchandise account includes two items: (1) the decrease of the asset, as indicated by the cost price of the goods sold; and (2) the amount of profit on the sale, that is, the amount of the increase in proprietorship.

The record of merchandise transactions is thus seen to be rather complex and will be explained fully in Chapter XIII. The above schedule is simply an indication of the types of transactions recorded in the Merchandise account and will be sufficient for the present. It will be seen that the sale of goods results in a debit to the customer's account and a credit to Merchandise.

Accounts with Fixed Assets.—Accounts with fixed assets are those with land, buildings, and equipment of all sorts.

(NAME OF ACCOUNT)

Debit: *Credit*:

(1) For full cost to the business   (a) For sale or loss,

     in position ready for use.   at cost price.

The debit to this account is not for invoice or first cost only, but should include all expenditures necessary to secure full title or to place the equipment in position for use by the business, such as abstract of title costs, freight, drayage, and, in the case of machinery, setting-up and placement costs. The corresponding credit is usually to Cash, or to Notes or Accounts Payable.

The account is credited for the sale of all or a portion of the asset at the same price at which it was originally charged, so that the balance in the account shows the pro rata cost of the part left. A loss from fire or otherwise is treated similarly. If the asset is sold at a profit (an unlikely occurrence), the account is credited with its cost price, while the excess of the sale price over the cost price is credited to a proprietorship account, such as Profit on Sale of Machinery. The debit corresponding to these two credits is usually to Cash or some other asset received in payment. Where the asset is sold at a loss, the account is credited with: (1) the sum received, and (2) the difference between this sum and the cost of the asset, which difference represents a loss. The loss or deficiency is debited to a proprietorship account, such as Loss on Sale of Machinery, and the additional debit is to Cash or some other asset received. This latter debit amount plus the debit to Loss on Sale of Machinery must, of course, equal the two amounts credited to the fixed asset account and representing the cost of the asset sold.

Fixed asset accounts are further considered in Chapter XIII, where the manner of recording loss through depreciation is shown.

Accounts with Notes Payable.—When we issue our own note, the credit is to Notes Payable and the debit is either to the liability account reduced or to the asset account increased. When we call the note in, either by paying it or by canceling our claim against the person returning the note, Notes Payable is debited and Cash or the person returning the note is credited.

Accounts Payable

(NAME OF CREDITOR)

Debit:	*Credit*:
(1) For money we pay him on account.	(a) For amount we owe him at beginning.
(2) For notes we give him on account.	(b) For goods he sells us on account.
(3) For goods we return to him.	
(4) For discounts he gives us.	
(5) For claims he allows us.	

As will be noted by reference to the customer's account, the entries to the creditor's account, being viewed from the opposite standpoint, are exactly the reverse of the entries to the customer's account.

Other Liability Accounts.—Accounts with other liabilities, such as Mortgages, Bonds, Expenses Payable, and the like, follow in the main the general principles laid down (pages 81 to 83). Specific treatment will be given them as they are met in the discussion. In the case of long-time notes payable supported by mortgages, record should be made under the title "Mortgages Payable" rather than "Notes Payable."

CHAPTER XII
DEBIT AND CREDIT AS APPLIED TO PROPRIETORSHIP ACCOUNTS

Proprietorship Accounts Defined.—Proprietorship accounts are the accounts which record the effects, both temporary and ultimate, of business transactions upon proprietorship. The study of the two preceding chapters has made clear the fact that transactions which involve the receipt of income or the payment of expenses result respectively in an increase or decrease of proprietorship, and that these increases or decreases are temporarily recorded in suitable income and expense accounts until the close of the fiscal period, at which time the accounts are summarized to determine the net effect of all transactions upon proprietorship or the capital invested in the business. Therefore, the proprietorship accounts are of two general kinds: temporary and vested. Temporary proprietorship accounts make temporary and immediate record of the results of the agencies or forces at work within the business to produce a profit. They set forth the efforts to increase the net worth of the business. They record the costs of the effort and its yield in earnings, the record being made under appropriate titles to show the kind of cost and the source of the yield. Vested proprietorship accounts record the ultimate or summarized results of business transactions. They therefore record the original investment and its subsequent net increases and decreases.

Fundamental Consideration of Proprietorship Debits and Credits.—Income and expenses comprise the temporary proprietorship items which, after being summarized, show their ultimate effect upon vested proprietorship. In other words, they are proprietorship items set up temporarily to furnish detailed information for aiding in efficient management and control and are later transferred to the ultimate or vested proprietorship records. Since, from the mathematical necessity of the proprietorship equation, proprietorship items normally have credit balances, it is evident that all income, or earnings, must be placed on the credit side of their appropriate accounts. Cost of management and all expenses of operation are deductions from that income and must therefore be recorded on the left or debit side of appropriately named accounts.

Income Debits and Credits.—With regard to their debits and credits, income accounts follow this rule:

INCOME
(under appropriate titles)

Debit: *Credit:*

(1) For all deductions from the   (a) For the yield.

yield shown contra.

Income accounts normally have entries only on the credit side. They are debited, however, for the purpose of deducting from the yield shown on the credit side, (1) because of overstatement of the amount of the yield in the first place; (2) because of error in the original placing of the item of income, which is now transferred to its proper account; and (3) for the purpose of summarizing when it becomes necessary to transfer all income and expense items to one summary account. The entries made for the purposes of transfer and summarization are sometimes called "adjusting" and "closing" entries.

Expense Debits and Credits.—With regard to their debit and credit, expense accounts follow this rule:

EXPENSE
(under appropriate titles)

Debit: *Credit*:

(1) For the cost.   (a) For all deductions from the cost, shown contra.

Expense accounts normally have entries only on the debit side. Their credits are for purposes similar to the debits to income accounts as stated just above.

Examples of temporary proprietorship items can be found in Chapters V, VI, and VII, where the profit and loss summary is treated.

Vested Proprietorship Debits and Credits.—Two accounts should be kept on the ledger with the proprietor, a capital and a personal account, i.e., "John Doe, Capital" and "John Doe, Personal." The capital account records the original investment or the amount of capital now in the business as shown by the last financial statement. The personal account shows all direct changes made in the capital during the fiscal period either through withdrawal or the additional investment of funds or properties. The capital account, therefore, shows no change until the close of the fiscal period, when the increase or decrease in net worth is transferred to it.

An exception to this is sometimes made when there is evident intention to withdraw during the period some of the invested capital, in which case such withdrawal is shown in the capital account as a debit or subtraction item. Also, if there is evident intention to increase the investment during the fiscal period, record of it is sometimes made in the capital account. Practice in this regard is not uniform.

The ordinary transactions with the proprietor, such as more or less regular withdrawals of cash or goods and other similar transactions, are recorded in his personal account. This is his current account as distinguished from his more permanent capital account. Both of these accounts may be termed vested proprietorship accounts. Their debit and credit schedule appears as follows:

(NAME OF ACCOUNT)

Debit:	*Credit*:
(1) For amounts or values withdrawn.	(a) For amounts or values invested.

The capital account usually shows only one item throughout the period until its close; the personal account shows both debits and credits, made according to the above schedule. The personal account ordinarily shows transactions of the following kind: on the debit side, withdrawals in funds or goods, the payment or assumption by the business of the personal debts of the proprietor, and his retention of any funds or properties belonging to the business, such as collections from customers; on the credit side, the investment in the business of any funds or properties, the retention by the business of any funds or properties belonging to the proprietor, as where the business collects and retains a debt due him personally, and the payment or assumption by him personally of any debts of the business.

Further Consideration of Expense Items.—In explaining the debits to fixed asset accounts it was pointed out that all costs necessary to place the asset in position for use by the business constituted a part of the value of the asset and should be recorded in the asset account. Similarly, it was explained that in the Merchandise account there was included as a part of the value of the merchandise all the costs incident to putting the merchandise in position for sale by the business. Costs of this kind are classed as incoming costs and are almost without exception treated as additions to the value of the asset. The costs incurred from this point on, in the course of business operations, are classed as expenses or proprietorship decreases.

It might sometimes appear that all these operating costs—the kind shown in the profit and loss statement—also add to the value of the assets of the business. Such is not the case. In a mercantile concern, business is conducted for the purpose of selling merchandise. Profit arises through the purchase of merchandise at one price and its sale at a price sufficiently higher to pay for all operating expenses and leave a margin. The cost of merchandise to the customer reimburses the proprietor for his original outlay in merchandise and for a fair portion of the operating expenses incident to the maintenance of the store. The customer is willing to pay this additional amount because it is cheaper for him to pay the merchant a margin over the cost of the merchandise sufficient to induce the merchant to conduct a market for merchandise, than to undergo the necessary expenditures—of time, expense, and inconvenience—entailed in making the purchase from the original vendor.

The economic organization of business is based on this hypothesis. In the management of a business there is a very large element of risk. The sale price of commodities at a given time is not always determined on the basis of the original cost of the commodity plus the costs of maintaining a store for its sale. Competition sometimes enters in to drive the price down below this amount. While every merchant *expects* in the long run to receive from the sale of his merchandise not only what he himself has paid for it but also the cost of conducting his store and a fair margin of profit, for a given period and for a given item of merchandise he may not be so fortunate.

In recording business transactions, therefore, prudence demands that the costs of operating the business be not recorded as increases in the value of the merchandise dealt in, but rather that they be set up separately and charged against the income received from the sale of the merchandise before the increase (or decrease) in the value of the assets is determined and made a part of the asset record. As merchandise is converted into cash the amount received is recorded as an increase in the asset cash. This cash includes the original cost of the merchandise plus some of the costs of operating the business. These are costs which must be incurred and they add value to the business as indicated by the willingness of the customer to pay the merchant for them. Because the added value is problematical at the time the costs are incurred, they are recorded as expenditures which must be made good out of the sale of the merchandise at a sufficiently enhanced price to cover them, i.e., they are *expenses* which are to be treated as deductions from sales income.

The net difference between the income and the cost of securing the income, as indicated by the expense accounts, will represent the value added to the assets of the business, and will therefore be reflected tangibly in an increase in the value of the assets by that amount. This increase will usually be reflected either in the cash holdings or in claims against customers.

It may not be out of place at this point to call attention to the fact that, as the bookkeeping record is usually handled, the only relationship between asset increases, liability decreases, and expenses (proprietorship decreases) arises from the fact that all of them are debits and are so placed because of the mathematics of the fundamental equation on which double entry rests. Assets, liabilities, and proprietorship are three distinct and separate groups of accounts related only by the logic of the proprietorship equation. As the subject of accounting is developed the student will see the increasing importance of drawing sharply the lines of division among these groups and he will see also the difficulty at times of maintaining this distinction.

CHAPTER XIII
DEBIT AND CREDIT AS APPLIED TO MIXED ACCOUNTS

Mixed Accounts Defined.—In the course of business operations certain accounts which at the beginning of the period belong definitely to some one of the three groups, asset, liability, and proprietorship, with the progress of the period take on a mixed character. That is, included under one account title there is a mixed record of asset and expense, or other combination of two or more groups. For example, the machinery which belongs to the asset group at the beginning of the period depreciates in value day by day, both through use and the lapse of time. This daily decrease in value is of slight amount and in the management of the business it is not necessary that it be shown on the books. While it is theoretically possible to record this daily loss, practically nothing would be gained by so doing. Hence, the machinery account is allowed to carry both the asset value of the machinery at a given time and the amount of its depreciation. Only periodically, usually at the close of each fiscal period, is the account separated into its two parts, the one which shows the true asset value and the other which indicates the amount of depreciation and which is therefore the expense or proprietorship-decrease portion of the account.

In the previous chapter the way in which the Merchandise account takes on a mixed character was briefly explained. It was shown that the credit side reflected both a decrease of the asset and an increase of the proprietorship by the amount of the gross profit on the goods sold. Thus, because of the way in which accounts are kept practically, as distinguished from a theoretically correct method, which would maintain at all times a sharp line of division between assets, liabilities, and proprietorship, certain accounts are allowed to become mixed. It is the purpose of this chapter to discuss the proper handling of the more common mixed accounts.

Analysis of a Sale Transaction.—The impracticability of immediately separating each sale of goods into its two elements of cost and profit and the taking of a physical inventory as a means to this end, was discussed in Chapter VI. The necessity for this later separation may be made clear by analyzing a sale transaction.

Suppose an article costing $10 is sold for $12. At the time of its purchase a debit was made to Merchandise account and a credit, say, to Cash. When the article is sold, it would seem that the credit should be to Merchandise to show the decrease in that asset. However, in the sale price of $12 is included something more than the amount by which the stock of merchandise is decreased. This additional amount is the profit of $2. Hence, a credit to

Merchandise of $12 would result in too large a subtraction from the asset Merchandise, if it is intended that the Merchandise account shall always show by its balance the value of the unsold stock. Theoretically the best method of entering this sale would be to debit Cash for $12, and to credit Merchandise with $10 and Profit with $2.

The Old Merchandise Account, Its Content and Significance.—It is impracticable, however, to compute and record the cost of every unit sold. Using the above illustration, instead of crediting Merchandise with $10 and Profit with $2, the entire $12 may be credited to the Merchandise account. There is a disadvantage in this procedure, in that the Merchandise account then no longer represents the one asset Merchandise, but is a mixture of an asset element, merchandise, and a proprietorship element, profit; two elements which must be separated at the close of the period.

Originally, the Merchandise account was kept in this way; it was a *mixed* account and followed the rules of debit and credit as shown below, the amounts being given for purposes of illustration:

(A)

MERCHANDISE

Debit:		*Credit:*	
(1) For goods on hand at beginning.	10,000.00	(a) For sales.	25,000.00
(2) For purchases, sometimes including freight-in, drayage-in, etc.	20,000.00	(b) For returned purchases.	2,000.00
(3) For returned sales	1,000.00	(c) For purchases rebates and allowances.	100.00
(4) For sales rebates and allowances.	500.00		

Where the account is kept in this manner it is usually burdened with the additional data listed under (3), (4), (b), and (c). Sales being a credit item, it is plain that subtractions from sales (3) and (4), must appear on the debit side, and, purchases being a debit item, subtractions from purchases (b) and (c) must appear on the credit side. If these subtractions were actually performed instead of being indicated in the account, the debit side would show net goods to be accounted for, viz., goods on hand at the beginning, $10,000, plus *net* purchases, $17,900, making a total of $27,900; and the credit side would show *net* sales, $25,000 minus $1,500, or $23,500.

If, now, the cost value of the goods on hand at the close of the period (as determined by a physical inventory) equals $8,000, it is evident that the cost price of the goods sold is equal to the cost value of the goods to be accounted for, minus the cost value of the goods left on hand, that is, $27,900 minus $8,000, or $19,900. To secure this subtraction within the account, it is necessary to enter on the credit side this $8,000, the cost value of the final inventory. Accordingly, an additional credit item (d) is inserted, after which the account will show:

(B)

MERCHANDISE

Debit:		*Credit*:	
(1) For goods on hand at beginning.	10,000.00	(a) For sales.	25,000.00
(2) For purchases, sometimes including freight-in, drayage-in, etc.	20,000.00	(b) For returned purchases.	2,000.00
(3) For returned sales	1,000.00	(c) For purchases rebates and allowances.	100.00
(4) For sales rebates and allowances.	500.;00	(d) For goods on hand at end.	8,000.00

The account is now a pure proprietorship account, the balance showing the gross profit on sales, amounting to $3,600.

Modern Practice in Showing Merchandising Transactions.—Actual subtraction, however, within the account is contrary to the method of showing subtractions in the account. Therefore, the mixed Merchandise account cannot show the figures representing "net purchases," "net sales," "total goods to be accounted for," and "cost of goods sold"—information which is very essential to proper management. While containing all the data necessary to give the final information, viz., the "gross profit," the mixed account does not show the separate factors leading up to it. Analysis of the mixed account is necessary to find the elements of which it is composed. The best accounting practice provides for this analysis as the transaction takes place. The old Merchandise account is no longer used; in its place separate accounts are set up to represent the various elements mentioned above. Each account thus contains only one kind of item as indicated by its title. These accounts are:

(1)

    Merchandise Inventory

(2)

    Purchases

(3)

    Inward Freight and Drayage

(4)

    Returned Purchases

(5)

Purchases Rebates and Allowances

(6)

SALES

(7)

RETURNED SALES

(8)

SALES REBATES AND ALLOWANCES

Accounts **(1), (2), (3), (7),** and **(8)** correspond to the four classes of debits shown above in the mixed Merchandise account, and accounts **(1), (4), (5),** and **(6)** correspond to the credits. Explanation of the use of account **(1)** for both the initial and final inventories is given in detail in Chapter XV.

The advantage of the use of these accounts instead of the one Merchandise account is in the availability of the information they contain and in the saving of labor, because now there is no need to analyze the Merchandise account for information relating to returns, allowances, and so forth. By later transferring the totals of the Returned Sales and of the Sales Rebates and Allowances to the Sales account, the balance of this account will show the "net sales." A similar transfer of the Inward Freight and Drayage, the Returned Purchases, and the Purchases Rebates and Allowances to the Purchases account, and a transfer to it of the initial and final inventories, make it show by its balance the "cost of goods sold" which set over against "net sales" shows the figure of "gross profit."

The student will understand that the use of these detailed accounts does not free the record of merchandise transactions from the mixture of different elements, decrease of the asset and increase of the profits. It does, however, make the record more valuable because of the information it makes available.

Accounts with Assets Subject to Depreciation.—Another kind of mixed account requiring explanation is that of the fixed asset subject to depreciation. Due to ordinary wear and tear, and some other causes, most fixed assets lose part of their value as time goes by. At the end of each fiscal period the amount of this loss and the present value of the asset must be estimated, after an inventory has been taken, when necessary, of their number, weight, or other units of measurement. Such an estimate is called an appraisal. The difference between the present appraised value of the asset and its former cost or appraised value constitutes the loss from wear or other causes, and is termed depreciation.

Since depreciation takes place day by day, but for practical reasons cannot be recorded daily, fixed asset accounts, as they stand valued in the ledger, represent true asset values only for the date of their entry. Except on that date, these accounts, then, include depreciation and hence are mixed accounts including both asset and proprietorship elements. As with the Merchandise account, an adjustment is made periodically to separate the two elements. Since the asset account is a debit account, entry of the amount of the depreciation to the credit side would result in the account showing, by its balance, the appraised value of the asset at any given time. It is, however, desirable to leave the account in its original condition, in order not to lose sight of the cost of the asset. Therefore the usual practice is to enter this figure of depreciation to the credit side of a separate account called Depreciation Reserve for the particular asset, using the word "reserve" in the sense of "estimate."

If the latter method is followed, each asset has two accounts, one showing original cost and the other estimated depreciation, and it is necessary for a true valuation of the asset to read the two accounts together; that is, from the asset account showing original cost, the amount credited to the reserve account must be deducted to show the true value of the asset. Because of this, the reserve account is often called a valuation account or an offset account, as it gives the amount of the offset to the original asset account necessary to show its correct value. Similarly, when an increment in the value of an asset is kept separate from its face or par value—as when the premium paid for stock or bonds is shown separately from the par value of the stock or bonds—the account showing the increment is called an adjunct account and must be read with the asset account to secure true valuation. The offset account, then, is a subtraction item and the adjunct an addition item to the corresponding asset account. The showing of the asset and its periodic valuation is made as follows:

MACHINERY

1921

Jan. 1 5,000.00

DEPRECIATION RESERVE MACHINERY

1921

Dec. 31 500.00

1922

Dec. 31 500.00

A reading of the two accounts taken together shows the original value of machinery as $5,000, the value after one year's use $4,500 and after two year's use $4,000. The contra debit for the credit in the reserve account is made to an account called Depreciation, which represents the expense of the depreciation for the period, that is, the deduction from profit or proprietorship. Sometimes, this charge is made direct to Profit and Loss, as will be shown in a later chapter.

Capital and Revenue Expenditures.—The fixed asset accounts usually show the investment of some of the original capital and therefore are sometimes called capital asset accounts. A fundamental distinction must be made between expenditures for the purchase and installation of the asset itself and expenditures for expenses in connection with its repairs, maintenance, and upkeep. These two classes of expenditures are usually called "capital expenditures" and "revenue expenditures" respectively.

The asset account itself is chargeable with all costs incurred up to the point of putting the asset in shape for use in the business. It may be charged also with subsequent expenditures resulting in an increase in its value. Expenditures, however, which are for the purpose of repairs or of keeping the property from too rapid depreciation without adding anything to its original value, must be charged to a properly labeled *expense* account. These revenue expenditures for expenses, such as repairs, maintenance, upkeep, together with depreciation, are subtractions from profit and proprietorship, while asset expenditures usually constitute an exchange of the asset cash for some other asset, which exchange has no effect on proprietorship.

Sometimes two items of expenditure are seemingly of the same nature, while in fact they belong to separate groups, as the original painting cost of a building and the cost incurred later for repainting. In the first instance the expenditure is an asset, a part of the original cost necessary to put the building in a finished condition; in the other instance, it is an expense necessary to maintain the asset in something near its original condition. In order to secure accuracy in the records, careful discrimination between capital and revenue expenditures is a matter of great importance.

CHAPTER XIV
PERIODIC WORK ON THE LEDGER

The work preliminary to summarizing the record of transactions for a period and preparing the balance sheet and profit and loss statement is comprised under three heads: (1) the Trial Balance, (2) Adjusting Entries, and (3) Closing Entries. These three steps will be discussed at this point sufficiently for practice work in closing the ledger. Fuller treatment of the subject is reserved for later chapters, after the nature of the transactions that may complicate the closing of the ledger have been explained.

The Trial Balance.—When all transactions for the fiscal period have been entered on the ledger, it is desirable to make sure that the ledger is in equilibrium, i.e., to make sure that for every entry on the debit side there is an equal credit entry, and that for every credit entry there is an equal debit entry; in other words, that the ledger equation explained in Chapters IX and X is maintained. This proof of the mathematical correctness of the ledger is accomplished by means of a device called the "Trial Balance," which consists of a debit and credit list of either all account totals or of all account balances. If the total debits equal the total credits, the mathematical equilibrium is demonstrated. A trial balance is usually set up somewhat as follows:

TRIAL BALANCE, June 30, 19—

	Dr.	Cr.
Cash	$ 1,000.00	
Notes Receivable	1,500.00	
A. B. Casey	500.00	
B. C. Darby	450.00	
C. D. Ebbets	200.00	
D. E. Field	300.00	
E. F. Gall	150.00	
F. G. Hiller	350.00	
Merchandise Inventory	4,000.00	
Store Equipment	500.00	
Depreciation Reserve Store Equipment		$ 75.00
Notes Payable		1,000.00

Hill & Innes	350.00
Jones & Kanter	175.00
Lunt & Mason	200.00
Noble & Oberly	150.00
P. I. Richards, Capital	5,000.00
P. I. Richards, Personal	1,000.00
Sales	20,000.00
Purchases	12,000.00
Salaries	2,500.00
Insurance	500.00
General Expenses	2,000.00
	$26,950.00 $26,950.00

Work Preliminary to the Trial Balance.—Before taking a trial balance, the accounts should be totaled on each side. These totals are shown in small but legible pencil figures immediately beneath the last entry, sufficient space being left for a regular entry on the line immediately below the pencil footing. Reference to the illustration in Form 3 makes this bookkeeping detail clear. The difference between the totals of the account should now be shown in pencil in the explanation column on the side of the larger amount. Taking the trial balance thus becomes merely a transcription of pencil balances, debit or credit as the case may be, from the list of accounts.

Balancing an Account.—Sometimes it is desirable, as in the Cash account, to show on the face of the account the difference between the total debits and credits, i.e., the balance of the account. This may be accomplished by writing the balance on the side with the smaller total, and by formally ruling up the account and entering in ink the totals on both sides, which totals, of course, are now equal. It should be noted that the total rules in the money columns are drawn on the same line on both sides of the account, thus leaving several blank lines on the debit side. This is done so that the entries in the new section of the account will start on the same line for both debits and credits. On the next line below the double ruling, the balance item is brought down to its proper side. The account is now said to have been closed as to all items above the rulings and shows its open balance in the one item beneath the rulings. The method of balancing and ruling accounts is illustrated in the Cash account shown in Form 3.

It is important to bear in mind that the closing balance of the account is on the side showing the smaller *pencil* total, whereas the opening balance which appears beneath the ruling is on the opposite side. The only purpose of the entry on the smaller side is to force an equality of the two sides, thus formally closing all entries to that point and showing the "balance" as a single item in the new portion of the account.

It should be noticed that this "balance" entry does not disturb the equilibrium of the books, because it is entered on both the debit and credit sides of the same account.

Use of Red Ink.—The total and closing rulings and the balancing entry are sometimes made in red ink, but black ink is preferable. The use of red ink is usually reserved for recording subtraction items in the same column with those from which the subtraction is to be made. Where red ink is so used, the total of the "red" is subtracted from the total of the "black" amounts and the net result is shown in the total of the column. When there are only a few "red" items, this method of recording obviates the use of a separate column for them. Such red ink entries are not found in the standard ledger, being confined to special ledgers and columnar statements of various kinds.

Form 3. Account Balanced and Ruled

Rulings.—The single lines above the totals, indicating the addition, extend only through the money columns and are on the same line on both debit and credit sides. The closing rulings beneath the footings are double and extend through the date columns, the money columns, and the posting reference columns. The diagonal line on the debit side from the total line to the date column for the last entry is for the purpose of filling all blank lines, and preventing any further entries on them after the account is formally closed, as such entries would have the effect of falsifying the totals shown. Thus the diagonal line which may be on either debit or credit side serves as a safeguard against fraud. Diagonal rulings, however, are not used so extensively as formerly.

Transferring.—When for any reason it is desirable to transfer an account from one page to another, the transfer is made by means of an entry similar to the "balance" entry shown in the Cash account above. Instead of the word "Balance," the word "Transfer" or "Forward" is used, and in the column between the explanation and money columns is entered the number of the page to which the transfer is made. On that page the account name appears, and the first entry is the amount transferred from the old account, with a page reference to the old account in the reference column. In making the transfer it is customary to close the portion of the account on the old page in the manner explained above, and to transfer only the balance.

Sometimes an entry may be made in an account in error and for this or some other reason may need to be transferred. Assuming, for the purpose of illustration, that such an entry is a credit, its amount is first written as a subtraction item on the debit side in the old account, with proper reference to the page to which it goes. On the new page it appears on the credit side, like the original item, and may be considered as the contra to its transfer record in the old account. In the new account the old page number must be entered. Great care should be exercised in all transfer entries to show correct cross-indexing.

Sometimes it is desired to transfer not the balance but the total debits and credits of an account. In this case the total debit amount may be entered on the credit side of the old account and the total credit amount on the debit side, with proper page and explanatory references. This forces the equality of the two sides and the account may now be totaled and ruled off. The total debit amount of the old account is then entered on the debit side and the total credit amount on the credit side of the new account.

A much simpler and more workable method, however, is to treat the new account as a continuation of the old. There is then no necessity of formally balancing the old account. The transfer is effected by totaling both sides of the old account and indicating the new page to which these totals are transferred, taking care to enter the totals on the proper side of the new account, with proper references to the old account page. This procedure is illustrated in Form 4.

Rulings and Entries in Personal and Note Accounts.—Some peculiarities met with in the entries and rulings of personal and note accounts, both receivable and payable, will be discussed here.

In John Adams' personal account (Form 5) notice that his address is included in the heading, that the terms of credit extended to him on each sale are shown in the explanation space on the debit side, and that his payments are entered on the credit side according to the date on which they are received. If a payment appears directly opposite the corresponding charge, with no other credits intervening, lines are ruled underneath both the debit and the credit items to show that down to that point the account balances. The record of dealings with each customer should be as full as possible in order to furnish an accurate basis for credit rating. If he is prompt in his payments, taking advantage of the discounts offered him, the account should show this.

Form 4. Transfer of Account to New Page

Form 5. Personal and Notes Payable Accounts

- 96 -

A convenient method of showing clearly the taking of discounts, without the need of calculating the time between dates of charge and payment, is to enter the discount in small ink figures above the net amount received. When two partial payments are made, as on October 1 and 15, to settle the charge of September 20, and there are no other credits intervening, the two credits, with the total in small figures, may be ruled off against the single charge. At the time the trial balance is taken—in the illustration on August 31, September 30, and October 31—the balance of the account is calculated and shown in pencil on its proper side, debit or credit, just to the left of the reference column on the line of the last entry on that side.

Sometimes, when payments are made out of order or on account and it is desired to show to what particular charges they apply, an index number or letter showing the cross-reference is used, as shown in the Notes Payable account. As notes are issued by the business, they may be numbered, and when it pays a particular note, the entry should show the number of that note.

These remarks apply also to notes receivable. If full payment is received on each note as it comes due, the entry may be made on the same line on which the note was first recorded. This may result in the entries to the account appearing out of chronological order, but it assists in an easy determination of the outstanding notes. Numbering, or preferably lettering, the entries in an account may be applied with advantage also to the entries in personal accounts, as it aids in locating unpaid items, especially where payments cannot be recorded in the order in which the items to be settled have been entered.

The method of ruling and thus canceling items as explained above, is usually limited to notes and accounts receivable and payable, that is, to the accounts on which particular payments are received or made and the balance of which it is desirable to ascertain at frequent intervals. On the other hand, it is advisable that the method of showing periodic balances, by means of small pencil figures for use in the trial balance, be applied to all accounts.

CHAPTER XV
PERIODIC ADJUSTMENTS AND SUMMARIZATION

Why Current Records of the Ledger Need Adjustment.—At the end of the fiscal period the ledger does not present a true record of financial condition. The fixed assets of the business are constantly depreciating in value; merchandise tends to become out of date, shopworn, stale, or soiled; some merchandise has been sold, while some is still on hand; some of the accounts receivable may prove uncollectible, and some of the notes receivable may be dishonored. Also, at the end of the period liabilities such as taxes, salaries, rent, and the like may have been incurred, but because there is no creditor's invoice or other business paper as evidence of such liability they are not usually entered on the books until payment is made.

Again, it may be that the services paid for during this period, as shown by the various expense accounts, have not been entirely used, as where a supply of coal for heating purposes remains on hand, or when, as in the case of insurance bought for a given period of time, a part of the protection period extends beyond the close of the current fiscal period. In these and similar cases, the items must be separated into their two component elements, one part belonging to the current period, and the other part to a later period. The part of the expense to be deferred and used up in a later period represents an asset at the close of the current period and must therefore appear on the balance sheet under the heading of "Deferred Charges."

Similarly, income is sometimes received in advance to cover services which have not yet been rendered, or rendered only in part, as when rent is received in advance to cover a given number of months, some of which belong to the next fiscal period. Consequently, only a part of this income applies to the current period, the balance being deferred to later periods.

For these reasons certain asset accounts need to be adjusted and certain liability accounts must be opened to bring the ledger into accord with the actual condition of things and show the true financial status of the business. The entries required for this purpose are called "adjustment entries" to distinguish them from the closing or summarizing entries to be described later in this chapter.

First in importance among the adjusting entries are those required to show the correct value of the stock-in-trade, the fixed assets, and the accounts receivable. Whether the merchandise items are kept in one or several accounts, the value of the stock on hand is not shown at any given time during the fiscal period. Goods have been purchased at one price and sold at another, and no record of the value of the merchandise inventory on hand is available. Similarly, no current record has been made of the depreciation of buildings, furniture, fixtures, or other equipment, nor has any provision been made for the accounts receivable that may prove uncollectible.

Basis of Adjustment Entries.—These items, then, merchandise, asset depreciation, bad debts, prepaid and accrued expenses and income, are the occasion of the adjustment entries. An inventory is required to find the value of the stock-in-trade; an appraisal is made of the depreciating assets to determine the amount of depreciation for the current period; and proper consideration must be given to the prepaid and accrued income and expense items for the period under review. The following illustrations are concerned with the several classes of adjustment entries. The detail of the account is not shown in each case, but only the balance.

Adjusting and Closing the Merchandise Records.—Unlike the method shown in the debit and credit schedule for merchandise in Chapter XIII, the modern practice is to keep the merchandise record by means of the separate accounts used in the profit and loss statement, viz., Merchandise Inventory, Purchases, Inward Freight and Cartage, Returned Purchases, Purchases Rebates and Allowances, Sales, Returned Sales, and Sales Rebates and Allowances. It should be understood that this detailed record of merchandise transactions is preferable to the single merchandise account only because it gives more information. The detailed record does not in any way maintain a sharper separation of the asset and income elements of the merchandise transactions than does the single merchandise account. It does, however, make immediately available information as to volume of business, purchases, returns, and so forth—items which in any well-managed business are watched carefully. These detailed accounts taken together comprise the merchandise record and are equivalent to the single merchandise account.

It is apparent from a consideration of the single merchandise account that at any given time it includes these three items: (1) the net cost of the total goods to be accounted for; (2) the decrease in the asset merchandise brought about by sale; and (3) the profit on the goods sold. In order to bring about the separation of the merchandise records into the two elements (a) goods still on hand, that is, the asset element, and (b) the profit on goods sold, that is, the income element, it is necessary to bring the detailed accounts together for the purpose of summarization. This summarization is accomplished in much the same way as in the profit and loss statement. The net amount of sales and the net cost of goods sold are determined and set up against each other in order to indicate the gross profit. In arriving at the cost of goods sold it is necessary to bring together the opening inventory, the purchases, the inward freight and cartage, and from their sum to subtract the purchase returns, the purchase rebates and allowances, and the final inventory. How this is accomplished in the ledger is explained by an illustration, in which the adjustments or transfers between accounts are traced by means of cross-index letters.

Assume the following facts: Goods on hand January 1, 19—, $10,125.67; purchases for six months $47,897.42; inward freight and cartage $560.25; returned purchases $2,125.40; purchase rebates and allowances $267.92; sales $65,283.21; returned sales $3,924.83; sales rebates and allowances $392.48; and goods on hand June 30, 19—, $11,267.40. Each of these items appears as the first entry on the proper side of its account, and is distinguished by not being marked with a bracketed letter. The items comprise the ledger record previous to summarization at the close of the fiscal period.

Merchandise Inventory

19—			19—		
Jan. 1		10,125.67	June 30 Purchases (B)		10,125.67
June 30 (E)		11,267.40			

Purchases

19—			19—		
June 30 (Total purchases)		47,897.42	June 30 Returned Purchases (C)		2,125.40
Inward Freight and Cartage (A)		560.25	Pur. Rebates & Allow (D)		267.92
Mdse. Inventory, Jan. 1 (B)		10,125.67	Inventory, June 30 (E)		11,267.40
			Profit & Loss (F)		44,922.62
		58,583.34			58,583.34

Inward Freight and Cartage

19—			19—		
June 30 (Total)		560.25	June 30 Purchases (A)		560.25

Returned Purchases

19—			19—		
June 30 Purchases	(C)	2,125.40	June 30 (Total)		2,125.40

Purchases Rebates and Allowances

19—			19—		
June 30 Purchases	(D)	267.92	June 30 (Total)		267.92

Sales

19—			19—		
June 30 Returned Sales	(G)	3,924.83	June 30 (Total)		65,283.21
Sales Rebates & Allow	(H)	392.48			
Profit & Loss	(I)	60,965.90			
		65,283.21			65,283.21

Returned Sales

19—		19—		
June 30 (Total)	3,924.83	June 30 Sales	(G)	3,924.83

Sales Rebates and Allowances

19—		19—		
June 30 (Total)	392.48	June 30 Sales	(H)	392.48

Profit and Loss

19—   19—

June 30   Purchases (F) 44,922.62   June 30 Sales   (I) 60,965.90

To show the total cost of goods bought during the period, the freight-in of $560.25 is transferred or closed into Purchases. To show the "*gross* cost of goods to be accounted for," amounting to $58,583.34, the inventory of January 1 of $10,125.67 is transferred to the debit side of Purchases account. To show the *net* cost of goods to be accounted for, the returned purchases and allowances are deducted from this gross cost by being transferred to the credit side of Purchases. The balance in Purchases account at this point, viz., $58,583.34 minus $2,393.32, or $56,190.02, indicates the net cost of goods to be accounted for.

This item of $56,190.02 is not indicated in the account, however, but is given here simply to make the discussion intelligible. Part of this $56,190.02 (net cost of goods to be accounted for), amounting to $11,267.40, is the cost value of the unsold goods according to the inventory of June 30, and the balance of $44,922.62 ($56,190.02 minus $11,267.40) constitutes therefore the *cost of the goods sold*. This final inventory is also shown as an asset on the debit side of Merchandise Inventory in the new section of the account, i.e., the portion of the account following the *initial* inventory section which has now been closed and ruled off as shown on page 118.

Put in a somewhat different form, we may say that the cost of goods sold is found by subtracting from the gross cost of goods to be accounted for, $58,583.34, first the returns and the rebates, $2,393.32, and then the amount of the closing inventory of June 30, $11,267.40. The balance left of $44,922.62 represents the *cost of goods sold*. This balance is now transferred to the debit of Profit and Loss account.

All the transfer entries given above have their debits and credits determined as explained in Chapter XIV. The student should note that the same additions and subtractions are thus brought about in the Purchases account as are made arithmetically in the section of the profit and loss statement given over to cost of goods sold.

The Sales account is debited with the balances of the Returned, Sales and Sales Rebates and Allowances, thus showing a balance of net income from sales which is transferred to the credit of Profit and Loss. The Profit and Loss account then shows net income from sales on the credit side, and cost of goods sold on the debit side. The difference between the two sides is gross profit on sales. All of the merchandise accounts, except the Inventory account, are now balanced, and should be ruled off in the manner explained in Chapter XIV.

The second illustration covers the case where the stock-in-trade record is kept in one mixed account called Merchandise. Using the same data as in the other illustration, the account appears as follows:

MERCHANDISE

19—			19—		
Jan. 1	Inventory	10,125.67	June 30	Sales	65,283.21
June 30	Purchases	47,897.42		Returned Purchases	2,125.40
	Returned Sales	3,924.83			
	Sales Rebates and Allow	392.48		Purchases Rebates and Allow	267.92
	Inward Freight and Cartage	560.25		Inventory, June 30	11,267.40
	Profit and Loss	16,043.28			
		78,943.93			78,943.93
June 30 Inventory		11,267.40			

When the merchandise record is kept under separate accounts the freight-in is *transferred* to the debit of the Purchases account; but when a single mixed account is kept with merchandise, freight-in is usually entered directly to the debit of that account. To adjust the account when kept in this manner, the new inventory is entered to the credit of Merchandise. The balance of the Merchandise account now shows the gross profit on sales, $16,043.28. This is transferred to the credit of Profit and Loss. (It will be noted that this *transferred* item is identical with the *balance* of the Profit and Loss account of the first illustration.) The Merchandise account is now totaled and ruled off. On the debit side, beneath the ruling, the new inventory is entered, being the contra to the credit entry of $11,267.40 above the ruling. The equilibrium of debits and credits is thus maintained. In this open item of $11,267.40 the account shows an asset, the goods on hand June 30.

The handling of merchandise transactions according to the second illustration is not considered good accounting but is shown because it is frequently met with in bookkeeping practice.

Underlying Theory in the Adjustment of Merchandise Records.— Careful analysis and study of the adjustment of the merchandise records should be made in order to see the way in which the logic of the trading section of the profit and loss statement is worked out in the ledger. The record of the merchandise asset should be kept, in strict theory, in the same way as that of every other asset, namely, the accounts should be charged with the full cost of the asset and credited at cost price with the portion sold, the profit or loss on the sale being carried in a separate account. The balance of the Merchandise account would then show the value of the asset merchandise on hand at any time.

Theory, however, gives way to the practical difficulties of handling the account in this way. Therefore, periodically the mixture of asset decreases and income increases brought about through this practical method of handling merchandise records must be corrected, or "unmixed," so that these elements will appear separately. The Purchases account, after the opening inventory, the inward freight, and the purchase returns, rebates, and allowances are transferred to it, gives the net total of the merchandise asset for the period. This net total represents two things: (1) merchandise still on hand, and (2) merchandise sold. By way of adjusting the records, the goods on hand, as shown by the physical inventory, are separated from the total and put into the Merchandise Inventory account, which shows by its title that it is an asset. That leaves in the Purchases account the cost of goods sold. The credits which should indicate the decrease in the asset, equal to the cost of goods sold, are found in the net merchandise sales, as shown by the Sales account after transferring to it the sales returns, rebates, and allowances. But these credits are here mixed with the gross profit. The portion of the net sales representing the cost of sales of merchandise should now, in strict theory, be transferred from the Sales account to the Purchases account. This transfer would effect the balancing of the Purchases account, indicating that there are no merchandise asset values in that account, these having been transferred to the Merchandise Inventory account. The result of this theoretically correct procedure would be to bring about a segregation of the merchandise records into their two elements, the asset element as shown by the Merchandise Inventory account and the income element as shown by the remaining balance in the Sales account.

Once again, however, strict theory gives place to the more practical need of requiring the accounts to give full information for management purposes. Accordingly, instead of handling them in the way just indicated, the adjustment procedure explained on pages 118 to 120 is followed.

Handling Depreciation of Fixed Assets.—As shown in Chapter XIII, the method of handling depreciation of assets consists of nothing more than separating the expense element from the asset element, both of which are carried currently under the title of the asset. For reasons explained in Chapter XIII, the credit to the asset which effects the separation is not recorded in the asset account but in a supplementary account entitled "Depreciation

Reserve" for the particular asset. This reserve account is an integral part of the asset record and must always be considered in connection with the asset account in determining the value of the asset. The credit entry in the reserve account is a sort of suspended credit, recorded there temporarily for purposes of information. The offsetting debit to this credit is made in the expense account Depreciation.

The adjustment entry thus effects a separation of the asset account into the two elements, (1) present value of the asset as shown by the asset account and its depreciation reserve account, and (2) the expense element recorded under the Depreciation expense account. The following illustration indicates the bookkeeping procedure:

FURNITURE AND FIXTURES

19—

Jan. 1   750.00

DEPRECIATION RESERVE FURNITURE AND FIXTURES

                                                          19—

                                       June 30 (A)   75.00

DEPRECIATION

19—   19—

June 30 (A)   75.00   June 30 Profit & Loss   75.00
                                            (B)

PROFIT AND LOSS

19—

June 30 Depreciation   75.00
(B)

The asset Furniture and Fixtures, valued at $750 at the beginning of the year, is estimated by appraisal to have depreciated 10%, or $75, during the half-year. This cost or expense is charged to an account called Depreciation, and credited not to Furniture and Fixtures, but to the valuation account "Depreciation Reserve Furniture and Fixtures." The Furniture and Fixtures account and its valuation account, *taken together*, show the appraisal value of $675. Thus the credit adjusting entry is made to record a decrease in asset values. The Depreciation account, carrying the debit of $75, is an expense account and is closed into Profit and Loss, just as any other expense account is closed.

The Estimate for Doubtful Accounts.—At the close of a fiscal period, when an accurate statement of the financial condition of the business is to be drawn up, all assets must be very carefully valued. The bookkeeping procedure necessary to show the correct value of fixed assets subject to depreciation has been explained. The outstanding claims against customers also require evaluation. Every business man knows from past experience that he will be unable to collect all of his outstanding accounts. He may not know which of the accounts will prove uncollectible, but he does know that there will be a loss in the sum total of these claims against customers. The amount of this estimate is based on past experience in each business.

A standard basis for the estimate is not possible because in some businesses credit is extended much more carefully than in other businesses and in some collections are followed up more vigorously than in others. In making the estimate two methods are used, one being a certain percentage of the outstanding accounts, the other being a certain percentage of the sales made during the period. Where experience shows the necessity, the loss from both outstanding accounts and notes receivable is provided for.

The same bookkeeping procedure is used here as with the estimate of depreciation. An expense account, usually entitled "Bad Debts," is debited, and an account called "Reserve for Doubtful Accounts" is credited for the amount of the estimated loss. The effect of the entry is to separate the claims against customers into their two elements, namely, the true asset element, represented by the difference between the asset account and its valuation reserve account, and the expense element as indicated by the Bad Debts account.

The following illustration sets forth the method of handling bad debts on the books of account:

ACCOUNTS RECEIVABLE

19—

June 30   100,000.00

Reserve for Doubtful Accounts

		19—	
		June 30 (A)	2,000.00

Bad Debts

19—		19—	
June 30 (A)	2,000.00	June 30 Profit and Loss (B)	2,000.00

Profit and Loss

19—			
June 30 Bad Debts (B)	2,000.00		

It is known, from past experience, that the asset Accounts Receivable, $100,000 in this instance, will not be collected in full. To bring this book value down to its real value, the estimated loss, which it is thought will be 2% of the outstanding accounts, is reserved from their value, that is, credited to a reserve account, which is to be taken in conjunction with the asset account. The offsetting debit is to Bad Debts, an expense account. It represents an expense which the current period has to bear, and is closed into Profit and Loss with other expense accounts.

Handling Prepaid and Accrued Expenses and Income.—The method of handling the estimates or inventories of prepaid and accrued expenses and income is very similar to that shown for handling the mixed Merchandise account. Illustrations follow:

Insurance

19—			19—		
Jan. 1 (Paid)		150.00	June 30 (Unexpired)		125.00
			Profit and Loss		25.00
		150.00			150.00

June 30	(Deferred)	125.00				

RENT INCOME

19—			19—		
June 30	(Unearned)	250.00	June 15	(Received)	300.00
Profit and Loss		50.00			
		300.00			300.00
			June 30	(Deferred)	250.00

WAGES

19—			19—		
June 30	(Paid)	2,125.00	June 30	Profit and Loss	2,325.00
(Accrued, unpaid)		200.00			2,325.00
		2,325.00			
			June 30	(Accrued)	200.00

INTEREST INCOME

19—			19—		
June 30	Profit and Loss	145.00	June 30	(Received)	127.50
				(Accrued, due us)	17.50
		145.00			145.00
June 30	(Accrued)	17.50			

The first account, Insurance, shows the method of handling a deferred or prepaid expense. At the close of the period the account is a mixed account, the unexpired portion of the insurance representing an asset to be shown on the balance sheet as a deferred charge, the expired or consumed portion representing an expense for the period to be closed into Profit and Loss. Insurance has been paid, in this case for a three-year term; hence only one-sixth of it is chargeable to the first half-year, the remainder being deferred to later periods. The amount of the inventory or unexpired portion is entered to the credit of the account in order to effect subtraction of the amount, the balance of $25 thereby showing the insurance cost for the current period. This balance is carried to Profit and Loss. After closing the account, the inventory is entered to the debit side below the ruling, thus showing the so-called "deferred asset" portion which will appear in the balance sheet.

The next account, Rent Income, is a mixed account with income and liability elements. It shows that rent has been received for a period which extends beyond the current fiscal period. On June 15, rent for the period of, say, June 15 to September 15 was received. Only one-sixth of this income applies to the term January 1 to June 30; therefore the balance of $250 must be deferred or carried over to the next fiscal period. The adjustment is made by an entry of $250 for unearned rent on the debit side to effect its subtraction from the earnings for the current period, thus reducing them to $50. This income of $50 is transferred to the credit of the Profit and Loss account. After the Rent account is ruled off, the deferred income is entered below the ruling on the credit side, forming a part of the earnings of the next period. It is shown among the liabilities in the balance sheet for the current period, usually under the caption of "Deferred Income."

The third account, Wages, shows wages paid to June 30 of $2,125. At that date wages earned but not yet paid, perhaps because the pay-day did not coincide with the date of closing the books, amounted to $200. This item is obviously an expense of the current period incurred during the short interval between the last pay-day in June and June 30. The adjustment is therefore made by entering $200 on the debit side of the Wages account, to effect the *addition* of this sum to the expense already shown there. The total amount of the account is transferred to Profit and Loss and the account is ruled off. The amount of unpaid wages, $200, is shown on the credit side beneath the ruling. In the balance sheet it appears as a liability, usually under the caption of "Accrued Expense."

Similarly with the fourth account, Interest Income. Income to date is $127.50; earned but not yet due on June 30, $17.50, showing full earnings of $145 for the current period. This total is transferred to Profit and Loss, the account is ruled off, and the earned but not received portion is shown as a debit beneath the ruling, and as an asset in the balance sheet.

Great care must be exercised in the adjustment of all inventories to maintain the equilibrium of the ledger by the entry of each amount to both the debit and credit sides.

Besides the four illustrations given above, there are many other accounts requiring the same kind of adjustment entries. In certain special cases it may be necessary to make adjustments on both sides, as for example in a general expense account or in a mixed interest account showing both interest income and interest expense. For illustration a mixed interest account is shown. The debit opening item of $100 in the new section of the account represents an asset, an interest claim against outsiders, while the credit opening item of $50 represents the liability to others for interest due them but not yet paid. For the sake of accuracy and clarity, however, the better bookkeeping practice is to keep separate accounts for Interest Income and Interest Cost.

INTEREST

19—			19—		
June 30	(Paid)	400.00	June 30	(Received)	500.00
	(Unpaid)	50.00		(Accrued, due us)	100.00
	Profit and Loss	150.00			
		600.00			600.00
June 30	(Accrued)	100.00	June 30	(Unpaid)	50.00

Summarizing the Ledger—The Profit and Loss Account.—After all the types of adjustments have been made, the accounts in the ledger are restored to their fundamental classifications, namely, assets, liabilities, and proprietorship. There is now no intermixture of these basic elements. The proprietorship group of accounts shows both the vested proprietorship, that is, the capital at the beginning of the period, and the temporary proprietorship, that is, the increases and decreases (as indicated by the income and expense accounts) which have taken place during the current period.

At the close of the fiscal period, when the temporary proprietorship accounts have served their purpose by showing the day-to-day changes in proprietorship and the results must be summed up, these accounts are closed for the current period so as to keep the records separate from those of the next period. For the purpose of summarizing the profit and loss group of accounts, an *account* called Profit and Loss is opened in the ledger and to it the balances of all temporary proprietorship accounts are transferred.

The Profit and Loss *account* in the ledger must not be confused with the formal *statement* of profit and loss, made up outside the ledger just as is the balance sheet. On the credit side of Profit and Loss will appear all credit or income account balances, and on the debit side will appear all debit or expense account balances. Accordingly, if the balance of the Profit and Loss account is a credit balance, it shows a net profit for the period; if a debit balance, it shows a net loss for the period.

The net profit or net loss shown by the Profit and Loss account represents either an increase or decrease in proprietorship, and as such is transferred to the proprietor's personal account. As explained in [Chapter XII](), this account usually shows his drawings during the period against these profits as they were assumed to be accruing. The personal account thus indicates whether the amount which he has drawn out is larger or smaller than the net profits as determined by the Profit and Loss account. If his profits are larger than his drawings, his capital has been increased by the amount of the credit balance in his personal account and the transfer of this balance to the credit side of his capital account will then show the total net worth of the business. If his drawings are larger than the profits, there is a decrease in capital, as shown by the debit balance of his personal account, and the transfer of this balance to the debit side of the capital account reduces the former capital amount.

The summarization of results at the close of a period is called "closing the ledger." The procedure consists, first, in a transfer, i.e., in a closing out, of all the temporary proprietorship accounts to the Profit and Loss account; second, in the transfer of the balance of this account to the owner's personal account; and third, in the transfer of the balance of the personal account to the owner's capital account. After all temporary proprietorship accounts, the Profit and Loss account, and the owner's personal account have been closed, the only accounts remaining open on the ledger are those showing either assets, liabilities, or capital. A formal statement of the balances of these accounts constitutes the balance sheet. The accounts through which the income and expense records of the business are closed, summarized, and transferred to the vested proprietorship account, are shown below, with typical entries:

PROFIT AND LOSS

19—			19—		
June 30	Purchases (Cost of Goods Sold)	15,000.00	June 30	Sales (Net income from sales)	30,000.00
	Sales Salaries	5,000.00			
	Delivery Expense	500.00			
	Office Salaries	2,400.00			

Supplies, Postage, etc.	200.00		
Insurance	150.00		
Bad Debts	500.00		
Interest	150.00		
Depreciation	200.00		
John Doe, Personal (Balance)	5,900.00		
	30,000.00		30,000.00

JOHN DOE, PERSONAL

19—		19—	
Jan. 5 Cash	300.00	June 30 Profit and Loss	
Feb. 10 "	250.00	(Net profit)	5,900.00
Mar. 3 "	150.00		
Apr. 1 "	200.00		
May 10 "	300.00		
June 3 "	250.00		
30 John Doe, Capital (Balance)	4,450.00		
	5,900.00		5,900.00

JOHN DOE, CAPITAL

19—		
Jan. 1		75,000.00
June 30 John Doe Personal		
(Net increase in proprietorship)		4,450.00

CHAPTER XVI
SOURCES OF DATA FOR THE LEDGER

Insufficiency of the Ledger Record.—In an earlier chapter a business transaction was defined as an exchange of values, and the ledger as the book in which transactions are grouped under predetermined titles or names. Thus, all transactions relating to machinery are grouped under the title "Machinery"; those relating to cash under the title of "Cash"; those to purchases under the name "Purchases"; etc. Even in a small business the ledger may contain a large number of accounts, all necessary to give a clear-cut presentation of the volume and significance of business transactions.

The ledger record presents an analysis of transactions into their component elements, each transaction being classified and recorded, usually, in at least two ledger accounts, and frequently in more. Consequently, in order to learn the nature of a given transaction, to see it in its entirety, it may be necessary to refer to a number of separate ledger accounts. This process, even if the ledger is small, is not always easy; and when the ledger contains a large number of accounts, it becomes practically impossible. Accordingly, another kind of record is needed.

The Book of First Record.—This other record shows in one place the transaction in its entirety; it gives a complete statement of the conditions and all other data relating to the transaction. It also shows the fundamental analysis of the transaction into its debit and credit elements under appropriate titles. It is called the original or first record. Usually it is not the very first record made of the transaction but it is the first record made in the books of account. The book in which this record is kept is called the "Journal." The record as kept in the ledger is a secondary record based on the original or first record in the journal. Because of its secondary nature, courts will not accept the ledger as evidence without verification.

Posting to the Ledger.—The act of transferring the original entry from the journal into the ledger is called posting to the ledger. In order not to lose sight of the original record in the journal it is important that the ledger entry show by letter and number the book and page where the original entry can be found. This index is entered in what is called the reference column of the ledger account, which is just to the left of the money column. In this manner every entry in a ledger account has a reference to the original entry pertaining thereto.

The Journal.—A journal may be defined as a diary or log in which the happenings or transactions of a business are recorded in chronological order; that is, consecutively day by day as they arise. Formerly it was sometimes called a day-book or blotter. As usually operated, however, the day-book or blotter contained a rough record giving all the essential data relating to each transaction without regard to accounting terminology, i.e., without regard to the formulation of the debit and credit of each transaction. The day-book entry was a sort of memorandum from which a formal record was made in the journal. This day-book or blotter, though still in use in some places, has very largely been discarded and only the formal journal is used. This latter was originally a single book but in modern accounting practice it has become separated into many special journals.

Characteristics of the Journal.—1. Being of the nature of a diary, the journal shows each day's transactions in consecutive order with little regard to grouping. The first characteristic, therefore, of the journal is that it is a book of chronological entry, a record of each transaction just as it took place, with the entries made according to the dates of the transactions.

2. Another characteristic of the journal entry is that it is an analytical and classifying record. Before the entry is made, the transaction is analyzed into its two elements of debit and credit, determined according to the effect the transaction has in increasing and decreasing assets, liabilities, or proprietorship. The account titles used in the journal are the same as those used in the ledger and are selected on the basis of a detailed subclassification of the three fundamental groups of accounts. The degree of detail in classification depends on the desired minuteness of the information required. The guiding principle in giving these titles is to use such names as will tell truthfully and accurately what kind of information is recorded under each head. A journal entry is therefore an analytical record as to debit and credit, which classifies the different elements of the transaction under such titles as will later be used in the ledger.

3. A final and a very essential characteristic of the journal is that every entry should carry in addition to account titles, with their debit and credit amounts, a brief but complete summary of all the conditions and data relating to the transaction, so that, if referred to in the future, the journal record will call to mind the essentials of the entire transaction.

Because of these three characteristics, and particularly the last two, the journal record is of prime importance.

Equilibrium of the Journal Entry; Compound Entries.—As explained in a preceding chapter, the debit and credit elements of all transactions must be equal in amount. Since the journal entry is an analysis of the transaction, it must obviously show equal amounts in the debit and credit columns. In case the analysis and classification require an entry consisting of more than one debit and one credit item, the total of the several debit items must equal the total of the several credit items. Such an entry is called a compound journal entry.

Standard Form of Journal.—The standard form of journal provides spaces for the following information: date, classification as to debit and credit, ledger index column, money columns to show both the debit and credit amounts, and full record of the essentials of the transaction. The following form illustrates a complete journal entry:

19—

Jan.	10	Notes Receivable	10	1,000.00	
		James Jackson	14		1,000.00
		60-day note, payable at First National Bank,			
		Perryville, Maryland, with interest at			
		6% per annum. Due March 10, 19—			

Form 6. Standard Form of Journal

The date is sometimes shown in the middle of the first blank line; but it is better to place it at the extreme left. The account titles are placed on separate lines unencumbered with other data, because they are of first importance in posting. The name of the debit account is shown on the extreme left of the explanation column, with a uniform margin to the right for the credit account. The debit and credit amounts are placed in the left and right money columns respectively. Data giving full explanation of the entry are shown directly below the classified debit and credit entry, slightly to the right of the margin of the credit account title, and a uniform margin is maintained down the page. The column to the left of the money columns shows the ledger pages to which the entry is posted. The entry is read thus: Notes Receivable, debit; James Jackson, credit, $1,000.00.

CHAPTER XVII
THE SUBDIVISION OF THE JOURNAL

Inadequacy of the Old Journal.—As explained in the previous chapter, every business transaction was formerly entered in the journal. This necessitated the making of a formal debit and credit entry for every item, many of which were of the same kind. As the object of every business is to sell something, during any business day a large number of sales, in consequence, had to be analyzed, classified, and entered separately. The entry in each case was a credit to Sales, and either a debit to the customer if the sale was "on time," or a debit to Cash if the sale was for cash. It was soon perceived that instead of making a separate entry for each sale, one entry could be used for bringing into the books all the sales for a given day. This was accomplished by carrying a memorandum of the individual transactions until the close of the day when a formal summary or compound entry was made in the journal. Such a summary or compound journal entry is illustrated below:

A. Jackson	175.00	
D. Hayes	25.00	
J. M. Marshall	132.50	
T. P. Pollard	79.40	
I. M. Cranston	93.20	
M. V. Johnson	17.15	
Sales		522.25

To record the day's sales.

The memorandum of each sale was made in a blotter to record the quantities and kind of goods sold but such entry formed no part of the double-entry record, being merely the source of information for the formal summary entry.

The Special Journal a Labor-Saving Device.—This use of the journal can also be made in connection with other transactions, with similar great saving of labor. Throughout the day in every business there is a large number of cash transactions—receipts and disbursements—which require a debit and credit record. Also purchases of merchandise, although not numerous for any particular day, comprise a large number of entries during the course of a month or year. To save the labor of so many entries, the original journal is divided into separate books known as special journals, each containing the original entries for a particular group of similar transactions, the number of books corresponding to the number of groups into which the various transactions are divided.

For instance, where the policy of the business is to encourage the settlement of outstanding customers' accounts by notes, the use of a notes receivable book or journal effects a very appreciable saving of labor. Through the use of such a book, limited to a record of nothing but notes receivable, it is unnecessary to write each time a note is received, a complete journal entry as follows:

- Notes Receivable 1,500.00
- James Jackson 1,500.00

Instead, the entry of Jackson's name in the notes receivable journal is in itself evidence of a debit to Notes Receivable account. Thus only the credit side of the entry need be shown, with appropriate explanation and detail, the formal debit being suppressed. When, however, the books are closed at the end of each regular period, the total of all these entries in the notes receivable journal is formally labeled "Notes Receivable, Dr." and posted to the debit of the Notes Receivable account. This procedure brings on the ledger one debit entry for the transactions of the entire month. The corresponding credits have been posted in detail day by day from their journal record.

So also, when it is the practice of the business to issue many of its own notes either in payment of purchases or for discount purposes, a "Notes Payable Journal" may be used. The method of handling this book is similar to that of handling the notes receivable journal as described above. A similar procedure is followed in the case of sales, purchase, and cash transactions referred to above. The method of handling these four groups of transactions will be explained in detail in the chapters which follow.

Basis of Subdivisions.—The basis for dividing the one general journal into special journals is the relative frequency with which transactions of a similar nature occur. It would evidently be of no utility to create a special journal if the number of transactions to be recorded in it was small, as the saving in the labor of making the entries would be more than offset by the trouble of using an extra book.

Customary Subdivisions.—The special journals most frequently met with are those for purchases, sales, and cash. The Purchase Journal contains the original entry of purchases, the Sales Journal the original entry of sales, and the Cash Journals the original entry of cash transactions. All *other* original entries are made in the general journal. For the sake of brevity, the general journal is usually designated by the single term "Journal."

It should be thoroughly understood that no matter how many special divisions of the journal may be in use, such books combined with the general journal comprise the *journal* record of transactions. None of them is merely a memorandum record to be summarized and to be formally recorded later. The record made in each is formal, although abbreviated, and each must be posted completely, both debit and credit, in order to secure in the ledger a full record of all business transactions.

A brief explanation will be given in following chapters of the more simple forms of special journals.

CHAPTER XVIII
THE PURCHASE AND THE SALES JOURNALS

Types of Purchase Journal.—For recording purchases of stock-in-trade, a separate special journal called "Purchase Journal" is used. Sometimes this special journal takes the form of what is called an "Invoice Book," explanation of which is given in a later chapter. The purchase journal is sometimes used to record all sorts of purchases, as for example, purchases of store and office supplies, of advertising and printing, and even of services such as labor, and of uses, such as the use of a building. Such use of the journal is more commonly made by manufacturing concerns than by mercantile houses and the journal is then known as a "Voucher" or "Accounts Payable Register," which is explained in Volume II. The present discussion is limited to the purchase journal as a record of purchases of stock-in-trade by a mercantile firm.

Analysis of the Purchase Transaction.—The debit and credit analysis of a transaction covering a purchase of stock-in-trade may result in either one of two groups of entries: (1) if the transaction is on credit, a debit to Purchases and a credit to either a personal account payable or to Notes Payable account; or (2) if the transaction is for cash, a debit to Purchases and a credit to Cash. Whether the purchase is on open account, on a note, or for cash, it is often desirable to keep the accounts in such a way as not only to indicate the vendor in each instance, but also to show the volume of business done with each creditor. This is accomplished when the purchase is for cash or for a note, by opening an account with the creditor in much the same way as when it is on open account.

Thus every purchase transaction is first recorded as follows:

- (1) Purchases
- Vendor

If the purchase is a cash purchase, the liability to the vendor is immediately canceled by the entry:

- (2) Vendor
- Cash

The vendor's account is canceled by being credited and then immediately debited with the same amount. This leaves on the books as the net result of these two entries a debit to Purchases and a credit to Cash. This record of the transaction is seen therefore to agree with the analysis of the cash purchase transaction as previously explained.

Instead of opening individual accounts with each vendor, in the case of cash purchases, the same result is sometimes accomplished by the use of one account called "Sundry Cash Creditors." To it all such cash purchase transactions are posted both from purchase journal and cash book. This method records the combined liability to all vendors in one account. It does not, however, show the volume of business done with each creditor.

If the purchase is on a note, the liability to the vendor as set up in entry (1) is immediately canceled by the entry:

- (3) Vendor
- Notes Payable

The net result of these entries, (1) and (3), is seen to be a debit to Purchases and a credit to Notes Payable—a record which corresponds with the original analysis of the transaction.

Since a purchase on open account also results in a debit to Purchases and a credit to Vendor, it is seen that all types of purchase transactions may be recorded as a debit to Purchases and a credit to Vendor. Accordingly, in making the current record in the purchase journal, the debit element may be omitted, since it is always the same, and only the credit element, which differs in each case, may be set up. Periodically, usually at the close of each month, the debit element is formally set up for the total amount of purchases for the period. (See Form 7, a typical purchase journal.) Thus the one formal debit is made to offset the numerous credits set up during the month. The purchase journal is thus seen to be as fully a debit and credit journal as the general journal, even though in making its day-to-day record the debit element is, for the sake of economy in labor, omitted.

Other methods of handling the cash and note purchase transaction are explained on page 152.

Form and Method of Using the Purchase Journal.—The simplest form of purchase journal is the same as that of the standard journal. It provides space for date, classification, explanation, ledger index, and two money columns. In the purchase journal the money columns do not have "debit" and "credit" significance, but the first may be used for the detailed extensions and the other column for the total of each purchase. Assume, for the sake of illustration, that the following purchases have been made:

January 10, 19—, from S. C. Bontell, terms 2/10, n/30:

    5 tons hay   @ $12.00

    100 bu. corn   @   .90

1,000 bu. wheat @ 1.10

30 tons coal @ 4.50

January 18, 19—, from P. V. Stewart, terms 2/10, n/30:

50 tons hay @ $12.00

130 tons coal @ 5.00

January 22, 19—, from I. S. Van Doren, terms n/30:

100 tons coal @ $ 4.50

600 bu. wheat @ 1.00

January 28, 19—, from S. M. Sax, terms 2/10, n/60:

510 bu. wheat @ $ 1.10

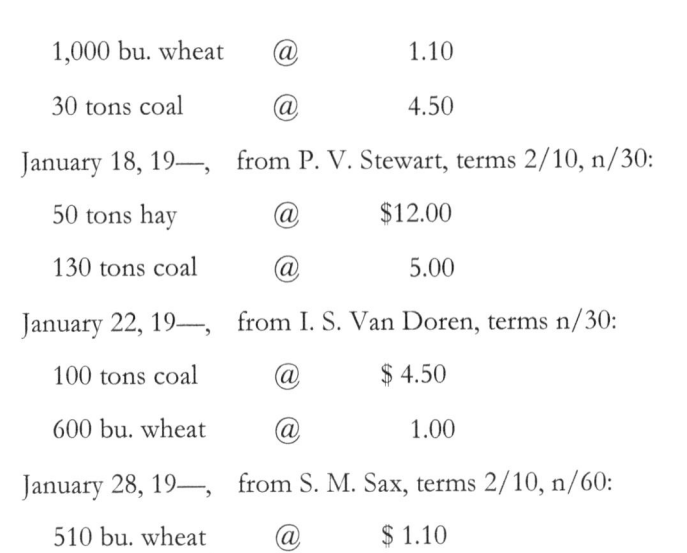

The purchase journal record, using the simple form of the standard journal, would be as follows:

DATE		ACCOUNT CLASSIFICATION	L. F.		
19—					
Jan.	10	S. C. Bontell			
		Terms, 2/10, n/30			
		5 t. hay @ $12		60.00	
		100 bu. corn @ 90c.		90.00	
		1,000 bu. wheat @ $1.10		1,100.00	
		30 t. coal @ $4.50	120	135.00	1,385.00
	18	P. V. Stewart			
		Terms, 2/10, n/30			
		50 t. hay @ $12		600.00	
		130 t. coal @ $5	125	650.00	1,250.00
	22	I. S. Van Doren			
		Terms, n/30			
		100 t. coal @ $4.50		450.00	
		600 bu. wheat @ $1	140	600.00	1,050.00
	28	S. M. Sax			
		Terms, 2/10, n/60			
		510 bu. wheat @ $1.10	131		561.00
	31	Purchases, Dr.	10		4,246.00

Form 7. Purchase Journal

Usually, however, a form of purchase journal is used which is better adapted to its purpose. In this, instead of giving the detailed explanation, the file number of the original invoice is written as part of the explanatory matter, which usually comprises only this file reference and the terms of the purchase. This modern type of journal is illustrated below.

DATE		INV. NO.	NAME	TERMS	FOLIO	
19—						
Jan.	10	15	S. C. Bontell	A7190 2/10, n/30	120	1,385.00
	18	16	P. V. Stewart	A9364 2/10, n/30	125	1,250.00
	22	17	I. S. Van Doren	A7005 n/30	140	1,050.00
	28	18	S. M. Sax	A8423 2/10, n/60	131	561.00
	31		Purchases, Dr.		10	4,246.00

Form 8. Modern Type of Purchase Journal

Posting the Purchase Journal.—In posting the purchase journal, it is customary to post daily the credits to the various vendor accounts as they are entered from day-to-day in the journal. In this way the true status of the amounts due these creditors may be known at any time by reference to their ledger accounts. The offsetting debit to Purchases account is posted only at the end of the month when the purchase journal is summarized. In the meantime the ledger is out of equilibrium because only the credit side of all purchase transactions has been entered in the ledger. This equilibrium is restored, however, by the monthly posting of the debit to Purchases account which must always be made before the trial balance is taken.

An essential part of posting is the cross-indexing of the two records, the journal and the ledger. The cross-reference column in the ledger account must show the initial and page of the journal from which each item is posted. For example, "P. 10" in the ledger would refer to purchase journal, page 10. Likewise the ledger folio (L.F. or Folio) column in the journal must show the ledger page of the account to which the item has been posted. Thus, in the illustration, Stewart's account is on page 125 of the ledger, where he is credited with $1,250. At the end of the month the purchase journal is footed and the summary entry, "Purchases, Dr.," is made and posted to the debit of Purchases account on page 10 of the ledger. This one debit item in the ledger brings about the equilibrium with the individual credits posted to the various personal accounts payable. The purchase journal is then ruled off and thus made ready for new entries for the next month immediately below the rulings.

Departmental Analysis of Purchases.—When it is desirable to separate various classes of purchases so as to determine the profit from each class, particularly in a business which is departmentized, a purchase journal similar to the one shown in Form 9, which has an additional money column for each class of purchases, may be used. If there are three classes or departments, at least four money columns are required. The entry in the first column is for the total amount of the purchases; and the entries in the other three columns, which are headed each with the name of a class or department, are for the total purchases of the respective departments. It is evident that the totals of these three columns, added together, must at all times be equal to the total of the first column. This affords a check on the accuracy of the distribution. At posting time a separate account is opened in the ledger corresponding to each of these classes of purchases. The summary entry in a purchase journal of this kind appears as follows:

	L. F.	TOTAL	DEPT. 1	DEPT. 2	DEPT. 3
		10,125.40	4,269.80	3,197.25	2,658.35
Purchases, Dept. 1, Dr.		4,269.80			
" " 2, Dr.		3,197.25			
" " 3, Dr.		2,658.35			

Form 9. Departmental Purchase Journal

Purchases are classified under separate titles, usually because it is desirable to make a corresponding classification of sales and so secure departmental results of operation.

The Sales Journal—Analysis of the Sales Transaction and Method of Record.—For recording sales of stock-in-trade, a record called the "Sales Journal" is used, which is limited to sales of merchandise. A sales journal practically identical in form with the purchase journal serves this purpose. Its columns are ruled and current entries are made in it just as in the purchase journal.

The analysis of a sales transaction shows a credit to Sales and a debit either to Customer, Cash, or Notes Receivable, according as the sale is "on time," for cash, or against a note given by the customer. In handling cash sales and sales against the customer's note, the same procedure is followed as with purchases, i.e., accounts with customers are opened for *all* sales, and are immediately closed off if cash or a note is received at the time of the sale.

The current entry in the sales journal shows only the debit item, i.e., the charge to the customer's account, the credit to Sales account being omitted. At the end of the month, however, the total of all sales is indicated by the summary entry and is posted to the credit side of the Sales account in the ledger. In order to keep the customers' accounts up to date, the current entries in the sales book, giving the names of the customers and the amounts, are transferred to the customers' accounts in the ledger at the close of each day.

Summarization of the Sales Journal.—At the end of the month or other posting time, the sales journal is totaled and the summary entry is made and posted, thus bringing the ledger into equilibrium by one credit to Sales account for the sum of all the debits to customers accounts made day by day. The closing rulings are then made. The treatment is exactly similar to the work in the purchase journal, the only difference being in the summary entry, where "Sales, Cr." takes the place of "Purchases, Dr." If it is desired to keep the sales record by departments or classes of commodities, analysis columns will effect the distribution. In this type of sales record the closing summary indicates the various departmental or other sales accounts to which postings are to be made, instead of the one general account, Sales, precisely as the departmental purchase journal (Form 9) indicates the departmental or other purchases accounts to which purchase entries are to be posted.

Goods Sold to the Owner.—The treatment of goods sold to the owner of the business requires brief consideration. The proprietor usually withdraws goods at cost price. There is thus no element of profit in the transaction as there is in other sales. A strict analysis of the transaction shows that it brings about only a decrease of the asset unmixed with any element of income. Theoretically, then, such transactions should not be recorded with the regular sales, but should be shown as a credit to Purchases account. In practice, however, entering them in the sales journal is the easiest method of recording them, and since they are not usually large in volume, this method does not vitiate the total sales figure as a basis for estimating percentages of profit. This matter is discussed in detail on page 273.

CHAPTER XIX
THE CASH JOURNALS

The Cash Book.—For recording transactions involving cash, two journals are used. One of these records receipts and the other disbursements of cash. They are known respectively as the "Cash Receipts Journal" and the "Cash Disbursements Journal." Instead of being separate books, however, they are usually bound together and comprise what is called the "Cash Book." When bound together their pages alternate throughout the book. The cash receipts journal occupies the left-hand pages, i.e., the even numbered pages—2, 4, 6, etc.—and the cash disbursements journal the right-hand pages—3, 5, 7, etc.— page 1 not being used. This method sets up the cash record, receipts and disbursements, on facing pages and the movement of cash is thus under easy and constant review.

The Cash Receipts Journal—Analysis of a Cash Receipt.—If $100 cash is received on account from John Doe, a customer, an analysis of the transaction shows "Cash" debit and "John Doe" credit.

- Cash 100.00
- John Doe 100.00

So with all receipts of cash; the "cash" element is a debit. The record of cash receipts being made in a journal devoted exclusively to receipts of cash, the "Cash, Dr." element of the entry may be omitted and only the "credit" element need be shown; the very fact that the entry is made in the cash receipts journal is sufficient to indicate that "Cash" is a debit. The cash receipts journal (Form 10)—the left or debit side of the cash book—is operated, therefore very much like the purchase journal.

DR. CASH

DATE	ACCOUNT CLASSIFICATION (CREDIT)	EXPLANATION	L. F.	AMOUNT COLUMNS	
19— July 1	Balance	Bro't forward	✓		5,000.00
2	Sundry Customers	Cash sales	15	125.00	
3	Commissions Earned	Sale of real estate	20	150.00	
5	J. B. Jackson	On account	25	15.00	
	Sundry Customers	Cash sales	15	140.00	
6	Interest Income	1 year on mortgage	21	175.00	
	Cash, Dr.		1		605.00
					5,605.00
July 8	Balance				5,240.00

Form 10. Cash Book (left-hand page)
(Cash Receipts Journal)

The Cash Disbursements Journal—Analysis of a Cash Disbursement.—If $10 is paid for expenses of some kind, the analysis gives "Expense" debit and "Cash" credit.

- Expense 10.00
- Cash 10.00

So with all disbursements of cash. A separate journal being devoted exclusively to cash disbursements, the "Cash, Cr." element of the entry may be omitted and only the debit shown. The cash disbursements journal is thus seen to be operated in the same way as the sales journal.

Thus, all left-hand pages in the cash book show receipts and all right-hand pages show disbursements. Because it is unnecessary to *write* the debit element of cash received and the credit element of cash paid out, a great saving of labor is effected. Nevertheless, it must be remembered that the entry on either side of the cash book is essentially a journal entry, and that the missing elements—cash debit on the left page and cash credit on the right page—are supplied at the end of the period by the totals when the two journals are summarized in preparation for posting to the Cash account in the ledger.

CASH   CR.

DATE	ACCOUNT CLASSIFICATION (DEBIT)	EXPLANATION	L. F.	AMOUNT COLUMNS	
19—					
July 1	Rent	Store rent July	18	50.00	
2	Stationery		20	10.00	
3	Sundry Creditors		16	250.00	
5	A. Conners	Withdrawal	10	15.00	
6	Salaries	Clerks	19	40.00	
	Cash, Cr.		1		365.00
	Balance		✓		5,240.00
					5,605.00

Form 11. Cash Book (right-hand page)
(Cash Disbursements Journal)

Form of the Cash Journals.—In the cash journals, just as in all other journals, provision is made for date, account classification, explanation, ledger posting index, and money columns. In a simple form of cash book, just as in the purchase and sales journals, two money columns are usually provided, the one for detail—a day's or week's detail—and the other for totals. Such a form is shown in Forms 10 and 11. The student should note carefully how the cash receipts journal is summarized. The balance of cash brought forward from the previous week is entered in the second or total column so that the detail column shows only the current week's receipts. Inasmuch as the Cash account in the ledger already shows the balance of cash at the beginning of the week, i.e., $5,000, this amount must not be included in the summary entry for the current week. In summarizing the cash receipts journal, therefore, the total only of the detail column, showing the cash received since the last summary, is set up as a "Cash, Dr." item. In summarizing the cash disbursements journal, since there is normally no balance carried over from the previous week, the total of the journal—representing the cash disbursed since the last summary—is set up as a "Cash, Cr." item. This is shown as $365, the amount being posted to the credit of the ledger Cash account on page 1.

Cash Book Taking the Place of the Cash Account.—Because the two cash journals are set up on facing pages, the record contains essentially the same information as a detailed Cash account in the ledger. The double page record brings together both the receipts and the deductions from receipts—cash being normally a debit account. For this reason the cash book record is itself sometimes used as a ledger account and when it is so used its totals are not posted to the ledger account. The balance of the cash book must, however, be included in the trial balance of the ledger, because when so used the cash book is not only a *journal* but a *ledger account* as well.

When, however, the totals of both cash receipts and disbursements are posted to a Cash account in the ledger, the balance used in the trial balance is taken from the ledger account and not from the cash book, although of course the balances in both are the same.

Whichever of these two methods is used, it must always be remembered that the cash book is essentially a journal and that therefore its classifications of business transactions must be transferred to their proper accounts in the ledger.

Best accounting practice, however, requires that a Cash account be carried in the ledger so that the ledger will be a complete record of all transactions and will be independent of all other records for proof of its equilibrium.

Posting the Cash Book.—In posting the debit side of the cash book to the ledger, it is important to remember that the debit element of the transaction is merely indicated by the fact that the entry appears on the left-hand page of the cash book. The account name written in the Account Classification column is the credit element and must be posted to the credit of the corresponding account in the ledger. Similarly, on the right-hand side of the cash book, the cash credit element of the entry is suppressed and the named account should be posted to the debit of the corresponding ledger account.

After the posting of the individual items has been completed, the "Cash, Dr." and the "Cash, Cr." as shown by the summary entries must be posted to the ledger Cash account, as explained on page 143.

As stated above, each side of the cash book is, in reality, a journal in itself—a cash receipts journal and a cash disbursements journal—and it is only because these two journals are shown side by side that the cash book is sometimes made to serve the purpose of a ledger Cash account.

Balancing and Ruling the Cash Book.—The cash book in its simple form is balanced and ruled in the same manner as a ledger account. When the balance is brought down to the new section it is usually entered in the second or total column, thus reserving the first or detail column for the daily or weekly cash receipts, and separating these items from the balance brought down from the previous period. (See Forms 10 and 11.)

When the record is to be transferred to a new page, either the current page (double page) is balanced and ruled and only the balance is carried forward, or the current page is totaled and both debit and credit footings are carried forward as shown in Chapter XIV for the ledger cash account. The cash book is closed, ruled, and transferred as of the same date and on the same line for both sides, although usually there is room for more entries on one side or the other, which may be closed by diagonal ruling. This is done in order to keep the record of the receipts of a given period and that of the disbursements in nearly exact juxtaposition, and thereby facilitate a review of the cash movements for that period.

The Cash Short and Over Account.—It sometimes happens that when the cash book is balanced, the amount which ought to be on hand as shown by this balance, does not agree with the amount of cash on hand as shown by actual count. The discrepancy may be due to failure to enter some items of receipts or disbursements in the cash book, or to errors in making change; or it may be due to petty thieving by the cash clerk. If the error cannot be rectified at the time, an entry is made in the cash book, on whichever side necessary, in an amount sufficient to bring the book balance into agreement with the actual cash balance. The account to be debited or credited, as the case may be, is entitled "Cash Short and Over." If the correct charge or credit is afterwards determined, the item or items should be transferred from Cash Short and Over to their proper accounts. Usually the Cash Short and Over account is treated as an income or expense account and closed into Profit and Loss at the close of the period. Sometimes it is treated as an asset or liability account, depending upon the nature of its contents, i.e., the amount of the discrepancy shown and its probable cause.

The Cash Purchase and Sales Transactions.—A standard method of handling the cash purchase transaction when it is desired to keep a record of the volume of business done with each vendor, was explained on page 140, where the purchase was shown to be "washed" or cleared through the vendor's account. A more direct method is sometimes used.

When purchases are made for cash, a complete record of the transactions is made by the entry:

- Purchases
- Cash

Here there is evidently a conflict of places of original record. The transaction being a purchase, record should be made in the purchase journal; and since it is also a cash transaction, record should also be made in the cash book. However, if an independent record were made in both places, a duplication of the transaction would result, since entry in either journal is a complete debit and credit record. The transaction would be entered twice in full, causing an inflation of the purchases and cash disbursements. In the purchase journal, the credit to Cash would be set up at the time of the transaction and at the time of summarization the debit to Purchases would be included in the total of the Purchases, thus completing the ledger record. In the cash book the debit to Purchases would be set up at the time of the transaction, and when the summary was made the credit to Cash would be in the Cash total. Entry in both journals would, when posted to the ledger, bring about two debits and two credits for the same transaction.

To overcome this difficulty the following methods are commonly employed:

1. The record is made complete in both journals, but the credit to Cash from the purchase journal record is not posted, because that credit will be posted from its record in the cash book. Similarly, when posting the cash disbursements journal, the debit to Purchases is *not* posted, because that will be posted from the purchase journal. In this way original record may be made in both journals and each journal will then show by its total what it is intended to show, viz., total purchases and total cash disbursed, respectively. In the secondary record, the ledger, only half of each journal entry is set up, the debit to Purchases from the purchase journal and the credit to Cash from the cash book. This prevents the inflation mentioned above and does not destroy the equilibrium of the ledger because there is omitted, when posting from the cash book, a debit equal in amount to the credit omitted when posting the purchase journal.

2. The method explained on page 140 is used with this variation: The record in each journal shows the individual vendor's account, but at posting time no vendor account is set up in the ledger, neither the credit to the vendor's account shown in the purchase journal nor its offsetting debit shown in the cash disbursements journal being posted.

It is necessary, when making the original entries in the journals, to indicate all postings which are to be omitted, by entering a check mark, ✓, or a cross, ✗, in the ledger folio column of the journal.

The purchase on a note payable, one method of recording which was explained on page 140, may also be handled more directly by either of the methods explained above for a cash purchase. In the case of the note, however, the journals used are the purchase and general journals.

Similar methods are employed, also, for handling the cash sale and the sale against a customer's note.

Columnar Analysis of Cash Receipts and Disbursements.—As illustrated in the chapters on purchase and sales journals, additional money columns are often used for the purpose of analyzing the purchases and sales by departments or classes of commodities. A similar analysis of both the cash receipts and cash disbursements may aid in segregating certain classes of cash items and thus save labor in posting. Of cash receipts, two classes are usually more active than all others combined. More cash is received from cash sales and from customers on account than from any other source. Accordingly, two additional columns may be used with these headings. *All* cash receipts must be entered in the Total, Bank, or Net Cash column, as it is variously termed, and then distributed into any special columns provided. Thus all "Cash Sales" would be extended, both in the Net Cash and in the Sales column, and all receipts from customers would be entered in the Net Cash and in the Accounts Receivable column.

In the case of cash disbursements, the number of columns depends upon the degree of analysis desired. At least two additional columns are frequently found, one for creditors and one for expenses. Where cash purchases are numerous they may be segregated, or where any particular *class* of expense is of frequent occurrence it may be shown in a separate column. Where one ledger is used for customers, creditors, and general accounts, there is little gain in segregating customers and creditors by special columns in the cash book, except as a slight aid in posting. Where separate ledgers are used, it is important to have separate customers and creditors columns in the cash book, as will be shown later in connection with the subject of controlling accounts. Illustration and explanation of the columnar cash book are given on pages 158 and 159.

Cash Discounts Analyzed.—Sales and purchase discounts are another class of transactions best handled through the cash book, although, strictly speaking, they are not cash transactions. When a customer buys goods on account, he is usually offered two bases of settlement, depending on the length of the credit term allowed. Thus, 2% off is frequently allowed if payment is made within 10 days; otherwise the full amount of the invoice must be paid. Because the vendor does not know, at the time of entry on his books, on which basis settlement will be made, he makes the charge at the full invoiced amount. If the customer takes advantage of the discount offered, he pays less than the amount at which his account stands debited, yet the vendor must credit his account for the full amount of the original charge, in order to cancel his entire claim against the customer. To illustrate, a customer buys $100 worth of merchandise, with 2% off if paid within 10 days. On the 10th day he pays $98. The sale entry would be:

- (1) Customer 100.00
- Sales 100.00

The cash entry would be:

- (2) Cash 98.00
- Customer 98.00

But this does not cancel in full the $100 claim against the customer. The $2 discount, an allowance for early payment, is an expense to the business and must be charged to an expense account called "Sales Discount," and the customer must be given $2 additional credit, the entry being:

- (3) Sales Discount 2.00
- Customer 2.00

Entries (2) and (3) are usually combined in one as follows:

- (4) Cash 98.00
- Sales Discount 2.00
- Customer 100.00

Entry (4) is known as a compound entry. If entry (2), which is the part involving cash, is made in the cash book, then the additional entry (3) will have to be made in the general journal because there is no cash element in it and theoretically nothing but cash should be recorded in the cash book.

Handling Discounts in the Cash Book.—This recording in two separate places of what is really one transaction has led to the introduction into the cash book of a non-cash column in order to bring the whole transaction together. The customer's payment being a receipt of cash, the record must be made on the debit side of the cash book. Reference to entry (4) shows that Sales Discount is also a "debit." Where the cash book is limited strictly to cash transactions, the cash debit record shows only the "credit" element of the entry. The use of a Sales Discount column on the debit side of the cash book for the sake of making a complete record in one place thus introduces an extraneous element, one out of harmony with the other entries made there. In posting, great care must be exercised not to transfer Sales Discount to the credit side of its ledger account but to the *debit* side.

Alternative Treatment for Cash Discounts.—Sometimes another treatment of sales and purchase discounts in the cash book is met with. This treatment for sales discount is based on the fiction that the full amount of the original charge is received from the customer and that an immediate return is made to him of the amount of the discount. To use the example cited on page 155, the entries would be:

- Cash 100.00
- Customer 100.00

showing receipt of the full invoice price and therefore full credit to the customer; and

- Sales Discount 2.00
- Cash 2.00

representing the fictitious payment in cash of a discount on sales of $2. In the cash book these two entries would appear as follows:

Dr.	CASH	CASH	Cr.
Customer	100.00	Sales Discount 2.00	

This method of entering discount on sales would have the same ultimate result in the ledger as the columnar method, but the objection to it is that it makes the cash book show more money received and paid out than has actually been the case, thus making it difficult to check the cash against the bank record of deposits and checks. Another objection is that by this method the cash book does not show in one place a full record of the transaction, since the two items are shown on opposite sides of the cash book. Moreover, these items are seldom on contiguous lines because one side of the cash book is often considerably "ahead" of the other. Cash discount on purchases is sometimes handled by a similar unsatisfactory method.

The first method shown, requiring special discount and net columns on either side of the cash book, is the approved method.

Illustration and Explanation of the Analytic Cash Receipts Journal.—An example of a columnar cash book debit side is given (Form 12) for the purpose of illustrating some points in the discussion. It should be understood that there is little uniformity in the columnization of cash books. The needs of the business govern the ruling suitable in any given case. The illustration shown is therefore not presented as a standard form but is given only for the purpose of illustrating the method of analysis of cash receipts.

†This balance is taken from the credit side of the cash record appearing on page 159.

Form 12. Columnar Cash Book—Debit Side

Form 13. Columnar Cash Book—Credit Side

As shown in the illustration, all *actual cash receipts* are entered in the Net Cash column, which in connection with the Sales Discount column comprises the total corresponding to the Total column of the other subsidiary journals

- 133 -

when an analytic record is made. All items received from customers are entered in the Accounts Receivable column; but it is important to note that the *amount* entered in that column is not the *actual cash receipt* but the *full amount* of the original charge to the customer. Sales discount, if any, is entered in the Sales Discount column, and the *net* amount, the actual cash received from the customer, is the amount appearing in the Net Cash column. Cash sales are entered in the Cash Sales column and also in the Net Cash column. All other kinds of receipts are extended to the Sundry column.

In the ledger folio column, checks are placed for the individual cash sales entries, the posting usually being made from the summary in the sales journal, as explained a little later, or from the total of the Cash Sales column in the cash book if the other method is not employed. In the summary entry of the illustration, it is assumed that a Cash account is kept in the ledger. Hence "Cash, Dr." is shown posted to ledger Cash account on page 4; and the total Sales Discount, also *debit*, on page 20. The student should note the method of showing the amount of cash received during the current week, this amount comprising the "Cash, Dr." posting to the ledger Cash account. Of course, the itemized credits, except the cash sales, are posted to their respective accounts, as indicated in the ledger folio column.

The use of the Sundry column for extension of the miscellaneous items makes proof of the distribution possible. The sum of "Net Cash" and "Sales Discounts"—both debit items—must equal the sum of all the other columns.

Handling Columnar Analysis of Cash Sales.—If all sales, both cash and "on time," are entered in the sales journal, the totals of these two classes of sales are posted to the ledger Sales account from the summary in the sales journal. In this case there is no need of a separate Cash Sales column in the cash book, because such a column would simply duplicate the Cash Sales entry in the sales journal. Needless to say, cash sales always appear in the Net Cash column of the cash book, because they are cash receipts, but the "Ledger Folio" must be checked.

Sometimes two sales accounts are kept in the ledger, one for cash and the other for "time" sales. Here, also, if there is a Cash Sales column in the sales journal, no posting of cash sales from the cash book is necessary. On the other hand, if cash sales are omitted from the sales journal, then the cash book should provide for a Cash Sales column and the posting must be made from the total of this column in the cash book.

Illustration and Explanation of the Analytic Cash Disbursements Journal.—The cash disbursements columnar record corresponding to the cash receipts shown above, would appear as in Form 13. As with cash receipts, the illustration is not presented as a standardized form but merely for the purpose of showing the method of analysis. Postings are made or omitted, and the same considerations govern the making and posting of the summary entry, as in cash receipts. Being few in number, cash purchases are not shown in a separate column. The treatment of discounts received on purchases is exactly parallel to that of sales discount.

Since all net cash appears in Net Cash column on either side of the cash book, the cash balance is found by taking the difference between these two columns. The two sides must be ruled up and closed on corresponding lines and as of the same date.

CHAPTER XX
THE MODERN JOURNAL

Matter Left for Record in the Journal.—By the use of a cash receipts, a cash disbursements, a purchase, and a sales journal, four principal classes of transactions are taken out of the old-time journal and entered in separate books of record. If transactions of any other class are numerous enough to justify the use of a separate book of record, such a record should be set up. Although the number of subsidiary journals, each recording one kind of transaction, may become very large, nevertheless in practically all cases it is necessary to retain the general journal (often referred to simply as "the Journal"), in order to take care of such miscellaneous items as are not recorded in any of the special journals.

The standard form of journal was illustrated in Chapter XVI, where it was stated that a journal must provide space for date of entry, account classification, ledger folio index, debit and credit money columns, and explanation. As an explanation of the form, method of use, proper observance of margins, etc., was made there, it need not be repeated here.

Kinds of Transactions Recorded in the Journal.—When the number of subsidiary journals used is limited to the cash receipts, cash disbursements, purchase, and sales journals, as is frequently the case, all items not affecting these four books should be entered in "the Journal"; i.e., transactions involving notes receivable and notes payable; adjustments with customers and creditors resulting from return of goods or claims and allowances thereon; and all formal opening, adjusting, and closing entries. Furthermore, there is usually a number of other transactions, which because of their special and unusual nature cannot be grouped with the items of the special journals and must therefore be entered in the general journal.

Journal Explanations.—When these various classes of transactions are entered in the Journal, a very complete explanation should be given the entry. In fact, all entries covering settlements and adjustments with outsiders and within the business itself are of primary importance and the explanation should be so carefully worded as to make the intent of the entry plain and intelligible.

Closing and Posting the Journal.—No particular formality attaches to the closing and posting of the ordinary standard form of journal. There is no summary entry, no totaling, and there are no rulings to be made. Ordinary care must be exercised to see that the debits and credits are correctly posted. Since the entry in the Journal is given in its complete form and no debits or credits are suppressed, as is the case in the special journals, posting is not difficult.

The Analytic Journal with Divided Columns.—One form of the journal has its debit and credit columns separated, the debit money column appearing at the extreme left of the page, followed in order across the page by columns for date, account classification, ledger folio, and credit money amount. This kind of journal is called a divided or split-column journal and is ordinarily used to collect the totals to be posted to controlling accounts and thus to secure control over subsidiary ledgers. This matter will be fully discussed in later chapters. When the journal is so used it is provided with additional debit and credit analysis columns on each side according to the subsidiary ledgers employed. A divided-column journal with three debit and three credit columns is shown in Form 14. There is always a general money column on each side, the other columns depending on the kind of analysis required by the business.

Form 14. Divided Column Journal

In the illustration referred to, an Accounts Receivable and an Accounts Payable column are provided. It is obvious that the Accounts Receivable column should usually appear on the credit side and the Accounts Payable column on the debit side; although in some cases provision is also made for an Accounts Receivable column on the debit and an Accounts Payable column on the credit side. The account of S. J. White, a customer, which is paid by his note, should be credited for the amount of $510.20 and consequently the item is extended to the Accounts Receivable column.

Illustrations—Opening Entries.—Illustration will be given of a few typical transactions requiring journal entry. The standard two-column journal will be used.

For the purpose of illustrating opening entries, assume the following data:

On September 30, 19—, Jack Gibson started in business, with the following assets and liabilities: Cash $3,500; Notes Receivable $800; Merchandise $4,000; Furniture and Fixtures $450; Accounts Receivable $2,100; Accounts Payable $1,500; and Notes Payable $1,200.

An analysis of this transaction shows that no part of it belongs to either the purchase or sales journals. The part relating to cash is entered in the cash receipts journal. However, in order to show the complete investment in one place, the entire transaction including the cash part, is entered in the Journal and posted from there, with the exception of the cash item. The reason for this exception is that the cash investment is also entered in the cash book and will find its way to the ledger Cash account through the total cash debits at the end of the period. Because of this the cash item in the *Journal* should be checked and not posted to the Cash account in the ledger.

Likewise, the investment item in the *cash book*, showing a credit of $3,500 to Jack Gibson, Capital account, should be checked and not posted to the credit of his account in the ledger because this item forms a part of the total investment of $8,150 posted to his credit from the Journal entry.

If the student has difficulty in determining the debits and credits of entries of this kind, it may be helpful to set up the data informally first, in the form of a balance sheet. Using this as a *guide*, he should then make his journal entry, debiting the asset items and crediting the liability and net worth items.

JOURNAL

DATE	ACCOUNT CLASSIFICATION	L. F.		
19— Sept. 30	Jack Gibson opened up a general merchandise business at 375 Decatur Street, Ansonia, Conn., investing assets and assuming liabilities as shown by the following entry:			
	Cash	✓	3,500.00	
	Notes Receivable	2	800.00	
	Accounts Receivable	3	2,100.00	
	Merchandise Inventory	4	4,000.00	
	Furniture and Fixtures	6	450.00	
	Notes Payable	8		1,200.00
	Accounts Payable	8		1,500.00
	Jack Gibson, Capital	10		8,150.00

Dr.   CASH

DATE	ACCOUNT CLASSIFICATION	EXPLANATION	L. F.		
19— Sept. 30	Jack Gibson, Capital	Cash investment posted from Jr.	✓		3,500.00

Form 15. Opening Entries on Books

The above entries bring the transaction completely on the books of original entry and show the ledger folios to which the various items are posted. Notice the check in the L. F. column in the Journal opposite "Cash" and in the cash book opposite "Jack Gibson, Capital," which is inserted to prevent posting the same item twice.

For opening entries full explanation and details, where necessary, should be given in the Journal, covering lease agreements and contracts entered into when commencing business, and other similar data. It should be noted that with *opening* entries it is customary for the explanation to precede the formal showing of debits and credits, rather than to follow it as in the case of all other journal entries.

Adjusting and Closing Entries.—Other typical entries to be illustrated are those made at the close of a fiscal period: (1) to adjust the books in accordance with certain data that were not obtainable before; (2) to transfer all temporary proprietorship accounts to the summary account, Profit and Loss; and (3) to transfer the net profit, i.e., the balance of the Profit and Loss account, to the proprietor's personal account, and the balance of this latter account to the proprietor's capital account.

The debits and credits of the entries necessary to effect the record of the data and transfers mentioned, can be determined as in the operations with ledger accounts previously shown.

The following data relate to Jack Gibson's business and are given to illustrate the three classes of entries mentioned above:

During the year, sales amounted to $33,000; purchases to $25,000; selling expenses to $3,500; and general administrative expenses to $2,025. It is estimated that of outstanding accounts $350 are uncollectible; that furniture and fixtures have depreciated in value $45. Merchandise inventory shows $5,000 on hand. Gibson drew $1,000 during the year.

The first thing necessary is to make the adjustments on account of depreciation, bad debts estimate, and present inventory. These adjustment entries are made in the Journal as follows:

19—

Sept. 30	Depreciation		20	45.00	
	Depreciation Reserve Furniture and Fixtures	6		45.00
	To bring on the books the expense due to estimated depreciation and to effect the proper valuation of Furniture and Fixtures.			
	Bad Debts	21	350.00	
	Reserve for Doubtful Accounts	3		350.00
	To bring on the books the expense due to estimated loss from uncollectible accounts.			
	Purchases	16	4,000.00	
	Merchandise Inventory	4		4,000.00
	To transfer the goods on hand at the beginning of the year to Purchases.			
	Merchandise Inventory	4	5,000.00	
	Purchases	16		5,000.00
	To transfer the inventory of merchandise now on hand to Merchandise Inventory account.			

The first two entries, when posted, will bring on the book valuation accounts for furniture and fixtures and accounts receivable, and will set up the expense accounts, Depreciation and Bad Debts. The third Journal entry, when posted, will transfer the goods on hand at the beginning of the year so that they can be added to the Purchases made during the year. In this connection it will be remembered that the sum of these two items, old inventory plus purchases during the year, constitutes the primary factor of "cost of goods to be accounted for." The fourth entry shows the asset Merchandise now on hand and, by its credit to Purchases, effects a subtraction from Purchases, so that the balance of Purchases, $24,000, shows the "cost of goods sold."

The books are now adjusted and ready for summarization by means of the Profit and Loss account. The following Journal entries, transferring all temporary proprietorship items to the Profit and Loss account, will effect the closing operation:

19—

Sept. 30	Sales		15	33,000.00	
	Profit and Loss		14		33,000.00
	To close.				
	Profit and Loss		14	29,920.00	
	Purchases		16		24,000.00
	Selling Expense		18		3,500.00
	General Administrative Expense		19		2,025.00
	Bad Debts		21		350.00
	Depreciation		20		45.00
	To close.				29,920.00
	Profit and Loss		14	3,080.00	
	Jack Gibson, Personal		11		3,080.00
	To transfer net profit for the year.				
	Jack Gibson, Personal		11	2,080.00	
	Jack Gibson, Capital		10		2,080.00
	To transfer the portion of the year's net gain left in the business.				

The first entry transfers the sales income to the credit of Profit and Loss. The second entry charges the Profit and Loss account with the cost of goods sold and all other expenses for the fiscal year. When the posting has been completed up to this point, the balance of the Profit and Loss account shows a net gain of $3,080, which, belonging to the proprietor, is transferred to the credit of his personal account, as shown by the third entry. He has drawn against prospective profits to the extent of $1,000, leaving $2,080 of profit remaining in the business as an addition to his permanent investment. Hence, this balance is transferred to Gibson's capital account by the fourth entry.

Objection to the Direct Ledger Method of Adjusting and Closing the Books.—These adjustment and closing transactions are sometimes recorded directly in the ledger without first entering them in the Journal. Usually this is not satisfactory because it does not show in one place a complete record of all the adjustment and closing summaries necessary at the close of a fiscal period. These summaries are matters of sufficient concern to the business to warrant their entry in the Journal where full and complete explanations can be given. The more complex entries often needed to adjust and close the books of a business where numerous income and expense accounts are kept, follow the same general principles as those discussed above. Adjusting and closing entries are given fuller treatment in Chapters XXVII and XXVIII.

The two illustrations given above cover certain types of Journal entries which are of a more difficult character than the customary purchases, sales, and cash entries. A keen analysis is often required to formulate the debits and credits of these entries, and the explanatory matter should be worded with sufficient care to render them intelligible even after the immediate interest in them has been lost and their recording ink has become "cold."

Entries Affecting Several Journals.—Transactions sometimes require entry in two or more journals. A basic principle of bookkeeping is that there should be no duplication of entry in the various journals. A transaction that can be completely entered in one journal should not be entered in any other journal. The one exception to this principle is made in the case of an investment transaction, as explained on page 171. Sometimes, however, there may be a conflict of places of entry, as in the case of cash purchases and sales, already explained, where entry is made in both journals in order to allow each journal to perform its proper function. Two examples will illustrate the proper method of handling such transactions.

PROBLEM 1. Assume that a customer, James Robbins, buys $1,000 worth of goods, paying $300 cash, giving a note for $500 and leaving the balance on open account.

The following entries should be made:

(a) James Robbins	1,000.00	
Sales		1,000.00
(b) Cash	300.00	
James Robbins		300.00
(c) Notes Receivable	500.00	
James Robbins		500.00

- 142 -

It will be noted that three journals are involved. Entry (a) is recorded in the sales journal; entry (b) in the cash receipts journal; and entry (c) in the general journal. The net effect of the three entries is:

James Robbins	200.00	
Cash	300.00	
Notes Receivable	500.00	
Sales		1,000.00

Because special journals are used, however, the transaction must be split up as indicated above.

PROBLEM 2. Assume that the business purchases from the Investment Trust Co. a building site valued at $5,000, paying for it $2,000 cash and a note for the balance supported by a mortgage.

Two methods are used to record this transaction, neither having any special advantage over the other.

FIRST METHOD:

(a) Land	2,000.00	
Cash		2,000.00
(b) Land	3,000.00	
Mortgage Notes Payable		3,000.00

Entry (a) is made in the cash disbursements journal, and entry (b) in the general journal. This method of entry requires the splitting of the land value into two parts and breaks up what is really a unit transaction by recording it in two places. Because of this, the general journal portion of the entry should be followed by a very full explanation of the *entire* transaction, in which reference to the partial cash payment should be made. In the cash disbursements journal the only explanation needed will be a reference to the general journal entry.

SECOND METHOD.—To bring about a complete record of the land item in one place, the following method is often used:

(a) Land	5,000.00	
Investment Trust Co.		5,000.00
(b) Investment Trust Co.	2,000.00	

Cash		2,000.00
(c) Investment Trust Co.	3,000.00	
Mortgage Notes Payable		3,000.00

Entry (a) in the general journal sets up an account with the vendor, the Investment Trust Co. Entry (b) in the cash disbursements journal and entry (c) in the general journal show the cancellation of the liability to the vendor through the payment of cash in the one case and the giving of a mortgage in the other. The net effect of the entries is:

Land	5,000.00	
Cash		2,000.00
Mortgage Notes Payable		3,000.00

It will be noted that this method sets up a formal account with the vendor—a desirable thing—but that it requires one more entry than the first method.

The other entries recorded in the Journal ought not to give the student any particular difficulty.

CHAPTER XXI
BUSINESS PAPERS—NEGOTIABLE INSTRUMENTS

The books of original entry, i.e., the journals, having been explained, the attention of the student will be directed next to the sources of information on which the entries in the various journals depend. Accordingly, some of the important papers and methods used in business will be discussed, after which further accounting principles and methods will be given adequate treatment.

Use of the Note Receivable.—The purpose of sales is the ultimate conversion of stock-in-trade into cash to provide for the payment of services and for the purchase of commodities for future sale. This conversion of stock-in-trade into money may be immediate, as when goods are sold for cash, or deferred, as when goods are sold on account. In the latter case the conversion is indirect, because the charge against the customer must be collected before conversion is complete.

Frequently the "note receivable" acts as an intermediate step in the process of converting stock-in-trade into cash. It is an instrument in which the customer formally promises to pay his debt at a fixed time in the future. The kind of claim represented by a note receivable is, legally, different from the open account claim; generally speaking, a note is considered *a better* claim than an open account. This is because the note implies a prima facie acknowledgment of the correctness of the original charge, and in event of suit relieves the holder from proving the original items of the claim.

Accordingly, when a promissory note is received from a customer, the open account claim against him ceases to exist and a different kind of claim evidenced by his promissory note is acquired. Therefore the open account is credited to show cancellation of the original charge, and Notes Receivable is debited to show the new claim. It may be well to remark here that the same instrument which is a *note receivable* to the vendor is a *note payable* to the customer.

In some businesses, it is the policy to encourage customers to give notes. In such cases it is often advantageous, particularly for the credit information shown, to set up the note transactions with each customer under individual names, e.g., "John Doe, Notes Receivable." Such a title plainly indicates the nature of the items listed under it; viz., claims against John Doe, witnessed by his promissory notes. As a general rule, however, the notes received from any one customer or all customers are usually relatively small in number and for this reason they are for the most part brought together under one class title, Notes Receivable.

Negotiable Instruments—Their Use and Requisites.—Notes receivable belong to a class of business papers termed negotiable instruments, the distinctive feature of which is that in many ways and for many purposes they *take the place of money*. The negotiable instrument, usually of small size but often representing a large sum of money, is used in the commerce of the world as a *medium of exchange*, in place of heavy and bulky coin or valuable bank notes which when lost or stolen can be passed as currency.

From a legal standpoint a negotiable instrument is one which gives a bona fide holder an absolute right to it, whether the preceding holder had acquired it lawfully or not. It is in this respect distinguished from other objects of value, as a horse, for example, the present possessor of which is the legal owner only if he acquired it in good faith from one who in turn had acquired it lawfully.

To be negotiable, an instrument must have the following requisites:

1. It must be in writing and signed by the maker or drawer.

2. It must contain an unconditional promise or order to pay a fixed sum of money—and the payment must be made in legal tender.

3. It must be payable on demand or at a time which is either fixed or can be determined.

4. It must be payable to bearer or to order.

Negotiable Instruments—Kinds and Definitions.—Any formal or informal written promise to pay possessing these essentials is a negotiable instrument. Examples are: promissory notes—notes receivable and notes payable—drafts, checks, money orders and, with certain restrictions, warehouse receipts.

A promissory note may be defined as an unconditional promise to pay a specified sum of money at a certain time. It usually has a form similar to the following:

```
$500.00                                          Jacksonville, Fla., Sept. 9, 19—
Sixty days......................after date....I....promise to pay to
the order of Henry Smith.................................................
Five Hundred and no/100..........................................Dollars
At the First National Bank of Jacksonville, Fla.
For value received with interest at 6% per annum.
No. 35.  Due Nov. 8, 19—                                    John Johnson
```

Form 16. Promissory Note

The Draft.—A draft is a written order by one party on a second party to pay to a third party the amount of money named. To be negotiable, it must be so drawn as to meet the requirements of negotiability named above. A draft may have a form similar to the following:

```
$125.75                                        Hoboken, N. J., Oct. 5, 19—
Sixty days after sight..................................pay to the
order of......James Stanley Jackson and Company...................
One Hundred Twenty-five and 75/100........................Dollars
Value received and charge to the account of
To George S. Perkins      }
  No. 93. Providence, R. I. }              Bert V. Robbins
4
```

Form 17. A Draft

It will be noticed that there are three parties to a draft—the drawer, the drawee, and the payee. The drawer is the person who draws the draft and whose signature appears at the lower right-hand corner of the draft. The drawee is the person on whom the draft is drawn, George S. Perkins, above. He is sometimes called the payer. The payee is the person who is to receive the payment ordered, James Stanley Jackson & Co.

To understand the use of the draft as an instrument of business, suppose the following relations exist between the three parties named above:

1. George S. Perkins bought goods from Bert V. Robbins on account for $175.

2. Robbins bought goods from James Stanley Jackson & Co. to the amount of $125.75 on account.

The problem will be discussed from the standpoint of Bert V. Robbins. From the above data it is clear that Robbins has a claim against Perkins for $175 and owes $125.75 to Jackson & Co. Instead of collecting the claim against the former and paying his debt to the latter, he writes out a draft for $125.75 on Perkins, with Jackson & Co. as payee, thereby requesting (or ordering) Perkins to pay $125.75 to Jackson & Co. This draft he sends to Jackson & Co. and they present it through their bankers to Perkins. Under ordinary circumstances Perkins acknowledges the correctness of the draft and writes his acceptance *on the face of it*, thereby promising to pay the amount when due. Acceptances are usually worded in the following manner:

Accepted, Oct. 6, 19—
Payable at First National Bank
of Providence
GEORGE S. PERKINS

It should be said that the three-party draft is not usually made use of without the consent of the drawee previously obtained, as in the case of a bank check, which is a draft on the bank drawn by the depositor. Very often in ordinary drafts, particularly when drawn against an export of goods, the drawer makes out the draft in favor of himself and indorses it in blank, thus making it transferable to bearer.

The Accepted Draft.—When accepted, the draft becomes, to all intents and purposes, an ordinary promissory note—Perkins' promise to pay Jackson & Co. $125.75. Until the draft is accepted by Perkins, it simply constitutes a request from Robbins to Perkins to pay the amount named and the draft as such does not bind Perkins in any way. Hence, no entry is made on the books of account of any of the three parties until acceptance. Of course, a memorandum is kept of all drafts drawn.

Illustrative Entries.—Upon acceptance by Perkins, the following entries are made:

1. On the books of Jackson & Co., the payee:

Notes Receivable   125.75
    Bert V. Robbins   125.75
        Robbins' draft on G. S. Perkins,
        accepted by Perkins, payable December 5.

Perkins' acceptance, in possession of Jackson & Co., constitutes a claim against Perkins, and Jackson & Co. therefore debit Notes Receivable. They credit Robbins because this draft was sent to them by Robbins in payment of Jackson's open claim against Robbins for $125.75.

2. On the books of Perkins, the drawee:

Bert V. Robbins   125.75
    Notes Payable   125.75
        Accepted Robbins' draft at 60 days' sight,
        favor of J. S. Jackson & Co.

This entry cancels Perkins' liability on open account to Robbins, and shows as a substitution therefor the amount of his acceptance in favor of Jackson & Co. at Robbins' request.

3. On the books of Robbins, the drawer:

James Stanley Jackson & Co.   125.75
    George S. Perkins   125.75
        To record the cancellation of our liability
        to Jackson & Co. on open account, and to

credit Perkins with his acceptance of our
draft on him at 60 days' sight.

From the point of view of Bert V. Robbins, the acceptance by Perkins means two things: (1) the cancellation of a part of Robbins' claim against Perkins, and for this reason Robbins credits Perkins with $125.75; (2) the cancellation of Robbins' debt to Jackson & Co., hence Jackson & Co. is debited on Robbins' books for $125.75.

It is important to note here that in case Perkins fails to pay the note at maturity, Robbins becomes liable to Jackson & Co. Robbins may therefore be considered the first indorser of the accepted draft. The discussion of the manner of booking Robbins' liability contingent upon Perkins' failure to pay is deferred to Chapter XLIII.

Entries After Payment of the Draft.—Upon payment by Perkins, the following entries are made:

1. On Perkins' books, a debit to Notes Payable and a credit to Cash.

2. On Jackson & Co.'s books, a debit to Cash and a credit to Notes Receivable.

Draft and Cash Compared as Instruments of Payment.—The following two diagrams may further illustrate the utility of the draft as an instrument of trade.

1. Showing the settlement of the several claims in *cash*—in case Robbins had collected $125.75 from Perkins and had paid $125.75 to Jackson & Co., the payments being made independently in each case:

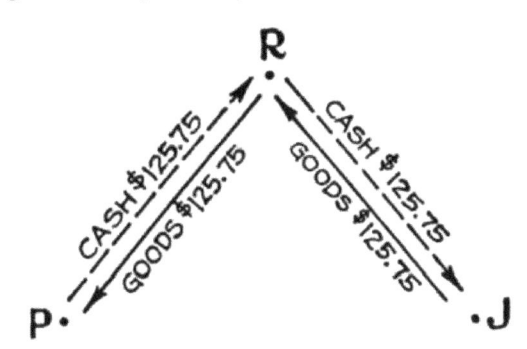

2. Showing a settlement by draft—a clearing house method:

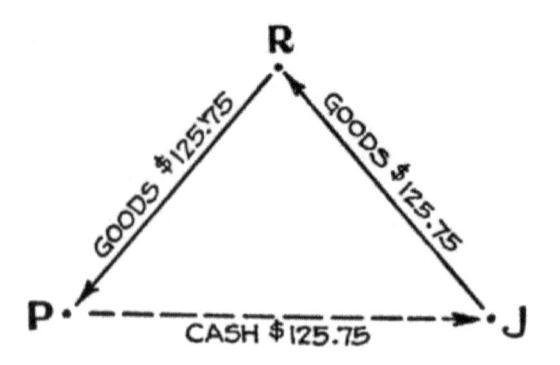

The commercial, three-party draft is little used now. With the larger function of banks in the conduct of modern business, other kinds of drafts as discussed below have come into use. The three-party relationship is the basis of all draft transactions, however, and must therefore be thoroughly understood.

Classification of Drafts.—There are several kinds of drafts, which may be either sight or time instruments. A draft drawn "at sight" is a request on the drawee to pay at sight, i.e., immediately upon presentation to him. The use of the sight draft in making collections is quite common. A delinquent customer is drawn on at sight and collection is attempted through the bank. The method is oftentimes effective because refusal to pay may reflect on the drawee's credit with his own bank. Usually no formal book entry is made of such drafts until paid. A draft drawn, say, "at 60 days' (or 30 days') sight" is a request to pay 60 (or 30) days after presentation. Hence, the dating of the acceptance of such a draft is of prime importance. Such a draft is, of course, a time draft.

A draft drawn "60 (or other number) days after *date*" is called a date draft and is payable 60 days from the date of the instrument—not, as in the first case, 60 days after presentation or acceptance. It also is a time draft. It is not necessary, although customary, to present time drafts for acceptance.

Drafts may be "commercial" or "bank" according as the drawee is a merchant or a bank, respectively. B. V. Robbins' draft on Perkins shown above is a merchant's draft. A bank draft is a request by one bank on a correspondent bank to pay a given amount of money to a named payee. A customary method of remitting money is by the purchase and remittance of a bank draft, for the issuing of which banks usually charge a fraction of a per cent. To illustrate its use, take the following situation:

L. W. Roberts of Denver owes Field & Co. of Chicago $210 on account. Roberts goes to his Denver banker and buys a bank draft which may read as follows:

FIRST NATIONAL BANK   No. *37849*
                  Denver, Colo., *Aug. 16*, 19—
Pay to the order of *L. W. Roberts*........................$*210.00*
Two Hundred Ten and no/100........................Dollars
To *Second National Bank,*   *F. G. Moffit,*
     Chicago, Ill.   Cashier

Form 18. A Bank Draft

Before sending this draft to Field & Co., Roberts indorses it in favor of Field & Co., who upon its receipt deposit it with their own bank and through it secure its collection from the Second National Bank. Roberts pays his bank for the draft $210 plus exchange.

Drafts may be foreign or domestic. They are domestic when they are drawn and payable within the same state or country; otherwise they are foreign. According to the present usage, the term "draft" is used whenever the parties concerned live within the United States, although they may reside in different states, and the term "bill of exchange" is applied to all such instruments where some of the parties live abroad.

The Trade Acceptance.—The Federal Reserve Board defines a trade acceptance as "a bill of exchange drawn by the seller on the purchaser of goods sold and accepted by such purchaser." The chief characteristic of this document as contrasted with the ordinary draft is the showing on its face of the origin of the transaction giving rise to the draft, usually by means of the following statement: "The obligation of the acceptor hereof arises out of the purchase of goods from the drawer." The following requirements to make a trade acceptance eligible for rediscount by the federal reserve banks have been laid down by the Federal Reserve Board:

1. It must have arisen out of an actual commercial transaction, usually the purchase and sale of commodities.

2. It must have been drawn under a credit opened for the purpose of conducting or settling accounts resulting from business transactions involving the shipment or storage of goods.

3. At the time of presentation to a federal reserve bank for discount or as collateral for the loan of money, it must have a maturity of not more than three months exclusive of days of grace.

Trade acceptances are promissory notes just as are any other accepted drafts. Because they comprise a very liquid asset, it is not unusual to record them in an account, Trade Acceptances, and so distinguish them from other notes and drafts. If they are few in number, they are more usually recorded as Notes Receivable.

Checks.—A check is a draft on a depositary bank. It is an individual's order to his bank of deposit to pay a named or designated payee a certain sum of money. Two illustrations are given below, somewhat different in form but identical in nature. In the first, likeness of the check to a draft is very evident.

(1)

S. E. KELLAR LUMBER COMPANY   No. 575
Hoboken, N. J., *Feb. 7,* 19—
Pay to the order of *H. B. Claflin & Co*..............................*$525.79*
Five Hundred Twenty-five and 79/100.........................Dollars
To THE FIRST NATIONAL BANK,   S. E. KELLAR LUMBER COMPANY,
  Hoboken, N. J.   By *S. E. Kellar, President*

(2)
No. *575*   Hoboken, N. J., *Feb. 7,* 19—
THE FIRST NATIONAL BANK
Pay to the order of *H. B. Claflin & Co*..................................
Five Hundred Twenty-five and 79/100..........................Dollars
$525.79   S. E. KELLAR LUMBER CO.,
                        By *S. E. Kellar, President*

Form 19. Forms of Checks

The *certified check* is usually an individual's or firm's check bearing the certification of the bank's cashier that the check is good. This certification is evidenced by writing across the face of the check these or similar words:

Good
when properly indorsed
FIRST NATIONAL BANK
F. G. MOFFITT, CASHIER

Such a certification makes the bank responsible for its payment.

A cashier's check is a bank's own check drawn on itself in favor of a third party and signed by its cashier. As a medium of exchange it ranks higher than the check of a private person, due to the superior credit of the bank and to the fact that the bank is usually more generally known in a community.

Other Negotiable Instruments.—*Express* and *postal money orders* are drafts payable at sight, drawn respectively by one express agent on another and by one postmaster on another.

A warehouse receipt is a receipt from a warehouse, elevator, or other storage concern acknowledging the receipt of goods or property. Such a receipt usually contains the contract agreements entered into by the parties, covering the conditions according to which the goods are accepted for storage. The warehouse receipt is usually negotiable, or partially so, in that title to the property may pass with its transfer.

Principles Governing the Writing of Commercial Paper.—Ordinary prudence requires commercial paper to be drawn in a way that will make forgery difficult if not impossible. To this end the following two rules should be observed:

1. Leave no blank spaces, particularly where the amount is written. This is not so important when the amount is perforated, with a perforated star at each side.

2. Write the indorsement at the top margin. Unless this is done, some statement might be inserted which would change materially the effect of the signature; e.g., the payer might later write above the signature that the check is accepted in full payment for a definite bill.

Kinds of Indorsement.—An indorsement is usually for the purpose of transferring title. There are several kinds of indorsement, as follows:

1. A *blank* indorsement, which consists only of the payee's signature; this renders the instrument payable to bearer.

2. A *full* indorsement, which reads as follows: "Pay to the order of . . . .," giving the name of the indorsee, i.e., the person to whom the instrument is transferred, and followed by the signature of the indorser, who before his indorsement was the payee.

3. A *qualified* indorsement, which is either a blank or full indorsement with the words "without recourse" added to it. This kind of indorsement transfers title with no liability attaching to the transferor in case of non-payment by the maker at maturity.

4. A *restrictive* indorsement, giving the name of the party to whom the check is transferred, the words "for collection" or "for collection and deposit" being added and followed by the signature. This indorsement does not transfer title but merely appoints the person or bank named as agent for the purpose of collection.

CHAPTER XXII
BUSINESS PAPERS—THE GOODS INVOICE AND BILL OF LADING

Definition.—When a business transaction takes place, a record or memorandum of its amount and nature is usually made out. Thus, the amount of cash received for a sale may be rung up on the cash register or a sales clerk may make out a duplicate sales ticket and turn over the carbon copy as a sales memorandum to the bookkeeper; for cash disbursed a receipt, to be the basis for formal entry on the books, may be demanded from the person to whom the payment is made.

These memoranda of business transactions are called "business papers." They comprise all of the more or less formal and informal documents which constitute the firsthand evidence of most transactions. Among the most common business papers may be mentioned: the goods invoice for purchases or sales; negotiable paper, including the check, note, draft, money order, and warehouse receipt; the statement and account sales; the shipping order and bill of lading; the bill of sale; the lease agreement; and contracts of all sorts. A few of the business papers most frequently used will be explained.

The Invoice.—When a merchant sells goods to a customer he writes out an itemized "bill" which is sent along with the goods. This bill, loosely called an "invoice," is from the seller's viewpoint more accurately described as a sales invoice, and from the customer's or buyer's viewpoint as a purchase invoice. It is an itemized statement of goods bought or sold, and should state the names of vendor and vendee, the address of the vendor and the date of sale, the quantities, kinds, and prices of the goods, the terms of sale, and additional information as to method of shipment, etc.

Handling the Purchase Invoice.—When goods are bought the purchase invoice should be verified or audited. The method of audit depends upon the organization of the business. In a small business, if the invoice is received before arrival of the goods, it is usually held till their arrival and then checked against them as to quantities, quality, and price. The extensions and total are verified and entry made in the purchase journal, using the audited invoice as a basis. The invoice should then be placed in a temporary file till paid, after which it is usually filed under the vendor's name for future reference. The check in payment of the invoice, when returned canceled by the bank, is frequently attached to the invoice for which it was issued as evidence of its settlement. At any rate the paid invoice should bear on its face a notation to show the payment.

In a large business where the clerical work is divided among departments, several copies of the original purchase order sent to the vendor are usually made out—one copy, for instance, for the purchasing department, one for the receiving room, one for the auditing department and so on. The procedure of auditing is then more complex. The copy furnished the receiving room is usually left blank as to quantities, and sometimes the description of the goods ordered is also omitted. When the goods are received, quantities and kinds are filled in by the receiving department, and the copy is sent to the auditing department where it is checked against the auditor's copy of the original order and the purchase invoice from the vendor. If found correct as to quantity, kinds of goods, extensions, and additions, the invoice becomes the basis for entry in the purchase record—journal or voucher register as the case may be—after which it follows the customary routine as to filing. The invoice remains in a temporary file as long as it is unpaid. Upon payment it is placed in a permanent file, either under the name of the vendor, by invoice number, or according to whatever system may be in use.

Handling the Sales Invoice.—Practically all systems of handling sales require that at the time of the sale some record or memo of the transaction be made. In retail establishments the use by each salesman of a book of sales tickets with provision for duplicate or triplicate impression is very general, whether the sale be cash or charge. The cash and charge tickets are usually put up in separate books and a different color of paper is used for each. At the close of the day the total cash tickets are checked against the cash received from cash sales, and the total charge tickets give a controlling figure for charges to customers. The total of the cash tickets plus that of the charge tickets gives the total credit to Sales.

These sales tickets are usually entered on a daily sales sheet provided with distributive columns for analysis according to departments or kinds of commodities. A recapitulation giving the totals of each of these columns is made and posted to the ledger, while the customers ledger accounts may receive their charges direct from the sales ticket. This recapitulation really constitutes the sales journal record, as is explained in Chapter XLVII.

Where the number of charge accounts is not large, a folder system is sometimes used. Each charge sales ticket is placed in the folder which takes the place of that customer's account, thus avoiding the necessity of making a formal entry on the ledger. When the customer pays this bill, the sales ticket is so marked and is either left in the folder or transferred to a permanent file. The successful operation of the folder system presupposes that the customer will pay the exact amount of his bills shortly after the date of the ticket, no provision being made to care for overlapping credits. Whatever the system, the sales ticket is the original record of the transaction and therefore valuable as evidence in case of dispute. These tickets should be filed away and kept until all danger of dispute is past.

Credits and Returned Goods Invoices.—If for any reason goods purchased prove unsatisfactory and are returned, record of their return should be kept by the shipping clerk and used as a basis for securing proper credit from the vendor. The vendor usually sends a returned goods invoice, which, though similar in form to the purchase invoice, constitutes a *credit* to the purchaser instead of a charge. These credit memos, as they are termed, are always of some distinctive color, frequently red, in order to distinguish them readily from the regular invoice.

Similarly, when dissatisfied customers return goods, or when the business makes them an allowance on goods sold, a credit invoice or credit memo is sent them and the duplicate copy of this memo retained in the office becomes the basis for entering the transaction on the books.

Shipping Goods—The Bill of Lading.—The purchase and sale of goods usually involve dealings with railroads. It is not the purpose of this chapter to give an extensive system or method of handling shipments, but merely to explain the purpose of the railroad documents and their use as business papers.

A shipment of goods is evidenced always by a "bill of lading," a contract under which the railroad accepts freight for carriage, defines its liabilities as a transportation company or warehouseman, and states its duties and those of the shipper. Its standard content is prescribed by the Interstate Commerce Commission, although any additions to it not in conflict with the standard content are not forbidden. If the shipper so desires, he may have bills of lading printed to conform in size with his own files, instead of using those furnished by the railroad. There are two standard forms, the *straight* bill of lading which is not negotiable and the *order* bill of lading which is negotiable.

The bill of lading is always made out in triplicate, the original and the two copies being identical except as to titles and signatures. The original is signed by the shipper and the railway agent, and constitutes the shipper's receipt for the goods delivered to the railroad. The second copy called the "shipping order," is signed by the shipper only. It is his order to the railroad to ship the goods, and is held by the railroad as evidence of its authority. The third copy or memo is an exact duplicate of the original. Like the first copy, it is signed by the shipper and the agent, and is held by the shipper as a duplicate receipt. Sometimes it is forwarded with the invoice to the customer, but otherwise should be filed by the shipper with the original bill of lading. In case of claim against the railroad for loss or damage to goods in transit, the original bill of lading is required as evidence and should therefore always be kept in the shipper's possession.

Freight Notice and Expense Bill.—A notice, called "freight notice," is sent by the railroad to the consignee upon arrival of the goods. A more or less formal order is given by the consignee to the teamster or drayage company to call for the freight. This order authorizes the railroad to deliver it to the teamster or drayage company. Upon its delivery, an "expense" or freight bill is sent to the consignee itemizing the freight charges due on the shipment. The freight notice and the freight bill are usually made at one impression, the heading on the one being a notice of the arrival of freight, while on the other the heading is that of an ordinary invoice or bill showing the freight charges on the designated goods. Some railroads make three copies at one impression, consisting of (1) the freight notice, (2) the delivery receipt, and (3) the freight bill. Copy (2) is a receipt surrendered by the consignee upon delivery of the goods.

C. O. D. Shipments.—C. O. D. shipments are handled through the agency of an express company, the post-office, or a bank. Express companies accept for shipment freight which is to be paid for upon delivery, agreeing to collect and remit the amount of the invoice to the consignor less collection and remittance charges. This method of shipping sometimes gives the consignee the privilege of examination before acceptance. It is used with customers who are unknown to the shipper or with those whose credit is doubtful.

When the parcels post service is used for shipping goods C. O. D., the post-office makes the collection for the shipper. The shipper must, of course, always prepay the postage, although this may by agreement become a charge against the customer.

When a bank is made the shipper's agent to collect on delivery, a draft is drawn on the consignee and sent to the bank along with a special C. O. D. bill of lading, the *order* bill referred to above. This original C. O. D. bill together with the attached draft is sent by the bank to its correspondent located in the same city as the consignee. The correspondent bank presents the draft to the consignee for acceptance or payment, as the case may be, and thereupon delivers the special bill of lading to him. The shipper's order to the railroad provides that the goods are to be delivered only upon presentation by the consignee of this special bill of lading. In the use of the order bill of lading, it is customary for the original copy to show the goods consigned to the order of the shipper himself. This copy, indorsed by the shipper, and the attached draft are the documents used by the bank in making the collection.

Duties of the Traffic Department.—In a large business a special department known as the traffic department is authorized to handle all shipments. Briefly, its duties are to look after all incoming freight, its receipt in good condition and its proper distribution to the several departments; to handle all outgoing freight, its proper routing so as to secure lowest tariffs and speedy delivery; and to secure the adjustment of claims for damage or loss of goods in transit.

The Statement of Account.—When goods are sold, an invoice or bill showing terms of sale, quantities, items, prices, and total amount of sale is sent to the customer. Periodically, frequently the last of the month, a statement is rendered each customer whose account shows a debit balance. Frequently the date of sending the statement is recorded in the explanation column of the ledger account, which, from a credit point of view, is a desirable practice.

The statement of account is a transcript, sometimes a summary, of the customer's ledger account, i.e., it contains all charges and all credits for the period covered. If there is a balance outstanding at the beginning of the month, the current statement opens with the balance item and is followed by lists of all charges, payments, and other credits for the current period; the total credits are subtracted from the total charges and the balance constitutes the amount now due and owing. Sometimes a statement of account is made out in detail, giving a copy of the original invoices which evidence the several sales transactions. Statements of account are issued in many different forms, but the following illustration shows all the essentials:

STATEMENT OF ACCOUNT

New York, N. Y., May 31, 19—

Mr. J. P. Norton,
    1031 Blvd. F, Saratoga, Va.
In account with
    D. COHEN & COMPANY
    Manufacturers of Ladies' Waists and Suits

May	1	Balance	$ 325.40	
	5	Mdse. per bill rendered	1,000.00	
	14	" " " "	575.60	
	27	" " " "	121.25	$2,022.25
		CR.		
	4	Cash	$ 500.00	
	10	Mdse. ret'd, per credit memo	50.75	
	20	Note	1,000.00	1,550.75
		Balance due		$ 471.50

Form 20. Monthly Statement of Account

CHAPTER XXIII
BANKS AND THEIR METHODS

Service of the Bank to the Community.—Practically all business houses at the present time take advantage of the banking facilities to be found in every community where there is enough business transacted to justify the establishment of a bank. A bank is sometimes defined as an institution which deals in money and credit. One of its chief functions and the one on which its main income is *based* is that of acting as a place for the deposit of moneys, these deposits forming the basis for its loans and discounts. Among its other important functions and services are to collect drafts and checks drawn on other banks; to issue and sell its own drafts on other banks, thereby enabling its customers to make payments to out-of-town creditors; to discount commercial paper, i.e., to loan money to its patrons on approved security; and to issue paper currency.

Opening an Account with the Bank.—Because so much of the bank's business is based on the honor and integrity of its customers, a prospective depositor is usually required to present a card of introduction signed by a customer of the bank or someone else known to it. A depositor who wishes to open a checking account is asked to file a "signature" card bearing the signatures which he will use in signing checks. As considerable expense attaches to handling depositors' accounts, some banks require that the balance of the account shall never fall below a fixed minimum.

The Deposit Ticket.—When an account is opened, the depositor is provided with a pass-book and check book. All deposits are made by means of deposit tickets, discount memoranda, or collection notices. The deposit ticket is in form similar to the following:

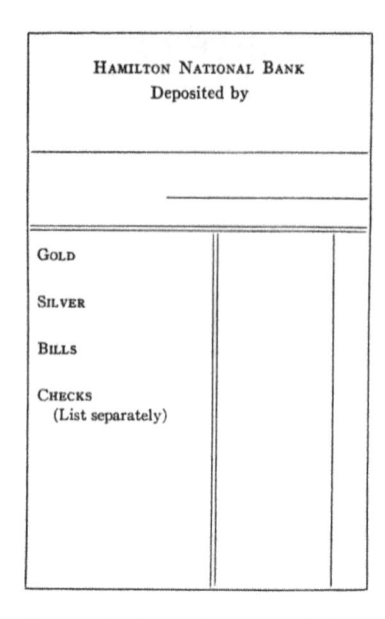

```
┌─────────────────────────────────┐
│      HAMILTON NATIONAL BANK     │
│           Deposited by          │
│                                 │
│  ─────────────────────────      │
│                                 │
│  GOLD        │         │        │
│              │         │        │
│  SILVER      │         │        │
│              │         │        │
│  BILLS       │         │        │
│              │         │        │
│  CHECKS      │         │        │
│  (List separately)               │
│              │         │        │
└─────────────────────────────────┘
```

Form 21. Bank Deposit Ticket

All moneys and checks deposited are listed on this ticket under the indicated classifications. The deposit is handed to the receiving teller of the bank, who, after verifying the ticket, makes an entry of the amount in the depositor's pass-book. Duplicate deposit tickets are usually kept by the depositor. It is important to note that checks must be indorsed before they are deposited, so as to make them collectible by the bank.

The Pass-Book.—The pass-book is the record of the depositor's dealings with his bank and, although written up by the bank teller, it is usually kept from the depositor's viewpoint, i.e., the bank is debited with all deposits and credited with all checks presented for payment. At stated intervals, say monthly, the book is left with the bank for balancing, at which time the *total* amount of checks paid by the bank is entered in the pass-book and the canceled checks are returned to the depositor. Sometimes the pass-book is kept in account form, the left page indicating deposits, and the right page payments by the bank. More frequently, however, the pages of the pass-book do not have debit and credit significance but constitute a continuous record. In this case, at the end of the period, the deposits are footed and the total of the checks is *subtracted* from the total deposits, thus showing the balance due the depositor.

A method coming into quite general use among banks is to send a monthly statement of account just as trading concerns do. This statement is a transcript of the bank's ledger account kept with each depositor, showing deposits and withdrawals. When this is done, withdrawals are not entered on the pass-book, which thus serves only as a memo or receipt of the moneys deposited.

The Check Book.—The check book is provided either with a stub, counterfoil, or interleaf, for making a duplicate record of the check drawn. Provision is usually made in the check book for the entry of the deposits. Sometimes each check is subtracted from the previous balance and the amount of the new balance shown; more often, total checks and total deposits are shown separately and in this way, while it is an easy matter to find the balance by subtracting the total checks from the total deposits, the actual figure does not appear and hence is not available to curious eyes.

The balance shown in the monthly statement or by the periodic balance of the pass-book is seldom the same as that shown in the depositor's check book, due to the fact that certain checks issued by the depositor have not yet been presented for payment to the bank. The method of reconciling the pass-book with the bank balance is treated in Chapter L, "Accounts Current."

Securing a Loan through the Discount of a Note.—A common practice of business men in borrowing money is to discount or sell to their bank or to a broker their own promissory notes and those received from customers. When merchants discount their own notes at a bank, the notes bear only one signature, that of the merchant, and for this reason they are called "one-name" paper. If a merchant receives a note from a customer, indorses it, and then discounts it at the bank, two signatures appear on it—that of the original maker and that of the indorser. Notes of this kind are called "two-name" paper. Banks usually prefer two-name paper because, if the maker fails to pay the note at maturity, the indorser can be held liable for its payment, while in the case of one-name paper the bank has recourse to no one except the maker.

When a merchant makes out a promissory note of, say, $1,000 due 90 days after date, and discounts it at his bank, the bank usually deducts interest at, say, 6%, from the face of the note; i.e., the merchant is credited not for the full $1,000 but only for $985, and when the note matures he either pays the amount, $1,000, or his account is debited with it. The $15 is called "discount" because it is "subtracted" from the face of the note; but since this item is paid for the use of the amount loaned by the bank, it is of the same nature as interest. There is no reason, therefore, for keeping two separate ledger accounts, one for discount and one for interest paid, the two usually being combined under one title, "Interest and Discount" or "Interest."

Principles to be Observed in the Calculation of Interest.—In connection with interest computations it is important to observe the following points, the principles involved in each case being best explained by making use of suitable illustrations.

1. In commercial practice, when the interest period is expressed in months, the interest for each month is one-twelfth of the annual interest, i.e., a note for $1,000 dated April 11, 19—, due "three months from date," matures July 11 and the interest at 6% is 6% of $1,000 divided by 12 multiplied by 3, or

$$\frac{\$1,000 \times .06 \times 3}{12} = \$15$$

2. Were the same note worded "ninety days from date," it would mature *July 10* instead of July 11, the number of intervening days being 19 in April, 31 in May, 30 in June, and 10 in July; total 90 days. The interest would amount to

$$\frac{\$1,000 \times .06 \times 90}{360} = \$15$$

3. If a note is dated March 6, 19—, and matures, say, on April 30, the interest period is 55 days (25 in March and 30 in April). Usually, in computing the number of days in the interest period the opening date is omitted but the closing date is included. In some instances the practice is to include both days.

It is important to note that it is almost a universal custom to use 360 as a denominator in all these cases, although the theoretically correct number is 365. This is done for the reason that the use of 360 greatly facilitates the computation. The government of the United States makes an exception to this rule and counts the year as 365 days, and disregards the month as a unit base; i.e., instead of counting the month of January as $1/12$ of a year, its computation requires the use of the fraction $31/365$ as the multiplier. Interest on $1,000 for, say, 12 days, by this method, amounts to

$$\frac{\$1,000 \times .06 \times 12}{365} = \$1.97$$

instead of

$$\frac{\$1,000 \times .06 \times 12}{360} = \$2$$

The incorrectness resulting from the commercial method (using 360 days as denominator) usually is negligible and is fully justified by the economy of time in computation. It may be noted that under this practice the amount of annual interest is $1/72$ more than under the method used by the government.

4. When paper is discounted by a bank, even though its term be given in months, the bank invariably counts the exact number of days in estimating the amount of the discount. Take a note dated June 25 with a term of 3 months and due therefore on September 25, but discounted at the bank on July 25. The term of discount, instead of being 2 months, would be for 62 days, a gain to the bank of 2 days on a 360-day basis.

Short Methods of Interest Computation.—In calculating interest or discount, the so-called 12% or 6% method seems the easiest of application. Its base is taken as $1. In the 12% method the interest for a year is therefore 12 cents, for a month 1 cent, and for a day $1/3$ mill. In the 6% method, the interest for a year is 6 cents, for a month $1/2$ cent, and for a day $1/6$ mill. Using these fractions with the years, months, and days as multipliers, the result is the interest on $1 for the given period. This result multiplied by the face of the note gives the required interest, assuming that the interest rate is 12% or 6%.

A variation of the above gives the following rule, somewhat easier to apply. Reduce the time to days—using a 360-day year, 30-day month basis; multiply the time by the face, point off three places (i.e., treat the product as mills), and divide by 3 or 6 according as the calculation is on a 12% or 6% basis. If the basis used is 6%, but the actual rate is different, add or subtract whatever aliquot part the given rate is more or less than 6%; i.e., if the rate is 8%, add $2/6$ or $1/3$; if 5%, subtract $1/6$; etc. The following example will illustrate:

A note for $1,000 dated June 10, 19—, for 4 months, with interest at 7%, was discounted July 30 at 8%. Find the net proceeds. The note when due will be worth $1,000 plus 4 months' interest at 7%. That becomes the basis for the discount calculation.

Applying the 6% method:

4 months =	120	days
Multiplied by	1,000	(face of note)
	120,000	
Marking off 3 points	120	
Take $1/6$ (index for 1 day)	$1/6$	

	20	= interest @ 6%
Add ¹/₆	3.33	
	23.33	= interest @ 7%
Add	1,000	
Value of note on October 10	1,023.33	
This amount (1,023.33) is the basis on which the discount is to be figured.		
Multiply by the term of discount (72 days[2])	1,023.33	
	72	
	2,046.66	
	71,633.1	
	73,679.76	
Marking off 3 points	73.68	
Take ¹/₆ (day index)	¹/₆	
	12.28	= discount @ 6%
Add ²/₆ or ⅓	4.09	
	16.37	= discount @ 8%
Value of note on October 10	1,023.33	
Less discount	16.37	
Net proceeds on July 30	1,006.96	

CHAPTER XXIV
METHODS OF POSTING

The Journal and Ledger Records Differentiated—Posting.—When a correct and complete record of business transactions has been made in the various journals, practically all the current information needed by the business has been secured. However, because this information is recorded in chronological order, it is not available for use. It requires sorting, grouping, and indexing. To meet this requirement the original chronological record must be transferred to other records which provide for the desired grouping. The separation of the general journal into journals for different classes of transactions such as sales, purchases, and cash, results in making certain kinds of information somewhat more available, but more than this is required for business management. The original records must be grouped and summarized under proper account titles, so that the total results for the period may be had under review at one time. The book containing these account titles is called the ledger, and the transfer of the original record to the ledger is called posting.

Time of Posting.—Where subsidiary journals are used, it is not customary to post all entries at the same time. The entries affecting personal accounts, i.e., those of customers and creditors, should be posted daily. Inquiries from customers as to their balances are received every day, and in order that this information may be given promptly and correctly, customers ledger accounts should be kept up to date in every respect. This is a matter of great importance because, if the information desired by the customer is not given promptly, or if an error is made in giving it, thus calling for correction at a later date, the customer's good-will may be lost and his trade transferred to others. For this reason personal accounts, especially those with customers, should be posted daily, and great care should be exercised in doing the work.

All other accounts may have their postings made periodically—once a week or once a month—the frequency depending upon the need of the business for the information furnished by the accounts. The flow of cash—always of importance—is shown daily by the cash book record; the volume of sales each day can be had from the sales journal; but information as to expenses can usually be had only from the ledger after completing the weekly or monthly postings.

Methods of Posting.—Knowing that errors in posting are easily made and that when made they may cause great confusion, it is important for the bookkeeper to know what kinds of errors occur most frequently, and to study means of avoiding them. Certain methods of posting have been found to produce a minimum of error. Some points in connection therewith will be considered here.

One of the chief errors in posting is to make entry on the wrong side of the account, i.e., to post a debit as a credit, or vice versa. The use of subsidiary journals has done away with a large part of errors of this kind, yet it is advisable to keep the following points constantly in mind when posting:

1. The sales journal is a "charge" journal, i.e., the individual items represent debits and must therefore be posted to the debit side of the proper ledger accounts. The sales *summaries*, however, are credits and must be posted as such.

2. The purchase journal is a "credit" record and all postings, except summaries, are made to the credit side of the respective accounts.

3. In the cash receipts journal, each individual item represents a credit, as explained in a previous chapter, and each individual item in the cash disbursements journal represents a debit. Hence, postings of the individual items on the debit side of the cash book must be made to the credit side of the ledger account, and postings of items on the credit side of the cash book must be made to the debit side of the ledger accounts. The posting of the summary entries of the cash book follows the debit and credit designation made at the time of summarization. The principles here involved were fully discussed in Chapter XIX.

4. In the Journal the debits and credits of each entry are fully expressed, i.e., neither element is suppressed. In posting from this record it is best to transfer all the debits consecutively and then all the credits. The possibility of posting a debit item as a credit is thereby greatly reduced.

Cross-Indexing the Entries.—An essential part of posting, in addition to recording the date and the amount, is to cross-index every entry, i.e., to index it both in the book of original entry and in the ledger. The "folio" column in each book is used for this purpose. The index in the ledger consists of the first letter of the book of original entry followed by the page number, and the index in the book of original entry shows the number of the ledger page to which the item is posted. (See Form 22.)

In this way, when the indexing in both books is completed it is possible without loss of time to trace the entry from the journal to the ledger, and vice versa. Usually the ledger folio is entered in the book of original entry immediately after each item is posted. When this is done the absence of a reference number in the journal indicates that the item has been omitted in posting. This check is frequently helpful in tracing errors. Some bookkeepers, however, before doing any posting, go through the book of original entry and from the account index of the ledger enter in the ledger folio column of that particular journal the ledger page numbers. By this method, much time is saved in finding the account in the ledger, but a *check mark* should be placed after each item as soon as it is posted, to indicate the fact. Then the absence of the *check mark* indicates an unposted item.

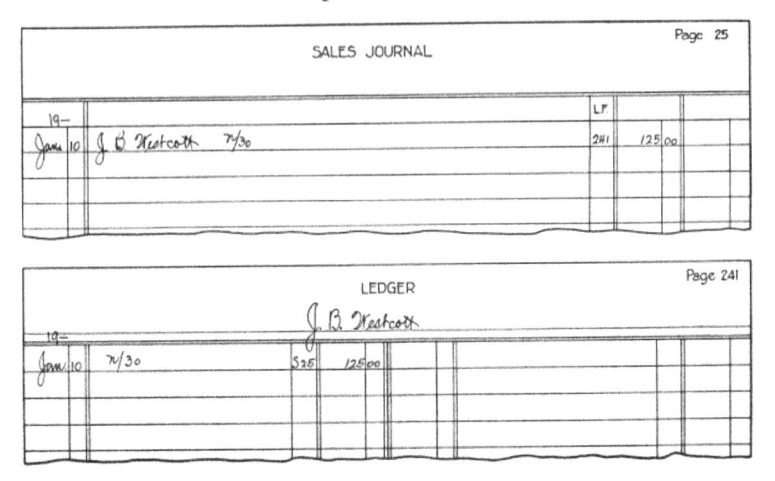

Form 22. Cross-Indexing in Posting

Explanatory Matter in the Ledger.—In posting personal accounts it is customary to show the terms of credit in the explanation column of the account. In this way the face of the account shows whether the customer pays promptly or not, and affords a basis for his credit rating.

Notes Payable and Notes Receivable accounts in the ledger should show essential data, such as due date, interest rate, etc. However, when a separate note or bill book is used, these data are given therein and may be omitted from the account in the ledger.

With all other accounts, except sometimes the Profit and Loss account, little or no explanatory matter is carried. However, when a posting is made that is at all unusual, it is well to enter explanatory matter in the ledger. From the business man's point of view, the ledger is the most important book of account, and if its record can be so made as to require a minimum of reference to original books, it serves its purpose so much the better. Where possible, the Profit and Loss account should carry the names of the accounts closed into it; in fact all transfers, whether made on the face of the ledger or by journal entry, should carry the account title and the ledger folio to which and from which the item is transferred. It is a fundamental principle that every entry must be indexed in such a way as to render reference to it easy at any time.

CHAPTER XXV
THE TRIAL BALANCE AND METHODS OF LOCATING ERRORS

The Trial Balance.—In Chapter XIV the trial balance was defined as a list of account *totals*, debit and credit, or account *balances*, debit or credit, for all the *open* accounts in the ledger. This list is set up in two columns, debit and credit, and if the original entries in the journals and the postings to the ledger have been done correctly, the totals of these two columns should be the same.

Neither method of showing the trial balance has any inherent advantage over the other. Some concerns desire the account totals to be shown in the trial balance, as that indicates to some extent the volume of business. This would be true of all accounts which had been opened during the current period. As to those carried over from a previous period little current information would be given. As a general thing, however, the status of *customers'* accounts is better indicated when both total charges and total credits are shown. Where only the balance is shown, it does not provide any basis for determining whether that balance is normal for that particular account. In judging a request for a further extension of credit there is a rather close relationship between the volume of trade with a customer and the amount of his unsettled balance.

Sometimes, even the totals of accounts that *balance* are shown in the trial balance, thus giving the status of *all* accounts appearing in the ledger. Again, concerns desirous of knowing the net amount owing on customers' accounts and the net amount owed on creditors' claims, require *balances* of all personal accounts and cash, but debit and credit *totals* of all other accounts. No unalterable rule can be given. The manner of showing the accounts in the trial balance is governed by the way in which the trial balance is to be used and the purpose it is to serve. Manifestly, however, the trial balance cannot give information of every kind desired by a manager. As personal accounts are usually handled by canceling offsetting credits against corresponding debits and carrying only balances forward, the trial balance cannot well show at the same time both total transactions and outstanding balances. Only in small concerns could the trial balance give the information which in larger concerns would be gathered statistically and furnished in addition to the trial balance.

The tendency in modern accounting is to make the ledger record so detailed that all accounts are *currently* "uniphase," i.e., have entries on but one side, and in connection with such accounts the two methods of entering them in the trial balance are identical, because the total of the one side of the account is at the same time the balance of the account. It must be observed that as a matter of course this modern tendency does not apply to personal accounts nor to adjustment and closing accounts.

Errors in the Trial Balance.—The manner of entering the small pencil footings of both sides of each account and also the account balances previous to taking the trial balance, was explained in an earlier chapter. This preliminary work should be done carefully so as to reduce errors to a minimum.

It is not purposed here to discuss all the kinds of errors that find their way into the accounting records. Errors are frequently made in the original analysis and classification of the transaction, which, as previously stated, result in an entirely incorrect showing of financial condition. Such errors do not affect the balance of the books and are not detected by the trial balance. Their detection is one phase of the professional auditor's work. This discussion has been qualified by saying that *if* the work of original and secondary entry has been done correctly, then the ledger should prove. Some points in connection with errors which often occur in posting will be treated here.

The equality of the two totals of the trial balance proves that for every debit entry on the books there has been made an equal credit, or at any rate that the sum of all debit entries equals the sum of all credit entries; i.e., it proves only the *mathematical* correctness of the work.

It might happen that an item, though posted to the *correct side* of the ledger, has been entered in the *wrong account*. The trial balance would not detect an error of this kind. For example, John Doe's account might be debited with a charge belonging to Richard Roe, both being customers. This of course would make the books show wrong balances in those particular accounts, but would not cause an incorrect showing in the *total* assets. However, more serious results may come from an error caused by posting to the wrong account.

According to the schedules shown earlier, all transactions bring about increases and decreases in the three main groups of accounts, viz., assets, liabilities, and proprietorship. A transaction resulting in an increase of assets may have its credit in any of the three classes—decrease of assets, increase of liabilities, or increase of proprietorship. A credit entry in any one of these would result in an exact offset to the debit and would therefore so far as that transaction was concerned, result in equal debits and credits in the trial balance; but were entry made to the wrong group of accounts, it would bring about absolutely false results. This would be the case if a proprietorship account were credited, resulting in an increased profit, when the credit should have been to the liability group with a resulting increase of the liabilities—two divergent results.

Thus, while the trial balance does not detect errors in posting to the wrong account, it has great value in that its equality is considered as good evidence of the correctness of the books. This is so because errors of the kind just referred to are not of so frequent occurrence as those involving only the mathematics of the work.

Suggestions for Locating Errors.—Where trial balance totals do not agree, it is certain that one or more errors have been made somewhere. The following suggestions may be useful in locating them:

1. If there is a difference of 1 in any column, i.e., .01, .10, 1.00, 10.00, etc., the error very likely results from wrong addition. Check additions of the trial balance and if the error is not located there, those of the ledger accounts must be checked as well.

2. If the difference between the two trial balance totals is an even number, divide this difference by two and look through the trial balance for an item of that amount but entered as a debit instead of a credit or vice versa. The amount of the error must be divided by two because the placing of a given item in the wrong column would result in a difference of *twice* this amount in the totals of the trial balance. If the error is not located in the trial balance, it may be necessary to look through the ledger accounts because the wrong placing may have occurred there.

In checking through the ledger for an error of this kind, some aid is afforded by the fact that all postings from *even* pages in the cash book (i.e., the cash receipts) appear on the *credit* side of the ledger accounts, and all postings from the *odd* pages in the cash book appear on the *debit* side of the ledger accounts. If, therefore, in any of the *credit* reference columns in the ledger is seen a reference like "C 13" or "C 29," or in any of the *debit* reference columns an index like "C 40" or "C 58," it is probable that the error is due to posting to the wrong side.

3. If the mistake has not been found in this way, the trial balance should be checked against the ledger to be sure that no open accounts have been omitted. Examine all closed accounts to see that they balance.

4. Examine the posting index column of all books of *original* entry to see that no items have been omitted in posting.

5. When the totals of the trial balance are unequal, the error may lie either in the debit total or in the credit total, or both may be wrong. Even when the trial balance "proves," both totals may contain the same error. In order to determine what is the correct footing, the following method may sometimes

be applied: Take the total of the previous trial balance, add to it the current totals from the several journals, and deduct the total of all accounts closed during the period. The result shows the correct footing for the present trial balance. Where the number of accounts closed during the period is large, the work entailed by this method may be prohibitive. The method is of easy application only when the trial balance is taken by means of debit and credit totals.

It may be left to the student to prove why this is a correct method for determining the present trial balance total. Suffice it to say that it is based on the fundamental fact that for every credit item in any of the journals there is of necessity a debit or group of debits the total of which corresponds with the credit item. Duplicating entries in two or more journals must be eliminated from the journal total.

The following table will serve to illustrate the above method:

Previous trial balance total	$12,967.30
Sales journal total for current period	8,429.60
Purchase ” ” ” ” ”	5,627.40
General ” ” ” ” ”	564.90
Cash receipts ” ” ” ”	2,572.60
Cash disbursements ” ” ”	1,962.75
	$32,124.55
Closed accounts total	1,211.41
Correct trial balance total	$30,913.14

6. If the difference between trial balance totals is divisible by 9, the error may be due to a *transposition* of figures or to a *transplacement*, sometimes called a *slide*. A transposition is an interchange of figures, as 96 for 69, 215 for 512, 6,274 for 4,276, etc. The first is called a simple or one-column transposition, the second a two-column, and the last a three-column transposition. One-column transpositions may also occur in numbers of three or more figures, as 172 for 712, or 3,129 for 1,329.

Transpositions.—The following rules will be of help in locating errors of transposition. To determine divisibility by 9, the easiest way is to "cast out" the 9's.

(a) If the difference between the trial balance totals is divisible by 9 and consists of less than three figures, i.e., 9, 18, 27, 36, a one-column transposition may be the cause of the error. Divide this difference by 9. If the quotient is 1, the difference between the two transposed figures is 1. If the quotient is 2 or 3 or 4, the difference between the transposed figures is 2 or 3 or 4, etc. For instance:

Correct Number	Transposed Number	Difference		
54	45	9	divided by 9	= 1
87	78	9	" " 9	= 1
75	57	18	" " 9	= 2
97	79	18	" " 9	= 2
30	03	27	" " 9	= 3
85	58	27	" " 9	= 3

Thus the figures in the last column indicate the difference between the figures of the original item.

(b) If the difference is divisible by 9 and consists of two significant figures followed by one or more naughts, the error may be caused by a *one-column* transposition between columns of a higher order. For instance:

The correct amount being	6,394
and the transposed amount	3,694
the difference is	2,700

which divided by 9 gives 300. This indicates a transposition between figures in the "100" and "1,000" columns, the difference between these figures being 3. Reference to the example given will show this to be the case.

(c) When the difference between the trial balance totals is divisible by 9 and lies between 99 and 1,000, the error may be due to a *two-column* transposition.

Here the middle figure of the error is always a 9, e.g., an error of 297 resulting from writing 512 as 215. Dividing the number (27) formed by the two outside figures of the difference by 9, the quotient (3) is the difference between the two transposed figures, i.e., the 5 and the 2. For instance:

Correct Number	Transposed Number	Difference				
514	415	99	9 divided by 9	=	1
735	537	198	18 " " 9	=	2
981	189	792	72 " " 9	=	8

Thus, the figures in the last column (1, 2, 8) indicate the difference between the two transposed figures in the correct item. Instead of dropping the middle figure of the difference and dividing by 9 as above, the entire difference figure may be divided by 99 with the same result.

(d) Similarly, when the difference is 999 or a four-figure amount with two 9's in the middle, a three-column transposition may be indicated thereby. For instance:

Correct Number	Transposed Number	Difference			
5,174	4,175	0,999	09 divided by 9 = 1
6,392	2,396	3,996	36 " " 9 = 4
7,081	1,087	5,994	54 " " 9 = 6

the figures in the last column (1, 4, 6) again indicating the difference between the transposed figures in the original.

Instead of dividing the number formed by the outside digits (9, 36, 54) by 9, we might divide the full amount of the difference (999, 3,996, 5,994) by 999; this would give the same result.

The reason for the divisibility of this difference by 999 in an error of this kind is apparent when a number is given algebraic notation instead of Arabic. The Arabic number 2,197 expressed algebraically would be 2,000 + 100 + 90 + 7. Generalizing, we may formulate any number of four figures by 1,000a + 100b + 10c + d, in which a, b, c, and d may have values from 0 to 9 inclusive. A transposition between the thousands and units digits, the "a" and the "d," would result in the following number: 1,000d + 100b + 10c + a. The error would therefore be:

Original number	1,000a + 100b + 10c + d
Transposed number	a + 100b + 10c + 1,000d
Difference	999a - 999d

This error is plainly divisible by 999, and the resulting quotient (a-d) is the difference between the two transposed digits.

It may be shown similarly why 99 is a divisor of the error cited under case (c) above.

Transplacements.—A transplacement or slide occurs when some or all of the digits of a number are moved one or more places to the right or left without change in the order of the figures; for instance, 736 written as 73.60, as 7.36, or as 700.36. The first is called a one-column slide, the second and third two-column slides. The error caused by a one-column slide is always divisible by 9, a two-column by 99, a three-column by 999, etc. The division by 9, 99, 999, etc., disregarding decimals, always gives the figures whose transplacement has caused the error. Thus the error caused by writing 736 as 73.60 is 662.40, which divided by 9 is 736; or 736 written as 7.36 produces an error of 728.64, which divided by 99 gives 736; or 736 written as 700.36 causes an error of 35.64, which divided by 99 gives 36, the part transplaced. The reason is similar to that given above for the transposition.

When a whole number of dollars is written as cents, the resulting error is divisible by 9 and moreover the cents *added to* the dollars gives 99 in each case. For instance in writing:

.73 instead of 73.00, the resulting error is 72.27

.58   ”   ”   58.00, ”””””   ”   57.42

.16   ”   ”   16.00, ”””””   ”   15.84

When the error in the trial balance is of this kind, the amount transplaced may be found by subtracting the cents of the error from 100. In the above examples this difference would be 100-27, 100 -42, 100-84, or 73, 58, and 16 respectively, which are in each case the figures of the transplaced amount as seen in the example. Having determined this, the trial balance and ledger accounts should be gone over to look for a slide of the given number.

Checking the Postings.—From the above discussion, the impossibility of determining in all cases the nature of the error is quite evident—particularly as to whether it is one caused by a transposition or a slide. Unless the kind of error is readily discernible, it is usually advisable to employ the method of checking, i.e., going over all the work of posting to determine its correctness—or other methods to be discussed in Chapter LI. After all, careful work in making the record with legible figures and in proving additions and subtractions, wherever possible, more than pays for itself in the time saved hunting for errors caused by slovenly and inaccurate work.

CHAPTER XXVI
THE CLASSIFICATION OF ACCOUNTS

Accounting Routine Related to Account Classification.—The basic relationships between the accounts and the statements of financial condition were explained in Chapter IX, where a chart of accounts was given to illustrate the fundamental equation of the ledger. The complete record-making routine, comprising the use of business papers for memorandum entry, the use of the journals for the first formal record of transactions, and the use of the ledger for the classified entry, has now been explained. There remain, however, two classes of entries, the adjusting and closing, whose relationship to the journal-ledger routine has not yet been fully discussed although their relationship to each record has been separately considered. Since the closing of the books contemplates the drawing up of financial statements and since all record-keeping must have in view from the very beginning a proper classification of accounts giving the desired information to be reflected finally in the statements, it seems best at this point to consider some phases of account classification before proceeding with a detailed explanation of the method used in adjusting and closing the books.

The Need for Classification.—As explained in preceding chapters, accounts may be broadly classified into the three main divisions of assets, liabilities, and proprietorship. This threefold division, however, is inadequate for the purpose of presenting detailed information as to the kinds of assets owned by the proprietor, the nature of his liabilities, and the causes that have produced increases or decreases of proprietorship. Subdivisions of the three main groups must, therefore, be made, the minuteness of subdivision being determined by the amount of detailed information desired.

One of the main purposes of account-keeping is to summarize results on the financial statements. The items which appear on these statements represent the balances of one or more groups of accounts. Items, for instance, such as "Land" and "Buildings," may each represent a single ledger account recording the value of the land, the factory, and the office buildings respectively; whereas the item "Accounts Receivable" represents the group of customers' accounts, the number of which may run into the hundreds and even thousands and which may be kept in a ledger devoted exclusively to the recording of their detail. The reasons for grouping assets and liabilities on the basis of degree of liquidity, and the advantages resulting from such grouping when drawing up the summary statements of the period, were discussed and illustrated in Chapter III.

It is evident from the above that the classification or grouping of the ledger accounts is reflected in the items on the financial statements; and that, conversely, the kind of information which it is desirable to present on the statements will to a large extent govern the groupings in the ledger. This dependence of the account titles and groupings in the ledger upon the end and aim in view makes it necessary to draw up the original classification with great care. To aid in securing a record correct in the first instance, certain fundamental groupings or classification of accounts must always be made.

Basic Classification.—While other groupings of accounts have been made, the classification used here has been from the beginning a three-phase one, consisting of an asset, liability, and proprietorship nomenclature. The third group of accounts, proprietorship, is further divided into the two subclasses, temporary and vested, as explained in Chapter XII. At the end of the fiscal period, after the ledger has been closed, there appear only asset, liability, and vested proprietorship accounts; but during the fiscal period, the temporary proprietorship accounts come into being and certain asset and liability accounts take on a mixed character resulting from the method in which the record is kept. This method is dictated not by a pure accounting theory, but by a theory designed to accommodate itself to the practical requirements of the average business. It is because the practical method of making the record falls short of the theoretically exact method, that adjustments must be made before summarizing.

For this reason, a record is not made daily of the portion of assets which has been consumed each day, but the asset accounts are adjusted at the close of each fiscal period to separate their asset and proprietorship elements. Also, when a note is discounted at the bank, its entire face value is set up as a liability. From the standpoint of accurate accounting, however, the face value of the note overstates the liability for the current fiscal period, if the note falls due in the following period, by the amount of the prepaid interest charge belonging to that next period. Only on the due date of the note does the record show the true condition of the liability. Thus, a "practical" method of keeping the record necessitates the use of certain "mixed" accounts. Fundamentally, however, the three-group classification given answers every necessary purpose.

Fundamentals of a Good Classification.—In judging the fitness of a particular classification, the end and purpose for which it is made must always be the criterion. Any classification of accounts must, therefore, have in view the fact that all accounts lead up to the balance sheet and profit and loss statement, and that they must provide the data necessary for the summaries of these statements. Classifications may be made from many different viewpoints and for many different purposes, but a classification which is logical and carries titles clearly indicating the purpose for which the accounts are intended, and which therefore needs little or no explanation, is a satisfactory classification. The three-group classification—assets, liabilities, and proprietorship—meets these requirements.

A two-group classification—real and nominal—is frequently used. Under this classification, asset and liability accounts are grouped as real, and proprietorship accounts comprise the nominal class. This is the standard classification. The student should be familiar with it, although the meaning of the groups is not so apparent as in the case of the three-group classification, referred to above.

Classifying Business Transactions.—When making the record of business transactions on the books of account, it is necessary, first, to determine the main account group or groups affected by the transaction. After this is done, it is usually easy to determine which particular account in the group is affected. Great care must be used in the determination of the main groups, since a wrong classification results in an incorrect showing in the summary statements at the close of the fiscal period.

To illustrate, in Chapter XIII reference was made to the fundamental distinction between capital and revenue expenditures. When making the original entry of some transactions this difference is frequently lost sight of and what should be charged to an asset account is charged to some expense account or vice versa. This charging to an asset account, of items which are rightly expense items and therefore cut down the proprietorship element of the business, is one of the easiest ways of inflating the profits for a period and so of making a better showing than would be the case if the facts were recorded correctly.

Correct classification of transactions is a matter of vital importance. An accurate analysis of every transaction must therefore be made before bringing it on the books. After determining the *main* group of accounts in which record is to be made, further analysis as indicated above is necessary in order to fit a particular transaction into its place under a suitable *account* title belonging to the main group.

Detailed Classification.—In dealing with account classification, the more detailed groupings must also be considered. Such consideration deals, (1) with account titles in detail and even with the kinds and classes of transactions to be recorded under particular titles, and (2) with the arrangement and use of these detailed accounts in the various sections of the summary statements at the close of the fiscal period. Certain broad principles have already been laid down which are to be followed in the selection of the account title, and the objection to the inclusion of unlike items under the same title, and the care to be exercised against a more detailed analysis than is required by the needs of the business, have also been explained. That system of accounts which groups only one kind of data under each particular account title is better than a system which mixes its records by grouping dissimilar data under a single head. Yet, caution is always to be exercised against too great detail and an unnecessary multiplication of accounts. Oftentimes essential facts and forces of business activity are lost sight of in a maze of detail.

Below is given a somewhat detailed classification of accounts in accordance with the two considerations stated above. No attempt is made at completeness; only the more usual titles are presented. This classification will be used throughout the rest of the volume.

CHART OF ACCOUNTS

- *Asset Accounts*
- CURRENT
- Cash
- Petty Cash
- Notes Receivable
- Accounts Receivable
- *Reserve for Doubtful Accounts*[3]
- Merchandise Inventory
- Stocks and Bonds (for current investment)
- Accrued Income
- DEFERRED CHARGES TO OPERATION
- Shipping Supplies
- Insurance
- Interest
- Office Supplies
- Etc.
- FIXED
- Furniture and Fixtures
- *Depreciation Reserve Furniture and Fixtures*
- Delivery Equipment
- *Depreciation Reserve Delivery Equipment*

- Buildings
- Depreciation Reserve Buildings
- Good-Will
- Etc.
- *Liability Accounts*
- CURRENT
- Notes Payable
- Accounts Payable
- Dividends Payable
- Accrued Expenses
- DEFERRED INCOME
- Rentals
- Interest
- Subscriptions
- Etc.
- FIXED
- Mortgages Payable
- Long-Time Notes Payable
- Bonds Payable
- Debentures
- Etc.
- *Proprietorship Accounts*
- VESTED
- Proprietors, Capital
- Proprietors, Personal
- Capital Stock
- Surplus (Profit and Loss)
- Reserves of Profit (not valuation items)

- TEMPORARY
- Income, Operating
- Sales
- *Sales Returns and Allowances*
- *Cost of Sales*:
- Initial Inventory
- Purchases
- Inward Freight and Cartage
- *Purchases Returns and Allowances*
- *Final Inventory*
- Expenses, Operating
- Selling Expenses
- Salesmen's Salaries and Commissions
- Salesmen's Traveling and Entertainment Expenses
- Delivery Expense (wrapping, shipping room, horse
- and motor expenses, delivery salaries, etc.)
- Outward Freight
- Sales Management Salaries and Expense
- Advertising
- Depreciation on Salesroom Equipment,
- Delivery Equipment, etc.
- Sundry Selling Expenses
- General Administrative
- Officers' Salaries
- General Salaries
- Stationery and Printing
- Legal Expense

- Postage
- Telephone and Telegraph
- Sundry Office Expense and Supplies
- Depreciation on Office Building, Equipment, etc.
- Light, Heat, and Power[4]
- Taxes
- Insurance[5]

- Financial Management Expense and Income
- Interest Expense
- Rent[6]
- Bad Debts
- Sales Discount
- Collection Expenses
- *Interest Income*
- *Purchase Discount*
- Non-Operating Expense
- Non-Operating Income

Method of Arranging Accounts in the Ledger.—As to the order of arrangement of accounts in the ledger, one principle governs: Arrange all accounts in such a manner as to facilitate the drawing up of the final statements. Thus, assets should come first, arranged in the degree of their liquidity or availability, and each valuation account following its particular asset. Liabilities, coming as they do after the asset accounts, should be arranged in a similar order. Next should come the proprietor's accounts, the summary Profit and Loss account, and the income and expense accounts in the order in which they are to be used in the statement of profit and loss. Where only one ledger is kept, the personal accounts receivable and payable are usually recorded in distinct groups, after all the other accounts, towards the back part of the ledger rather than in the position required by the principle just stated.

A trial balance taken from a ledger in which the order of arrangement of the accounts is strictly in accordance with this principle, is called a "classified trial balance."

CHAPTER XXVII
THE WORK SHEET AND SUMMARY STATEMENTS

Procedure Preliminary to Adjusting and Closing.—Before tracing the detail of the adjusting and closing entries through the books, explanation will be given of the usual method of insuring the accuracy of this periodic work preliminary to the formal closing of the books. This preliminary work comprises the technical procedure employed in drawing up the balance sheet and profit and loss statement before the books are closed. It thus brings about a summarization of the period's results made *outside* the books instead of *in* them. Therefore, a proof of the accuracy and correctness of the work of adjusting and closing can be secured before the summarization entries are made in the books. After proof of accuracy has thus been secured, the statements are used as a guide in making the formal adjusting and closing entries.

The information for the balance sheet and profit and loss statements comes mostly from the regular monthly trial balance taken at the end of the period just *before* the adjusting entries are made. This trial balance must of course be modified in order to include the effect of the adjustments. For the purpose of incorporating the adjustments in the trial balance and then separating the accounts into the two groups, namely, those which are to be summarized in the profit and loss statement and those which are to be used for the balance sheet, a regular form is used known as the accountant's "work sheet." This form and the method of its use will now be explained.

The Work Sheet.—For the work sheet "analysis" paper is used, which is ruled in its simple form as shown in the illustration on pages 226 and 227, space being provided for:

- 1. Account titles
- 2. Trial balance items
- 3. Adjustment items
- 4. Profit and loss items
- 5. Balance sheet items

For the purpose of illustration, a trial balance and a list of adjustments are given below, followed by the work sheet and the necessary explanatory detail.

The student must understand that the work sheet is no part of the formal accounting record, nor is the procedure employed by it a part of the formal work of closing the books. It is only a means by which a rough summarization of the period's results may be made *outside* the regular accounting records and all the data needed for the formal statements be brought together. Its purpose is to secure and prove the accuracy of results before the formal adjusting and closing work is entered on the books. Where many or complicated adjustments are to be made, with a resulting probability of error and difficulty in an orderly arrangement of the adjusting entries, the method of the work sheet is almost indispensable. The formal adjusting entries are then made up from the adjustment columns of the work sheet.

Illustration

Trial Balance, December 31, 19—

1	New York National Bank	$ 17,600.00	
2	Petty Cash	100.00	
3	Notes Receivable	15,000.00	
4	Trade Customers	35,000.00	
5	Reserve for Doubtful Accounts		$ 875.00
6	Liberty Bonds	3,000.00	
7	Merchandise Inventory	30,000.00	
9	Office Furniture and Fixtures	2,800.00	
10	Depreciation Reserve Office Furniture and Fixtures		700.00
11	Store Furniture and Fixtures	12,000.00	
12	Depreciation Reserve Store Furniture and Fixtures		3,000.00
13	Delivery Equipment	4,500.00	
14	Depreciation Reserve Delivery Equipment		2,250.00
15	Buildings	35,000.00	
16	Depreciation Reserve Buildings		7,000.00
17	Land	15,000.00	
18	Notes Payable		12,000.00
19	Trade Creditors		25,000.00
20	Mortgages Payable		17,500.00
21	U. R. Smart, Capital		90,000.00

22	U. R. Smart, Personal	10,500.00	
24	Sales		195,000.00
25	Sales Returns and Allowances	1,850.00	
26	Purchases	135,000.00	
27	Purchases Returns and Allowances		5,400.00
28	In-Freight and Cartage	1,350.00	
29	Salesmen's Salaries	13,500.00	
30	Selling Supplies and Expense	1,600.00	
31	Advertising	4,800.00	
32	Out-Freight	400.00	
33	Delivery Expense	3,300.00	
34	Office Salaries	5,000.00	
35	General Expense	2,000.00	
36	Office Expense	4,500.00	
37	Printing and Stationery	750.00	
38	Taxes	2,840.00	
39	Insurance	1,750.00	
40	Interest Cost	900.00	
41	Collection and Exchange	85.00	
42	Sales Discount	850.00	
43	Interest Income		1,500.00
44	Purchase Discount		1,300.00
45	Sub-Rentals Income		650.00
46	Special Police on Strike Duty	1,200.00	
	Total	$362,175.00	$362,175.00

ADJUSTMENT DATA, December 31, 19—

Inventory of Merchandise	$26,500.00

Estimated Depreciation:

    Office Furniture and Fixtures, 10% of original cost

    Store Furniture and Fixtures, 10% of original cost

    Delivery Equipment, 16⅔% of original cost

    Buildings, 4% of original cost

Doubtful Accounts, ¼% of Net Sales

Accrued Income:

Interest Accrued on Notes Receivable	150.00

Deferred Expenses:

Insurance Unexpired	250.00
Advertising Paid in Advance	300.00
Printing and Stationery Supplies on hand	150.00
Selling Supplies and Expense	200.00

Accrued Expenses:

Taxes	340.00
Salesmen's Salaries	175.00
Interest on Notes Payable	50.00
Special Police on Strike Duty	150.00
Office Salaries	100.00

Deferred Income:

Sub-Rentals Paid in Advance	50.00

The initial step in the use of the work sheet is to enter the trial balance in the first two columns, as shown on pages 226, 227. The accounts in the trial balance should be arranged in classified form before being entered on the work sheet, as this aids greatly in drawing up the statements. The various adjustment entries, debit and credit, which are almost the same as in the ledger, are then entered in the adjustment columns. The work sheet may be looked upon somewhat as a ledger, entries in whose accounts are to be made horizontally instead of vertically. The analogy to the ledger cannot be carried too far, however. It should be noted that when it is necessary to adjust any account in the trial balance by increasing its debit, this is accomplished by entering the item in the debit adjustment column on the same line with the account to be adjusted. On the other hand, if a subtraction is to be made from a debit amount shown in the trial balance, the amount to be deducted is entered in the credit adjustment column. A complete debit and credit entry must be made in the adjustment columns for each adjustment.

There is given below a debit and credit *list* of these entries as they are to appear on the work sheet. The manner of making and cross-indexing these adjustment entries is indicated by the cross-reference letters used. It will be noted that, while in most instances these entries are exactly the same as the formal adjusting journal entries, there is a difference in the case of the merchandise inventories.

The student should understand that the *list* of adjustment entries given below does not appear anywhere in the formal accounting records. It is shown here in *journal form* only to indicate the debits and credits of the entries to the work sheet. Entries of the adjustment transactions are always made direct to the work sheet, never being set up in journal form. Each of these entries should be traced into the adjustment columns of the work sheet. The figures in parentheses just preceding the debit and credit amounts are, of course, not *ledger folios* but refer to the similarly numbered items on the work sheet so that the student will have no difficulty in tracing them.

(a) Merchandise Inventory—Final		(8) 26,500.00	
(a) Merchandise Inventory—Final		(8)	26,500.00
(b) Depreciation Office Furniture and Fixtures	(51)	280.00	
(b) Depreciation Reserve Office Furniture and Fixtures	(10)		280.00
(c) Depreciation Store Furniture and Fixtures	(51)	1,200.00	
(c) Depreciation Reserve Store Furniture and Fixtures	(12)		1,200.00
(d) Depreciation Delivery Equipment	(51)	750.00	
(d) Depreciation Reserve Delivery Equipment	(14)		750.00

(e) Depreciation Buildings	(51)	1,400.00	
(e) Depreciation Reserve Buildings	(16)		1,400.00
(f) Bad Debts	(50)	482.88	
(f) Reserve for Doubtful Accounts	(5)		482.88
(g) Interest Income (Accrued)	(52)	150.00	
(g) Interest Income	(43)		150.00
(h) Insurance (Deferred)	(53)	250.00	
(h) Insurance	(39)		250.00
(i) Advertising (Deferred)	(53)	300.00	
(i) Advertising	(31)		300.00
(j) Printing and Stationery (Deferred)	(53)	150.00	
(j) Printing and Stationery	(37)		150.00
(k) Selling Supplies and Expense (Deferred)	(53)	200.00	
(k) Selling Supplies and Expense	(30)		200.00
(l) Taxes	(38)	340.00	
(l) Taxes (Accrued)	(54)		340.00
(m) Salesmen's Salaries	(29)	175.00	
(m) Salesmen's Salaries (Accrued)	(54)		175.00
(n) Interest Cost	(40)	50.00	
(n) Interest Cost (Accrued)	(54)		50.00
(o) Special Police on Strike Duty	(46)	150.00	
(o) Special Police on Strike Duty (Accrued)	(54)		150.00
(p) Office Salaries	(34)	100.00	
(p) Office Salaries (Accrued)	(54)		100.00
(q) Sub-Rentals Income	(45)	50.00	
(q) Sub-Rentals Income (Deferred)	(55)		50.00

U. R. SMART, WORK SHEET, DECEMBER 31, 19—.

Account Title	Trial Balance Dr.	Trial Balance Cr.	Adjustments Dr.	Adjustments Cr.	Profit and Loss Dr.	Profit and Loss Cr.	Balance Sheet Dr.	Balance Sheet Cr.
1 New York National Bank	17,600.00						17,600.00	
2 Petty Cash	100.00						100.00	
3 Notes Receivable	15,000.00						15,000.00	
4 Trade Customers	35,000.00						35,000.00	
5 Reserve for Doubtful Accounts		875.00		(f) 482.88				1,357.88
6 Liberty Bonds	3,000.00						3,000.00	
7 Merchandise—Inventory—Initial	30,000.00				30,000.00			
8 Merchandise—Inventory—Final			(a) 26,500.00	(a) 26,500.00		26,500.00	26,500.00	
9 Office Furniture and Fixtures	2,800.00						2,800.00	
10 Depreciation Reserve Office Furniture & Fixt.		700.00		(b) 280.00				980.00
11 Store Furniture and Fixtures	12,000.00						12,000.00	
12 Depreciation Reserve Store Furniture & Fixtures		3,000.00		(c) 1,200.00				4,200.00
13 Delivery Equipment	4,500.00						4,500.00	
14 Depreciation Reserve Delivery Equipment		2,250.00		(d) 750.00				3,000.00
15 Buildings	35,000.00						35,000.00	
16 Depreciation Reserve Buildings		7,000.00		(e) 1,400.00				8,400.00
17 Land	15,000.00						15,000.00	
18 Notes Payable		12,000.00						12,000.00
19 Trade Creditors		25,000.00						25,000.00
20 Mortgages Payable		17,500.00						17,500.00
21 U. R. Smart, Capital		90,000.00						90,000.00
22 U. R. Smart, Personal	10,500.00						10,500.00	
24 Sales		195,000.00				195,000.00		
25 Sales Returns and Allowances	1,850.00				1,850.00			
26 Purchases	135,000.00				135,000.00			
27 Purchases Returns and Allowances		5,400.00				5,400.00		
28 In-Freight and Cartage	1,350.00				1,350.00			
29 Salesmen's Salaries	13,500.00		(m) 175.00		13,675.00			
30 Selling Supplies and Expense	1,600.00			(k) 200.00	1,400.00			
31 Advertising	4,800.00			(i) 300.00	4,500.00			
32 Out-Freight	400.00				400.00			
33 Delivery Expense	3,300.00				3,300.00			
34 Office Salaries	5,000.00		(p) 100.00		5,100.00			
35 General Expense	2,000.00				2,000.00			
36 Office Expense	4,500.00				4,500.00			
37 Printing and Stationery	750.00			(j) 150.00	600.00			
38 Taxes	2,840.00				3,180.00			
39 Insurance	1,750.00			(h) 250.00	1,500.00			
40 Interest Cost	900.00		(n) 50.00		950.00			
41 Collection and Exchange	85.00				85.00			
42 Sales Discount	850.00				850.00			
43 Interest Income		1,500.00		(g) 150.00		1,650.00		
44 Purchase Discount		1,300.00				1,300.00		
45 Sub-Rentals Income		650.00	(q) 50.00			600.00		
46 Special Police on Strike Duty	1,200.00			(o) 150.00	1,350.00			
50 Bad Debts			(f) 482.88		482.88			
51 Dep. Office			(b) 280.00		280.00			
" Store			(c) 1,200.00		1,200.00			
" Delivery Equip.			(d) 750.00		750.00			
" Buildings			(e) 1,400.00		1,400.00			
52 Accrued Income: Interest Income			(g) 150.00				150.00	
53 Deferred Charges: Insurance Prepaid			(h) 250.00				250.00	
Advertising			(i) 300.00				300.00	
Printing & Stationery			(j) 150.00				150.00	
Selling Supplies			(k) 200.00				200.00	
54 Accrued Expenses: Taxes				(l) 340.00				340.00
Salesmen's Salaries				(m) 175.00				175.00
Interest Cost				(n) 50.00				50.00
Special Police on Strike Duty				(o) 150.00				150.00
Office Salaries				(p) 100.00				100.00
55 Deferred Income: Sub-Rentals Income				(q) 50.00				50.00
56 Net Profit to U. R. Smart, Personal					14,747.12			14,747.12
Total	362,175.00	362,175.00	32,527.88	32,527.88	230,450.00	230,450.00	178,050.00	178,050.00

Form 23. Work Sheet

In order to set up some of these adjusting entries, it becomes necessary to add some new accounts on the work sheet. The student will note these appended at the end of the regular trial balance shown on the work sheet. They are, first, Bad Debts and Depreciation, under the latter of which the detail of the fixed assets subject to depreciation is given, and then follow in order the balance sheet classifications of Accrued Income, Deferred Charges to Operation, Accrued Expenses, and Deferred Income, provision being made to show under each of these titles the detail of the accounts involved.

It will be noted that some of the adjusting entries are not set up in the adjustment columns in exact accord with the way in which the same items are entered on the ledger, but rather in accord with the use to be made of the particular items in drawing up the periodic statements. The purpose of the columns is not to make the adjustments and summarization in a formal manner as is done in the books, but to gather together all the adjusting data so that a correct separation of the balance sheet and profit and loss items can be made for use in the formal summary entries and in the statements. Thus, instead of transferring the initial inventory to the Purchases account, it is allowed to remain under its own title, because it will be needed as a separate item in drawing up the cost-of-goods-sold section of the profit and loss statement. Similarly, the final inventory is not shown deducted from Purchases, but is set up, debit and credit, in the adjustment columns, opposite the title "Merchandise Inventory—Final," which is inserted immediately following the account "Merchandise Inventory—Initial." At the time of summarizing, the debit item goes into the balance sheet, while the credit item goes into profit and loss. This method of handling provides in the profit and loss columns the detailed information needed for the cost-of-goods-sold section of the statement, comprising Initial Inventory, Purchases, In-Freight, Purchases Returns and Allowances, and Final Inventory.

The bad debts adjustment is entered in the adjustment columns as a debit to Bad Debts and a credit to Reserve for Doubtful Accounts. Similarly, the depreciation entry is shown as a debit to Depreciation in detail, the credits going to the various depreciation reserve accounts.

The adjustments covering deferred charges are shown as debits to the "Deferred Charges to Operation" classification in detail, the offsetting credits being to the various expense accounts as shown in the trial balance. These credits in the adjustment column will, when combined with the corresponding debit in the trial balance column, indicate the net amount of the charge to profit and loss. The other classes of adjustment entries follow the same procedure.

After all adjustments have been made, a complete distribution of the items in the trial balance and adjustment columns is made either to the profit and loss or the balance sheet columns. The difference between the profit and loss columns will thus show the net profit or loss for the period and must be transferred to the balance sheet as a vested proprietorship item. Instead of being shown as a definite addition to the proprietor's capital, the transfer is indicated as the final item on the work sheet, being a debit in the profit and loss columns to balance them, and a credit in the balance sheet columns. This difference, $14,747.12 in our illustration, constitutes the net profit for the period, and when added to the credit side of the balance sheet columns should give a total equal to the total of the debit balance sheet column. This transfer of net profit effects a proof of the accuracy of the work.

When this proof has been secured, the formal profit and loss statement should be drawn up, all of the material for which will be found in the profit and loss columns of the work sheet, where it is arranged in almost the exact order needed for the formal statement. The information for the balance sheet is found similarly in the balance sheet columns, all of the detail being properly grouped but a rearrangement of the order of some items being necessary. Thus, while the detail of the deferred charges to operation has been gathered together in one place in the work sheet, in the formal balance sheet this group of items must appear immediately after the current asset section. See page 234 for the profit and loss statement and page 232 for the balance sheet.

It is thus seen that the work sheet provides a convenient method of passing through the trial balance the adjustments necessary to a summarization of the results of the period and of effecting a rough summarization of these results. The work sheet becomes the source of information for the formal statements and a preliminary stage to the adjustment and closing of the books.

The purpose of the formal adjusting entries and the manner of framing them are fully explained in Chapter XXVIII. After the information on which they are based is brought together and entered on the work sheet and after the work of summarization has been proven, the adjustment columns of the work sheet are made the source for these entries. The formal adjusting entries as they appear in the journal are given on page 245. They should be compared with the debit and credit list for the work sheet as given above and the differences noted.

Need for the Summary Statements.—Before setting up the formal journal entries necessary to adjust and close the books, the balance sheet and statement of profit and loss will be shown. These two periodic statements do not form an integral part of the books of account. They are drawn up periodically and submitted to the proprietor, because the latter does not always have ready access to the books of account and often lacks sufficient knowledge of accounting to interpret correctly the information shown by the journal and ledger. The periodic statements are intended to show the results of the year in a concise, non-technical form, so that a proprietor, even though not versed in the science of accounts, can readily understand them.

The Two Forms of Balance Sheet.—The balance sheet may be arranged in either of two forms. The first form (illustrated on page 232) follows the principles already laid down in Chapter III. This is called the "report form" and is based on the proprietorship equation when written

$$\text{Assets - Liabilities = Proprietorship}$$

Being non-technical, it is perhaps more favored by executives not versed in technical account-keeping.

The second form (illustrated on page 233) follows the proprietorship equation when written

$$\text{Assets = Liabilities + Proprietorship}$$

This form shows financial condition by means of the account form, the subtraction of the liabilities from the assets being indicated by their respective debit and credit positions in the account. It will be noticed, however, that this method of showing the subtractions is not strictly adhered to, some deductions being actually performed, as for instance in the case of the valuation reserves which are subtracted from the respective assets to which they apply. This is done in order to render the statement more intelligible. The same principles govern the arrangement of the items and groups of items as in the first form, viz., degree of liquidity for the assets and a similar arrangement for the liabilities. The account form is used almost always when the statement is submitted for publication.

Two Forms for the Profit and Loss Statement.—The statement of profit and loss is also made up in either of two forms, called the report form and the account form, based on the same principles as the two forms of balance sheet just discussed. Explanation of the report form has already been given in Chapters V and VI. The account form (illustrated on page 235) is very nearly a transcript of the ledger Profit and Loss account. It differs chiefly in that the information concerning "sales" which is summarized in the Sales account on the ledger is here set up in an inner column and shown summarized on the face of the statement. The information as to cost of goods sold is similarly summarized.

U. R. Smart
Balance Sheet
December 31, 19—

Assets

Current Assets:			
Cash—New York National Bank		$17,600.00	
Petty Cash		100.00	$17,700.00
Notes Receivable	$15,000.00		
Trade Customers	35,000.00	$50,000.00	
Less—Reserve for Doubtful Accounts		1,357.88	48,642.12
Merchandise Inventory			26,500.00
Liberty Bonds			3,000.00
Accrued Income (interest due but not paid)			150.00	$ 95,992.12
Deferred Charges to Operations:			
Insurance Prepaid			$ 250.00
Advertising Prepaid			300.00
Printing and Stationery Supplies			150.00
Selling Supplies and Expense			200.00	900.00
Fixed Assets:			
Office Furniture and Fixtures		$ 2,800.00	
Less—Depreciation Reserve		980.00	$ 1,820.00
Store Furniture and Fixtures		$12,000.00	
Less—Depreciation Reserve		4,200.00	7,800.00
Delivery Equipment		$ 4,500.00	
Less—Depreciation Reserve		3,000.00	1,500.00
Buildings		$35,000.00	
Less—Depreciation Reserve		8,400.00	26,600.00
Land			15,000.00	52,720.00
Total Assets				$149,612.12

Liabilities

Current Liabilities:			
Notes Payable			$12,000.00
Trade Creditors			25,000.00
Accrued Expenses:			
Taxes	$340.00		
Salesmen's Salaries	175.00		
Interest Cost	50.00		
Special Police on Strike Duty	150.00		
Office Salaries	100.00	815.00	$37,815.00
Deferred Income:			
Sub-Rentals Income			50.00
Fixed Liabilities:			
Mortgages Payable			17,500.00
Total Liabilities				55,365.00

Net Worth

Represented by:			
U. R. Smart, Capital, January 1, 19—			$90,000.00
Profit for the Year	$14,747.12		
Drawings	10,500.00		4,247.12	$94,247.12

Form 24. Balance Sheet—Report Form

U. R. SMART
BALANCE SHEET
December 31, 19—

Assets				Liabilities			
Current Assets:				**Current Liabilities:**			
Cash—N. Y. National Bank		$17,600.00		Notes Payable		$12,000.00	
Petty Cash		100.00	$17,700.00	Trade Creditors		25,000.00	
Notes Receivable	$15,000.00			Accrued Expenses:			
Trade Customers	35,000.00	$50,000.00		Taxes	$340.00		
Less—Reserve for Doubtful Acc'ts		1,357.88	48,642.12	Salesmen's Salaries	175.00		
Merchandise Inventory			26,500.00	Interest Cost	50.00		
Liberty Bonds			3,000.00	Special Police on Strike			
Accrued Income			150.00	Duty	150.00		
			$95,992.12	Office Salaries	100.00	815.00	$37,815.00
Deferred Charges to Operation:				**Deferred Income**			
Insurance Prepaid		$250.00		Sub-Rentals Income (Paid in Advance)			50.00
Advertising Prepaid		300.00		**Fixed Liabilities:**			
Printing and Stationery Supplies		150.00		Mortgages Payable			17,500.00
Selling Supplies and Expense		200.00	900.00	Total Liabilities			$55,365.00
Fixed Assets:					*Net Worth*		
Office Furniture and Fixtures	$2,800.00			U. R. Smart, Capital		$90,000.00	
Less—Deprec. Reserve	980.00	$1,820.00		Profit for the Year	$14,747.12		
Store Furniture and Fixtures	$12,000.00			Drawings	10,500.00		
Less—Deprec. Reserve	4,200.00	7,800.00		Net Increase		4,247.12	94,247.12
Delivery Equipment	$4,500.00						
Less—Deprec. Reserve	3,000.00	1,500.00					
Buildings	$35,000.00						
Less—Deprec. Reserve	8,400.00	26,600.00					
Land		15,000.00	52,720.00				
Total Assets			$149,612.12	Total Liabilities and Net Worth			$149,612.12

Form 25. Balance Sheet—Account Form

U. R. SMART
STATEMENT OF PROFIT AND LOSS
For the Year Ending December 31, 19—

SALES..			$195,000.00	
Sales Returns and Allowances.........................			1,850.00	
NET SALES...				$193,150.00
COST OF GOODS SOLD:				
Inventory of Merchandise, January 1, 19—.............			$ 30,000.00	
Purchases during the year..................	$135,000.00			
In-Freight and Cartage.....................	1,350.00		136,350.00	
Less:		$166,350.00		
Purchases Returns and Allowances...........	$ 5,400.00			
Inventory, December 31, 19—...............	26,500.00		31,900.00	
Cost of Goods Sold............................				134,450.00
GROSS PROFIT..				$ 58,700.00
SELLING EXPENSES:				
Salesmen's Salaries.........................		$ 13,675.00		
Selling Supplies and Expense................		1,400.00		
Advertising...............................		4,500.00		
Out-Freight...............................		400.00		
Delivery Expense..........................		3,300.00		
Depreciation:				
Store Furniture and Fixtures....	$1,200.00			
Delivery Equipment...........	750.00	1,950.00	$ 25,225.00	
GENERAL ADMINISTRATIVE EXPENSES:				
Office Salaries............................		$ 5,100.00		
Office Expense............................		4,500.00		
General Expense...........................		2,000.00		
Printing and Stationery.....................		600.00		
Taxes....................................		3,180.00		
Insurance.................................		1,500.00		
Depreciation:				
Office Furniture and Fixtures....	$ 280.00			
Buildings....................	1,400.00	1,680.00	18,560.00	
FINANCIAL MANAGEMENT EXPENSES:				
Interest Cost..............................		$ 950.00		
Sales Discount............................		850.00		
Bad Debts................................		482.88		
Collection and Exchange....................		85.00	2,367.88	
Total Operating Expenses.......................			$ 46,152.88	
FINANCIAL MANAGEMENT INCOME:				
Interest Income............................		$ 1,650.00		
Purchase Discount.........................		1,300.00	2,950.00	43,202.88
OPERATING PROFIT.......................................				$ 15,497.12
NON-OPERATING EXPENSE AND INCOME:				
Expense—Special Police on Strike Duty................			$ 1,350.00	
Income—Sub-Rental Income...........................			600.00	750.00
NET PROFIT FOR THE YEAR.................................				$ 14,747.12

Form 26. Statement of Profit and Loss—Report Form

U. R. SMART—STATEMENT OF PROFIT AND LOSS
For the Year Ending December 31, 19—

Inventory, January 1, 19—			$ 30,000.00	Sales	$195,000.00	
Purchases during the year	$135,000.00			Less—Sales Returns & Allowances	1,850.00	
In-Freight and Cartage	1,350.00	136,350.00		Net Sales		$193,150.00
		$166,350.00				
Less:						
Purchase Returns & Allow.	$ 5,400.00					
Inventory, December 31, 19—	26,500.00	31,900.00				
Cost of Goods Sold		$134,450.00				
Gross Profit (down)		58,700.00				
		$193,150.00				$193,150.00
Selling Expenses				Gross Profit		$ 58,700.00
Salesmen's Salaries		$ 13,675.00		**Financial Management Income**		
Selling Supplies and Expense		1,400.00		Interest Income	$ 1,650.00	
Advertising		4,500.00		Purchase Discount	1,300.00	2,950.00
Out-Freight		400.00				
Delivery Expense		3,300.00				
Depreciation:						
Store, Furn. & Fixt.	$1,200.00					
Delivery Equipment	750.00	1,950.00	$ 25,225.00			
General Administrative Expenses						
Office Salaries		$ 5,100.00				
Office Expense		4,500.00				
General Expense		2,000.00				
Printing and Stationery		600.00				
Taxes		3,180.00				
Insurance		1,500.00				
Depreciation:						
Office Furn. & Fixt.	$ 280.00					
Building	1,400.00	1,680.00	18,560.00			
Financial Management Expenses						
Interest Cost Notes Payable	$ 950.00					
Sales Discount	850.00					
Bad Debts	482.88					
Collection and Exchange	85.00	2,367.88				
Net Operating Profit (down)		15,497.12				
		$ 61,650.00		Net Operating Profit		$ 15,497.12
Non-Operating Expense				**Non-Operating Income**		
Special Police on Strike Duty		$ 1,350.00		Sub-Rentals Income		600.00
Net Profit to U. R. Smart, Personal		14,747.12				$ 16,097.12
		$ 16,097.12				

Form 27. Statement of Profit and Loss—Account Form

Interim Statements.—In many businesses, where the fiscal period is six months or a year, it is often desirable and important that at least approximate results be secured at interim periods. This can be accomplished by means of the work sheet without entailing the burdensome work involved in a formal closing of the books. At the time of the taking of any trial balance, the work sheet can be used as a means of making the necessary adjustments before securing results as to financial and operating condition. Accurate results would of course require as careful work as at the end of the regular fiscal period. The purpose of interim summaries is to indicate trends rather than to show accurate and definite results. At such times, therefore, the inventory is usually estimated, oftentimes the same amount being used as at the beginning of the period. Accruals and deferred items are not so carefully estimated nor in so great detail. Bad debts and depreciation must be taken into account. In this way approximate results for any period—frequently every month—may be secured without interfering with those for the regular fiscal period.

CHAPTER XXVIII
ADJUSTING AND CLOSING THE BOOKS

Adjustment Entries—Kinds and Place of Record.—In Chapter XV it was shown that the records as they are usually kept do not reflect the true condition of the business at any time *during* the fiscal period. For this reason before summarizing the book record for the current period it is necessary to bring onto the books a number of entries the purpose of which is to "adjust" the mixed accounts and thus make the ledger reflect the true condition. These adjustments may be effected by entry made directly on the face of the ledger, but it is better to run them through the journal, thus making it possible to give ample explanation. A further advantage of first recording the adjustment entries in the journal is that in this way all such entries appear in one place in the books of account. The ledger should always be kept as a book of *secondary* entry, with supporting data in some book of *original* entry.

Seven types of adjustment entries are needed for the ledger of a mercantile concern. They are:

- 1. Merchandise Inventory
- 2. Depreciation
- 3. Bad Debts
- 4. Accrued Income
- 5. Deferred Expenses
- 6. Accrued Expenses
- 7. Deferred Income

All such items must be given consideration and entered upon the books before the final results for the period can be correctly shown. It is oftentimes necessary to make correcting entries for items the improper entry or the omission of which are not detected until the close of the fiscal period. These errors, whenever discovered, should of course be corrected at once. Because entries of this kind are in the nature of adjusting entries, consideration of them is included in this chapter.

It may be observed here that if a business manager has an intelligent insight into the development of his enterprise, and carefully watches the volume of sales, purchases, and expenses, he may be able to forecast with some degree of accuracy the approximate results for a given period; but only by making the actual count of stock now on hand and by carefully estimating the classes of items just mentioned, can accurate and dependable results be assured.

All these types of adjustment entries are not always found in every such business, however. Each type will be discussed in turn.

Inventory of Stock-in-Trade.—One of the most important adjustment entries is that by which the inventory of stock-in-trade is set up separately on the books. By reference to Chapter XIII it will be seen that none of the accounts connected with merchandise, viz., purchases, sales, returns, etc., contain any definite and up-to-date information as to the value of merchandise on hand. To determine the gross profit on sales this value must be known, and until the gross profit is determined the net profit cannot be ascertained. The balance sheet, the statement of profit and loss, and the Profit and Loss account, call for this information. Therefore, before these statements are made, and before the books can be closed, the value of goods on hand must be determined. The process by which this is done is called "inventory-taking."

Without discussing the detail of a system of inventory-taking, three fundamental principles can be stated relative thereto:

1. Make sure that all goods belonging to the firm on the date of the inventory are included.

2. Make equally sure that there is no duplication of count, i.e., that no goods are counted twice.

3. See that the condition of the goods, viewed from the standpoint of salability, is indicated.

Two factors of importance enter into the determination of the inventory, viz., the quantity of the goods on hand and their value per unit. Inaccuracy in either factor may lead to a gross error in the final amount. By falsifying the count of the goods the inventory can, of course, be inflated. A usual and more elusive method, often resorted to, consists in raising the price per unit, since the addition of even a fraction of a cent per unit may have the effect of converting an actual loss into an apparent profit. Without further indication of the reason for such valuation, it is now generally required that the inventory be valued on the basis of cost, or market if market is lower than cost. The term "cost" should include all costs, incurred up to the point of placing the goods in condition ready for sale, not only the purchase price, but also duties, freight, drayage, insurance during transit, etc.

After the amount of the inventory has been determined, it is placed on the books. However, before this is done it is necessary that the Merchandise Inventory account be cleared of the goods on hand at the *beginning* of the period by transferring the amount to Purchases. The following journal entry effects the transfer:

- Purchases
- Merchandise Inventory
- To transfer the opening inventory
- to Purchases.

The posting of this entry automatically clears the Inventory account and, by its addition to Purchases, causes that account to show the "total goods to be accounted for." Purchases, as it now stands, contains both the cost of goods which have been sold during the current period and those which are still on hand as shown by the inventory just taken. Accordingly, to separate the two items, the following journal entry is necessary:

- Merchandise Inventory
- Purchases
- To set up the inventory of
- goods now on hand.

This entry when posted shows in the Merchandise Inventory account the asset element, and leaves in the Purchases account the cost of the merchandise sold. The effect of these two entries, then, is to adjust the books to true conditions so far as the merchandise is concerned.

Depreciation, and Loss on Doubtful Accounts.—As indicated in Chapter XV, the amount of depreciation of particular assets and the losses due to bad and doubtful accounts are carefully estimated at the close of the fiscal period. The individual depreciation items are all summarized in a *single* depreciation account—an *expense* account—whose total debit is closed out to Profit and Loss. The *depreciation reserves*, however, which are credit items, are handled under separate account titles, and constitute the valuation account of the corresponding assets. The journal entry covering depreciation reads as follows:

- Depreciation
- Depreciation Reserve Buildings
- Depreciation Reserve Furniture and Fixtures
- Depreciation Reserve Delivery Equipment
- Depreciation Reserve Machinery

The Reserve for Doubtful Accounts is the valuation account of Accounts and Notes Receivable. Assume, for instance, that the debit balances of the latter two accounts are $15,900, and the credit balance of their valuation account is $600. The difference between these two accounts, viz., $15,300, represents the present estimated value of Accounts and Notes Receivable. The journal entry made *periodically* to record the estimated loss from uncollectible items is:

- Bad Debts
- Reserve for Doubtful Accounts

When the two entries above, for estimated depreciation and bad debts, are posted, the present appraised values of those particular assets are brought on the ledger; i.e., from the values, as shown by the respective asset accounts, are taken the portions estimated to have been used up, lost through depreciation, or uncollectible. These lost portions are set up as expense items, leaving in the adjusted asset accounts true asset values as existing at the close of the period.

Accrued Income.—As to the asset portion of items of this kind, it is indicated in the account in a manner similar to deferred expenses, as explained on page 242. Take the case of interest income earned but not due. The entry for adjusting it is:

- Interest Income (Accrued)
- Interest Income

The credit part is posted immediately, thereby showing an addition to the income already recorded as earned during the current period. The debit part is posted after the current account is adjusted and allowance made for the closing transfer entry to Profit and Loss. The debit part of the adjusting entry is then entered on the debit side of the *new* portion of the account. Assume this debit item to be $50, and the interest received during the next period to be $170. The new account will indicate a *credit balance* of $120, which is the amount actually earned during that period, since the previous period took credit for the $50 accrued or earned during *that* period.

Deferred Expenses.—When a part of the expense paid during the current period applies to the next period, the prepaid portion must be taken out of the current expenses and held over—deferred—as a charge to the expenses of the next period. Taking insurance as an example, the following journal entry effects the required adjustment:

- Insurance (Deferred)
- Insurance

In posting this entry, the credit part is posted first in order to take out of the excessive cost shown chargeable to this period the portion equitably belonging to the next period. When this is done, the *debit balance* of the

Insurance account indicates the amount to be charged to the current period and is the correct charge against the Profit and Loss for the period. After making allowance for the space needed for closing the account, the debit side of the above entry is posted, this debit becoming the first charge in the account for the next period. Note that the use of the bracketed "Deferred" is as a guide in posting. It indicates that that portion of the entry is not to be posted until provision has been made for closing the account. After posting is completed, the Insurance account appears as follows:

INSURANCE

Jan. 2   125.00   Dec. 31 200.00

Apr. 10 250.00

Aug. 15 300.00

               675.00

Jan. 1   200.00

There remains, of course, the transfer to Profit and Loss of the current balance before the account is *closed*. This closing work is treated later in the chapter.

Accrued Expense Items.—These items cover expenses which the business has incurred but has not yet paid, and which are properly chargeable to this period but have not yet been charged on the books. For instance, salaries earned up to the close of the period but not paid at its close constitute an additional charge to the period's operations which must be entered on the books before they will show true conditions. This amount also constitutes a liability of the business. Accordingly, the journal entry is:

- Salaries

- Salaries (Accrued)

thus charging the Salaries account with the amount due but not paid, and bringing this amount down as a credit balance to the new account for the next period. Assuming this unpaid amount to be $72, the account after closing will show this $72 as a liability on the *closing date*. Its effect, however, during the next period will be to *reduce* the amount charged to salaries during that period, because this $72, although paid during that period, has already been charged to the previous period.

The credit to Salaries, therefore, serves two purposes, viz., that of showing the outstanding liability at the *close* of the current period, and that of effecting a reduction of what would be, without this credit, an overcharge to *next* period's salaries. For example, if the total salary paid during the next period is $600, the *balance* of $528 is the amount applicable to that period, although the amount actually paid is $600.

Deferred Income.—Income received by the business during the present period which, however, belongs to the subsequent period is called "deferred income," as for instance, rent received in advance from a tenant. As to the liability portion of items of this kind, it is indicated in a manner similar to the accrued expense items. In this case the journal entry is:

- Rent Income
- Rent Income (Deferred)

the effect being to decrease the amount of rent income for the current period and to show the portion belonging to the next period deferred to that period's account.

Corrections.—When an error has been made in any entry on the books, it should not be erased or scratched out, because by so doing suspicion may be raised as to what was expunged. The wrong item should be ruled out and the correct item written above it or wherever it belongs. This applies particularly to books of original entry whose use as evidence has often been destroyed because many erasures appeared in them.

Another way of making a correction, when an amount has been posted to a wrong account, is first to cancel the wrong posting through a similar entry on the *other side* of the same account, and then to post it to the correct account. Cross-reference to the two accounts must be made.

When an amount has been posted to the *wrong side* of *the correct account*, e.g., $100 to the credit side of John Doe's account, when it should have been posted to the debit side, the incorrect credit may be canceled by a debit of $100, and after this the original $100 should be entered on the debit side; or the cancellation and correction may be combined by entering $200 on the debit side. Better still, the incorrect posting may be ruled out and a correct posting made of the *original entry* whose wrong posting caused the error. Adequate cross-reference should be given so as to make the tracing of the items easy and to indicate exactly what was done.

As these entries are of a somewhat unusual nature, their exact purpose should be plainly indicated in the explanation columns. According to the methods mentioned above, the various correcting entries are made directly on the face of the ledger. It is often preferable, however, first to make the required correction entries in the journal with full explanation, and then to post them to the ledger.

Adjusting Entries Illustrated.—In order to indicate clearly the routine and method to be followed in summarizing the books at the close of the fiscal period, the formal adjusting and closing journal entries needed for the books of U. R. Smart will now be set up, the illustrative data being the same as were used for the work sheet in Chapter XXVII to which reference should be made. In connection with the work sheet it was stated that the adjustment columns of the work sheet are used as a guide to making the adjusting entries. As to sequence in the journal, these follow immediately, without break, the last current entry for the month. The adjusting entries for U. R. Smart are:

Purchases	30,000.00	
Merchandise Inventory		30,000.00
Merchandise Inventory	26,500.00	
Purchases		26,500.00
Depreciation	3,630.00	
Depreciation Reserve Office Furniture and Fixtures		280.00
Depreciation Reserve Store Furniture and Fixtures		1,200.00
Depreciation Reserve Delivery Equipment		750.00
Depreciation Reserve Buildings		1,400.00
Bad Debts	482.88	
Reserve for Doubtful Accounts		482.88
Interest Income (Accrued)	150.00	
Interest Income		150.00
Insurance (Deferred)	250.00	
Insurance		250.00
Advertising (Deferred)	300.00	
Advertising		300.00
Printing and Stationery (Deferred)	150.00	
Printing and Stationery		150.00

Selling Supplies and Expense (Deferred)	200.00	
Selling Supplies and Expense		200.00
Taxes	340.00	
Taxes (Accrued)		340.00
Salesmen's Salaries	175.00	
Salesmen's Salaries (Accrued)		175.00
Interest Cost	50.00	
Interest Cost (Accrued)		50.00
Special Police on Strike Duty	150.00	
Special Police on Strike Duty (Accrued)		150.00
Office Salaries	100.00	
Office Salaries (Accrued)		100.00
Sub-Rentals Income	50.00	
Sub-Rentals Income (Deferred)		50.00

Purpose of Summarizing.—After the adjusting entries are posted, the ledger reflects the true financial condition as of the date of these entries. However, at this stage the information contained in the ledger is usually scattered over a large number of accounts. To obtain a concise view of the results of the business, it is necessary to summarize this information. The Profit and Loss *account* is the means by which the temporary proprietorship accounts are summarized and the net results as to profits or losses are indicated.

In this connection it will be remembered that the adjusting entries have already effected a separation of the elements of the mixed accounts, so that the temporary proprietorship items—expenses and income—applicable to the current period are now separately shown. The transfer of these *temporary* proprietorship items to the *vested* proprietorship accounts constitutes the work of closing. The use of the Profit and Loss account as a place of summary—a clearing house—through which the *net* result can be passed on or transferred to the vested proprietorship accounts, constitutes a part of the method or technique of closing.

The Closing Entries.—The student is already familiar with the principles of debit and credit involved in making the closing entries. As indicated above, these are transfer entries and merely effect a transfer of all temporary proprietorship items to the Profit and Loss account for summary there and for the transfer of the net result to some vested proprietorship account or accounts. Like all other entries, these are made first in the journal and are posted from there to the ledger. The current sections of the various expense and income accounts are then ruled off and the ledger is said to be "closed."

Method of Closing the Books.—As explained on page 129, the Profit and Loss account in the ledger is used for summarizing the temporary proprietorship accounts before transferring them, i.e., their net result, to the vested proprietorship accounts. The use of Purchases and Sales accounts for a partial summarization of the various merchandise accounts has also been explained. After this partial summarization has been made, the debit balance of the Purchases account, showing cost of goods sold, is transferred to the Profit and Loss account; and similarly, the credit balance of the Sales account, representing net sales, is transferred to the Profit and Loss account. Profit and Loss then shows on the credit side net sales and on the debit cost of goods sold, the difference being the income portion, i.e., the gross profit of the merchandising activities for the period. If it is desired to show on the face of the account the actual figure of gross profit, the Profit and Loss account may be balanced at this stage, though this is not usually done. The rest of the work of summarization is accomplished directly through the Profit and Loss account.

Closing Entries Illustrated.—The formal journal entries necessary to effect this summarization in the ledger are given below, being based on the illustration used for the work sheet and being made up directly from the various sections of the formal profit and loss statement shown on page 234. The way in which this is done should be carefully noted. As to their sequence in the journal, these closing entries will, of course, immediately follow the formal adjusting entries illustrated above.

Purchases	1,350.00	
In-Freight and Cartage		1,350.00
Purchase Returns and Allowance	5,400.00	
Purchases		5,400.00
Profit and Loss	134,450.00	
Purchases		134,450.00
Sales	1,850.00	
Sales Returns and Allowances		1,850.00

Sales	193,150.00	
Profit and Loss		193,150.00
Profit and Loss	25,225.00	
Salesmen's Salaries		13,675.00
Selling Supplies and Expense		1,400.00
Advertising		4,500.00
Out-Freight		400.00
Delivery Expense		3,300.00
Depreciation		1,950.00
Store Furniture and Fixtures	1,200.00	
Delivery Equipment	750.00	
Profit and Loss	18,560.00	
Office Salaries		5,100.00
Office Expense		4,500.00
General Expense		2,000.00
Printing and Stationery		600.00
Taxes		3,180.00
Insurance		1,500.00
Depreciation		1,680.00
Office Furniture and Fixtures	280.00	
Building	1,400.00	
Profit and Loss	2,367.88	
Interest Cost		950.00
Sales Discount		850.00
Bad Debts		482.88
Collection and Exchange		85.00
Interest Income	1,650.00	

Purchase Discount	1,300.00	
Profit and Loss		2,950.00
Profit and Loss	1,350.00	
Special Police on Strike Duty		1,350.00
Sub-Rentals Income	600.00	
Profit and Loss		600.00
Profit and Loss	14,747.12	
U. R. Smart, Personal		14,747.12
U. R. Smart, Personal	4,247.12	
U. R. Smart, Capital		4,247.12

It will be noted that after the net sales and cost of goods sold are transferred to the Profit and Loss account, all expenses directly connected with sales, such as Salesmen's Salaries, Advertising, Delivery Expense, Depreciation of Delivery Equipment, of Store Furniture and Fixtures, and similar items, are closed into the Profit and Loss account.

The groups of accounts closed next are those covering General Administrative Expenses, Financial Management Expenses, Financial Management Income, Non-Operating Expense, and Non-Operating Income. It will be noticed that the *order* of closing follows the order in which the same items appear in the profit and loss statement.

The Profit and Loss account now shows on the credit side the items of income and on the debit side the costs and expenses applicable to the current period. Its balance then gives the net profit (or loss) covering the period's transactions.

Throughout the period, as the profit accrues, the proprietor may have drawn against it for personal use, as shown in his Personal account. To show the amount of profit remaining in the business, the balance of the Profit and Loss account is transferred to the Personal account, the balance of which then gives the amount of undrawn or overdrawn profit. The balance of the Personal account is closed into the Capital account, the credit balance of which then represents the net worth of the business at the end of this period and at the commencement of the next.

The Profit and Loss Account.—In posting the closing journal entries to the Profit and Loss account in the ledger, usually only the group totals as indicated by the entry will appear. In small concerns where expenses and income are not classified in much detail, the individual items composing the group total are often shown. These items are, of course, the same as appear in the part of the journal entry which is contra to the group total charged or credited to Profit and Loss. The ledger Profit and Loss account for the illustration will appear as follows when completely posted:

PROFIT AND LOSS (23)

19—			19—		
Dec. 31	Purchases............	$134,450.00	Dec. 31	Sales..............	$193,150.00
	Selling Expenses.....	25,225.00		Financial Management Income.....	2,950.00
	Administrative Expenses...........	18,560.00		Sub-Rentals Income.	600.00
	Financial Management Expenses....	2,367.88			
	SpecialPolice on Strike Duty............	1,350.00			
	Net Profit, to U. R. Smart, Personal...	14,747.12			
		$196,700.00			$196,700.00

Form 28. Profit and Loss Account in Ledger

Profit and Loss Not an Account for Current Entry.—It should be kept clearly in mind that the process of closing the books is merely a method or device by which the transactions for the year are *summarized* and the net result determined. This net result, whether a profit or a loss, belongs to the proprietor and must ultimately be shown in his account. It is, therefore, manifest that the Profit and Loss account is *only* a summary account and should never be used for current entry. It is the means by which the *temporary* proprietorship accounts are summarized and the medium through which the net result is cleared into some vested proprietorship account or accounts.

Effect of Closing the Ledger.—The transfer of net profit to a vested proprietorship account completes the work of closing the ledger, all temporary proprietorship accounts for the *current* period being closed out. All open balances now shown on the ledger constitute either assets, liabilities, or vested proprietorship. A post-closing trial balance contains only the accounts shown on the corresponding balance sheet. The income and expense accounts, having been cleared of their current record, are prepared to receive the record of the next period. The business cycle for this particular business has been completed and its correct history recorded.

CHAPTER XXIX
TYPES OF ACCOUNTING RECORDS AND THEIR DEVELOPMENT

Evolution of Analytical Journals.—Though the only books absolutely necessary for an accounting record under the double-entry method are the journal and the ledger, even the small business finds some subdivision of the journals advantageous, and so makes use of sales, purchases, and cash receipts and cash disbursements journals. As a business grows and its transactions increase in volume and complexity, further subdivision is needed. When the scope of its organization becomes too great for a personal oversight, a method or system must be devised for keeping the proprietor or manager in close touch with the various departments and lines of business endeavor. This is accomplished by means of reports from the accounting department, which exists largely for the purpose of furnishing this kind of information.

Principle to be Followed in Securing Analysis.—In an earlier chapter it was laid down as a fundamental principle that the information desired by the management should be furnished from analytical records made at the time of original entry, rather than by analyzing a composite record at the time the information is wanted. Such analytical records make possible a quicker and more up-to-date report to the management, and they save labor in securing the information by making the analysis at the time of record when all the facts related to it are readily available.

Types of Sales Journals and Methods of Handling.—The first step in the analysis of business transactions is the subdivision of the general journal into separate journals, and this analysis is carried still further by the use of columnar journal records. Reference has already been made, in Chapter XVIII, to the use of additional columns in the sales and purchase journals. Here a brief sketch will be given of the methods of recording sales in various kinds of sales journals.

1. The earliest type of sales journal, not often used today, consisted of a letter impression book containing the press copy of invoices sent to customers, with columns for the extension of the amounts and sometimes with additional columns for purposes of analysis. Such a journal has the advantage that the original entry is an exact copy of the invoice. Oftentimes, however, the impression is poor and nearly or quite illegible; it takes much room; the detail shown is not often used; and it increases the work of making and handling the record.

2. Another method makes use of a perforated invoice book with a columnized interleaf solid-bound between the perforated invoice sheets. The

sales invoice is written on one of the perforated sheets and a carbon underneath gives a duplicate on the interleaf, the latter constituting the formal sales record. The advantages and objections are practically the same as for the impression book method.

3. Another method is to make a separate carbon copy of each invoice and use the duplicate as the source of entry in the sales journal. The journal entry gives only the file number of the duplicate invoice so that in case of need the duplicate can easily be referred to. Such a sales journal may, of course, contain analytical columns with any desired heads.

4. Still another method uses the duplicate invoice for posting to the customer's account, after which it is filed in binders. The latter are usually provided with recapitulation sheets which show the totals and analysis for each day, week, or month as the case may be. Just as above, the invoice file provides the detail in support of the ledger account and the recapitulation sheets constitute the journal from which credits to the various sales accounts are made. Either one of these last two methods eliminates most of the objections and embraces most of the advantages of the other methods mentioned above.

Where several sales ledgers are used, the sales journal is sometimes subdivided on the same basis as an aid in posting and for the purpose of securing controlling figures as explained in following chapters.

The Sales Returns and Allowances Journal.—The use of any special form of sales journal, particularly if it provides for an analysis of the sales, requires a similar record of sales returns and allowances. Either a separate book, similar in form to the sales journal, may be employed for recording these items or the pages in the back of the sales journal may be used instead.

Development of the Purchase Journal.—The development of the purchase records from the old-time scrapbook for invoices to the modern analytic voucher record resembles the development of the sales journal. The old-fashioned invoice book was usually a big, loose-bound, coarse paper volume in which were pasted the invoices for goods bought. An extension column was provided for the amount of the invoice, and the total of this gave the purchases for a given period. The use of columns for various classes of purchases provided the required analysis, but, as it was a cumbersome, nondescript record, it was bound to give place to something better—the formal purchase journal or register of today.

The purchase journal or register consists of a bound or a loose-leaf book ruled to suit individual needs and purposes. Where sales are analyzed by classes, an exactly similar analysis of purchases must be made in order to secure a gross profit figure for each class. Therefore its form follows very closely that of the sales journal. Entries are made in the purchase journal of the name of the creditor, the amount of his invoice, and the number of the file where the invoice can be found in case of need.

Where a separate purchasing department is maintained, the duplicate purchase orders, corrected if necessary to correspond with the purchase invoice received, may be used as the basis of the purchase journal. In this case recapitulation sheets are inserted just as with the sales journal. The handling of purchases is simplified by the fact that as a rule they are much smaller in number than sales. The same general considerations apply to the handling of returned purchases as to returned sales.

Handling Expenses through the Purchase Journal.—It is the practice of some concerns to treat expenses such as labor, rent, salaries, supplies, etc., as purchase transactions. Under this method, instead of postponing the entry until the item is paid, it is made at the time of securing the service or supplies. The basis for the entry may be either: (1) the bill or purchase invoice; (2) a formal purchase memo or voucher made out for each transaction; or (3) the fact that the expense has been incurred may suffice for the entry on the books with no formal paper to vouch for it. The use of such formal papers as the basis for entry is known as the voucher record system. The details of this system are fully explained in the second volume. Discussion is here limited to a brief outline of the method and of the advantages of its use.

When expense invoices are entered and analyzed in the voucher record form of purchase journal, their posting requires debits to the various expense accounts and credits to the individual creditors' accounts in the ledger. If the ledger contains only a controlling account, this account must be credited with the total of the expense and other purchases, while the individual accounts in the creditors subsidiary ledger must be credited with the details which make up the total. When the bill is paid, entry in the cash book will not be, as usual, to the debit of the expense account in the general ledger, but to the debit of the creditor's account in the subsidiary ledger. The reason for this procedure will be made clear in the discussion of controlling accounts to follow.

The entry of expense invoices in the above manner secures an immediate record of all liabilities as incurred and therefore makes the books show at all times the true state of affairs as regards liabilities. The method, however, necessitates a little more work in making the record, and for this reason many concerns do not enter expenses until paid, making the debit to them through the cash book. In this latter case all unpaid expense bills should be kept in an expense file for reference when information as to the unrecorded liabilities is desired.

Note Journals.—As explained previously, note journals are sometimes used instead of the general journal for the record of note transactions, where these are sufficiently numerous. Provision is sometimes made for securing a proper analysis in order to distinguish between notes from customers and notes from other sources. It will be seen later that such an analysis is necessary when controlling accounts are operated.

Analysis in the Cash Book.—The cash journals may be ruled to furnish any desired analysis, showing on the debit side (i.e., the cash receipts journal) the sources of receipts, and on the credit side the objects of expenditure. As the sources of cash receipts are usually more limited than the objects of expenditures, they do not require so much analysis. The analysis may be very detailed, the only limit to the number of columns being the width of the page. A minute analysis of expenditures, however, is usually made, not in the cash journal, but in the purchase or voucher record, which thus relieves the cash book of a mass of detail.

The chief advantage of using additional columns in books of original entry lies in the fact that time and labor are saved in posting. The column total is posted in one item, whereas each of the numerous items composing it would have to be posted separately to the account named in the column heading if no analytical column were provided. Hence it would be a waste of space to provide separate columns for items which recur so infrequently as to make their summarization unnecessary. Care should be taken to avoid needless columnization.

It is customary to have the following columns on the debit side of the cash book: General or Sundry, Accounts Receivable, Sales Discount, and Net Cash or Bank; on the credit side: General or Sundry, Accounts Payable, Purchases Discount, and Net Cash or Bank. (See page 282 for illustration.) The proof of the distribution is secured by checking the sum of the net cash and discount columns against the sum of the totals of the other columns. In both receipts and disbursements journals every item must appear in the respective Net Cash columns, and from these distribution is made to the other columns. For example, in the cash receipts journal, receipts from customers are distributed into the Accounts Receivable column for the gross amount of each item, and into Sales Discount for the discount, if any is taken. All other items are carried into the General or Sundry column. Where several sales ledgers are kept, additional columns may be provided so that instead of having one accounts receivable column, there are columns for each ledger. Similar treatment is given to the disbursements.

Analysis in the General Journal.—Where the general journal is used for returned goods, allowances, and other adjustments with customers and creditors, use is made of analytic columns with these captions for both the debit and credit: Accounts Receivable, Accounts Payable, and General. Here, however, there is no column in which to enter all items for distribution to the other columns. If a customer's or a creditor's account is affected, entry is made in that column in the first place. All *other* entries are in the General column. (See page 281 for illustration.)

With regard to analysis columns in the general journal, some accountants maintain, with good reason, that if the number of transactions of a particular kind is sufficiently large to justify their segregation in a separate column, this in itself would be ample justification for the use of a separate journal to record these items. Whenever the analysis of recurring transactions in the general journal is facilitated by the use of separate columns, the advisability of opening a new journal for the record of such items as appear in the general journal most frequently should be considered.

Subdivision of the Ledgers.—The next step in the subdivision of the records is made in the ledgers. The general or impersonal accounts of the business are of a more permanent character than the accounts with persons—customers and creditors. Consequently, when once it is determined under what account titles information is desired and those accounts are set up, there is usually little need to change their titles. Personal accounts, however, are constantly changing as some customers are lost and new ones are added, and also because creditors change with purchases in new markets. Hence, when a business outgrows its small beginnings, it is customary to keep these changing accounts in separate books. The basis for the first subdivision of the ledgers, therefore, is the separation of the accounts into personal and impersonal. The accounts with customers are carried in a separate ledger called variously the sales, customers, or accounts receivable ledger, and those with creditors in a ledger called purchase, creditors, or accounts payable ledger. All other accounts are kept in the main ledger known as the general ledger. One advantage of this subdivision is that several bookkeepers can work on the various ledgers at the same time.

A further subdivision of the customers ledger is frequently made into "city" and "country," the former containing the accounts with customers located within the city where the business is situated, and the latter the out-of-the-city accounts. Other subdivisions may be made on an alphabetical basis, i.e., customers ledger No. 1, containing all accounts from A to G; customers ledger No. 2, H to M, etc. Sometimes the concern's sales territory is divided into arbitrary districts and the ledgers are subdivided to correspond with such districts.

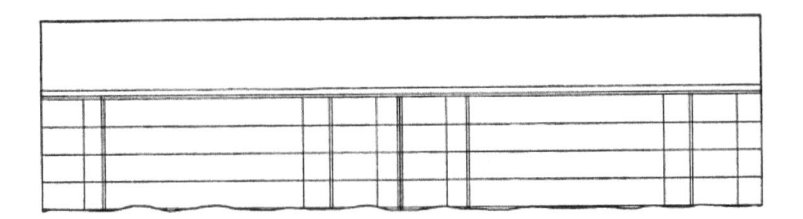

Form 29. Standard Ledger—Divided Column

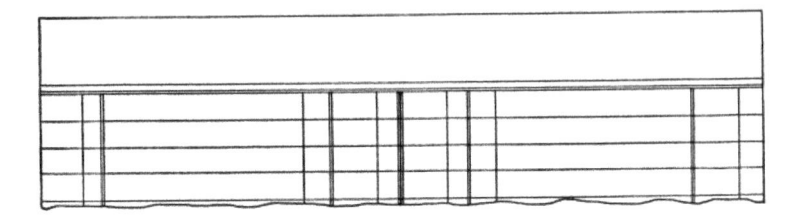

Form 30. Standard Ledger—Center Column

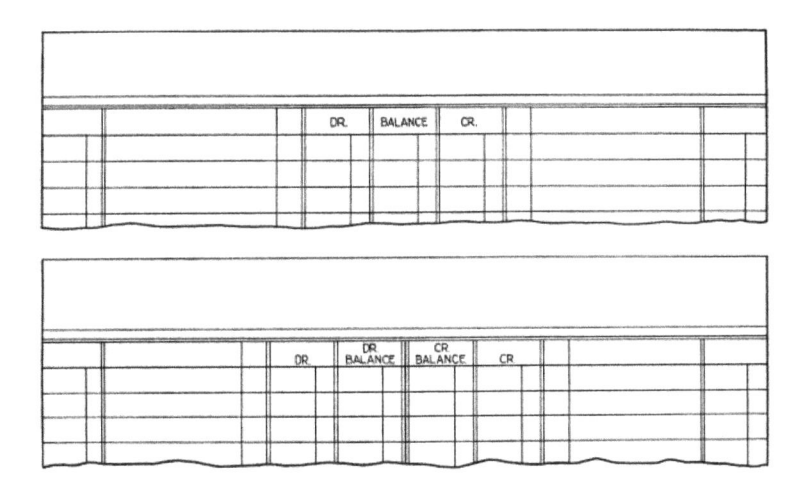

Form 31. Balance Ledger Rulings

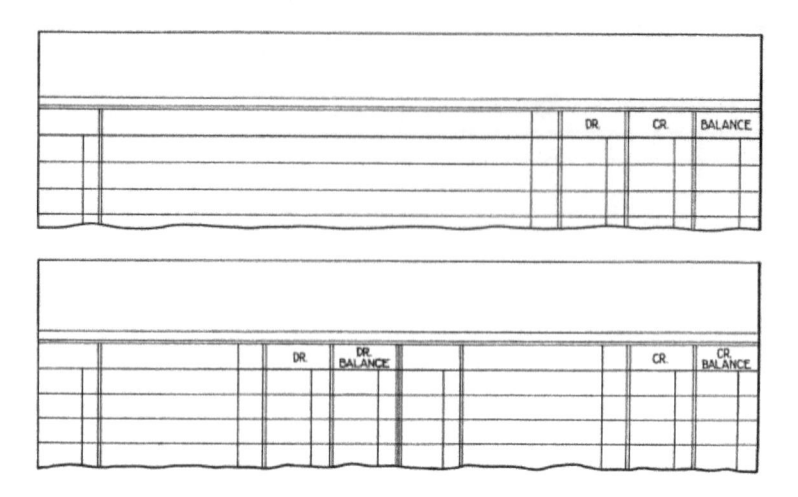

Form 32. Balance Ledger Rulings

Kinds of Ledgers.—There are several kinds of ledgers, which may be classified (1) as to their rulings, and (2) as to their bindings.

1. RULINGS. As to their rulings, ledgers are either standard, balance, or progressive. The standard ruling has two duplicate parts, a debit and a credit, and is usually divided in the center of the page, one money column appearing at the extreme right of each part, although sometimes the arrangement is symmetrical with both debit and credit money columns at the center, and the date columns at either side of the page. (See Forms 29 and 30.)

The balance ruling is a three or four-column ledger with the money columns either at the center or at the right-hand margin, or at both the center and the right-hand margin. The extra columns are for the account balances. If the balance is usually either a debit or a credit, only one balance column would be necessary; where it is apt to be a debit at one time and a credit at another, a debit balance column and a credit balance column are advantageous. The balance ruling is used particularly with personal accounts where there is need for an up-to-date balance. Where this kind of ledger is used, entry of new debits or credits should always be on the next blank line as shown in the balance column, so as to allow the extension of the new balance opposite the last entry even though this should leave blank several of the preceding lines on the debit and credit sides. Typical forms of some of these are shown in Forms 31 and 32.

The Boston, progressive, or tabular ledger, as it is variously called, makes provision for a *horizontal* progress of the account as to sequence of time; the title of the account is written at the left-hand margin, and one or more lines are allowed to each account according to the degree of its activity. The account title is written once at the left margin of the master or main sheet, and is sometimes repeated at the right margin if the sheet is very wide. The page is divided into columns for each day of the period. To effect this, short-margin insert sheets must be bound in to give the desired room for accommodating a whole period's record. This style of ruling was formerly much used in banks where a daily balance for each depositor's account was necessary. It is capable of adaptation to other uses, however. One form is shown, Form 33.

DEPOSITORS NAMES	BALANCE	MONDAY			TUESDAY			WEDNESDAY		
		CHECKS	DEPOSITS	BALANCE	CHECKS	DEPOSITS	BALANCE	CHECKS	DEPOSITS	BALANCE
John Smith	500 00	200 00		300 00	150 00	1000 00	1150 00	etc.		

Form 33. Boston Ledger Sometimes Used for Depositors

2. BINDINGS. Ledgers may be classified also as solid-bound, loose-leaf, and card, the titles being self-explanatory. One of the great advantages of the loose-leaf and card ledgers over the solid-bound ledger is their flexibility. They lend themselves easily to any desired grouping of the accounts; they may be numerically arranged where accounts are numbered instead of named; they may be arranged as to classes and each class made self-indexing; or a geographical grouping may be made. Another great advantage of this form of ledger is the ability to discard or file away in other binders all "dead" accounts, thus making for ease and facility in the use of the "live" ledger. Also it is possible for several clerks to work simultaneously, since the leaves or cards are removable and may be distributed among any number of clerks. There is always the danger, however, of failure to return a leaf or card, or of placing it out of regular order when returning it, or of destroying it, if it were desired fraudulently to do away with any particular account. The use of loose-leaf and card ledgers for personal accounts is pretty thoroughly established, notwithstanding the disadvantages just mentioned.

CHAPTER XXX
CONTROLLING ACCOUNTS

Introductory.—Reference to controlling accounts has been made several times in preceding chapters. It is purposed now to define them and explain their use. The separation of the various journals on the basis of an analysis of transactions frees the general journal of a vast mass of detail it formerly carried. This separation, however, in no way affects the underlying debit and credit scheme of the whole system. Each journal is an integral part of the whole; every entry therein has its equal debit and credit which are in due course posted to its proper account, thus maintaining the equilibrium of the ledger. The separation of the ledger into three or more special ledgers in the interest of economy of effort and ease of use has also been mentioned. Still, each of these special ledgers is an integral part of the whole ledger and the accounts in the special ledgers must be entered in the trial balance to secure proof of equilibrium.

The customers ledger is usually the most active of the various ledgers, i.e., more postings are made in it because the majority of business transactions involve dealings of various sorts with customers, and more accounts are required to keep the records with customers. It is usually, therefore, the largest part of the whole ledger, but its accounts are all of the same kind, viz., accounts receivable. When taking a trial balance, the total of the balances of the customers ledger accounts is usually set up under the title "Accounts Receivable," leaving the details to a supplementary list or schedule.

Advantage of a Controlling Account.—The advantage of thus condensing the trial balance is apparent and suggests the desirability of obtaining the "accounts receivable" balance independently of the customers ledger. If this is done the bookkeeper in charge of the general ledger can not only draw up his trial balance without reference to the customers ledger, but has also the correct figure for the total of the account balances in the customers ledger. In other words, he has a figure which controls the customers ledger and which therefore furnishes him with a check on the accuracy of the ledger clerk or bookkeeper who keeps that ledger. The most convenient method of recording the accounts receivable figure is evidently by means of a formal account on the general ledger. When such an account is kept, the effect is to make it a summary account whose detail is carried in the customers ledger.

Controlling Account Necessitates Changed Idea of Ledger Equilibrium.—By having a customers controlling account (or "Accounts Receivable" as it is commonly called, though other terms are also used) in the general ledger, the customers ledger is no longer used as an integral part of the whole ledger and becomes a "subsidiary" ledger; that is, its function is reduced to that of a supporting schedule or list of detail for the summary controlling account. The equilibrium of the general ledger is now maintained by summary posting to the controlling accounts. Though the customers ledger has ceased to be a "ledger" in the proper sense of the term, it is still a vital part of the system, carrying as it does the detail of the summary controlling account. Moreover, it is linked up to the system by being provable against its summary account. Yet it should be borne in mind that its scheme of debit and credit is now an independent one and is not linked up to the debit and credit equilibrium of the general ledger; that is, the postings in the subsidiary ledger are merely memorandum entries of the detail posted in summary form to the general ledger. Thus the mathematical basis of the controlling account is simply that the whole is exactly equal to all its parts, the balance of the summary account being equal to the total of the balances of all the customers' accounts of which it is the summary. To illustrate, if we have customers' accounts whose balances are $1,000, $2,000, $3,000, $4,000, and $5,000 respectively, then the summary account must have a balance of $15,000.

Debits to the Controlling Account.—The principle and the purpose of the controlling account having now been explained, the next problem to consider is how best to gather the summary figures for its debits and credits. If every debit to a customer's account must be posted also to the controlling account and every credit to a customer's account must be shown as a credit in the controlling account the work involved would be almost doubled and little would be gained by thus duplicating the postings in another ledger. Therefore it is important to secure the figures for entry in the controlling accounts with the least effort, i.e., in the form of debit and credit summaries. Hence, to determine the sources of these debits and credits of the controlling account, analysis must be made of the sources of the debits and credits to the customers' accounts.

Most of the debits to customers' accounts are from the sales journal. Additional debits may be from the cash disbursements journal when cash payments are made as a rebate or a refund for overpayment or some other similar transactions; still others from the general journal for adjustments of various kinds. The debits to customers, however, for cash paid them are very few in number, because such adjustments usually are not made by means of cash payments. The sales journal, as usually operated, carries a column for credit sales, whose total represents in one amount the total of all detailed debits to customers' accounts. The total of the credit sales column, therefore, controls the total debits to all customers on account of charge sales to them. In summarizing the sales journal the summary entry should show that this total is to be posted not only to the credit side of the Sales account but also to the debit of the controlling account in the ledger. This is so because the customers ledger has ceased to be an integral part of the general ledger, the controlling account having taken its place. Accordingly, the general ledger contains no record of either the debits or credits of the entire group of sales transactions until the end of the month, when this group must therefore be brought into the general ledger in summary form, both debit and credit.

Where the total sales in the sales journal include an analysis of sales into cash sales and credit sales, the following summary entry should be made:

- Accounts Receivable
- Cash
- Sales

The cash debit is set up only to show the equilibrium of the summary entry and is not posted, because it is entered also in the cash book and is posted from there. This debit posting to "Accounts Receivable" in the general ledger secures in one posting a debit amount equal to all individual debit postings to the customers ledger from this source. The controlling account in the general ledger is variously termed "Sales Ledger," "Accounts Receivable," "Trade Debtors," "Customers," etc.

The two other sources of debit posting to customers' accounts are the general journal and the cash book. The debit side of the journal is provided with an Accounts Receivable analysis column in which, as explained in the previous chapter, debits to customers' accounts are entered. At posting time the total of this Accounts Receivable column will therefore give in one figure a debit posting item to the general ledger Accounts Receivable account equal to all individual debit postings from the general journal to customers' accounts in the customers ledger.

Usually it is not necessary to provide an Accounts Receivable column on the credit side of the cash book, since debit postings from there to customers' accounts are very infrequent. Hence no total or controlling figure for entry in the Accounts Receivable account can be obtained. Every item which is posted from this source to the debit of a customer's account must be also posted—item by item—to the debit of Accounts Receivable in the general ledger. This is of course a double debit posting, but one of these debits is to a subsidiary ledger which is no longer a part of the equilibrium scheme and therefore does not throw the general ledger out of balance. Great care must be exercised to make sure that each of these items is posted both to a customer's account and also to the Accounts Receivable account.

Credits to the Controlling Account.—An analysis of the credits to customers' accounts shows four main sources:

1. The cash receipts journal for payments made by customers.

2. The sales returns journal, if one is kept, for goods returned by customers.

3. The note journal for notes received in payment.

4. The general journal for various adjustments and also for the purpose of recording notes and returned sales where special journals are not kept for these transactions.

Accordingly, analytic columns for accounts receivable are provided in the cash receipts journal and the general journal. The totals of their columns are posted to the credit of Accounts Receivable, and the detailed amounts to the credit of the various customers' accounts. The credit postings from these sources to the customers ledger accounts and to the general ledger Accounts Receivable account are therefore the same so far as totals are concerned. The sales returns journal is summarized at posting time by means of an entry similar to that in the sales journal, as follows:

- Sales Returns
- Accounts Receivable

In this case the credit posting to the Accounts Receivable account is equal to the detailed credits to customers' accounts.

Similarly, a summary entry for the notes receivable journal secures a controlling figure for Accounts Receivable. If the notes are all received from customers to apply on their accounts, the summary entry is:

- Notes Receivable
- Accounts Receivable

the amount being the total of that journal.

In this way the total of all debits and of all credits to the individual customers' accounts is represented by the summary items entered in the general ledger controlling account, Accounts Receivable. Consequently, the balance of this single account is equal to the balance of the customers ledger. For the trial balance, therefore, one account takes the place of hundreds or even thousands of customers' individual accounts. As a result of this, much time is saved and the possibility of error on the general ledger is greatly reduced.

Proving the Customers Ledger.—The use of a controlling account in the general ledger, however, does not eliminate the necessity of proving the accuracy of the customers ledger. It merely makes it possible to take a trial balance without bringing the numerous customers' accounts into it. It is just as much a part of the proof of the work to make a list of customers' accounts balances and check it against the balance of the Accounts Receivable general ledger account, as it is to prove the general ledger by means of a trial balance.

If there is a discrepancy between the subsidiary ledger and its controlling account on the general ledger that discrepancy does not necessarily prevent a trial balance of the general ledger, but it does show error in the work which must be searched out and corrected.

Accounts Payable Account.—A similar arrangement will make possible a controlling account on the general ledger for the creditors or purchases ledger. This account is variously termed Accounts Payable, Purchase Ledger, Creditors, or Trade Creditors account. Its mechanism is the same as for Accounts Receivable. Analysis of credit postings to creditors' accounts shows the purchase journal as their main source. Other credits come through the general journal and a very few through the cash receipts journal. The summary entry for the purchase journal is:

- Purchases
- Accounts Payable
- Cash

This shows a debit to the Purchases account for the total amount of the purchases, a credit to Accounts Payable for the liability to creditors, and to Cash for the amount paid on cash purchases. The cash item is not posted. The Accounts Payable column total on the credit side of the journal, and the separate items from the cash receipts journal, furnish the other credits to the Accounts Payable account in the general ledger.

The debits come from the Accounts Payable columns in the cash disbursements journal and in the general journal, and the summaries for the notes payable and purchases returns journals.

Basic Principle as to Postings to Controlling Accounts.—In the handling of controlling accounts, the one fundamental requirement is to make sure that every entry in books of original entry which affects any account in the subsidiary ledger is reflected in the postings to the controlling account in the general ledger. This principle resolves itself into the mathematical axiom stated above that a whole is equal to all—not just some—of its parts. Only thus can a true control be established.

Making the Subsidiary Ledger Self-Balancing.—Through the use of the two controlling accounts explained above, the trial balance is relieved of a large number of accounts, and the general ledger is made independent of the subsidiary ledgers. On the other hand, the subsidiary ledgers are dependent for their proof on the controlling account balances in the general ledger. In an effort to make every ledger "self-balancing," a further refinement of the controlling account idea is frequently incorporated in each subsidiary ledger. It is accomplished in the following manner: An exact duplicate of the controlling account on the general ledger is set up in the subsidiary ledger, *with this difference*, that the sides of the account are reversed so that the subsidiary ledger account has for its debits the credits of the general ledger account, and for its credits the debits of the general ledger account.

Take the Accounts Receivable controlling account for illustration. On the general ledger its balance is of course a debit balance representing the total outstanding accounts due from customers. Similarly, the schedule or list of customers' accounts taken from the sales ledger will represent debit balances whose total is the same as the controlling account balance. If, then, the controlling account itself is placed on the customers ledger as an additional account, the sides being reversed, the balance of this one account will be a credit equal to the total debit balance of all the other accounts in the customers ledger. Therefore, if the customers ledger is correct, its own balance will be offset exactly by the credit balance of the one additional account, and the ledger then is said to be self-balancing. There is no theory or principle of debit and credit involved in this; the device is simply introduced in order that the ledger may provide an internal proof of its correctness. The title of the balancing account on the subsidiary ledger is "Adjustment" or "Balance" and has no significance other than that mentioned. In a similar manner any subsidiary ledger may be made self-balancing.

CHAPTER XXXI
HANDLING CONTROLLING ACCOUNTS

Chapter XXX concerned itself with the statement and explanation of the principles on which the controlling account rests, the manner of its construction, its advantages, and with the changed application of the fundamental scheme of debit and credit under a system of records operating controlling accounts. The present chapter will be devoted to a consideration of the problems met with in the practical operation of these accounts.

Introduction of the Controlling Account.—Upon the installation of a new system or set of books, the controlling account feature may be incorporated from the start. The new system must provide for the separation from the general ledger, of the ledgers over which control is to be established. The method of securing controlling totals for posting to the general ledger controlling accounts was indicated in the preceding chapter.

Where it is desired to introduce controlling accounts into a system which has not formerly used them, certain adjustments must be made, i.e., the accounts to be controlled must be segregated and controlling account columns must be provided for in the books of original entry. With the transfer of these accounts to a separate ledger, together with the introduction of the controlling accounts into the general ledger, the equilibrium of that ledger is maintained. The opening entry in the newly established controlling account is of course the sum of the balances of the transferred accounts.

If it is desired to establish the new controlling account by journal entry, that entry would appear somewhat as shown on page 279, Form 34, with suitable explanation added. All these items should be posted to the general ledger as shown by the entry, and in addition the detailed items should be posted as debits to the accounts in the customers ledger. The effect of these postings would be, first, to close the individual customers' accounts formerly carried in the general ledger and open up in their stead the controlling account; and second, to set up on the subsidiary ledger the detail of the customers' accounts.

Recording Withdrawals of Stock-in-Trade.—The original basis for separating the main journal into its subsidiary parts was the analysis of transactions by kinds, such as sales, purchases, cash, etc. The sales journal was presumed to contain only sales of stock-in-trade. Departure from this principle was advisable in the case of goods drawn at cost, for use in the business or by the proprietor or for other purposes. This is done because withdrawals of stock-in-trade, at whatever price and for whatever purpose, can be recorded more conveniently in the sales journal than elsewhere.

It is theoretically incorrect, however, to enter such items in the Sales account because withdrawals at cost do not represent actual sales, and for this reason they should be regarded as deductions from purchases or from inventory. The only proper place for their record, under this view, is the general journal, entry in which would have to be by detailed debit and credit for each item. However, because this requires much more work than entry in the sales journal, this last method is more commonly employed. Usually the volume of such transactions is not large and would not seriously vitiate the use of the Sales account as the basis for estimating percentages of cost of goods sold, gross profit, selling expenses, etc. Moreover, as the total amount of these withdrawals is often fairly constant as between periods their record in the sales journal is countenanced.

The Problem of the Sales Journal Summary.—When withdrawals from stock at cost price are recorded in the sales journal, a new problem arises in summarizing the sales journal when operating under a controlling account system. The customers or sales ledger is usually limited absolutely to customers' accounts. Accounts with the proprietors, and with all other titles under which withdrawals for other purposes may be recorded, are almost invariably carried in the general ledger. Therefore, while most of the items entered in the sales journal are posted to the customers ledger, these withdrawal items must be posted in detail to the general ledger. Thus the total of the sales journal does not represent the correct debit to accounts receivable in the general ledger. Evidently an analysis of the content of the sales journal must be made in order to obtain the correct controlling figure.

Such analysis may be made in several ways. Where possible, three columns in addition to the departmental columns should be used. The column titles would be "Sales Ledger," "Cash," and "Sundry." The sum of these three would give the total to check against the total of the other distributive columns, but only the "Sales Ledger" total would be posted to Accounts Receivable, and the individual items in that column would be posted to the customers' accounts in the sales ledger. The items in Sundry column would be posted to their named accounts in the general ledger. This method secures an automatic separation of the controlling account total from other items, and should be used where possible.

If the number of these extraneous items is too small to warrant the use of a separate column, they may be recorded in the Sales Ledger column and indicated by means of an "✕" or some other mark. At summary time, the sales journal must be looked over and these items picked out. Subtraction of their sum from the Sales Ledger column total would give the correct controlling account posting.

Still another method requires a correcting general journal entry at the time the sales journal entry is made. Under this method these special items are included in the Sales Ledger column, thereby causing an overcharge to Accounts Receivable. The correcting general journal entry must therefore credit Accounts Receivable by the amount of the overcharge for each item. For instance, if stock has been drawn by the proprietor, the general journal entry at the time the sales journal entry is made would be:

- Proprietor, Personal
- Accounts Receivable

the debit to proprietor being checked here and posted from the sales journal, or vice versa. This method, however, results in a duplication of work. It would be preferable not to enter these items in the sales journal and to make the record only in the general journal, and so leave the Sales Ledger column total in the sales journal the correct controlling figure.

In a complicated controlling account system, where for current entry a simple bookkeeping routine must be established and all items of whatever kind be handled in the same way, the withdrawals by proprietors are recorded in accounts opened with them in the sales ledger just as with customers. At the end of the period, before closing the books, these proprietors' accounts are transferred by general journal entry to the general ledger, requiring one entry—like the one last shown above—for the drawings of the period.

Cash sales may also be handled without the use of a separate column in the sales journal. Two methods are used for this. Under the one, cash sales are included in the Accounts Receivable debit total of the sales journal, although the individual items are not posted to the subsidiary ledger, and they are also included in the Accounts Receivable credit total of the cash receipts journal. The inflated debit in the general ledger controlling account is thus offset by an equally inflated credit, the balance therefore being the correct amount to control the sales ledger.

Under the other method the postings to the general ledger controlling account are the same as in the first method. The two methods differ, however, in that under the second method an account is opened in the subsidiary ledger entitled "Cash Customers" or "Cash Sales," to the debit of which are posted in detail the cash sales items from the sales journal and to the credit of which are posted in detail the cash sales items from the cash receipts journal. The account is thus only a "wash" or clearing account. This method, however, prevents the inflated debits and credits in the controlling account.

The methods last described for handling proprietors' withdrawals and cash sales are the ones most frequently used in large businesses where simplicity of routine for current entry must be secured.

The Problem of the Purchase Journal Summary.—The practice of recording extraneous transactions in the purchase journal brings about at summary time a situation similar to that of the sales journal, when a controlling Accounts Payable account is maintained. The purchase journal is, and should be, the place of record for purchases made for the business. If the proprietor (or other person), for his personal account and use, purchases through the business merchandise which never goes into stock, accurate accounting requires such transactions to be charged direct to the proprietor and not to the Purchases account of the business. Inasmuch as the liability is assumed by the business and the creditor's account will appear in the purchase ledger, the use of the purchase journal total for credit to the Accounts Payable controlling account gives the correct figure. The trouble comes in because this same figure cannot be used as the debit to Purchases. Subtraction of these extraneous items must be made to determine the proper amount chargeable to the Purchases account, thus necessitating an analysis at summary time.

Accounts Both Receivable and Payable.—It frequently happens that purchases from, and sales to, the same party are made, i.e., goods are sometimes bought from and sold to a customer. If the account of this debtor-creditor is normally a purchase account, it is set up in the purchase ledger. If a sale is made to this debtor-creditor and charged to his purchase ledger account, such transaction should not be included in the Accounts Receivable controlling figure from the sales journal unless an adjusting entry is made through the general journal. Such entry would affect only the controlling accounts and would be:

- Accounts Payable
- Accounts Receivable

Or the item might be omitted from the sales journal controlling figure and stated separately in the summary entry for the sales journal.

A more satisfactory method is to set up two accounts with such parties—one as a creditor, the other as a customer. Then no adjustment need be made at the time of summarizing the journals, because the two accounts are treated as entirely independent of each other. The settlement of these two accounts may be handled separately or by a payment of the balance between the two. If settled by balance, an adjusting journal entry should be made to show on the books the two separate elements involved. This would of course affect both the controlling accounts and the two individual accounts.

The Problem of the Note Journals Summaries.—Of notes receivable the large majority are usually received from customers. The summary entry for such is:

- Notes Receivable
- Accounts Receivable

Where notes are received from other sources, as from officers, partners, or from outside parties to whom loans have been made, it is evident that these must not be included in the credit to Accounts Receivable, and it may be advisable also to eliminate them from Notes Receivable unless they are short-term, current items, as only such should be carried under Notes Receivable. These special notes may be carried in a "Notes Receivable Special" account.

If, as sometimes happens, interest is included in the face of a note, this must be adjusted by the summary entry, as follows:

- Notes Receivable
- Accounts Receivable
- Interest Income

The considerations stated above as applicable to the notes receivable journal, are of equal importance in handling the notes payable journal. A very careful analysis of the note journals should be made at a summary time, which analysis should be shown by the summary entry.

Summary Entries for Columnar Books.—Illustration will now be given of some standard forms for summarizing the columnar journals. Sometimes the summary entries for the various subsidiary journals are made in the general journal. This seems to accomplish no good purpose and is not usually recommended. Theoretically it is desirable to show a formal debit and credit summary for each journal footing posted to the ledger. If, however, the number of columns is small and it is readily seen that the debits and credits are equal, the formal summary is often dispensed with. So also, if there are many distributive columns of the same effect, i.e., debit or credit, as in the large departmental sales journal or the voucher register referred to on page 144, formal summary is not shown, the posting being made from the column totals as illustrated for Petty Cash on page 369.

The Sales Journal Summary.—An illustration of the sales journal summary is given in Form 35. The Sundry items should be posted in detail from their column and their total checked in the summary entry. Where a Sundry column is not used and the Sundry items are included in the Sales Ledger column, they must be separated before the summary entry can be made.

Accounts Payable	Accounts Receivable	General	Date		L. F.	General	Accounts Receivable	Accounts Payable
		15,000.00		Accounts Receivable				
				A (customer)		2,500.00		
				B "		5,000.00		
				C "		4,000.00		
				D "		3,500.00		

Form 34. General Journal

	Sales Ledger	Cash	Sundry	A	B	C
	(Detailed entries appear in this space)					
Totals	25,000.00	75,000.00	750.00	30,500.00	25,250.00	45,000.00
Accounts Receivable	25,000.00					
Cash		75,000.00				
Sundry			750.00			
Dep't A, Sales				30,500.00		
" B, "					25,250.00	
" C, "						45,000.00

Form 35. Sales Journal Summary

Where, also, a Cash column is not carried, as is so often the case, there being just one column for Sales Ledger, Cash, and Sundry items, from which distribution is made, the separation of the Cash items need not be shown in the summary entry, provided those items are entered also in the Sales Ledger column of the cash book. Where, due to the large number of distributive columns, the sales journal can ill afford the room for a Cash column, the above method offers the best solution of the problem.

The purchase journal summary is similar to that of the sales journal, and therefore no separate illustration need be given here.

The General Journal Summary.—As shown by the illustration in Form 36, in summarizing the general journal the Accounts Receivable and Accounts Payable columns are formally totaled, ruled off, and their totals brought into the General columns on both debit and credit sides and these columns are totaled and ruled off, thus showing the equilibrium of the journal. This summary entry is posted to the proper accounts in the general ledger. There is no particular advantage, however, in this formal summary entry because the postings could easily be made directly from the column totals.

The Cash Book Summaries.—As illustrated in Forms 37 and 38, the formal summary for each side of the cash book shows the equality of the Bank and Discount columns total against the General and Accounts Receivable and Payable columns. To show the correct debit to the bank for the present month, the balance brought forward from last month and entered in both the General and Bank columns on December 1, must now be subtracted from both.

On the disbursements side no explanation of the summary entry is necessary. It will be noted that, to show the balance of the bank account, a restatement of the Bank column total is necessary.

Accounts Receivable	Accounts Payable	General	Date		L. F.	General	Accounts Receivable	Accounts Payable
				(Detailed entries appear in this space)				
		10,250.00				8,050.00		
1,500.00	5,000.00	1,500.00	Dec. 31	Accounts Receivable			1,200.00	7,500.00
		5,000.00		Accounts Payable				
				Accounts Receivable		1,200.00		
				Accounts Payable		7,500.00		
		16,750.00		To close		16,750.00		

Form 36. General Journal Summary

Date		L. F.	General	Accounts Receivable	Sales Discount	Bank
Dec. 31	Totals		13,050.00	41,250.00	1,800.00	52,500.00
	Balance Dec. 1,		5,000.00			5,000.00
			8,050.00			
	Bank, Dr.					47,500.00
	Sales Discount, Dr.					1,800.00
	Accounts Receivable, Cr			41,250.00		
			49,300.00			49,300.00
Jan. 1	Balance		11,350.00			11,350.00

Form 37. Cash Summary Book—Receipts Side

Date		L. F.	General	Accounts Payable	Purchase Discount	Bank
Dec. 31	Totals		8,000.00	37,500.00	4,350.00	
	Bank, Cr.					41,150.00
	Purchase Discount, Cr.					4,350.00
	Accounts Payable, Dr.		37,500.00			
			45,500.00			45,500.00
	Bank, as above					41,150.00
	Balance					11,350.00
						52,500.00

Form 38. Cash Summary Book—Disbursements Side

Other Controlling Accounts.—It is frequently desirable to keep some accounts of the business private, such as those showing partners' investments, drawings, ratios of sharing profits, the adjusting and closing entries, the profit and loss, etc. This can be accomplished through the use of a private ledger supported by a private journal and sometimes a private cash book. For their operation a controlling account of the private ledger is set up in the general ledger, and similarly a controlling account of the general ledger appears in the private ledger. The use of private books is explained in Volume II of this work.

Sometimes subsidiary expense ledgers are used to carry a minute division of each expense group, with corresponding controlling accounts, such as Selling Expense, Office Expense, General Expense, Factory Expense. Similarly, if the consignment sales of a business are large enough to justify a separate record in a consignments ledger, a controlling account is set up in the general ledger. In a manufacturing business, Raw Materials, Goods in Process, and Finished Goods accounts are often controlling accounts for the stores, jobs, and finished stock ledgers. In a corporation the Capital Stock account (or accounts) is a controlling account over the stock ledger.

Principle Governing Content of Subsidiary Ledgers.—Before closing this chapter, it should be stated as a fundamental principle that no accounts should be carried in a subsidiary ledger except such as are of the same general kind and can without misrepresentation be carried under the group title of the controlling account.

CHAPTER XXXII
PARTNERSHIP FROM THE BUSINESS VIEWPOINT

Partnership Defined.—In Chapter II, reference was made to some of the features of a partnership—the purpose of its formation, advantages, disadvantages, etc. The laws of the state of New York define a partnership as follows: "A partnership, as between the members thereof, is the association, not incorporated, of two or more persons who have agreed to combine their labor, property and skill or some of them for the purpose of engaging in any lawful trade or business, and sharing the profits and losses as such between them."

This definition brings out in a general way the reasons for the formation of the partnership and its essential features. Under this type of organization, where several persons combine their capitals, it is possible to secure a larger fund of capital than under the sole proprietorship. This opens to the partnership avenues of business usually closed to the sole proprietor. The bringing together of the man with a special aptitude or skill, or of a man with a following in the community on account of social standing and acquaintanceship, with another who has money or a plant for the operation of a business, often makes successful an otherwise unpromising undertaking.

Operating Feature and Working Organization.—Mutual agency is the essential operating feature of the partnership. By this is meant that any one of the partners can act for the others, and in the eyes of the law all are equally responsible for the management of the business. Except in the case of a limited partnership, to be explained later, each partner has an equal voice in the management and control of affairs. Unlike the corporation where for management purposes the owners' powers are delegated to a controlling board, the essential character of the partnership is that each partner has, regardless of the amount of his investment, an equal right in the direction of its business. As between themselves, for purposes of division of duties and specialization of effort, definite power to exercise control over certain features of the business may be delegated to individual partners. But such delegation means nothing more than a method of dividing the work and is simply the working organization of the firm which may be changed at any time the majority of the partners see fit. Thus, while a partner may be limited in his actions for the firm by agreement among the partners, so that he is not a general agent for the firm, still as to outsiders who know nothing of this internal arrangement, he has power to bind the partnership by his acts, because an outsider has a right to expect that any partner has power to act as an agent for the firm. This is so because such power is of the essence of the partnership form.

Essential Characteristics of the Partnership.—Limited life is an essential characteristic of the partnership. The partnership relation is a very personal one. It can be terminated in a number of ways, but the death or retirement of any member automatically works a dissolution of the firm, even though another man takes his place. The legal theory is that the old partnership is dead and a new one, even though bearing the same firm name, has come into existence. Thus a partnership cannot be perpetual. The relationship between the partners is so intimate that the success of the undertaking depends fundamentally on the good faith and honor exercised by each partner towards the others, and therefore any addition to the personnel of a partnership can be made only with the consent of all members of the existing firm.

The partnership being the outgrowth of the sole proprietorship, certain of the aspects of its earlier form still cling to it. For suit at law it is looked upon as a collection of single owners, and action on contract must usually be taken against the individual members of the firm. Suit by or against the partnership cannot as a rule be brought in the firm name. Some states, however, allow this under recent enactments. Title to personalty can be held and transferred under the firm name, but realty must be in the name of the individual members or in the name of one member acting as trustee for the firm. Thus, while in the view of the business community the copartnership is a business entity under a firm name, in the sight of the law it is not an entity but merely a collection of single owners. This legal view accounts also for the full debt liability of every partner—except in a limited partnership. In case the firm assets are insufficient to meet the claims of creditors, any or all the partners' private resources may be levied upon.

Co-ownership of the profits of a business is another feature essential to the copartnership. No sharing in the profits on any other basis than that of co-ownership will constitute a partnership. When the question comes before the courts, the intention of the parties governs, and evidence showing that each acted as principal for himself and as agent for the others, and has shared profits as profits, would be sufficient to constitute the relationship.

The Partnership Contract.—A partnership being a contract relationship, all the requirements governing legality of contracts, such as agreement, consideration, lawful object, competency of contracting parties, etc., apply to the copartnership. The contract may be oral or in writing. In case of dispute an oral contract, on account of the difficulty of proof, is of little force in regulating the relations of the partners, and the general law of partnership would usually govern. Inasmuch as there is so great an opportunity for disputes in a relationship of this sort, it is imperative, if efficient working relations are to be maintained, that very carefully drawn articles of copartnership be agreed upon before active business is begun. These articles should contain, at least, the following:

1. The name of the firm and of the partners.

2. The kind and place of business.

3. The duration of the partnership.

4. The method of terminating it.

5. A detailed statement of the relations between the partners, such as duties and powers, capital contributions, withdrawals of capital, salaries, division of profits and losses, interest on capital, and the time of closing the books to secure a definite determination of the partners' interests.

Even when the utmost care is exercised in drafting the articles of partnership, it almost always happens that some portion is not understood alike by all or that some contingency arises not specifically provided for. Nevertheless, it is the only way in which a comparative avoidance of misunderstanding and dispute can be obtained.

Partnerships Classified.—As to the scope of their business operations, partnerships are usually classified into general and special. The general class embraces those for the conduct of some general or ordinary lines of business. The special class comprises those formed to undertake a definite task or some particular line of business. Joint ventures would come under this latter class.

As to the liability of their members, partnerships may be classified as general and limited. The general partner has the full liability, referred to above; the limited partner's liability never exceeds the amount of his investment. In a limited partnership one or more, but not all, members may limit their liability. This class of partnership can be formed only under direct authority of statute law. A limited partner is not active in the management of the business, being more in the nature of a lender of money to the firm, who gets his return in profits instead of interest. Should he become active in the firm's management, he will constitute himself an ordinary partner with full liability. The New York statute governing the formation of the limited partnership is as follows:

Two or more persons may form a limited partnership which shall consist of one or more persons of full age, called *general* partners, and also of one or more persons of full age who contribute in actual cash payments, a special sum as capital, to the common stock—or fund—called *special* partners, for the transaction within this state of any lawful business, except banking and insurance by making, severally signing and acknowledging and causing to be filed and recorded in the clerk's office in the county where the principal place of business of such partnership is located, a certificate in which is stated:

1. The name or firm under which such partnership is to be conducted and the county wherein the principal place of business is to be located.

2. The general nature of the business intended to be transacted.

3. The names, and whether of full age, of all general and special partners therein, distinguishing which are general and which are special partners, and their places of residence.

4. The amount of capital which each special partner has contributed to the common stock—or fund.

5. The time at which the partnership is to begin and end.

Affidavit of the payment of capital must be made and a notice of the formation of the partnership published in a paper of general circulation. The limited partnership is thus hedged about with safeguards for creditors, bankers, and other interested parties, particularly by the rule that a limited partnership cannot exist unless there are one or more general partners with full liability.

The Joint-Stock Company.—The joint-stock company is a partnership or association in which ownership, voice in the management, and profit-sharing ratio are evidenced by transferable shares of stock. Control and management are exercised through a board of directors chosen by the stockholders. If the company becomes bankrupt and the firm assets are insufficient to satisfy creditors, the members are personally liable to the full extent of their private property in the same way as in a general partnership.

The mining partnership is a form of joint-stock company which operates in mining communities. Usually the mining property itself is beyond the scope of such a partnership, only the development of this property by means of a lease being contemplated. Unlike the ordinary partnership, the members of a mining partnership may assign their shares of ownership. Upon their death or bankruptcy, their interests pass to others who take their place in the partnership without the consent of the remaining partners. Thus, the confidential relationship based on the right of selection of its members, characteristic of the ordinary partnership, is largely lacking in the mining partnership.

Partners Classified.—Finally, brief mention may be made of the following terms applied to partners to indicate varying degrees of activity within the ordinary partnership:

1. Ostensible partners—those who hold themselves out and are known to be partners.

2. Nominal—those who are known as partners but who have no real interest in the firm.

3. Dormant or silent—those who are not known to outsiders as partners and who take no active part in the management of the firm's affairs.

4. Secret partners—those who are not known as partners to outsiders but who have an interest and take active part in managing the firm.

For more detailed information as to a partner's rights, duties, and responsibilities to his copartners and to outsiders, a standard legal text on partnerships or business law should be consulted. The student should also read [Chapter II](#) in connection with this chapter and the next.

CHAPTER XXXIII
PARTNERSHIP FROM THE ACCOUNTING VIEWPOINT

From the fact that the law looks upon the partnership as a combination or collection of sole owners, some of the accounting problems arising out of the partnership form of organization are unique, and a partial or full treatment of some of these problems will be given in this chapter.

Profit-Sharing in the Partnership.—Of these problems perhaps the one occurring most frequently is that concerning the division of profits. Attention was called in Chapter XXXII to the need of explicit statement on this point in the articles of copartnership under the head of the intrapartnership relations. Since men combine their capitals for the purpose of realizing profits, it would naturally be supposed that all partnership agreements would be specific on that point. Yet it very often happens that many contingencies relating to the matter of profit-sharing have not been foreseen and as a result disputes arise.

The fundamental principles governing profit distribution may be stated as follows:

1. Where the agreement is silent, the law provides that profits shall be divided equally among the partners regardless of the amounts of their respective investments of capital. Some partners may have made no investments of money or property, setting up their particular skill and aptitude or standing in the community as their share and contribution to the profit-earning capacity of the organization. Unless it is specifically agreed otherwise, these will share equally in any profits.

2. Where profits are to be shared in the same ratio as capital, the agreement should specify whether the basis of division is to be the original investments or the capitals as shown at the beginning of each period, which would be the original investments plus profits left in the business. This latter interpretation would usually result in a changing ratio for succeeding periods, whereas under the former interpretation the ratio of profit-sharing would be always the same.

3. Provision should be made, either in the original articles or at a subsequent time, for a change in the profit-sharing ratio in the event of a partner's withdrawing some portion of his original investment if such withdrawal is allowed. It may be stated here that an agreement between the partners as to any ratio for division of profits can be made at any time and will govern such ratio, but must be on a determinable basis.

4. Where the articles are silent as to the division of losses, the profit-sharing ratio governs. Where a different ratio is desired, specific statement of it must be made. Of course, upon the inception of an undertaking losses are not contemplated, but the experience of others should cause provision to be made for apportionment of losses in order to avoid possible difficulties or disputes.

5. Unless the articles—or subsequent agreements—provide for the payment of salaries to any or all of the partners, none are allowed.

6. The conditions governing the partners' drawings should be explicit as to the amount to be drawn during a given period. It should be stated explicitly whether excess drawings shall be regarded as a charge against capital, or as the basis for an interest charge, or simply as an excess drawing standing in the partner's current account without penalty other than a disallowance of future drawings until lapse of time brings the total amount drawn within the agreed limitations.

7. The manner of handling undrawn profits should be made definite. Are they to be transferred to the capital account and so be made a part of capital, resulting in changing capital ratios; or are they to be carried as open balances in the drawing accounts and thus take on the nature of temporary loans subject to withdrawal at any time?

Average Investment as a Basis for Profit-Sharing.—Attention should be called to a basis for profit-sharing sometimes employed for special partnerships, entered into for the performance of a specific contract or for doing any special work. In these cases the capital needed may not be known at the start, or if known may not all be required then but is to be furnished by whichever partner may have available funds at the time of need. In such cases the basis of profit-sharing may be made the amount of capital furnished by each partner and the length of time of its use in the enterprise. Two methods of determining the ratio may be employed.

First Method. Each investment may be multiplied by the number of days occurring between the date on which the investment was made and the date of profit determination, giving a result which may be called "day-dollars" of investment in a sense similar to the term foot-pound in physics. From the total day-dollars of investment must be subtracted the day-dollars of withdrawals, arrived at similarly, thus showing net investment in terms of day-dollars. The sum of all the investments in day-dollars becomes the basis on which to prorate profits, each partner's share being the part which his individual net investments bear to this total net investment.

Second Method. The original investment of each partner may be multiplied by the time it remains unchanged, i.e., until it is added to or some portion is withdrawn. Similarly, this changed capital is multiplied by the time it remains fixed, and so for every change. The total of these items constitutes each partner's net investment, from which the profit-sharing ratio is determinable as above. In the problem given below, for purposes of illustration the dates are so taken that the calculation can be made on a month-dollar instead of a day-dollar basis, thus shortening the operation. The capital accounts of the partners, showing investments and withdrawals, are as follows:

A. B. CARD

19—	19—
Jan. 15 2,500.00	Jan. 1 10,000.00
Apr. 1 4,500.00	Mar. 15 7,500.00
June 15 1,500.00	June 1 5,000.00

D. E. FOLWELL

19—	19—
Feb. 1 3,000.00	Jan. 1 5,000.00
May 15 2,000.00	15 5,000.00
	Apr. 1 5,000.00
	June 15 2,500.00

Profits as on July 1, 19—, were $5,000. Determine each share.

SOLUTION
(Using the second method)

Amount	Months	Month-Dollars
A. B. CARD:		
$10,000 ×	½	$ 5,000
7,500 ×	2	15,000
15,000 ×	½	7,500
10,500 ×	2	21,000
15,500 ×	½	7,750

- 239 -

Amount	Months	Month-Dollars
14,000 ×	½	7,000
	6	$63,250

D. E. FOLWELL:

$ 5,000 ×	½	$ 2,500
10,000 ×	½	5,000
7,000 ×	2	14,000
12,000 ×	1½	18,000
10,000 ×	1	10,000
12,500 ×	½	6,250
	6	55,750

Total investment in month-dollars $119,000

Card's share of the profit: $\dfrac{63,250}{119,000}$ of $5,000 = $2,657.56

Folwell's share: $\dfrac{55,750}{119,000}$ of $5,000 = $2,342.44

The first method will, of course, give identical results. The second method has the slight advantage that the Investment Months column will always total the same as the length of the fiscal period, provided each partner makes his initial investment at the first of the period—which is not always the case—and acts as a check on the accuracy of that part of the calculation.

Interest on Partners' Investments.—A second problem of importance in connection with partnership accounting is the interest on partners' investments. The purpose of allowing such interest is twofold: First, it may serve as an indication of the excess of the profits in this enterprise over the return on the investment of a like amount in the money market, thus dividing the partnership profits into two parts, interest and management earnings; and second, it may serve as a method of distributing profits up to a certain amount on the basis of capital investments, where the agreed-on ratio is different from the capital ratio, thus distributing the period's profits on two different bases or ratios.

This is done sometimes to equalize somewhat the comparatively smaller-ratio profits of the partners who have made the larger investments. This problem, however, will be treated more fully in a later chapter where the methods of booking the interest, its treatment in case of a loss instead of a profit, and the computation of interest on drawings as well as on investments will be discussed and illustrated. Suffice it to say here that disputes frequently occur in connection with these problems and that detailed provision as to their handling should be made in the partnership agreement.

Valuation and Correct Booking of Original Investments.—A third matter of importance is the valuation and correct booking of the original investments other than cash. In the case of the sole proprietor this is of comparatively little importance because he will always reap the entire gain and therefore suffer no harm ultimately from present undervaluation of his property investments. In the partnership, however, where separate investment and personal accounts must be kept with each member, the correct valuation of the assets is of importance, inasmuch as the property of the partnership is the joint property of all partners and all will share ultimately in the effect of any under-or over-valuation at the time of investment. The partners' accounts are set up for the purpose of showing their respective interests in the enterprise, and after investments are once brought onto the books these accounts govern the equities of the various partners.

Distinction between Buying Out an Interest and Making an Investment to Secure an Interest.—The taking in of a partner by a sole proprietor or his admission as a new member to an existing partnership raises a point about which there must be a very definite understanding. A distinction must be made between purchasing from the owners an interest in the business as it stands at any given time and making an investment in a business to secure such an interest. The first transaction is of a personal nature between the owners and a third party who is a purchaser; in the other transaction the third party, who is an investor, puts in money to acquire an interest and his investment becomes the common property of all the owners of whom he is now one. In the one case the capital of the business is not increased, in the other case it is increased by the amount of the new investment. For example, if a balance sheet shows:

Cash	$ 5,000.00	Liabilities	$ 6,000.00
Other Assets	15,000.00	A. Jackson, Capital	14,000.00

and Jackson sells a half-interest to B. Killian for a given consideration, the new balance sheet becomes:

Cash	$ 5,000.00	Liabilities	$ 6,000.00
Other Assets	15,000.00	A. Jackson, Capital	7,000.00
		B. Killian, Capital	7,000.00

In this case no new capital has come into the business because the purchase price does not go to the business as such but to A. Jackson as a private individual.

If, however, Killian is admitted as a half-interest partner by making a cash investment equal to the amount of Jackson's interest on the basis of book values, the balance sheet of Jackson and Killian will read:

Cash	$19,000.00	Liabilities	$ 6,000.00
Other Assets	15,000.00	A. Jackson, Capital	14,000.00
		B. Killian, Capital	14,000.00

showing an investment of double the capital in the original Jackson business.

The question of good-will which frequently comes up when an interest in a going business is secured will be treated in Chapter XXXV, where also the manner of closing the books of the old business and opening those of the new firm will be shown.

Final Considerations.—From the foregoing discussion it is evident that the partnership relation gives rise to some of the most vexing questions which confront the accountant and the lawyer. It is a truism, therefore, that in drawing up the partnership agreement, all eventualities should be foreseen as nearly as possible and that they should be carefully provided for. As a final safeguard it is well to provide for the submission to arbitrators of disputes subsequently arising, the decision to be binding upon all the partners. This will avoid endless, expensive, and usually unsatisfactory actions at law and will more nearly secure justice to all. As a step in the same direction, it is suggested that provision be made for the drawing up of correct balance sheets and profit and loss statements, that sufficient time be allowed each partner to examine them as to their correctness and, if satisfied, that each be compelled to subscribe to them. This will localize any dissatisfaction within a limited time period and secure its adjustment while all salient points are still fresh in the minds of the interested parties.

CHAPTER XXXIV
CAPITALIZATION OF THE PARTNERSHIP

Sources of Capital.—From an accounting viewpoint, the capital of any business enterprise is the excess of its assets over its liabilities. Usually, the main fund of capital is secured by original contribution. In a partnership, the partners' investments provide the common partnership fund. Thereafter, additions to the capital may be secured in several ways:

1. Profits may be left in the business instead of being withdrawn.

2. Specific contributions may be made by the partners, which are either to be considered as additions to their capital investment, or are to be treated as more or less temporary loans to the business.

3. A new partner may be taken in, his contribution increasing the partnership capital.

The present chapter deals with original investments and with the first two types of additional capital mentioned above, while the next chapter discusses the admission of new members and the consolidation of partnerships.

Original Contributions.—It sometimes happens that the partnership agreement does not state specifically how much each partner shall invest in the business. For example, the agreement may state that partner A is to contribute certain properties, i.e., place of business and equipment; that B is to contribute a stock of goods, and that the investments of the remaining partners are to consist of cash, the exact amount of which is not stated because it depends upon the valuation to be placed upon the property and merchandise invested by A and B.

After such a valuation has been made and the amounts of the cash contributions have been determined, it may be found that the total investment is more than the business requires; or it may develop that some of the partners do not have sufficient funds available to pay their shares, while others may be able to contribute more than their respective shares. It thus happens that the partnership agreement is not always rigidly enforced, some partners contributing more, and others less, than the agreed amounts. At the time this is looked upon as a temporary arrangement, but it often results in a permanent condition. The partnership agreement should contain provision for such a contingency. If it does not, a later agreement should be made to regulate the relations between the partners.

Adjustment of Capital Contributions.—Whenever a partner contributes more than his agreed share, it is customary to allow him interest on the excess amount, and other partners whose investment may be less than the agreed amount are usually charged with interest. This is obviously an equitable method of meeting the situation.

As a rule, these interest adjustments are handled through the Profit and Loss account, i.e., the partners who invest less than the agreed share are considered to owe interest to the partnership, and those who invest more have an interest claim against the business—not against the other partners individually. The debit or credit balance in the Profit and Loss account resulting from these adjustments is in turn distributed among *all* the partners in the profit-or-loss-sharing ratios. It should be clearly understood, however, that although these adjustments are made through the Profit and Loss account, there is no element of business profit or expense involved. For this reason, these interest entries should be made direct in the appropriation section of the Profit and Loss, and should never be booked in the regular Interest accounts.

The following illustrations will bring out the different methods of adjustment:

PROBLEM. A, B, and C are equal partners under an agreement to contribute each $15,000. Provision is made that excess contributions are to be credited with interest at 6% and that deficits are to be charged at the same rate. The records show that actual contributions were: A, $18,000; B, $13,000; and C, $11,000.

Three methods of adjustment will be shown.

FIRST METHOD

A's excess is $3,000, interest on which is $180.

B's deficit is $2,000, interest on which is $120.

C's deficit is $4,000, interest on which is $240.

These three interest amounts are brought upon the books by the following journal entries:

Profit and Loss		180.00	
	A		180.00
B		120.00	
C		240.00	
	Profit and Loss		360.00

The Profit and Loss account then shows a credit balance of $180, which is distributed as follows:

Profit and Loss   180.00

    A   60.00

    B   60.00

    C   60.00

The net effect of these adjustments is a credit to A of $240, and debits to B and C of $60 and $180 respectively.

Note that A is credited with $180 for his excess of $3,000, and Profit and Loss is debited with the same amount, because it is the business that owes him this interest. If this Profit and Loss debit is distributed separately, A's share of it is $60, so that his real credit on his $3,000 excess is not $180 but $120. On the other hand, the combined debits to B and C result in a credit to Profit and Loss of $360, and if this item is distributed as such, A's share of it is $120, thus making his total credit on the complete adjustment $240. A similar explanation applies to the adjustments for B and C.

SECOND METHOD.

The first method was based on a consideration of the respective excesses or deficits on capital investments, but the same result may be obtained by comparing all contributions with the amount of the smallest investment, viz., $11,000 by C. This would show A's excess over C as $7,000, and B's excess over C as $2,000, and these two amounts may be treated as loans to the business. The result is that A is credited with 6% on $7,000, and B with 6% on $2,000, as follows:

Profit and Loss   540.00

    A   420.00

    B   120.00

The debit to Profit and Loss is charged in equal shares to the three partners as follows:

    A   180.00

    B   180.00

C		180.00
Profit and Loss		540.00

The final result shows a net credit to A of $240, a net debit of $60 to B, and a net debit of $180 to C, the same as by the first method.

THIRD METHOD.

The total capital contributed is $42,000. To be equal partners under the agreement, each should have contributed one-third of the common fund, or $14,000. Actually, A's investment is $4,000 in excess of this, while B's is $1,000 less, and C's $3,000 less. The excess contribution of A, $4,000, may be looked upon as a loan to B and C as individuals, bringing their shares up to the $14,000; viz., $1,000 to B and $3,000 to C. Instead of making the adjustment through the Profit and Loss account as in the first two methods, the interest is now adjusted between the three partners as private persons, the entries affecting only the partners' personal accounts. This adjustment results in a credit to A and a debit to B for $60, A having loaned B $1,000; and in a credit to A and a debit to C for $180, A having loaned C $3,000. A's total credit is $240, and B's and C's debits are respectively $60 and $180, the same as by the other two methods.

Thus it is seen that any of the three methods employed leads to the same results. It will be observed, however, that in the example given the contemplated investments are to be equal for the three partners ($15,000), and the profit and loss is to be shared on the same basis. The three different methods of adjusting interest lead to the same result only when the profit-sharing ratio is identical with the ratio between the contemplated investments.

Averaging Investments.—In temporary partnerships, organized for carrying out a particular undertaking, the amount of capital needed is often not known and may vary at different stages of the undertaking. Here the partners usually contribute as need arises, and withdraw when funds not needed in the business become free. Under such conditions, the partnership agreement should always state the manner in which the partners' interests are to be adjusted. A common method, as explained and illustrated in Chapter XXXIII, is to compute the average investment of each partner and to use these amounts as the basis for profit-sharing. In this way the problem of interest adjustment as such is completely eliminated.

Accretions of Capital through Profits.—At the close of the fiscal period, when results are summarized, the net profits are transferred to the partners' accounts. As the amount of profit left in the business usually differs for different partners, it is evident that the partners' capital accounts at the end of the period will show a different ratio from that existing at the beginning. Assume that a given partnership consists of two members, A investing $2,000 and B $1,000, and that profits are to be shared in the same ratio as these original investments, i.e., 2:1; assume further that A withdraws the greater part of his profits while B allows his share to accumulate, and that at the end of a number of years the capital ratios have completely changed, the capitals being, say, $8,000 for A and $24,000 for B. Obviously, under such circumstances it would not be just for A still to receive twice as much profit as B on the basis of the *original* investment ratio of 2:1.

Whenever it is intended that profits are to be shared on the basis of investments, the profit-sharing ratio should be changed from time to time in order to correspond with actual investments, and this should be plainly stated in the partnership agreement; or increments to capital through the accretion of profits should be treated as temporary loans subject to withdrawals and bearing interest until withdrawn. It should be the policy of the firm to offer an incentive to its members to leave their surplus profits in the business and so prevent the need of borrowing from outside.

Finally, it may be said that in the event of dissolution, accretions through profits constitute claims against the firm ranking before the partners' capitals. Such accretions partake of the nature of loans and for this reason they are sometimes carried in *partners' loan accounts*, to keep them separate from the original capital investments, or are left in the "Personal" accounts which are not then closed into the "Capital" accounts.

Additional Contributions and Loans.—When contributions are made by partners there should be a specific understanding as to whether such funds are to be considered as additional capital or as loans to the partnership. In the first case the items should be shown in the capital accounts of the partners, thus requiring a reconsideration of the profit-sharing ratio—although a change is not always made; in the second case they should be entered in the partner's loan accounts with corresponding interest adjustments, as has been explained.

Loans by partners may be evidenced by firm notes signed by all the partners. However, these notes should not be carried in the regular Notes Payable account because that account represents the firm's liability to outsiders, which must ordinarily be met promptly according to the terms of the instrument. At common law a partner may not bring suit against the firm of which he is a member; hence there is an essential difference between these two kinds of notes. For this reason a new account is opened entitled "Partners' Notes Payable," which is credited whenever the firm issues a promissory note to any of its members. Where the loan is not evidenced by a formal note, record should be in the partner's loan account. As stated on page 324, any loans made by partners to the business rank before regular capital claims, and this priority is not changed when such loans are evidenced by promissory notes.

Partners' Loans in Relation to Firm Credit.—Loans made by partners to the business may be viewed in two very different ways, depending upon the credit rating of the firm. If there is distrust as to the partners' standing and financial condition, the fact that they themselves, who know the real condition better than any outsider, are willing to put additional capital into the business, is the best evidence that the firm is not so badly off. Consequently, loans made by partners under such conditions help to increase the firm's credit.

On the other hand, if the integrity of any member of the firm is questionable, his loans to the business do not necessarily increase the credit of the firm; for in case of financial trouble he may attempt secretly to withdraw part of the assets from the business and to conceal the true condition of affairs from the creditors. Being on the inside, he is in a position to do this before outsiders can even scent trouble. Normally, however, the loan of a partner makes a better impression than a loan from an outsider, since in case of insolvency and dissolution the partner's loan ranks *after* the claims of outside creditors.

It sometimes happens that in a partnership one or more of its members lends the firm comparatively large amounts of money and accepts demand notes as evidence of such loans. If the partner holding such a note is unscrupulous, he may present it for payment at an unfavorable time and, if the business is unable to pay, may demand an "accounting." He may even go so far as to cause its dissolution, repurchase the business at much less than its true value and so "freeze out" his partners.

Borrowed Capital.—It may happen that a firm is obliged to borrow funds from outside in order to increase its working capital. For instance, the partners may have no available private funds for further investment and yet may not desire to admit new capital on a profit-and-loss-sharing basis. Such loans usually are on a long-time basis, and should not be included in the Notes Payable account. A special account should be opened, e.g., Notes Payable Special, Mortgage, or some other title plainly indicating the nature of the loan. Sharp distinction should be made between funds borrowed for the purpose of increasing the permanent capital, and money borrowed for current needs. The need for additional current funds usually results from seasonal fluctuations in business, slow collection of customers' accounts, or slow movement of stock, and is met by current borrowing at a bank; while the need for increased capital is caused by the original capital investment being insufficient to meet present conditions.

CHAPTER XXXV
OTHER PARTNERSHIP PROBLEMS

Admission of a New Partner.—In Chapter XXXIII a distinction was made between buying out an interest in a business and making an investment in a business. In the former case no new capital is acquired, while in the latter the capital of the firm is increased by the amount of the new partner's contribution.

When a new partner is admitted he usually acquires not merely the right to share in the profits, but he also obtains a share in the net worth (often called "net assets") of the enterprise. For this reason it is necessary that all the partners, including the new member, agree on the value of the net assets, and in this connection any of the following possibilities may arise:

1. Upon admission of the new partner the book accounts may be considered to represent the true status of the business. A balance sheet is drawn up and the new partner is admitted on the basis of the net worth it shows.

2. It may be agreed that the assets are not worth the amount at which they are carried on the books and that a new valuation be placed upon them.

3. The business may be considered to be worth more than the amount shown by the balance sheet.

First Case.—In the first case little difficulty is met in making the opening entry admitting the new partner. For instance, if the balance sheet shows a net worth of $30,000, and the new partner wishes to make an investment in order to secure a one-fourth interest in the firm, the amount to be contributed is manifestly $10,000. Assuming that he makes a cash investment of $10,000, the following entry meets all accounting requirements:

Cash	10,000.00	
A, Capital		10,000.00

As a result of this cash investment of $10,000, the net worth of the new firm is increased to $40,000 and the one-fourth interest belonging to A is evidenced by his capital account at $10,000. The new firm may now continue the old records and no further adjustments need be made.

Second Case.—In the second case it is necessary to place a new valuation upon the assets of the old firm and the accounts of the old partners must be adjusted accordingly. For instance, suppose A and B are equal partners and the financial status of the firm is shown by the following balance sheet:

Balance Sheet of A & B

Cash	$ 1,000.00	Notes Payable	$ 3,000.00
Accounts Receivable	10,000.00	Accounts Payable	5,000.00
Merchandise	6,000.00	Mortgage on Bldg	4,000.00
Building and Equipment	16,000.00	A, Capital	10,500.00
		B, Capital	10,500.00
	$33,000.00		$33,000.00

More capital is needed and C is invited to make an investment. Upon investigation he finds that there are included under Accounts Receivable many old items, of which it is estimated $1,000 will be uncollectible; that the merchandise is overvalued to the amount of $500; and that the building and equipment are worth $1,500 less than is shown on the books. He offers to make an investment to secure a one-fourth interest and his offer is accepted.

As a result of the new valuations placed upon the assets, the net worth of the firm is now $18,000, against the old showing of $21,000. Consequently, the capital accounts of A and B are reduced from $10,500 to $9,000 each. The new partner is to invest a certain sum sufficient to acquire a one-fourth interest in the new business. Hence the combined capital of A and B, amounting to $18,000, will represent three-fourths of the new capital, and consequently the amount to be invested by C is $6,000. Thus the new capital of the firm will amount to $24,000, one-fourth of which, or $6,000, is credited to C's capital account.

The balance sheet of the new firm will show:

Balance Sheet of A, B & C

Cash		$ 7,000.00	Notes Payable	$ 3,000.00
Accounts Rec.	$10,000		Accounts Payable	5,000.00
Less—Reserve	1,000	9,000.00	Mortgage on Bldg	4,000.00
			A, Capital	9,000.00
Merchandise		5,500.00	B, Capital	9,000.00

Building and Equipment	14,500.00	C, Capital	6,000.00
	$36,000.00		$36,000.00

The firm has thus secured $6,000 additional capital, on a basis somewhat unfavorable for the present, but inasmuch as the books now show conservative values, no real injustice results.

Third Case.—The third case shows the firm in a position to demand something more than book values as the basis for admission of the new partner. The presumption is that the old firm is favorably known, has an established trade and patronage, built by fair dealing and judicious advertising, by its favorable location, and the numerous other ways in which a substantial business may be developed. Its standing in the community is a factor of value to the firm because it brings trade to its doors. Other conditions being equal, a firm which enjoys a good reputation is worth more than a new venture. Such a reputation is known as "good-will" and constitutes an exceedingly valuable though an intangible asset. The essence of good-will is the ability to produce more than normal profits, i.e., profits above the average in that line. Consequently, whenever the members of a firm consider the admission of a new partner, good-will is regarded as one of the *assets* of the existing enterprise, thereby increasing its net worth.

The valuation of good-will, however, is a difficult matter and it is a well-established principle that good accounting will not allow the asset good-will to be set up on the books of a concern unless it has come into possession of it by purchase or unless a part of its own good-will is sold to a new partner. In this case the price received for the portion sold represents an outsider's valuation and may therefore become the basis for valuing the whole of it.

The following case will serve as an illustration:

PROBLEM. Assume that X has a one-half interest in a firm, and Y and Z a one-fourth interest each, the balance sheet showing the following summarized facts:

BALANCE SHEET OF X, Y & Z

Cash	$ 2,000.00	Liabilities	$10,000.00
Other Assets	48,000.00	X, Capital	20,000.00
		Y, Capital	10,000.00

                    Z, Capital   10,000.00

$50,000.00 $50,000.00

An outsider, R, is now to be admitted to a one-fifth interest by making an investment in the business. The relative shares of the others are to remain as before. Hence, after R's admission, X will have two-fifths, and Y, Z, and R one-fifth interest each. It is further assumed that no revaluation of the tangible assets is necessary.

The net worth of the old firm, according to the books, is $40,000, and if this were taken as the basis for admitting R, an investment of $10,000 would be sufficient to acquire a one-fifth interest in the new firm. However the business is considered to be worth $10,000 more than the $40,000 shown in the balance sheet, and for this reason, instead of paying $10,000, R is required to invest $12,500. The excess of $2,500 is paid by R as an offset to the shares of the others in the good-will of the firm.

There are three ways of treating this good-will element, viz.:

FIRST METHOD. Debit the Good-Will account for the amount actually paid for it by R, viz., $2,500, and credit the capital accounts of the old partners in proportion to their shares in the profits:

Good-Will   2,500.00

    X, Capital   1,250.00

    Y, Capital   625.00

    Z, Capital   625.00

As a result of this entry, the capital account of X is $21,250, and those of Y and Z $10,625 each. The capital account of R, however, shows a credit of $12,500. In other words, R's interest in the net assets—although not in the profits—of the business as shown by his account is *larger* than that of Y and Z, while as a matter of fact he is to have an equal share. For this reason, this method of treating good-will is not satisfactory.

SECOND METHOD. This method regards the matter from a different standpoint. Taking book values as a basis, the share bought by R is worth only $10,000. However, on account of good-will, the real value of this share is considered to be higher and R is required to pay $12,500 for it. Hence, in order that the books may show actual values, the good-will item must be added to the assets of the old firm, at the same time increasing the capital accounts of X, Y, and Z in proportion to their shares in the profits. The entry is:

Good-Will		10,000.00	
	X, Capital		5,000.00
	Y, Capital		2,500.00
	Z, Capital		2,500.00

As a result of this adjustment the capital of the old firm is shown as $50,000. R now invests $12,500, and the capital is thereby increased to $62,500. The capital accounts of the four partners now show $25,000, or two-fifths for X, and $12,500 or one-fifth each for Y, Z, and R.

THIRD METHOD. Under this method of handling good-will, the extra $2,500 invested by R is treated as a bonus for distribution among the members of the old firm, their capital interests in the new firm remaining the same as in the old and R's appearing at $10,000. There is no objection to this method if R is satisfied.

Of the three methods, the second usually proves the most satisfactory.

A similar problem involving the handling of good-will is encountered when a member of an existing firm sells out his interest, including a share of the good-will, to one who takes his place in the firm. Here the transaction may be looked upon as a private deal between buyer and seller, in which case the buyer merely succeeds to the seller's interest in the firm, his capital appearing on the books at the same amount as the seller's former capital figure even though the new partner pays more for it; or the good-will may be brought onto the books and the capitals of all the partners be shown at increased figures, as under the second method discussed above.

Consolidation of Partnerships.—There are various reasons why the consolidation of partnerships may be of mutual advantage to the individual firms concerned. When two or more firms consolidate, the competition which formerly existed between them is eliminated and co-operation takes its place. Also by uniting their businesses, many of the operations which were formerly performed separately are now amalgamated with resulting savings. Many other advantages may result from such consolidations.

From the standpoint of the accountant, the consolidation of partnerships is essentially the same as the admission of new partners, the same principles applying to both. Before actual consolidation takes place, it is necessary for each of the partnerships to place a new valuation upon its assets and for all concerned to agree upon the new figures. In almost all cases good-will is an important factor. The valuation of good-will requires an investigation of the profits and profit-earning capacity of the member firms. Conditions affecting the profits of the various firms must be equalized as nearly as possible so that the earning capacity of each can be compared on an equitable basis. Such questions as the way in which partners' salaries, interest on capitals, withdrawals, and loans have been handled; the relation of outside sources of income, if any, to the profit of any of the member firms; and whether the consolidation contemplates taking over such source of profits—these and similar questions must be considered and treated equitably for all concerned.

The following illustration is given to indicate the bookkeeping problems incident to consolidations:

PROBLEM. A and B, equal partners in an established business, consolidate with C and D, equal owners of an allied business. A and B are each to have a one-third, and C and D each a one-sixth interest in the new firm. The following balance sheets show their financial positions:

BALANCE SHEET OF A & B

Cash	$ 2,500.00	Notes Payable	$ 5,000.00
Notes Receivable	1,000.00	Accounts Payable	8,000.00
Accounts Receivable	22,000.00	Mortgage on Real Estate	4,000.00
Merchandise	10,000.00		
Furniture and Fixtures	2,500.00	A, Capital	16,000.00
Delivery Equipment	1,500.00	B, Capital	16,000.00
Real Estate	9,500.00		
	$49,000.00		$49,000.00

BALANCE SHEET OF C & D

Cash	$ 5,000.00	Notes Payable	$ 5,000.00
Accounts Receivable	15,000.00	Accounts Payable	7,750.00
Merchandise	8,000.00	C, Capital	9,000.00

Furniture & Fixtures	2,000.00	D, Capital	9,000.00
Horse & Wagon	750.00		
	$30,750.00		$30,750.00

A careful valuation of the various properties shows the figures of the balance sheet of C & D to be conservatively estimated. In regard to A & B's figures, however, it is decided to allow $2,000 for possible bad debts, and to value their merchandise at $9,000, delivery equipment at $1,000, and real estate at $9,000. Furthermore, it is agreed that C & D's good-will is to be valued at $5,000, and A & B's at $10,000.

After the adjustments the new balance sheets appear as follows:

BALANCE SHEET OF A & B

Cash		$ 2,500.00	Notes Payable	$ 5,000.00
Notes Receivable		1,000.00	Accounts Payable	8,000.00
Accounts "	$22,000		Mortgage on Real Estate	4,000.00
Less— Reserve	2,000	20,000.00		
Merchandise		9,000.00	A, Capital	19,000.00
Furniture and Fixtures		2,500.00	B, Capital	19,000.00
Delivery Equipment		1,000.00		
Real Estate		9,000.00		
Good-Will		10,000.00		
		$55,000.00		$55,000.00

BALANCE SHEET OF C & D

Cash	$ 5,000.00	Notes Payable	$ 5,000.00
Accounts Receivable	15,000.00	Accounts Payable	7,750.00

Merchandise	8,000.00	C, Capital	11,500.00
Furniture and Fixtures	2,000.00	D, Capital	11,500.00
Horse and Wagon	750.00		
Good-Will	5,000.00		
	$35,750.00		$35,750.00

It is agreed that C and D's capitals are each to be taken as representing one-sixth of the capitalization of the new firm, and A and B are each to contribute $4,000 in cash to bring their capitals up to the required amounts.

The opening balance sheet of the consolidated firm will then read as follows:

BALANCE SHEET OF A, B, C & D

Cash		$15,500.00	Notes Payable	$10,000.00
Notes Receivable		1,000.00	Accounts Payable	15,750.00
Accounts Receivable	$37,000		Mortgage on Real Estate	4,000.00
Less—Reserve	2,000	35,000.00	A, Capital	23,000.00
Merchandise		17,000.00	B, Capital	23,000.00
Furniture and Fixtures		4,500.00	C, Capital	11,500.00
Delivery Equipment		1,750.00	D, Capital	11,500.00
Real Estate		9,000.00		
Good-Will		15,000.00		
		$98,750.00		$98,750.00

CHAPTER XXXVI
PARTNERSHIP PROFITS

Ambiguity of Definition of Profits.—The term "profits" as applied to business is perhaps used with as little uniformity as any term met with. When a concern speaks of its profits, it is difficult to know exactly what is intended, because the meaning of the term depends very largely on the methods of accounting of that particular concern. The reported profits of different firms are not, therefore, a true basis for judging their relative worths. For instance, although the net profits of a single proprietorship and of a partnership are usually determined in the same manner, there is nevertheless variation in the treatment of some items such as salaries, drawings, interest on capital invested, etc. The partnership form, like the single proprietorship, contemplates an investment on the part of the owners not only of capital but also of time and effort. This is one of the differences in working organization between these forms of business and the corporation. Investment in the corporation is of capital only. If services are employed by the corporation, they are paid for and charged as services, salaries, etc.

Compensation for Time and Services.—In the partnership form of organization, the active and direct management of the business is usually vested in the owners. Where this is not the situation, as in a limited partnership, or whenever one or more of the partners does not take an active part in the management of the business, his share of the profit is usually curtailed by the allowance of salaries to the managing partners before any distribution of profits in the agreed ratio is made to the partners. Thus, partnership profits include not only the salaries of the owners but, in general, a recompense for the time and ability of the proprietors. The man who makes an investment in a partnership does so usually because he desires to invest his time as well as his capital. He expects, therefore, to receive not only a fair rate of interest on his money but also pay for the services he renders.

Interest on Investment.—The rate paid for the use of money is dependent both on the money market and on the element of risk involved in the particular investment. In mining ventures, for instance, where there is frequently considerable uncertainty as to the return of the principal, the interest rate is sufficiently high to offset, during the life of the loan, the possible loss of the principal at the end. So an investor in a partnership, because of the greater element of risk in comparison with other and safer investments, requires a higher rate of return in interest than he would ordinarily secure through the investment of his capital in sound securities.

Partnership Profits Defined.—Partnership profits, therefore, contain these two elements—interest and recompense for services. If profits are extraordinary or above normal, such excess may be and usually is the measure of the more-than-average ability of the partners, unless it results from the monopolistic character of the business.

In speaking of profits the term is used in a technical accounting sense and has reference to the manner of their showing in the Profit and Loss account and its content. That account or the Profit and Loss statement usually develops a so-called "net profit" which is distributed to the partners. Such profits are more easily defined by stating what should not be considered in their determination, than by attempting to give an itemized list of the income and expense items entering therein.

In accordance with the theory of the law of partnership, the net profit of a partnership is the balance of the Profit and Loss account before interest on owners' capital investments and the recompense to the partners on account of time and services are taken into account. In the accounting for an ordinary partnership, such items as interest on capital investments, salaries to partners, etc., are not to be considered as expense items to be deducted from profits before the net earnings are determined, but as a part of the net profits to be distributed to the several owners of the business. The payment of salaries and interest on capital is made simply for the purpose of distributing net profits according to certain methods agreed upon by the members of the firm.

Profit and Loss for Comparative Purposes.—For the purpose of comparing results between different periods, the Profit and Loss account should have a fairly uniform content from year to year. It should set forth the amount of the net operating profit, in the calculation of which account should be taken of all ordinary income and expenses incurred in the operation of the business. This will provide the basis for comparison, as between periods, of the ordinary normal activities of the business.

In the "Non-Operating" or "Other Income" sections any "outside-the-business" income and expense should be shown, such as income from outside investments, and expenses in connection therewith. Items of extraordinary income and expense, however, such as the profits arising through the sale of good-will, the sale of real estate, extraordinary losses from fire, etc., usually are taken directly into the partners' accounts so as not to destroy the value (for purposes of comparison) of the results shown by the Profit and Loss account from year to year.

In this way, while the purpose of the Profit and Loss account is to summarize the temporary proprietorship accounts, some proprietorship items may be omitted for the sake of making the summary of greater value to the proprietors. Such a method of handling does not conflict with principles previously laid down, but rests upon the general principle that accounting methods and forms must be flexible in order to conform to the requirements of particular cases; else they fail in fulfilling their full purpose.

Allowance of Salaries.—The allowance of salaries to partners is not so much for the purpose of measuring the excess of the profits of the partnership over what the individual owners might have earned by working for others, as it is for the purpose of equalizing or adjusting their interests on an equitable basis. When, on the one hand, men invest their abilities and services in addition to their capitals, and on the other hand, the profit and loss-sharing ratio is determined on the basis of capitals invested, the greater ability of a given partner may be recognized and compensated by a salary. Thus a partner of exceptional ability secures a larger share in the profits by receiving a fixed amount under the head of salary, the remaining part of the net profits being divided among all the partners in the profit and loss-sharing ratio.

Allowance of Interest.—As explained in [Chapter XXXIII](), it is not unusual in partnerships where the profit and loss ratio differs from the capital ratio, to allow interest on capital. The effect of such a provision is to secure a distribution of profits on a dual basis, viz., a part as interest on the capitals in the capital ratio and the remainder in the profit and loss ratio. Thus, two partners, A and B, whose capitals are $10,000 and $15,000 respectively, with a 6% interest allowance on capital and a subsequent half-and-half distribution of profits, share the profits in effect on two different bases. Suppose the profits are $6,000. The interest requirement will give A $600 and B $900, after which $4,500 will be divided equally. Interest on partners' capitals is thus in no sense an operating expense and should be handled always in the appropriation section of the Profit and Loss.

If the partnership agreement makes specific provision (but not otherwise), interest may be charged on partners' drawings. This is merely an additional device for adjusting the partners' interests, and causes a slight difference in the net shares of profits. Where interest is allowed on capitals and also charged on drawings, the partners' accounts, Personal and Capital, when considered together, comprise virtually an account current, and the interest computations may be made as will be explained in [Chapter L]() in connection with accounts current.

Another method of profit-sharing sometimes introduced in the partnership agreement is the device of an interest allowance for a contribution in excess of the agreed amount and an interest charge on partners' deficiency of capital. This method of equalizing unequal investments, as illustrated in [Chapter XXXIV](), is a fair arrangement to all concerned.

Interest on Partners' Loans.—Careful differentiation must be made between interest on partners' capitals and on partners' loans. If a loan is secured from outside parties, its interest cost is a business expense, to be taken into account before determining net profits. A loan from a partner does not in the least change the manner of showing its cost. Interest on partners' loans is not, therefore, to be handled in the appropriation section of the Profit and Loss account, but should be charged to the regular Interest Cost account, which is cleared in the regular way through Profit and Loss. The credit is to Cash if actually paid, or to the partners' personal accounts if unpaid, although the amount is sometimes credited to the partners' loan accounts in order to secure a compounding of the interest.

Reserved Profits.—In rare cases, before the partners' shares in the net profit are determined, a portion of it may be reserved for some specific purpose. The portion so reserved is transferred from Profit and Loss to some specified reserve account, to indicate the retention of the profits in the business. If the profits were transferred to the partners' accounts, they would be subject to withdrawal from the business. Even when shown in the reserve account, however, they belong to the proprietors and are just as much a part of the net worth of the business as if credited to the proprietors' accounts. Such reservation of profits may be for the purpose of providing for the replacement of some fixed asset when it wears out, as buildings, machinery, etc., or for meeting a liability when it comes due, or for some similar purposes. Such reservations, however, are seldom made in partnership accounting and a complete treatment of the subject is reserved for the work of the second year in connection with corporation accounting.

It should be noted that reserves created from profits are not to be confused with valuation accounts, such as reserves for depreciation and doubtful accounts. Valuation accounts in no sense represent a reservation of net profits. They represent the credit side of certain asset accounts. The contra debits—to depreciation or bad debts—of these credit reserves are expenses of the business which must be taken into account before the amount of net profit can be determined.

Closing Profits to Partners' Accounts.—The disposition of profits under a partnership does not differ materially from that under the single proprietorship form. When the net profits are determined, they belong to the proprietors and are usually transferred to their accounts. The method of transfer may be either by way of the partners' personal accounts or direct to the capital accounts. The principle involved in either treatment was discussed at the time of closing the books for the single proprietorship and will not be repeated here. Where the partners do not desire to have any change shown in their original capital accounts, the profits may be transferred to the loan accounts of the partners or stand as open balances in their personal accounts.

The Appropriation Section—Distributing a Deficit.—The appropriation section of the Profit and Loss account shows the distribution of net profits to the partners' accounts. A thorough understanding of the partnership agreement is necessary before the proper distribution can be made. If the agreement provides for salaries and interest on capitals and drawings, these requirements must first be met, even though the net profits are insufficient to satisfy them. Their purpose, as explained above, is to equalize conditions and interests among the partners preliminary to their sharing in the profit and loss ratio. If this equalization results in a deficit, such deficit will be distributed in the agreed ratio and to that extent nullify some portion of the profits distributed as salaries and interest. If specific provision in the articles of copartnership requires a different handling of the salaries and interest items, that provision of course governs. Otherwise these items should be treated as above.

If any of the partners leave profits in the business, this usually results in a changing ratio of the capital account balances. Where the distribution of profits is based upon the original contributions, it is advisable to transfer the profits left in the business to separate loan accounts for the partners. The partners' capital accounts then always show their original contributions.

Partners' Withdrawals.—Partners' withdrawals and salaries are usually handled in a very unsystematic way. The amount of the drawings allowed each partner during a given period—week or month—should be definitely determined by agreement, and regular checks should be issued for these amounts. The payment of partners' personal bills and the handling of any other personal items should, as a matter of standard practice, be made out of personal funds.

If the partnership agreement provides for salaries these should be credited, when due, to the partners' drawing accounts which will then be charged with all actual drawings, whether for salary or otherwise. The offsetting charge at the time the salary credit is made should be to a "Partners' Salaries" account, which at the close of the fiscal period is closed into the appropriation section of the Profit and Loss account, thereby showing in it the proper distribution of profits as salary.

Profits Determination upon Admitting a New Partner.—Particular care should be taken to determine as nearly as possible the correct net profit at the time of any change in the partners' relations. Upon the admission of a new partner, failure to make entry in the old partners' accounts of any profit rightfully belonging to them leads to its being shared with the new partner and consequently results in a loss to the old partners. In like manner the deferring of an expense charge—rightfully belonging to the period before the admission of the new partner—to the period after the admission, results in a wrongful charge to the new partner. Similarly, when a partner is admitted on a changing profit ratio basis (as when, for example, he is to receive a one-fourth share for three years, at the end of which time he is to have a one-third share), an incorrect determination of profits at the end of the three-year period may mean a loss either to him or to the old partners. So long as the same partnership and the same profit and loss-sharing ratios continue, no injustice results through failure to include some such items in their proper periods, as they are cumulative and their effect will be recorded in later periods. However, this is no excuse for the inaccurate determination of profits at any time.

CHAPTER XXXVII
PARTNERSHIP DISSOLUTION

Temporary Nature of Partnership.—Because of its personal character, a partnership has necessarily a limited duration. It must look forward to the time when its business will have to be closed up. The chief causes leading to a dissolution are briefly reviewed here.

Causes of Dissolution

1. The withdrawal of any partner. Under ordinary circumstances a partner cannot be held to a specific performance of his contract. If he becomes dissatisfied, suspicious, or desires for other reasons to withdraw from his contract before its expiration, he has that power. Such withdrawal cannot be looked upon as a right but only as a power to be exercised under unusual circumstances. If his withdrawal before the agreement terminates results in damage to his copartners, they have a lawful claim against him for the amount of the damage. Under extraordinary conditions, specific performance of the contract might be decreed, i.e., the partner would not be allowed to withdraw.

Withdrawal does not relieve a partner from liability for partnership debts incurred while he was a member of the firm. Any creditors not paid by the firm may hold the withdrawing partner liable for the debts. To be relieved from the liability on debts arising *after* his withdrawal, personal notice of withdrawal must be given to all the firms with which the partnership has been dealing; a published notice being considered sufficient for the parties not dealing with the firm until after withdrawal.

2. Sale of a partner's interest or admission of a new partner. When a partner, with the consent of his copartners, sells his interest in the firm to another, or when a new member is admitted to the partnership, in the eyes of the law the old partnership has ceased to exist and a new one has taken its place.

3. Limitations in the partnership agreement. The agreement may specify the period for which the partnership is to exist. If it is a special partnership, the object it is to accomplish may be stated and the law considers the firm automatically dissolved as soon as that object is attained.

4. Mutual consent of the partners. Whether or not the partnership period is limited by the agreement, the partners may at any time rescind their contract by mutual consent.

5. Misconduct, insanity, death, assignment, or bankruptcy of a partner. The happening of any of these contingencies effects a dissolution. By misconduct may be understood a member's failure to pay the agreed contribution of

capital, failure to perform his duties, his acting in bad faith towards his copartners, etc.

6. Illegal object. A partnership entered into for the pursuit of an object which later becomes illegal is automatically dissolved.

7. War between nations of which partners are citizens. This dissolves the partnership, though such dissolution may be more in the nature of a suspension, inasmuch as the relation may be resumed upon cessation of hostilities.

8. Bankruptcy of the firm. This results in the firm's assets being sold to satisfy the claims of its creditors and the firm as such ceases to exist.

9. Sale or transfer. A firm may sell out to another firm or change its form of organization to that of a corporation. The old firm, therefore, no longer exists.

Problems Incident to Dissolution.—It is purposed to consider some of the problems involved in winding up the affairs of a partnership. From the schedule of causes of dissolution given above it will be seen that a firm may be either solvent or insolvent at dissolution. The three statements sometimes set up in the case of insolvency—the Statement of Affairs, the Deficiency Account, and the Realization and Liquidation Statement—will not be explained here but results obtained through them will be taken into account. These statements are seldom met in practice and are not standardized either as to form or content. Their treatment is deferred to the work of the second year.

Partnership Provisions Covering Liquidation.—Because of the certainty of final dissolution, it is not unusual for the partnership agreement to make definite regulations concerning the method of liquidation. The appointment of one of the members as liquidating partner, the manner of distributing the proceeds from liquidation whether by instalments or otherwise, the manner of paying the liquidator for his services—all these contingencies should be provided for.

Where dissolution is forced by the death of one of the partners, to determine the interest of his heirs it is necessary to take inventory and make appraisal of the firm's assets. To avoid this inconvenience to the business, provision is sometimes made in the agreement that the remaining partners shall continue the business until the end of the regular fiscal period. The deceased partner's share in the profits for the current period up to the date of his death is determined by prorating the year's profit over the period in which the deceased had an interest. The method of calculating the firm's good-will is usually provided for in the partnership agreement so that the estate of the deceased partner will share in it also. Usually interest is allowed the estate of the deceased partner from the date of his death until the settlement of his share.

Partners' Rights and Procedure During Liquidation.—When dissolution is accompanied by liquidation, as happens in many instances, all the partners have an equal right to share in the work of liquidation. Since the work usually does not require the time of all the partners, a customary procedure is to appoint one member—or an outsider—as the liquidator. Notice of the dissolution, in which the name of the liquidator is given, is published in the leading newspapers. If liquidation is necessary because of the death of a partner, great responsibility rests upon the liquidator. He must act in strict good faith and endeavor to realize the best price possible for the assets of the firm in the interest of the deceased partner's estate. A similar responsibility rests upon him when liquidation is carried on in the interest of absent members.

The expenses and losses incident to liquidation must be borne by all in the profit and loss ratio. The liquidator may be paid either by means of a commission on the sums realized or by a salary. If the liquidator is a partner, settlement may take place privately between the partners but usually his commission or salary is charged to the firm's liquidation expenses.

Liquidation may proceed by sale of the assets in regular order and may even permit the purchase of additional goods where necessary to fulfil existing contracts or to complete partly manufactured goods, or where stock on hand can be disposed of to better advantage by the addition of side lines or specialties.

Distribution of Proceeds.—Upon the realization of the assets, application of the proceeds must be made in the following order: First, the claims of outside creditors must be met in full or by compromise where not fully recognized. Second, the claims of the partners on account of loans or advances made to the firm must be satisfied. Third, the partners share in the remainder, by first taking out their respective capital contributions and then, if there is a balance, by sharing it in their profit and loss ratios. If there is a loss, this must be shared in the profit and loss ratio before withdrawal of any capital contributions. The remainder, if any, is divided among the partners in the ratio of their capitals as diminished by the loss. Whether the net assets are either more or less than the total amount of the capitals, the difference is shared in the profit and loss ratio, and what remains is shared in the capital ratio. If a careful accounting is made of the profit or loss at the time of the sale of each piece of property and these profits and losses together with the dissolution expenses are summarized and distributed to the partners' capital accounts, those accounts will of course show the claims of the various partners on the net assets of the business after all assets have been converted into cash and all liabilities paid.

Instead of a complete liquidation of the firm's assets, certain of the assets may, by mutual consent, be taken over by each partner at agreed values and applied toward the satisfaction of his capital and loan interests. Such use of assets is spoken of as a *conversion* to that particular purpose. It must be distinctly understood that this is not a right which any partner can demand, but only a privilege granted by the mutual agreement of the partners. Any partner can demand that all the assets be sold and that the proceeds be applied in satisfaction of the interests concerned.

Sharing Losses.—In the case of insolvency, the partners are compelled to share the losses in the profit and loss ratio, not in capital ratio, and these losses are chargeable against their capital accounts. If the capital account of any of the partners is not large enough to satisfy his share in the losses, a deficit in that partner's interest results, which is represented by the debit balance in his capital account. This shows the amount which he must contribute to the firm in order that all claims may be satisfied. The rule that profits and losses in liquidation cannot be shared in the same ratio as capitals, unless this ratio is also the profit and loss ratio, is responsible for the fact that upon dissolution one or more partners may have to make additional contributions, while others may not be obliged to do so. This duty of contributing to make up a deficit is inherent in the partnership relation and can be enforced by the copartners.

A few illustrations will set forth the main problems in connection with the liquidation of partners' capitals:

1. Sharing Losses Equally

BALANCE SHEET OF A, B & C

Cash	$10,000.00	Liabilities	$10,000.00
Other Assets	60,000.00	A, Capital	15,000.00
		B, Capital	20,000.00
		C, Capital	25,000.00
	$70,000.00		$70,000.00

A, B, and C share profits and losses equally.

The above balance sheet shows, in summary form, the condition of the firm previous to liquidation, and also indicates the shares of the partners in the net assets as on that date, i.e., the partners share in the net assets in the ratio 15:20:25 or 3:4:5. Dissolution becomes necessary and in the course of liquidation the expenses and losses incurred amount to $15,000. After the net loss of $15,000 is divided equally among the partners, the capitals will amount to, A $10,000, B $15,000, and C $20,000. The result is that the capital ratio has changed from 3:4:5 to 10:15:20, or 2:3:4, and the net assets of $45,000 are to be shared in this new ratio.

2. Capital Deficit

BALANCE SHEET OF JONES & SMITH

Cash	$10,000.00	Jones, Capital	$20,000.00
Losses in Liquidation	15,000.00	Smith, Capital	5,000.00
	$25,000.00		$25,000.00

Jones and Smith share profits and losses equally.

The above balance sheet shows the condition of the firm after liquidation. It is necessary, first, to distribute the liquidation losses among the partners, after which they share in the net assets according to capital ratios. Accordingly, each capital account is debited with an equal share in the loss of $15,000, after which Jones' capital is $12,500 and Smith's account shows a debit balance of $2,500. This means that Jones not only gets the entire cash of $10,000, but Smith must contribute $2,500 to the firm and this also goes to Jones.

3. Personal Insolvency of One Partner

BALANCE SHEET OF SMITH, JONES & GREEN

Cash	$16,000.00	Smith, Capital	$15,000.00
Jones, Capital	9,000.00	Green, Capital	10,000.00
	$25,000.00		$25,000.00

Smith and Jones each have a ⅖ share and Green a ⅕ share in profits and losses.

The above balance sheet shows the financial condition of the firm after taking into consideration the losses incident to liquidation. From this it is seen that Jones owes the business $9,000. Assume that he is personally insolvent and cannot contribute the share due from him. The net assets available for distribution consist of $16,000 in cash. Inasmuch as Jones' interest is entirely wiped out and a contribution is due from him which he cannot pay, the amount of that contribution is an additional loss to be borne by the two remaining partners. Their respective shares in this loss are determined by their original profit and loss ratios ⅖ and ⅕, so that as between themselves Smith must bear ⅔ of the loss or $6,000, and Green ⅓ or $3,000; after which Smith's capital and share in the net assets is $9,000, and Green's $7,000.

Where a partner, in his private capacity, and the firm of which he is a member are both bankrupt, his personal creditors have first claim on his personal estate and the firm's creditors on the assets of the firm.

Distribution by Instalments.—Where the liquidation is of long duration, the partners may desire to receive what is due them by instalments rather than wait to receive their respective shares in one amount. Where the capital ratio differs from the profit and loss ratio, it is difficult to determine the proper ratio in which the instalments should be paid, due to the fact that expenses and losses have not yet been determined. Consequently it is impossible to tell what the ultimate ratios will be in which the partners are to share the net assets. As the payment of instalments on an arbitrary basis might result ultimately in an overpayment of some partners and an underpayment of others, the only safe method of handling the situation is to pay the first instalments to those partners whose capital ratios are in excess of their profit and loss ratios until their capitals are reduced to the point where the capital ratios of all the partners are the same as their profit and loss ratios. As soon as this point is reached, the proceeds of the assets may be distributed to the partners on the basis of their profit and loss ratios, because these are now identical with their capital ratios. A more complete treatment of this problem will be found on pages 650 to 654 of the author's second volume.

Treatment of Good-Will upon Liquidation by Sale.—When dissolution is brought about by the sale of the entire business, it may happen that the amount realized on the assets is smaller than their book value, and the difference must be treated as a loss in accordance with the principles previously stated. Similarly, where the assets are sold and the price realized is larger than their book value, the excess constitutes a profit and must be distributed among the partners in profit and loss ratio. Usually such an excess is treated as a receipt on account of good-will, and two standard methods of booking it are employed. When good-will is mentioned in the sale contract and its value has been determined, it is brought on the books as an asset and transferred immediately to the partners' accounts. Thus, if the value is $15,000 and the profit and loss ratio is ⅖ to A, ⅖ to B, and ⅕ to C, the entry is:

Good-Will		15,000.00
	A, Capital	6,000.00
	B, Capital	6,000.00
	C, Capital	3,000.00

Good-will is now shown as an asset, and the entry closing it off is the same as for the sale of the other assets, viz., a debit to Cash and a credit to Good-Will.

On the other hand, when good-will is not specified as such in the sale contract, but the amount realized on the sale of the assets is larger than their book values, this excess may be credited to Good-Will, which is then treated not as an asset account (as in the case given above) but as a profit and loss account. The balance of this account is closed out to the partners' accounts in profit-sharing ratios in the same way as above. The ultimate result is the same in either case; the first method is a little more complete since it shows the value of the asset good-will previous to its sale.

The formal entries by which the sale of any business is recorded on its books, whether single proprietorship, partnership, or corporation, are treated in Chapter XXXIX under corporations.

CHAPTER XXXVIII
THE CORPORATION

Definition.—The definition of a corporation, given by former Chief Justice Marshall as "an artificial being, invisible, intangible, and existing only in contemplation of the law," sets forth its fundamental characteristics, viz., artificial personality and creation by the law. Blackstone says, "A corporation is an artificial person created for preserving in perpetual succession certain rights which being conferred on natural persons only would fail in the process of time." Blackstone's definition lays particular emphasis on a characteristic not specifically mentioned by Marshall, that of perpetuity of succession. It is apparent that the corporation within the limits prescribed by statute has most of the attributes and powers of a person—it can sue and be sued, can hold and pass title to property, real and personal, can carry on business in its own name, is responsible to the extent of its entire property for the payment of its debts, etc.

Growth of the Corporate Form of Organization.—The corporate form of organization is being increasingly utilized for the conduct of business of almost every kind. It offers a much more attractive field to the investor who desires to place his surplus funds in productive enterprises and share in their profits without having the burdens of active management or the risk of losing his private fortune to satisfy the claims of business creditors should the undertaking prove unsuccessful. Just as the partnership is an advance over the sole proprietorship in point of business organization, efficiency, and ability to cope with larger undertakings, so the corporation in some of its forms represents an advance over the partnership form of business organization. Its advantages and disadvantages in comparison with the partnership will be reviewed briefly.

Advantages.—Some of its advantages are:

1. Limited liability. Only corporation property can be levied on to satisfy the claims of creditors; the private fortunes of the individual stockholders cannot be touched.

2. Continued existence. The death, withdrawal, or bankruptcy of any of its members does not interfere with its existence. Its life may be terminated by voluntary dissolution, insolvency, expiration of charter life, forfeiture of charter to the state for misuse, non-use, or abuse of its privileges.

3. Transferability of its shares, and their use as collateral for private loans without injury to the credit of the corporation.

4. Larger capital. A partnership becomes unwieldy and inefficient if the number of partners becomes too large. The number of stockholders in a

corporation is not limited and varies from one to many thousands in the larger corporations. Accordingly much more extensive fields of endeavor are open to the corporation because it can bring together and use advantageously the combined capitals of many persons.

5. Centralized control. Its method of internal organization is such that one man can be made the responsible head instead of the many heads of the partnership.

Disadvantages.—The chief disadvantages of the corporation may be summarized thus:

1. Comparative absence of personal interest of the managing officer. This is largely a theoretical drawback, inasmuch as it is usually required that the managing officer be a stockholder.

2. As a creature of the state, the corporation is subject to state legislative control. It is taxable by the state and is required to make periodic reports.

3. Its credit is dependent on the amount of its net assets and not on the fortunes of its individual owners.

4. Corporations are sometimes restricted as to the character of their business. In some states certain lines of business cannot be carried on by corporations.

5. In some states it is illegal for corporations to hold stock in other corporations.

In spite of these and other disadvantages, most of which are not serious, the advantages of the corporate form of organization far surpass those of the sole proprietorship or partnership.

The Formation of a Corporation.—Formerly a corporation could be brought into existence only by a special act of the legislature. As this method proved cumbersome and was subject to much abuse, it gave place in all states to general corporation statutes or enabling acts whereby an application in due form and according to statutory provisions is all that is necessary for organizing a corporation. Though the statutes differ for each state, they are uniform in the main points. The method of formation under the New York statute will be explained.

Certificate of Incorporation—New York State.—The form of application for a charter to do business as a corporation is known as a "certificate of incorporation." This document must be prepared by at least three natural persons, two-thirds of which number must be citizens of the United States and at least one of whom must be a citizen of New York State. These persons are called the "incorporators." Their certificate must be made out in the

English language, signed by each incorporator, acknowledged before a notary public, and must contain:

1. The name of the corporation, in the English language. This must be different from the name of any other domestic or foreign corporation doing business in the state and must not contain in its title the words, "bank, trust, insurance, etc."

2. The purpose or purposes for which it is created. There is practically no limitation as to the lines of endeavor the corporation may declare itself desirous of following, with the exception that banks, trust, transportation, and insurance companies, etc., come under special laws.

3. The amount of capital stock of the corporation, common and preferred if both are to be issued. Preferred stock of various classes may be authorized after incorporation. The minimum amount of capital required by the New York law is $500. One-half of the capital must be paid in within one year from the date of incorporation. The certificate must state also the amount of capital to be paid in before the corporation can commence business and this must not be less than $500. No debts can be contracted before that amount is paid in.

4. The number of shares into which the authorized capital is divided and the par value of each. This must not be less than $5 nor more than $100, although more recently capital stock has been authorized with no named par value.

5. The place in which the principal office is to be located, which must be within the state.

6. The contemplated duration of its life. This may be made perpetual.

7. The number of directors, which must not be less than three.

8. The names and post-office addresses of the directors for the first year. Directors usually are stockholders and at least one-fourth of the directors are subject to election annually.

9. The names and post-office addresses of the subscribers to the certificate of incorporation, and the number of shares in the corporation subscribed by each.

Filing the Certificate—New York State.—The certificate of incorporation is usually made out in triplicate. The original must be filed and recorded in the office of the Secretary of State; the duplicate certified by the Secretary must be filed with the clerk of the county in which the principal business office is to be located; and the certified triplicate is retained by the corporation in its own files. The fees for filing the certificate with the

Secretary of State are $10, and for recording 15 cents per folio. The county clerk's fees are 6 cents per folio for filing.

Organization Tax—New York State.—Before the filing of the certificate, an organization tax of 1/20th of 1% of the authorized capital stock must be paid to the State Treasurer. Record of this payment is forwarded to the Secretary's office.

Initial Acts of Corporation.—When the corporation is ready to commence business, its first act is usually to call a meeting of the incorporators and directors for the purpose of adopting a set of by-laws—although this matter may be delegated to the board of directors. This meeting also authorizes the issue of stock at or above par in exchange for cash, labor, or property.

State Control.—The outside control of the corporation is vested in the state. The state constitution, the general corporation law, the statutes relating to business organizations in general, and the specific contract between the corporation and state embodied in its charter or certificate of incorporation—these form the basis for state control and the limits within which the corporation may act as an authorized person. If the corporation does an interstate business, it is subject also to the regulations of the Interstate Commerce Commission.

Working Organization and Management.—The corporation's owners, that is, the stockholders, are the source of all authority and control. Unlike the partnership where control and voice in the management are equally shared by the partners regardless of any inequality in their investments, the corporation ownership is evidenced by shares of stock and each share is given one vote. Thus each owner's authority and voting power are dependent upon the amount of his ownership of stock. He has, however, the right to delegate this power to another person by "power of attorney," and in this way it frequently happens that one stockholder exercises a power far beyond the amount of shares owned by him. Delegation of voting power frequently occurs when the stock is widely distributed geographically and is owned in small lots. In theory the agent or attorney entrusted with the voting power of others is simply carrying out the will of his principal, the real owner of the stock.

Annual Election of Directors.—Because of the number of stockholders and because many of them are engaged in other pursuits, one of the characteristics of the corporate form of management is that the owners frequently do not have direct control of their enterprise. Accordingly, at regular times, usually annually, the stockholders elect directors to whom are delegated the general oversight and control of the business. The board of directors thus elected stands in the place of the stockholders during the period between the annual meetings at which it renders account of its management.

Officers.—The board of directors elects officers of the company—usually a president, vice-president, treasurer, and secretary—to undertake the active management of the business; or the directors may appoint a general manager or superintendent on whom rests the active management and who is the executive head of the corporation. Thus the chief characteristic of the working organization of the corporation is the delegation of authority to a responsible head. The accountability of the officers to the board of directors, and of the directors to the stockholders, has so far proved the most efficient method of conducting modern business.

The Showing of Proprietorship.—The chief difference, from an accounting viewpoint, between the corporate form and other forms of business organization is in the showing of proprietorship. Vested proprietorship in a sole owner or partnership business is carried under the title of the different owners' capital accounts, and credit is extended by the public to such owners, not on the basis of what the particular business is worth, but on the reputation of the owners and what they are known to be worth outside the business as well as in the business. On the other hand, the law has relieved the owners of a corporation of individual liability for the debts of the corporation. Only the corporate property can be held liable for the satisfaction of creditors' claims. For their protection, the corporation is not allowed to impair its capital stock by the payment of any portion of it in dividends to the owners or to change the amount of its capital stock without special authority. The outstanding capital stock, in theory, represents to the prospective creditor the minimum value of the corporation assets which are supposed to be sufficient to meet in full the claims of creditors. Accordingly, the portion of the capital of a corporation represented by its capital stock is a fixed amount, and the increments or decrements of proprietorship are usually shown in a separate account called Surplus. This account must always be read with the Capital Stock account to ascertain the current or present capital as distinguished from the original.

The Surplus account is sometimes divided and shown under such titles as Profits, Reserves, Undivided Profits, Working Capital, etc. To ascertain full proprietorship or net worth, all such accounts must be included.

RECORDS PECULIAR TO A CORPORATION

The Subscription Book and Subscription Ledger.—Upon the proper filing and acceptance of the certificate of incorporation, authority is given the incorporators to secure subscriptions to the capital stock. Subscription books or blanks may then be opened, which usually contain a form of agreement somewhat as follows:

We, the undersigned, do hereby subscribe for and agree to take the number of shares of the capital stock of the Blank Company, par value .... set opposite our names and pay for the same, ... per centum down, the remainder subject to the call of the board of directors.

Where the number of subscribers is large and especially if record must be made of the payment of calls, a Subscription Ledger or Instalment Book is used. This ledger has no set form but usually carries columns showing when the calls are to be made, when actually made, when paid, and the balance still due. A controlling account called "Subscribers" or "Subscription" is carried on the general ledger, with a special column in the cash book to gather the totals for posting.

The Stock Certificate Book and Stock Ledger.—A subscriber is, as such, a stockholder in the corporation even though his stock certificate may not yet have been issued to him. The stock certificate is merely evidence of ownership. It is usually issued from a book with perforated leaves similar to a check book, with stub to carry the essential data of the certificate. Directly from this stub, or through the medium of a stock journal, postings are made to the individual accounts in the stock ledger. This ledger which, in turn, is controlled by the Capital Stock account or accounts on the general ledger, carries the detailed information as to the number of shares issued, shares canceled, and balances held by each owner.

The Stock Transfer Book.—In the state of New York a stock transfer book must be kept, showing all the data in connection with transfers of shares, such as old and new stock certificate numbers, names of the parties, etc.

The Minute Book.—To preserve a record of the meetings of the directors and stockholders, and the business transacted thereat, use is made of a minute book kept by the secretary. This book, as the source of authority for all the important acts and policies of the corporation, is a most important record. The record should be a complete history of the corporation from its organization through the entire period of its existence.

Other Records.—When the stock is sold on the instalment plan, formal receipt of the payment of each instalment is sometimes made by means of an "Instalment Scrip Book," whose certificates or receipts are issued upon payment of each instalment. When full payment has been made, the instalment certificates are exchanged for the regular certificates of stock. A dividend book for recording the payment of dividends is sometimes kept, though the need for such a record has been largely eliminated through the use of dividend checks.

CHAPTER XXXIX
OPENING THE CORPORATION BOOKS

Corporation Accounting Records.—The method of recording the ordinary business transactions of a corporation is essentially the same as in the types of business organization previously discussed. The opening and closing of corporation accounts, however, as also the method of making the periodic summarization, call for the special treatment given in this chapter and the next.

Proprietorship and Capital Stock.—As stated before, the members of a stock corporation have their ownership evidenced by certificates of stock. The proprietorship or net worth of a corporation, as of the single proprietorship and partnership, is the excess of its assets over its liabilities. This excess is shown in the books by two accounts or two groups of accounts, viz., the Capital Stock account—or accounts—which represents the amount of outstanding shares; and the Surplus account—subdivided and carried under other titles, if desirable—which represents the excess of the proprietorship over the amount of capital stock. Each stockholder's share in the corporation is determined by the number of shares he possesses.

Common and Preferred Stock.—There may be various classes of stock. If only one kind is authorized at the beginning, the subsequent creation of other kinds requires an amendment of the charter. The usual classes of stock are common and preferred. As its name indicates, preferred stock has some kind of preference over the common or ordinary stock. This preference may be only in regard to dividends, or it may include preference as to ownership in the net assets in case of dissolution. Preferred stock usually carries a fixed dividend, payable before any dividend can be paid to the common stockholders.

Preferred stock is classified as cumulative and non-cumulative. The terms apply to the dividend liability of the corporation in the event that the continuity of dividend declarations is broken. The dividend on cumulative preferred stock accumulates and becomes a preferred claim for the amount accumulated since the time of the last dividend declaration. That is, the common shareholders are not entitled to receive any dividend until the preferred shareholders have received the amount of the accumulated total. Preferred stock that is non-cumulative does not possess this feature. A dividend once passed on such stock is not a preferred claim to profits as compared with the dividend rights of common stockholders, but lapses completely. Preferred stock is cumulative unless specified to the contrary.

The issue of No-par-value stock is authorized by thirteen different states. Very often in a corporation whose stock carries a stated par value, there is little real relationship between the actual value of the stock as indicated by the net assets of the corporation and its stated par value. The law requires that par-value stock be carried on the books at its stated par. If such stock has been sold or exchanged for assets of a lesser value, there is always the temptation to inflate the value of the assets in order to maintain it at the par of the stock issued for them. This tendency is not met in the use of stock carrying no par value. Such stock appears on the books at exactly the amount of the assets received in exchange for it. A purchaser of such stock, because of the fact that it carries no stated par value, is at once put on notice to investigate the values back of it. No-par-value stock may be either preferred or common. In the former instance, if the preference relates to the assets at the time of dissolution, each such share must state the amount of assets applicable to each share in case of liquidation of the corporation. This constitutes a preference claim, not over the creditors of the corporation, but only over the common stockholders.

Thus it is seen that there may be different classes of ownership of a corporation, the owners of one class having some advantages over the owners of the other classes. It should be understood, of course, that within each class the rights and duties of the owners are the same.

Opening the Books of a Corporation.—The opening entries of a corporation have to do with a correct treatment of capital stock, subscriptions, calls and instalments, payments by cash and by property, etc.

The charter to do business, granted a corporation by the state, gives it the right to sell shares of stock. These shares have no value in themselves and are worth only what the corporation can exchange them for, either in cash or other assets. There is, therefore, no reason for making a record on the books of account as distinguished from the corporation's minute book, of the corporation's right to issue stock and of the amount of the stock which it has a right to issue. Until the stock has been paid or subscribed for, no formal entry need be made on the books of account. Of course, full record of all deliberations and resolutions as to procedure and policy up to the time of the actual sale of the stock is carried in the minute book, and a concise narrative statement of the organization of the corporation, its purposes, the authorized capital stock issue, the number of shares, the par value of each share, if par value stock, and so forth, should always precede the formal opening entries in the journal. This record and that in the minute book should give all the information of this sort needed. There is a too prevalent tendency among bookkeepers to make all sorts of memorandum entries on the books of account. A memorandum entry is an entry which has no financial significance and is made merely as a reminder that transactions of financial significance may arise from that source.

Before a corporation can secure its charter it is necessary to make certain expenditures. These usually consist of fees paid to a lawyer for his services in assisting in drawing up the charter; fees for filing the certificate; the organization tax; the cost of the certificates of stock and stock records; and so forth. These expenditures must be met by the incorporators from their private funds but they are reimbursed from the funds received upon sale of the stock. It is, accordingly, customary in opening the books of a corporation to show first the sale of the stock before showing the expenditures for organization.

A number of different methods of opening the books are employed. The first of these does not make use of the memorandum entries referred to above, whereas the other two do use memorandum entries. The three methods will be illustrated by means of the problem given below. The entries are shown in journal form. It will be understood, of course, that those entries which involve cash will appear in the cash book only. All the other entries appear in the general journal.

PROBLEM 1. The Smith-Brown Company is incorporated with an authorized capital stock of $250,000, of which $150,000 is subscribed and paid for at par; the balance remains unissued for the present. The organization expenses are $1,000.

FIRST METHOD

THE SMITH-BROWN COMPANY

A corporation organized under the State of New York, with an authorized capital stock of Two Hundred and Fifty Thousand dollars ($250,000), divided into Two Thousand, Five Hundred (2,500) shares of the par value of One Hundred dollars ($100) each, with all powers necessary to carry on the business of manufacturing, selling, and distributing motors of all kinds.

Case 1. Where the subscription and payment are not simultaneous:

(a) Subscribers   150,000.00
      Capital Stock Subscriptions   150,000.00
           To record subscriptions to the
           capital stock as follows:
              A shares
              B"
              C"
              Etc.

(b) Cash   150,000.00

Subscribers		150,000.00

    To credit subscribers for the payment of their subscriptions.

(c) Capital Stock Subscriptions	150,000.00	
Capital Stock		150,000.00

    To record the issue of stock to all subscribers who have paid in full.

(d) Organization Expense	1,000.00	
Cash		1,000.00

    To record the payment of the costs of organizing the corporation.

Entry (a) sets up the claim under subscription contracts against the subscribers as an asset of the corporation, and is offset by the proprietorship account, carried under the title "Capital Stock Subscriptions," until payment has been made and the certificates of stock actually issued to the stockholders.

Entry (b) is self-explanatory.

Entry (c) shows the issue of the certificates and therefore transfers the proprietorship from Capital Stock Subscriptions to Capital Stock.

Case 2. Where the subscription and payment are simultaneous:

(a) Cash	150,000.00	
Capital Stock		150,000.00
(b) Organization Expense	1,000.00	
Cash		1,000.00

In a small corporation where a cash investment constitutes the entire original capital, the entries shown in case 1 above are sometimes abbreviated as here indicated. In such a case there is often no formal subscription contract entered into and there is therefore no need to set up accounts with Subscribers and Capital Stock Subscriptions.

Second Method.

This method makes use of the memorandum accounts, Unissued Capital Stock and Capital Stock Authorized. Omitting the narrative statement of organization, the explanatory matter after the various entries, and the organization expense entry, which are common to all methods, the other necessary entries are as follows:

(a) Unissued Capital Stock	250,000.00	
Capital Stock Authorized		250,000.00
(b) Subscribers	150,000.00	
Capital Stock Subscriptions		150,000.00
(c) Cash	150,000.00	
Subscribers		150,000.00
(d) Capital Stock Subscriptions	150,000.00	
Capital Stock		150,000.00
(e) Capital Stock Authorized	150,000.00	
Unissued Capital Stock		150,000.00

Entry (a) is a memorandum entry recording the amount of capital stock authorized by the corporation's charter. This entry has little or no financial significance. Not until stock is sold does the corporation have any real assets.

Entry (b) shows that of the stock which was unissued under entry (a), $150,000, has been subscribed for, thus giving the corporation a legally enforcible claim—an asset—for that amount.

Entry (c) is self-explanatory.

Entry (d) shows the issue of the stock when the subscriptions are paid.

Entry (e) adjusts the memorandum entry (a), to show the present amount of authorized stock still unissued, viz., $100,000. Both accounts under (a) continue as memoranda only, and as they exactly offset each other, they will not appear on the balance sheet.

Third Method.

This method also makes use of memorandum accounts before the sale of the stock. The difference between this and the second method should be noted.

It will be seen that the credit of entry (a) is here Capital Stock instead of Capital Stock Authorized. This is theoretically incorrect because as yet the corporation has no proprietorship. The best that can be said for it is that the debit represents a contingent asset and the credit a contingent proprietorship item. The other entries are self-explanatory.

(a) Unissued Capital Stock	250,000.00	
Capital Stock		250,000.00
(b) Subscribers	150,000.00	
Subscriptions		150,000.00
(c) Cash	150,000.00	
Subscribers		150,000.00
(d) Subscriptions	150,000.00	
Unissued Capital Stock		150,000.00

Premium or Discount on Stock.—The law requires that when stock of par value is issued, the Capital Stock account must be carried always at par. When stock is sold at a premium or at a discount, it necessitates, therefore, the use of supplementary proprietorship accounts to make the proper record. In the state of New York, a corporation cannot sell its stock at a discount, but in states where this is allowed the amount of such discounts should be charged to a "Discount on Stock" or some similar account. Sometimes the charge is made to "Organization Expense." The use of Organization Expense account for this purpose is contrary to the principle that the account title should show the exact nature of the items recorded under it. It is misleading and sometimes reprehensible. A full discussion of this matter is given in Volume II. When stock is sold above par, the amount of the premium is recorded in the account "Premium on Stock," which as usually handled constitutes a part of the permanent capital of the corporation. Premiums on stock sales should not be credited to Surplus account. The following illustration will show the kind of entries required:

PROBLEM 2. Of the $100,000 unissued stock of Problem 1, we will assume that $50,000 is later subscribed for at 98, and $50,000 at 102.

Entries to make the record according to the first method, Problem 1, are as follows:

(a) Covering stock subscribed for at a discount:

Subscribers	49,000.00	
Discount on Capital Stock	1,000.00	
Capital Stock Subscriptions		50,000.00

(b) For stock subscribed for at 102:

Subscribers	51,000.00	
Premium on Capital Stock		1,000.00
Capital Stock Subscriptions		50,000.00

Entries for payment of the subscription and issue of the stock follow the method of entry already shown on page 342. It will be observed that the Capital Stock Subscription and the Capital Stock accounts are always shown at par value.

Capital Stock on the Balance Sheet.—The net worth section of the balance sheet of a corporation will usually appear somewhat as follows for the capital stock items. Often, however, more detail is shown in connection with the surplus item. The student should note how full information is given concerning the capital stock.

(1) *Net Worth*

Represented by:

  Capital Stock:

Authorized	$250,000.00	
Unissued	100,000.00	
Issued and Outstanding		$150,000.00
Premium on Capital Stock		5,000.00
Surplus		60,000.00
Total Net Worth		$215,000.00

Where the discount on stock has not been charged off against Surplus either because sufficient profits have not been reserved, or because, although sufficient profits have been reserved, it is deemed desirable to build up a larger balance of Surplus before charging off the discount, the net worth section will appear as follows:

(2) *Net Worth*

Represented by:

Capital Stock:

Authorized	$250,000.00	
Unissued	100,000.00	
Issued and Outstanding		$150,000.00
Surplus		10,000.00
		$160,000.00
Discount on Capital Stock		15,000.00
Total Net Worth		$145,000.00

Discount on capital stock should usually be shown as above, although one sometimes finds it listed among the assets on a balance sheet. This is not wholly objectionable unless it is set up under a title which does not indicate its true nature.

Instalments.—The subscription contract sometimes provides for payment by instalments. The corporation usually issues to all such subscribers a "call," i.e., a notice that an instalment payment will come due at a given time. The subscriber is not considered delinquent until the call has been made and he has not responded. The accounts must therefore reflect the difference in status brought about by a "call." This is accomplished by transferring the claim against the subscriber carried in Subscribers account to a new claim against him carried under Call account. The illustrations below show the accounts required and their handling.

PROBLEM 3. Assume that the $50,000 of stock subscribed for at 102 is to be paid for one-half in cash and the remainder in two equal instalments at the end of successive three-month periods.

For the one-half cash payment the entry is as follows:

Cash	25,500.00	
Subscribers		25,500.00

At the end of the first three months, the record is:

Call No. 1	12,750.00	
Subscribers		12,750.00

To show the call issued.

Cash	12,750.00	
Call No. 1		12,750.00

To record payment of the first call.

Similar entries at the end of the second three months are:

Call No. 2.	12,750.00	
Subscribers		12,750.00
Cash	12,750.00	
Call No. 2		12,750.00

If the call is not paid in full at balance sheet time, the debit balance in the "Call" accounts constitutes an asset, i.e., the amount of unpaid instalments due from subscribers. Upon full payment of all subscriptions, certificates of stock are issued and recorded as shown on pages 341, 342.

Entries for Common and Preferred Stock.—Where more than one kind of stock is issued, such as common and one or more kinds of preferred, separate capital stock accounts—and usually other related accounts—should be kept for each class, as illustrated below:

PROBLEM 4. Assume that the stock of a corporation is $200,000 common and $50,000 preferred, and that $100,000 common and $50,000 preferred have been subscribed for. The entries necessary to record the subscription in accordance with the first method explained above, are:

Subscribers—Capital Stock Common	100,000.00	
Capital Stock Common, Subscriptions		100,000.00
Subscribers—Capital Stock Preferred	50,000.00	
Capital Stock Preferred, Subscriptions		50,000.00

The other entries for payment of subscriptions and issue of stock are essentially the same as explained above, but the record of the transactions affecting common and preferred stock should always be kept distinct and separate.

Entries for No-Par Stock.—When a corporation issues no-par stock, the amount of proprietorship resulting from its sale is exactly what the stock brings and is so recorded; there is neither discount nor premium. Booking it is, therefore, simple. The amount of capital so secured, i.e., secured from its sale, should, however, never be mixed with the accretions to capital from reserved profits or other sources. Such items constitute the Surplus just as in the case of stock of par value, and the legal requirement that these amounts be kept separate from the capital stock are just as strict. This is necessary so that the records will clearly show that dividends have not encroached upon the capital. Since the value at which no-par stock is carried on the books bears no relation to the number of shares issued, it is customary to carry on the balance sheet information as to the number of shares outstanding. The net worth section of the balance sheet of a corporation issuing no-par stock should appear as follows:

Net Worth

Represented by:

   Capital Stock—No Par:

Authorized	10,000 shares	
Unissued	3,000 "	
Issued and Outstanding 7,000 "		$369,465.00
Surplus		125,479.00
Total Net Worth		$494,944.00

Payment of Subscriptions by Property.—When payment of subscriptions is by property instead of by cash, the value at which such property shall be brought onto the books is entirely at the discretion of the corporation's directors, and unless fraud can be shown, their valuations are final. No difficulties are involved in recording such a payment; the paid properties are debited under suitable account titles, and the Subscribers account is credited. The following problem illustrates the change from a partnership to a corporation, at the same time showing how the payment of subscriptions by property must be treated.

Change from Partnership to Corporation

PROBLEM 5. A and B, partners, incorporate as the American Baking Company. The authorized capitalization is $250,000. Each partner subscribes for an amount of stock equal to his interest in the partnership, and C, an outsider, subscribes for the remainder of the stock at par. The corporation purchases the assets and assumes the liabilities of the partnership, paying therefor with stock as above. C pays his subscription in cash. The balance sheet of the partnership on that date was as follows:

BALANCE SHEET OF A & B

Cash	$ 20,000.00	Accounts Payable	$ 45,000.00
Accounts Receivable	150,000.00	Mortgage Payable	80,000.00
Merchandise	50,000.00	A, Capital	125,000.00
Plant	130,000.00	B, Capital	100,000.00
	$350,000.00		$350,000.00

Make the opening entries for the new corporation and also close the books of the partnership.

1. The entries to open the corporation's books:

(a) Subscribers 250,000.00
    Capital Stock Subscriptions 250,000.00
        To record subscriptions to
        the capital stock as follows:
        A 125,000

  B 100,000
  C 25,000

(b) Cash   20,000.00

 Accounts Receivable   150,000.00

 Merchandise   50,000.00

 Plant   130,000.00

  A & B, Vendors   350,000.00

  To record the purchase from A & B of their partnership assets.

(c) A & B, Vendors   125,000.00

 Accounts Payable   45,000.00

 Mortgage Payable   80,000.00

  To record partial payment to A & B for their assets by the assumption of their liabilities.

(d) A & B, Vendors   225,000.00

 Subscribers   225,000.00

  To record full payment to A & B for the balance due them, by the cancellation of their subscription indebtedness.

(e) Cash   25,000.00

 Subscribers   25,000.00

  To record payment by C of his subscription contract.

(f) Capital Stock Subscriptions   250,000.00

 Capital Stock   250,000.00

  To record the issue of stock to all subscribers, who have paid in full.

Entries (b), (c), and (d) are sometimes combined in the following compound entry:

Cash	20,000.00	
Accounts Receivable	150,000.00	
Merchandise	50,000.00	
Plant	130,000.00	
Accounts Payable		45,000.00
Mortgage Payable		80,000.00
Subscribers		225,000.00

Although this accomplishes the same result so far as the ultimate showing is concerned, it does not present the various steps of the transactions so clearly as the separate entries. The "A & B, Vendors" account in entry (b) indicates the liability of the corporation to A & B, arising from the purchase of their partnership properties. Entries (c) and (d) show the manner in which A and B are paid for this purchase, with consequent cancellation of that liability.

2. The entries to close the books of the partnership of A & B are:

(a) American Baking Company   350,000.00

Cash		20,000.00
Accounts Receivable		150,000.00
Merchandise		50,000.00
Plant		130,000.00

    To charge the American Baking Company with the assets purchased under contract of (date).

(b) Accounts Payable   45,000.00
    Mortgage Payable   80,000.00
        American Baking Company   125,000.00

    To credit the American Baking Company under their purchase contract for the taking over of the firm's liabilities.

(c) American Baking Company Stock   225,000.00

American Baking Company		225,000.00

    To credit the American Baking Company for
        the payment of the balance due by the issue of its stock at par to the firm.

(d) A, Capital	125,000.00	
B, Capital	100,000.00	
American Baking Company Stock		225,000.00

    To show the distribution of the stock.

Where the stock is issued to each partner directly (instead of to the firm and then distributed to the vendors), sometimes the issue is not shown on the partnership books, entry (c) above carrying debits to the partner's capital accounts in place of the debit to American Baking Company Stock. Whether the actual transaction follows one course or the other, entries as shown above seem to meet either requirement.

The student should make sure that the effect of the entries under (a) and (b) is thoroughly understood. It may be further noted that if good-will or shrinkage of values enters into the sale of a partnership, the necessary adjustments should be made in the partners' accounts before the sale takes place, after which the closing entries are as shown above.

CHAPTER XL
CURRENT AND CLOSING ENTRIES FOR THE CORPORATION

Relation between the Corporation and Its Owners.—It should be noted that the owners of a corporation are on a somewhat different basis in their relationships and activities to the business than are the owners of a partnership or single proprietorship business. The legal theory that the corporation is an entity, a person, separate and apart from its owners, necessitates a change in the status of accounts with owners as compared with similar accounts in the other types of organization. A charge against a stockholder as a customer of the corporation is on the same basis as a charge against any other customer. A stockholder may become a creditor of the corporation in exactly the same way as any other person. In a partnership, on the other hand, charges against a partner and credits to his account are looked upon as charges against and credits to his proprietary interest in the event of liquidation of the firm. This is not true in the case of a corporation, stockholders in such dealings being considered "outside" parties.

Current Record on Corporation Books.—After the corporation has been organized and the opening entries made on its books, the record of current transactions proceeds on practically the same basis as in all other types of business organization. Sales, purchases, cash receipts and disbursements, notes receivable and payable, and all the transactions arising out of them, are recorded currently in the same types of books and in the same manner as the similar transactions of a single proprietorship or a partnership.

While the record of current transactions is practically the same for all types of business organizations, there are some kinds of current transactions of a corporation which differ somewhat from those of the other types. They arise out of the nature of the corporation and are recorded under account titles peculiar to the corporate form. Some of these transactions and other accounting records will be discussed briefly.

Treasury Stock.—In some classes of enterprise and also under some methods of organizing and financing the corporation, no provision is made for the securing of a fund of working capital, all of the original capital being tied up in fixed assets—as a mine or some other plant. A similar condition is sometimes encountered even after a corporation has been operating for a number of years. Lack of business judgment and financial foresight sometimes brings about a condition in which the company has allowed an undue proportion of its current assets, and therefore its working capital, to become tied up in plant extensions.

In both such cases a frequent method of raising working capital is for the stockholders to donate to the corporation a pro rata portion of their holdings of stock to enable it to secure the needed working capital by selling the stock. When such stock comes back into the company's treasury, it is termed "treasury stock." Having once been issued and presumably fully paid for, it has this characteristic which does not attach to the original shares before their issue, viz., that it can be sold at a discount without the purchasers being liable to creditors, in case of bankruptcy, for the amount of the discount. Par-value stock which is originally sold at a discount or which is being sold on the instalment plan and has not therefore been paid for in full is subject to levy for the unpaid amount in the event of bankruptcy of the corporation. Thus, the man who buys a $100 share of original stock for $90, is subject to a $10 levy in the event that the assets of the corporation are not sufficient to pay its debts.

Accordingly, in financing highly speculative ventures such as mining, oil, and other similar companies, it is customary to issue the entire capital stock of the company to the owner or owners of the mining or oil property taken over by the corporation as the basis for its operations. Inasmuch as the value of the properties taken over is not determinable, it is usually impossible to show that the stock issued for them does not represent their true value. Accordingly, such stock is legally fully paid stock and not subject to the liability for additional assessment which attaches to stock sold at a discount. Working capital is provided through the donation of a portion of the capital stock to the treasury of the corporation, which is then in a position to sell to others the stock now fully paid and non-assessable. It is easier to find purchasers for this stock because it can be sold at whatever discount is necessary to dispose of it and carries with it no liability for future assessment.

Treasury stock may arise also through repurchase by the company. It may sometimes be desirable for a company to buy back some of its own stock. This is not allowed in all states but where allowed such stock repurchased becomes treasury stock.

The student should distinguish carefully between treasury stock and unissued stock.

Accounting for Treasury Stock.—The record of treasury stock transactions is not complicated. They are discussed under three heads as follows:

1. RECORD AT TIME OF ACQUISITION. Only the acquisition through donation will be explained here. Acquisition through purchase usually involves an adjustment of purchase price to par value and the vexed problem of valuation. This problem will be found discussed on page 18, Volume II.

Assume that a company has issued all its capital stock, $1,000,000 in amount, for the acquisition of a mining property, and that the shareholders donate to the treasury $400,000 of the stock to provide working capital. This stock donation will be recorded on the books as follows:

Treasury Stock   400,000.00
    Donated Surplus   400,000.00

Like any other gift, this gift of stock in theory creates additional capital and must therefore be recorded in a proprietorship account. The title "Donated Surplus" is used to indicate the source of this additional capital. Capital arising from this source should never be recorded in the general Surplus account, largely because of its problematical value but also because of the information which it gives concerning the financing of the company by making a separate record.

2. RECORD AT TIME OF SALE. Assume that $250,000 of the treasury stock is sold at 50. Inasmuch as the stock was brought on the books at par, the portion sold must be taken off at the same figure. The 50% discount, instead of being recorded in a Capital Stock Discount account, will be recorded as a charge against the Donated Surplus, thus adjusting a portion of this donated surplus, recorded originally at par value, to its realizable value. The following entry records the sale and adjustment:

Cash   125,000.00
Donated Surplus   125,000.00
    Treasury Stock   250,000.00

The student should understand that the customary procedure of opening the subscription books, making the entries with subscribers for treasury stock subscriptions, payment in cash or by instalments, and finally, the issue of the stock, may be the procedure followed in the sale of treasury stock just as in the sale of other stock. The net result will, however, be as shown by the above entry.

3. RECORD OF TREASURY STOCK ON THE BALANCE SHEET. On the balance sheet treasury stock is treated in the same way as unissued stock, namely, as a deduction item in the net worth section of the balance sheet. Using the above figures for illustration, the net worth section will appear as follows:

Net Worth

Represented by:
    Capital Stock:

Authorized	$1,000,000.00	
Treasury Stock	150,000.00	
Issued and Outstanding		$850,000.00
Donated Surplus		275,000.00
Total Net Worth		$1,125,000.00

Bonds Payable.—Generally, when a corporation borrows money on long-term notes secured by a portion of its fixed assets, chiefly its holdings of real estate, the notes (usually of uniform amounts so as to make them more marketable) are called "bonds." Thus, such notes or bonds are frequently in $100, $500, and $1,000 denominations, making it possible for one of limited means to take advantage of the mortgage offered as security for the loan. Bond issues are floated in pretty much the same way as capital stock issues, being offered for subscription at a price depending both on the interest rate which the bonds bear and the prevailing interest rate at the time of their offering. Thus, if the bonds bear 5% interest and the market rate for bonds of the same general character is 6%, an investor will naturally not be willing to pay par for them and the company will therefore have to sell them at such a discount as will put the yield to the investor approximately on a 6% basis. The company, by receiving for its bonds an amount less than par value but by being required to pay interest on the par amount, is thus paying higher than the nominal or agreed rate.

There is thus a very definite relationship between the bond discount and the interest rate which the bonds bear.

The accounting record of bond transactions is very similar to that of other liability transactions, and is shown under three heads as follows:

1. SALE OF BONDS PAYABLE. Assume that a $100,000 issue of bonds bearing 5% interest, payable semiannually, and maturing in 20 years, is sold at 90. The record will be:

Cash	90,000.00	
Bond Discount	10,000.00	
Bonds Payable		100,000.00

Bonds payable are always set up at par, since that represents the liability which must be met at maturity of the issue.

2. BOND INTEREST PAYMENT. At the close of the first six months, 2½% interest, or $2,500, will be paid to the holders of the bonds. Since the corporation will have to redeem its bonds at par, it has been deprived of the use of $10,000, represented by bond discount, because the issue was brought out at 5%. The $10,000 discount is therefore in the nature of a lump sum interest cost incurred in advance—prepaid—and must be spread equitably over the life of the bonds. Accordingly, at each of the 40 interest payments during the life of the issue, a pro rata share of this prepaid interest should be taken into account as bond interest. The distribution of bond discount over the interest payments made during the life of a bond issue is termed "amortization" of the discount. Scientifically, amortization is worked out on a compound interest basis, discussion and explanation of which are found on page 269, Volume II. Here, all we are concerned with is the principle involved and for the sake of simplicity the amortization is prorated evenly over the 40 interest periods, resulting in an additional interest charge of $250 each period. The record is therefore:

Bond Interest	2,750.00	
Bond Discount		250.00
Cash		2,500.00

3. CANCELLATION OR THE BONDS AT MATURITY. When the bonds come due and are paid, the record is the same as the cancellation of any other liability, viz.,

Bonds Payable	100,000.00	
Cash		100,000.00

Bond Premium.—Bonds are also often sold at a premium. As with discount, the premium is intimately related to the interest rate which the bonds bear. At the time of the sale of bonds, the premium is brought on the books as a credit, which together with the par value at which the bonds are booked, offsets the cash received from their sale. At the regular interest periods the premium is amortized over the life of the bonds and so results in a lessening of the periodic bond interest charge. The student should set up the entries to record the sale of bonds at a premium and the interest payment for such bonds.

Sinking Fund.—The sinking fund is a fund of liquid assets created by periodic sums, usually of equal amounts, set aside during the life of a bond issue or other liability to provide ready funds for the cancellation of the liability at maturity. This method is very commonly followed in public finance and is not infrequent in private corporations. It is not purposed here to explain the methods of determining what periodic sum is necessary to be set aside so that these principal sums and their interest accumulations will provide sufficient funds for the cancellation of the liability at maturity. Nor will the complicated problem of sinking fund investments in the hands of a trustee, and the expense and income arising out of it, be discussed here. These and related problems are covered fully in Chapter XXV, Volume II. Only the creation of the fund and its final disposition are treated here, under two heads as follows:

1. CREATION OF THE FUND. Assume that $1,000 cash is set aside at the end of each six months to provide for the retirement of the bonds at maturity. The entry for this, every six months, will be:

Sinking Fund   1,000.00

    Cash   1,000.00

2. CANCELLATION OF THE BOND LIABILITY. The student will understand that the cash set aside periodically for the sinking fund will be invested in securities in order to accumulate an income, which usually accrues to the fund. The securities in the fund must be sold just before the maturity of the bond issue, in order to provide cash. It will be assumed that in this instance the securities in the fund have been sold, that the cash in the sinking fund at the time of maturity is $101,500, and that the bond issue to be retired is $100,000. The entries will be:

(a) Bonds Payable   100,000.00

    Sinking Fund   100,000.00

(b) Cash   1,500.00

    Sinking Fund   1,500.00

Entry (b) returns to the general cash the unused cash in the sinking fund. In case of a deficiency in the sinking fund it will be necessary, of course, to draw on the general cash for the amount of the deficiency.

Sinking Fund Reserve.—It is often the policy of a corporation, which has to provide for the redemption of a bond issue, to reserve from the yearly profits a sum equal to the periodic payment into the sinking fund and the accumulations of the fund during that period. Such a policy prevents the distribution by dividends of all the current profits to stockholders, and insures that the increase in the assets represented by these profits will be held in the business and so provide each period an increased amount of assets for use in the business and ultimately, by conversion of the assets into cash, for the use of the sinking fund. The entries crediting the sinking fund reserve and showing its disposition at the maturity of the bonds are as follows:

(a) Surplus (or Profit and Loss)   1,000.00

     Sinking Fund Reserve   1,000.00

(b) Sinking Fund Reserve   100,000.00

     Capital Surplus (or Surplus)   100,000.00

The first entry shows the periodic reservation of profits. The second entry transfers the total profits so reserved during the life of the bonds, back to surplus—capital surplus if it is desired that these profits be made a part of the permanent capital of the corporation, or to general surplus in the event that these profits are to be made available for future dividends.

Closing the Books of the Corporation.—The results of the period's operations are summarized and the books closed in very much the same way as with the partnership. From what has been said above, it will be understood that there are some types of transactions to be considered at the time of closing the corporation's books that are not found in the partnership and single proprietorship. These concern largely the bond interest, the sinking fund reserve, and the dividend transactions. Bond interest is an expense. The sinking fund reserve is a reserve of net profits. Two methods are employed in showing the appropriation of net profits. Under the one method the total net profit is transferred to Surplus account, which then shows not only the profit for the current year but also the undistributed balance of previous years. The current appropriations of profits for whatever purpose are then booked as a charge against Surplus. Under the other method the current appropriations of profits are shown as charges against the net balance in the Profit and Loss account. Any unappropriated profit remaining is then transferred to the Surplus account.

Dividends.—A business is being operated always for the benefit of its owners, to whom the profits belong. In the case of a corporation, before the owners may secure any of the profits, a formal declaration of dividends must be made by the board of directors. During the term of its election the board is supreme in its management of the business. It is intimately in touch with the condition of the business. It knows the needs of the corporation and its obligations and must provide for them. If, after considering all the circumstances, it decides that some or all of the profits should be divided among the shareholders rather than be retained in the business for purposes of expansion, it meets in regular session and passes a formal dividend resolution.

Ultimate Control of Stockholders.—Thus it is seen that the board of directors is supreme during the period of its incumbency. Its actions are, however, subject to the review of the stockholders at their periodic meetings, which are usually held annually. If their policies are not favored by the shareholders, a new board, presumably one which will carry out the will of the majority of stockholders, is elected.

Dividends Out of Profits Only.—It is forbidden by law to pay dividends out of the capital of the corporation. Such payments would encroach upon the net assets of the organization and thereby weaken the creditors' security for the payment of their claims. Dividends need not be paid out of the profits of the current year, provided the undistributed profits of former periods are still available.

Distribution of Profits.—The appropriation of profits in a corporation differs, therefore, from that in a partnership. The entries recording the appropriation of profits cover in the main two kinds: (1) reserves, and (2) dividends. These entries are not necessarily the same for all corporations nor for all periods. No set disposition of profits is prescribed, authority resting with the directors. Their decision, therefore, as recorded in the minutes of their meetings is the basis for this group of entries. Some of the usual entries are illustrated in the following paragraphs.

Reserves and Dividends.—As stated above, the two methods for handling the appropriation of profits are: (1) as a charge against Surplus after the net profit for the current period has been transferred to that account; and (2) as a charge against the current Profit and Loss credit balance and a transfer of the remaining balance, if any, to the Surplus account.

A part of the profits may be retained in the business to provide funds for certain future needs, as for the payment of fixed debts, the extension of fixed plant, etc. Such items are transferred to the credit of properly named reserve accounts. Profits for distribution as dividends are similarly transferred to a Dividends Payable account. The dividend is always based on the amount of outstanding stock, not on the unissued or treasury stock. It is reckoned either as a percentage of the par value of each share, as a 6% dividend, or as a stated amount on each share, as a dividend of $4 or 10 cents per share.

The following illustration will show the necessary entries in accordance with the two methods.

PROBLEM. Assume that the net profits of Jackson & Co. are $25,000. The directors declare an 8% dividend on the outstanding capital stock of $100,000, and order $5,000 to be transferred to a reserve for buildings and $7,000 to a reserve for the cancellation of a bond issue.

FIRST METHOD

Profit and Loss	25,000.00	
Surplus		25,000.00

    To transfer net profits to Surplus.

Surplus	20,000.00	
Dividends Payable		8,000.00
Building Fund Reserve		5,000.00
Sinking Fund Reserve		7,000.00

SECOND METHOD

Profit and Loss	20,000.00	
Dividends Payable		8,000.00
Building Fund Reserve		5,000.00
Sinking Fund Reserve		7,000.00

    To appropriate profits as per resolution of the directors.

Profit and Loss	5,000.00	
Surplus		5,000.00

    To transfer balance to Surplus account.

Dividend Liability.—The student should note that the effect of a dividend declaration is to change a portion of the proprietorship into a liability. Surplus is decreased and liabilities are increased. The liability so created ranks with other liabilities, i.e., the assets of the corporation may be used to pay the liability to its stockholders equally with the payment of liabilities to outside creditors. The payment of such dividend is recorded by the cancellation of the dividend liability, as follows:

Dividends Payable 8,000.00

    Cash   8,000.00

Where there is more than one class of stock outstanding, it is customary to keep separate dividend accounts with each class.

Other Methods of Adjusting and Closing the Books.—It seems desirable at this point, although the material is applicable to any type of business organization, to discuss other methods of adjusting and closing the books than those heretofore explained. In Chapter XXVIII and previous chapters, the methods of handling deferred expense and income, and of summarizing the merchandising transactions were shown. The method given there of adjusting the ledger because of deferred expenses rested upon a classification of the various expense accounts to be adjusted as temporary proprietorship accounts. The method of adjustment effected a transfer out of the current part of the account, the asset portion of the expense, and carried it over into the next period. The balance remaining in the account after this adjustment shows the expense, that is, the amount of service or use, chargeable to the current period.

Another method of handling such items is based on an asset classification of the accounts recording them. Under this hypothesis such account titles as Postage, Stationery, Wrapping Supplies, and even Insurance (that is, unexpired insurance), are classed as asset accounts. At the close of the period when the adjustments are made, it is necessary to transfer from such asset accounts only the portions used or consumed during the current period. The balances left in the accounts represent the unused assets carried over into the next period. The difference between the two methods is indicated by the two sets of adjusting and closing entries given below.

PROBLEM. Assume that $1,000 of insurance has been purchased during the current period and that at its close unexpired insurance is $250.

FIRST METHOD.

The adjustment of the Insurance account classified as an expense account is here made by the following entry:

Insurance (Deferred) 250.00

    Insurance   250.00

The closing entry would be:

Profit and Loss 750.00

    Insurance   750.00

The ledger account would show as follows:

INSURANCE

19—		19—		
Jan. 15	500.00	Dec. 31	Deferred as unexpired	250.00
June 15	500.00		Profit and Loss	750.00

           1,000.00   1,000.00

19—

Jan. 1   250.00

SECOND METHOD.

The Insurance account is here looked upon as an asset account. The only adjustment necessary, therefore, is to remove from it the portion used, the portion remaining unused being an asset. This is effected by the following entry:

Profit and Loss   750.00

           Insurance   750.00

The ledger account would appear as follows:

                   INSURANCE

19—   19—

Jan. 15 500.00   Dec. 31 Profit and Loss 750.00

June 15 500.00

In favor of the first method it may be said that it brings out more sharply the difference between asset and expense accounts and the need for separating mixed accounts into their two elements of expense and asset. The second method requires less work.

The Trading or Selling Account.—For the purpose of summarizing the merchandising activities a separate account called Trading or Merchandise Trading is sometimes used to effect the partial summarization heretofore explained as being made in the Purchases and Sales accounts respectively. Where so used the Trading account becomes virtually the old Merchandise account with totals in place of details. The following entries will show its content and the method of handling it.

Trading   10,000.00

     Merchandise Inventory   10,000.00

          To transfer opening inventory.

Merchandise Inventory	12,000.00	
Trading		12,000.00
To set up new inventory.		
Trading	100,000.00	
Purchases		100,000.00
To transfer purchases for the period.		
Trading	3,000.00	
In-Freight and Cartage		3,000.00
To transfer in-freight and cartage expense.		
Purchase Returns and Allowances	5,000.00	
Trading		5,000.00
To transfer.		
Sales	150,000.00	
Trading		150,000.00
To transfer.		
Trading	6,000.00	
Sales Returns and Allowances		6,000.00
Trading	48,000.00	
Profit and Loss		48,000.00
To transfer the gross profit on sales.		

The Trading account is thus used as a means of separating the net sales into its two elements: (1) income, or gross profits; and (2) decrease of assets, or the cost of goods sold. This method makes the Profit and Loss account a purely summary account of income and expenses. Its chief disadvantage, however, is that a picture of the entire operations for the period is not presented in one account. One seldom finds the Trading account used in actual practice. It does serve, however, as an efficient teaching device to bring out clearly the way in which the merchandise accounts are adjusted and summarized in order to effect a separation of the income and decrease in asset elements.

CHAPTER XLI
HANDLING THE CASH

General Considerations.—In keeping record of the various properties of a concern, the greatest care is usually exercised in accounting for the asset cash. This is done because of the difficulty in tracing money that is lost or stolen and the ease with which the thief may get rid of it, due to its universal use as a medium of exchange, and due also to its great value in comparison with its small bulk. Merchandise, supplies, and the like, may be purloined or misappropriated, but not so easily and profitably. Oftentimes, however, unless care is exercised in safe-keeping it, large losses occur also in merchandise. Absolute prevention of losses cannot be expected even with the employment of all possible precautions, but experience shows that certain general safeguards may be placed about both cash and merchandise. In the ultimate analysis the best safeguard is the integrity of the employee; still the employer should not tempt the employee by making the abstraction of his cash an easy performance.

Principle of the Double Record.—A fundamental principle in the handling of cash is to secure a double—not a duplicate—record of its receipt and disbursement. The practice of depositing in a bank all cash receipts and making disbursements only by check should be followed invariably, because it secures this double record—the bank's record and the cashier's record. Any discrepancy is detected whenever comparison of the two records is made. When the bank's record is compared with the cash book record, the balances shown by each are seldom in agreement, chiefly because of the outstanding checks which have not yet been presented to the bank for payment. This requires a reconciliation of the two balances before proof of correctness is secured, which is usually accomplished by subtracting from the bank balance the amount of the outstanding checks. Other adjustments are sometimes necessary. These are explained and a form of reconciliation statement is shown on page 475.

Most concerns object, however, to issuing checks for small amounts, and set therefore a minimum below which they do not issue them. For the purpose of paying smaller amounts, a petty cash fund is provided from which disbursements are made in cash. This fund is established, in the first instance, by a check on the general cash and is from time to time replenished in the same way. In this manner the double record is maintained.

Handling the Petty Cash.—There are two general methods of handling the petty cash. Under the one, entry of the check creating the fund is made as an immediate charge to some expense account and no further accounting is required. This method is based on the theory that the cash is to be used for petty expenses anyway, and might as well be so charged now as later. Subsequent amounts for replenishment of the petty cash are treated in the same way. The objection to this method, from the accounting viewpoint, is that it results in an inaccurate record of expense distribution and a misstatement of the facts in that it charges to expense an item which at the time of the charge is still a part of the general cash fund. The second and chief objection is that it encourages in the petty cashier loose methods in handling and accounting for the fund, as usually no strict reckoning is required.

The second method, known as the "imprest method," is in more general favor. This charges the original check creating the fund to an account called "Petty Cash." The petty cashier is required to secure a receipted bill, sales ticket, or other voucher for every petty cash item of expenditure, so that at all times the amount of cash in his possession added to the receipted bills and vouchers must equal the original amount in the fund. Usually the fund is a fixed amount, its size depending upon the needs of the business for these small expenditures. When the cash in the fund becomes low, the petty cashier turns over his receipted bills to the general cashier, who issues a check for their exact total to replenish the petty cash by the amount of its depletion, thus restoring it to its original fixed amount.

The expenditures as shown by the receipted bills and vouchers are classified and entered by either of the following two methods: (1) as a charge to the several accounts through the general cash book, offsetting the petty cash replenishing check; in this case no charge appears in the "Petty Cash" account except the item covering the original check; or (2) by an entry through the journal debiting the various expenses and other items and crediting Petty Cash. This latter method necessitates charging in the general cash book the replenishing check to Petty Cash as an offset to the journal credit of the same amount. Most accountants consider the postings to the Petty Cash unnecessary—except the original—and so check both in cash book and journal. If, however, posting to the Petty Cash account in the general ledger is made whenever the fund is replenished, this will serve to indicate the activity of the fund on the face of the ledger account—information which could just as easily be obtained from the petty cash book. The imprest method thus effects a careful accounting of the petty expenditures.

The Petty Cash Book.—The petty cash book is usually a columnar record with the amount columns to the right of the explanation space. The first column is the receipts column, the second the disbursements column, and the others show under appropriate titles the distribution of disbursements. One form of the book is shown in Form 39, with typical entries and balancing.

Form 39. Petty Cash Book

Sometimes the classified summary which is made the basis of the general cash book or journal entry referred to above, is shown in the petty cash book, the account titles being written in the explanation column, with the amounts opposite in the credit column underneath the $100 total. The items of this summary are then posted to the ledger, and the debit of the replenishing check to Petty Cash on the general cash book is "checked" in the ledger folio column. Or if the distributive column titles give sufficiently analyzed account titles, their totals may be posted without formal summarization, posting being shown by the small-figure ledger page in each column, as in the illustration. Where the petty cash book is used as a posting medium, of course no summarization of it is made either in the journal or the general cash book.

Keeping the Bank Account.—Several different methods of keeping the bank account are in use. Sometimes the check stub is the only record kept; in Chapter XXIII reference was made to the two methods of keeping the account for the entry of deposits—either on the face or the back of the stub. When the entry is made on the face, each check is usually subtracted from the previous balance and the new balance is shown. When deposits are recorded on the back of the stub—or on a special deposit interleaf—check totals and deposit totals may be carried forward from leaf to leaf without showing any balance.

A better method is to use the stub only as a memo from which to make formal entry in the cash book columns—one for deposits on the debit side and one for checks on the credit side. These bank columns may be used, first, for the purpose of keeping the bank account, by showing the totals of deposits—but not the items composing each deposit—and the totals of the checks that have been drawn; and second, for the purpose of furnishing weekly or monthly totals for posting to a ledger account kept with the bank, thus making the ledger self-balancing without having to bring in the cash book balance.

If, however, the principle of double record (explained earlier in the chapter) is followed, there is no need of a *special* bank deposits column, since the total of the Net Cash column gives the amount of each day's deposits, and similarly the Net Cash column on the credit side shows the checks drawn against the bank. Thus the policy of depositing in the bank all receipts and disbursing only by check has an added advantage in that it simplifies the keeping of the record of cash as well as proving it. Under this method, the cash journals may be summarized, just as the other journals, and posted to a Cash account in the ledger. Detailed instructions for the handling of the entries, balancing, and closing under this method are given in Chapter XXXI.

Another and rather unusual method of keeping the cash book is to carry a Currency column on each side, supplemented by Bank columns for deposits and checks on the debit and credit sides respectively. In the debit Currency column are entered all receipts of money in regular course. When the bank deposit is made up, its amount is entered as a charge to the bank in the credit Currency column and also, as a memo, in the debit Bank column. As checks are drawn they are entered in the credit Bank column. Thus the balance of the Currency columns should show the actual amount of cash in the cash drawer at any time, and the difference between the Bank columns should show the balance in the bank. Though somewhat complicated, the method has its advantages under conditions where currency accumulates before being deposited in the bank.

Of course, under all methods of keeping the cash record, the requirement that all cash received be deposited and payment be made only by check should be strictly adhered to.

Entering Checks on the Cash Book.—When all disbursements are by check, every check drawn must be entered on the cash book and accounted for. Entry should be made in numerical sequence with suitable explanation of any spoiled checks. The amount of the spoiled check may be left blank or entered as usual, but in the latter case the spoiled check must also be included in the day's deposits, and the bank's cancellation stamp must be secured. Neither the deposit nor disbursement is posted, each entry being marked "contra" by way of explanation. This effects an inflation of the total receipts and disbursements, but inasmuch as the bank's record also shows the inflation, an adequate safeguard is secured. The new check replacing the one spoiled is entered in regular order.

The method just discussed is perhaps the best way of recording the exchange of checks for cash. Sometimes a concern is asked to exchange its check for currency, the party making the request desiring to send the check through the mails or for some other purpose. The entry is best made on both the debit and the credit side of the cash book with reference "contra" in each case, but neither entry need be posted. This makes the cash book record check against the bank record and shows the full history of the transaction. When a check is cashed in currency, or when a check of larger amount is received in payment of a debt and the difference is returned in cash, no record need be made of the check, as only the nature—not the amount—of the deposit for the day is changed and no disbursement is made which affects the bank account. When, however, a check is issued for "change" in lieu of currency, record should be made, debit and credit, as shown above.

Branch Cash—The Working Fund.—Frequently cash working funds must be provided for the current expenses of branches or of a factory located at a distance from the main office. When the branch or factory keeps a separate set of books, it must be charged with the advances of the working fund and a careful audit of the way the fund is handled must be made periodically, just as would be done with an independent concern.

Such cash transfers may also be handled by the imprest method as explained above. The original advance is charged to "Factory" or "Branch Cash," and is deposited in the branch's local bank to the credit of the head office, the branch having the privilege of using it. The branch may draw checks against the fund, sending the canceled checks to the head office as supporting vouchers for its disbursements. These canceled checks become the basis for the replenishing checks and also for the charges for branch expenditures made on the head office books.

If the branch is a selling agency making sales for cash and on account, a modification of the system is necessary. Daily reports should be required from the branch. Its cash receipts should be deposited daily and a duplicate deposit ticket should be forwarded to the head office by the bank. The bank should be asked also to forward all canceled checks. All collections on customers' accounts should be made from the head office. This does not prevent the abstraction of cash before deposit, but it at least places control or oversight of the bank cash account in the hands of the head office and secures a careful accounting of it.

Safeguarding Cash—General Principles.—Proper safeguards for the cash should always be provided. The method of the double record—the bank's and the owner's cash book—is good so far as it goes and acts as a check on cash transactions *after* the record is made, but does not insure that the cash book record will be made correctly in the first place. There are ways in which cash received may get into the cashier's or salesmen's pockets instead of the cash book. No system or method has yet been devised to prevent this entirely. Every system must rest at some point upon the integrity of the human agent, and will fail of its full efficiency and intended results if the agent fails in the trust reposed in him. Every effort should be made to prevent both petty thievery—the abstraction of small sums at every opportunity—and systematic robbery mapped out and planned with infinite care and detail. Only everlasting vigilance and a system of "checks" will secure satisfactory results, as occasionally it is the *trusted* employee who is not true to the trust placed in him.

Internal Check.—By internal check is meant the method by which employees check each other's records, control not resting entirely in any one clerk. Thus a system of record-making which combines the work of the cashier and bookkeeper under one clerk or which gives the cashier access to the ledgers is one which invites dishonesty.

Where the cashier has entire control of the cash, and besides opens the incoming mail, makes up his daily deposits, has his pass-books balanced periodically, and files the canceled checks, he has every opportunity to abstract cash and falsify his records. But where he must make detailed daily reports of the cash to the manager, treasurer, or some other officer; where he is denied access to the records—except his own cash record—and where his record is subject to periodic proof; where the mail is opened first and receipts listed by an independent clerk; where a careful system of proving receipts from cash sales and of allowing no unauthorized deliveries over the counter is employed; where every member of the office force is required to take a vacation during which his work and records are cared for by other employees—there is a very satisfactory system of internal safeguards and checks.

All these devices and systems are applicable in full only in large concerns where minute division of duties is possible. In smaller concerns where many duties have to be combined under one person, the problem of safeguarding the cash and providing other measures to prevent fraud of various sorts is more difficult. In such a concern, at least the cash received through the mail should be listed first by someone other than the cashier or bookkeeper, and the daily deposit slip should be compared with this list to see that all the cash items are included. The cash received from cash sales should also be proved daily against the sales tickets.

Statement of Receipts and Disbursements.—A periodic report of cash is usually made by means of a statement of receipts and disbursements. This statement is an abstract or summary of the cash book, showing the total receipts from various sources and the causes of the disbursements and their totals. A simple form is given below:

STATEMENT OF RECEIPTS AND DISBURSEMENTS

For Week Ending..........

RECEIPTS:
Cash Sales...........................	$10,129.40	
Accounts Receivable..................	25,464.50	
Notes Discounted.....................	1,500.00	
Miscellaneous: Interest, Rebates, etc..	519.20	
Total this week................	$37,613.10	
Previous Balance...............	2,319.40	$39,932.50

DISBURSEMENTS:
Accounts Payable.....................	$28,492.10	
Salaries and Wages...................	4,193.25	
Delivery Equipment...................	250.00	
Advertising..........................	1,300.00	
Miscellaneous: Interest, General Expense, etc.........................	920.15	35,155.50
Balance on Hand, as per cash book..........		$ 4,777.00

Form 40. Weekly Statement of Receipts
and Disbursements

To assist in checking past deposits, an itemized record of daily cash receipts is often kept, analyzed as to gold, silver, currency, notes and checks. To be of value this record should be filed with the daily deposit tickets and should be later available for purposes of comparison.

CHAPTER XLII
NOTES RECEIVABLE AND PAYABLE

Conditions Precedent to the Present Use of Notes and Bills.—During the twelfth and thirteenth centuries there was much bad money in circulation in Europe because of the widespread practice of coin-shaving and the entire lack of standards of purity of the coins. If a monarch needed funds for war or government purposes, his easiest way of getting them was to increase the amount of base alloy in the coins of the country or to increase the rate of seigniorage. As the former method might be resorted to several times during the reign of one sovereign, the weight and relative purity of metallic coins had no relation to the denominated value of the coins, and they fell under general suspicion. Consequently, only the money dealers, who could determine the actual value of coins by assaying them, were willing to trade for coins. These men gradually became the custodians of moneys for merchants, who were given receipts showing the assay value of the coins deposited. Because the receipt represented tested and proven value, it was a more acceptable medium of exchange than the coins themselves.

Medieval trade was subject to many perils, chief of which was that from robbers. Any safeguards placed about the transportation of money from one place to another, or any method devised for settling debts without the transportation of coin and bullion, were more than welcome. Out of these conditions arose the method of settling debts by means of drafts. The draft, not countenanced by law at first, had standing, however, under the "law merchant," the code of rules recognized by merchants as governing commercial relations. This code was later incorporated by statute into the law of the country.

These two kinds of paper, the one a receipt for coin which was in the nature of a demand promise to pay, the other a counterpart of the modern draft, were the forerunners of our promissory notes and bills of exchange of the present day. The law with regard to the bill or draft became settled as the result of the practice of merchants sooner than that relating to notes.

The Titles "Notes" and "Bills."—In this way, the word "bill" became an established term. The titles "bills receivable" and "bills payable" still cling to both classes of items. Inasmuch as the accepted bill is practically identical with the promissory note, and the title "bill" is so often used interchangeably with the word "invoice," it is advisable to use the terms *notes receivable* and *notes payable* instead of bills receivable and bills payable. Some advocate the use of the title "acceptances" in order to distinguish accepted bills from promissory notes. Unless these two classes of paper are large enough in volume to justify it, little advantage is secured by this separation of their bookkeeping record. However, in the case of trade acceptances, i.e., acceptances based on particular sales of goods and therefore evidencing bona fide commercial transactions as the basis for the extension of credit, it is advisable, because of their superior rating in the money markets, to segregate this class of acceptances from notes and other acceptances.

Relation of the Note to the Open Account.—In the preliminary discussion of the relation of the note to the open account in Chapter XXI, it was pointed out that both the note and account are claims against the person liable for payment; and that the one is carried under a class title "notes receivable," because the number of such notes is usually small, while each account receivable is carried under a separate title which designates the person liable for payment. The essential difference between the two kinds of claims is that the note is an acknowledgment of the justice of the claim and the correctness of the amount, whereas the claim under the open account may be disputed and in case of dispute requires outside proof; besides, the open account may always be offset by counterclaims and sometimes by a return of all or a part of the goods bought.

Any defenses of value under the contract for which the note was given are good defenses as between the original parties to a note; but not so as between the maker and a third party who is an innocent purchaser for value. To him the maker is liable according to the exact terms and tenor of the note. Only so could the element of negotiability be insured and the note pass from hand to hand as money. In no other sense is the note a preferred claim over the open account.

In case of bankruptcy a claim against the bankrupt under an open account and a claim under a promissory note or an acceptance made by the bankrupt before his insolvency, rank alike, both sharing pro rata in the net assets available for the satisfaction of the total claim of unsecured creditors.

Relative Liquidity of the Note and Open Account.—Compared with the liquidity of open accounts, promissory notes have a slight advantage in that they can more readily be turned into cash and at a better rate. Although an assignment of open accounts is possible by hypothecating them with a third party, the cost of such assignment is almost prohibitive and is resorted to only where the customary sources of credit are not available.

The legitimacy and the low cost of discounting notes greatly increase their liquidity. Oftentimes the question of risk, i.e., the degree of certainty of their payment when due, enters into the determination of the relative liquidity as between open accounts and promissory notes, but from this standpoint there is little, if any, difference between the two claims. Occasionally a firm, which refuses to pay its debts on open account, will meet its notes and acceptances in an effort to bolster its credit at the local banks. This phase of the question does not usually enter into the discounting operation, where the credit of the discounter is the determining factor in raising money. Of course, this may be only a temporary expedient if the note is dishonored and charged back to the bank. In some lines of business it is very common practice to secure notes for overdue accounts. If the Notes Receivable account contains many such items, its liquidity is seriously to be doubted. However, the note is usually classed as a more liquid asset than the open account.

Method of Recording Notes.—As to the accounting phase, a record is made of each note received or given, entry being to Notes Receivable or Payable, as the case may be. If the note transactions are few in number, the general journal is used for their record. Ample explanation must be given as to the essential facts of date, maker, for what received, rate of interest, due date, etc. Notes receivable must be watched carefully, as failure to present them when due releases all indorsers. There is nothing unusual in the entry when made in the general journal, its debit and credit being determined as indicated in Chapter XI.

The Note Journals.—Because the general journal does not lend itself to an easy record of the essential data pertaining to note transactions, a separate book is oftentimes kept for this purpose. This special book may be used merely as a memorandum record for carrying the detailed explanation of the Journal entry; or it may become a special journal that is used as an integral part of the accounting system, and, when so used, posting to the ledgers is made direct therefrom. The use of this special journal is always advisable when note transactions are numerous. A bills or notes receivable journal may be ruled as shown on Form 41. The notes payable journal differs but slightly from the notes receivable journal.

Form 41. Notes Receivable Journal
(left and right hand pages)

If the bill book is for memorandum use only, the "Amounts Credited" columns may be omitted. If it is a real note *journal*, its debit and credit equilibrium is shown through summary entry at posting time. The total debit is to Notes Receivable for the amount of that column's total. If it were not for the fact that sometimes notes are received in whose face amount is included not only the credit to the customer but an interest item as well, there would be no need of credit columns. The note journal would then be operated just as is any simple special journal, with a debit to Notes Receivable and the same amount credited to the customer; but when interest is included, the note is best recorded in an additional column, separating the credit to Customers from that to Interest. If notes are numerous, a distributive column in the cash book should be used for receipts from notes, in order to secure a total posting to the credit of Notes Receivable account.

Referring to the left-hand page of the illustrated ruling (Form 41), the face amount of the note receivable is entered in the Notes Receivable column, and the due date in one of the narrow columns headed "When Due," each of these columns representing a separate month. In this way it is easy to find the total of all the notes due in a given month and the amount of cash to be expected from their payment. For this purpose, however, it is best to use a note journal arranged by *months of maturity* on the principle of a "tickler." In such a journal one page is reserved for each month, and the notes are entered, not on the page for the month when received, but on that for the month when due. Thus a note received in January and due in March should be entered on the March page. To secure a summary of all notes received during each month for posting to Notes Receivable account at the end of each month, the various month pages are totaled and "recapped" on a special page. On this "recap" page, at the end of January, say, will be entered the total of the January page, giving the notes received in and maturing during January; the total of the February page, giving the notes received in January but maturing in February; etc., for each month during the year. The grand total is the amount to be posted to the general ledger, representing all notes received during January.

This type of journal gives easy control over maturities, and forecasts for a given month the amount of cash receipts from notes.

Notes Entered at Face Value Always.—Some notes are interest-bearing from their date of issue; others only after their due date when not paid. Even on non-interest-bearing notes, the law allows the charging of interest for their overdue period. From the standpoint of strict accuracy, a note payable at a future time is not worth its face value at the time of entry, unless it is interest-bearing from date at approximately as high a rate as the current discount rate. Its present value is such an amount as when placed on interest will equal the face at its due date. That value increases day by day until it reaches par or face on the due date. Because of the practical difficulties encountered in the numerous adjustments necessary under any other method of entry, universal practice countenances the bringing of the note onto the books at a slightly inflated value, i.e., face value, at the time of entry. Face value is the amount of the credit to the customer's account; it shows the amount to be collected on account of the note; and if interest-bearing, the amount on which the interest is based. Accordingly, the note transaction is entered at its face value. Where the note is interest-bearing and the face plus the interest is paid at maturity, credit is in two items, one to Notes Receivable for the face, and the other to Interest Income for the amount received as interest.

Occasionally, the interest for the period the note is to run is added to the amount of the debt, and the sum is made the face of a non-interest-bearing note. The purpose of such procedure is to secure a compounding of interest for the first period if the note is not paid at maturity. The entry of the note on the books is a debit to Notes Receivable for its face, and credits to the customer for the amount of the debt and to Interest Income for the amount of the interest. Only a credit to Notes Receivable is made when the note is paid. The credit to Interest Income, before the interest is actually earned and received, is necessitated by its pre-estimate and inclusion in the face of the note. Were a balance sheet drawn up on that date, the entire amount of this interest would be shown as deferred income.

The Interest Accounts.—As explained in Chapter XV, when interest items are numerous two interest accounts are usually carried on the ledger, one for Interest Income and one for Interest Cost. Sometimes, however, only the one account, Interest and Discount, is carried, and if it is desirable to separate the two classes of interest, it may be done by entering the debit and credit totals of the Interest and Discount account—instead of simply the balance—when the trial balance is taken. Needless to say, bank discount—interest paid in advance—is the only kind of discount recorded under this account title; it must not be confused with discounts on sales and purchases, which receive different accounting treatment.

CHAPTER XLIII
PROBLEMS ENCOUNTERED IN RECORDING NOTES RECEIVABLE AND PAYABLE

Entries in the Account.—The elementary discussion of entries to the note accounts in Chapter XIV will be reviewed and amplified here.

Where the Notes Receivable account in the ledger shows each note separately rather than the totals of the items, good practice countenances the recording of the *credits* in this account in non-chronologic order. Thus, when a customer settles his promissory note and the document is returned to him, the credit to Notes Receivable should be entered directly opposite the original debit item. This brings each complete note transaction on a single line and shows at a glance which notes are outstanding, as evidenced by the blank lines on the credit side of the account.

When, however, the credit items are entered in chronological order, the same purpose may be accomplished by the use of an index figure for the original debit and the corresponding credit item.

What has been said above applies equally to notes payable.

The Discounted Note.—In the booking of notes receivable discounted and accepted drafts, a problem arises because of the legal right accorded the holders of notes, in case of non-payment by the maker, to look for payment to any or all of the indorsers, provided certain formal requirements are complied with. Whenever a business house transfers a note by any method of indorsement (except the qualified), it incurs a *contingent liability*, which may become a *real liability* if the maker of the note fails to meet the obligation at maturity. Since it is the function of good accounting to present *all* the financial facts bearing on the business, it is evident that whenever a contingent liability is incurred, it should be entered in the books of account. Very frequently, however, this liability is ignored, with the result that it is eventually lost sight of altogether.

The usual, though incorrect, method of journalizing a note discounted transaction is as follows:

- Cash
- Interest Cost
- Notes Receivable

Usually when an asset is sold, a credit to the account of the asset sold is correct, but not so in the case of notes sold, i.e., of notes discounted. For the purpose of showing the complete facts, the entry at the time of discount should be made as follows:

- Cash
- Interest Cost
- Notes Receivable Discounted

and at maturity when the note is paid by the maker:

- Notes Receivable Discounted
- Notes Receivable

The effect of the first entry is to set up a suspense account, Notes Receivable Discounted, representing the contingent liability on the discounted note. The effect of the second entry is, first, to cancel the *credit* of the Notes Receivable Discounted account, because upon payment of the note by the maker the contingent liability ceases; and second, to cancel the original *debit* to the Notes Receivable account which was made at the time the promissory note was received but which remained *unchanged* when the note was discounted, because it was still needed to record the contingent asset which would become a real asset in case the contingent liability became a real liability.

It has been argued that the above treatment of discounted notes stretches the theory of debit and credit nearly to the breaking point. It must be observed, however, that unless accounting records are so kept as to give the necessary information, they are not serving the purpose which justifies their existence. Any theory which prevents the proper functioning of the records must be changed; there is no place for it.

It would be incorrect, however, to regard Notes Receivable Discounted as an independent liability account, because it only represents a contingent liability. The two accounts, Notes Receivable and Notes Receivable Discounted, must be considered together, the latter account being set up merely for the purpose of keeping notes discounted under review until their final status is determined. The purpose of the Notes Receivable Discounted account is in a way similar to that of the valuation accounts of depreciating assets. The asset account is held at its original figure, and in order to determine the present value of the asset, the valuation account must be referred to. Similarly, the asset account, Notes Receivable, is held at its original figure, even though some or all of the notes are discounted, and in order to know the amount of notes receivable actually on hand, the credit of the Notes Discounted account must be subtracted from the debit of the Notes Receivable account. In the balance sheet, Notes Receivable Discounted is not shown as a liability item, but appears as a deduction from Notes Receivable, only the difference, representing the amount of notes actually in possession, being extended among the assets. It should be noted, however, that this contingent liability is oftentimes shown on the liability side of the balance sheet, the corresponding asset, Notes Receivable, then being separated into two items, "Notes on Hand," and "Notes under Discount per contra." Banks uniformly follow this practice in showing these and similar items.

At maturity of the note the final entry (Notes Receivable Discounted debit and Notes Receivable credit) is placed upon the books as illustrated above. Usually no formal notice is received by the indorser that the note has been paid by the maker. In case the note is dishonored, prompt notice would be sent, and failure to receive such notice implies that the note has been duly paid.

What has been said above concerning notes applies equally to accepted drafts, the legal character of which is identical with that of notes, the status of the drawer of an accepted draft being the same as that of the first indorser of a promissory note. The contingent liability arising from the transfer of all negotiable instruments should usually be shown.

In some instances, however, there may be good practical reasons for not adhering to the above principle. When, for instance, a large number of notes and acceptances are handled and the experience of the business shows that few of them are ever dishonored, or if the matter is under constant review by the financial manager, it might be considered an unnecessary requirement to make use of a separate Notes Receivable Discounted account. It must be left to the judgment of the accountant to decide which method is preferable in connection with the needs of the business. However, if no current account is kept to show the contingent liability, at the end of the period the balance sheet must be made to show the amount of discounted notes still outstanding as of the closing date of the period.

The Dishonored Note.—A note is dishonored either when the maker refuses payment upon its legal presentation at maturity or when there is sufficient evidence that he intends to refuse. When a note is dishonored, a formal protest is required in order to hold the indorsers. The payee appears before a notary public or some other officer with notarial powers, and makes oath that legal presentment of the note has been made and that the payment was refused. The notary then takes the note and personally presents it for payment to the maker. If payment is still refused, the notary makes a certificate of protest and mails notices of the protest to all indorsers desired to be held. Such notice is sufficient basis for action to recover from the party or parties thus notified.

In making the accounting record of a dishonored note, a number of problems may arise. These problems deal with these two situations: (1) when the note is dishonored in the hands of the named payee; and (2) when the note has been discounted by him and is charged back on account of dishonor. To illustrate the entries required, take the following two cases:

PROBLEM. Case 1. Promissory note made by P. Canning for $100. Payee, D. Johnson. Due December 15. At maturity Johnson presents the note for payment, but payment is refused.

Case 2. Promissory note for $250 made by P. Canning. Payee, D. Johnson. Due December 15. Note was discounted by Johnson. Final holder is A. Andrews who presents the note for payment on December 15, but payment is refused.

The questions arising in connection with these two cases may be stated as follows: What record should be made on December 15—

- (a) By D. Johnson in case 1.
- (b) By A. Andrews in case 2.
- (c) By D. Johnson in case 2.

(a) D. Johnson, at the time he received the note from Canning, made the following entry:

Notes Receivable 100.00

  P. Canning 100.00

and on December 15, in order to show that the note is dishonored, he may make either of the following two entries:

(1) P. Canning   100.00

  Notes Receivable   100.00

     or

(2) Notes Receivable Dishonored 100.00

  Notes Receivable   100.00

Entry (1) takes the charge out of the note account and sets it up again as a claim on Canning's open account. Entry (2) transfers the charge to a Notes Receivable Dishonored account. Entry (2) is theoretically a better entry than entry (1), because from the latter it might be inferred that the nature of the claim has changed from a note claim to an open account claim. Such change has not taken place, however; Johnson's claim against Canning is still on the note. Therefore, entry (1) is not true to the facts.

On the other hand, entry (1) has an important advantage over entry (2), because by posting entry (1) Canning's personal account in the ledger is made to show the fact that one of his promissory notes was dishonored. This is a matter of very great importance, especially if Canning should again apply for an extension of credit.

If the second method is adopted, it is clear that the posting of the entry will not show the dishonor of the note on Canning's account. It is essential, therefore, that the bookkeeper should make a special memo of the fact in that account. If the bookkeeper could be depended upon to make such memorandum entry, the desired purpose of making Canning's account show a complete record of all dealings with him would be accomplished. Any treatment consistent with accounting principles and securing a complete history in one place of all dealings with the same individual satisfies all requirements.

(b) A. Andrews, who is the last indorsee of the note, should make the following entry at the time the note is dishonored:

Notes Receivable Dishonored 250.00

  Notes Receivable   250.00

The Notes Receivable Dishonored account represents Andrews' claim against any or all the indorsers whom he wishes to hold responsible. Instead of this, an entry might be made corresponding to entry (1) discussed above.

(c) In case the note should be charged back to Johnson, either by Andrews or by one of the other indorsers, he should make the following entries:

Notes Receivable Discounted   250.00

  Cash   250.00

P. Canning (or Notes Receivable Dishonored) 250.00

  Notes Receivable   250.00

It will be noticed that these two entries completely reverse the two original entries made by Johnson, viz.:

Notes Receivable 250.00

  P. Canning 250.00

at the time he received the promissory note from Canning, and

Cash   250.00

    Notes Receivable Discounted   250.00

when he transferred the note by indorsement.

It is to be understood that all expenses in connection with the dishonored note should be charged either to the personal account of the maker or to the Notes Receivable Dishonored account, as the case may be.

Where the Notes Receivable Dishonored account is used, it secures a good analysis of the claims against customers from the standpoint of probable realization and gives a relatively better basis for the bad debts estimate than that offered by the other manner of treatment. Of course, the use of such an account is limited to the ledger; it never appears as such on the balance sheet, being included there in the customers' accounts with ample reserve for uncollectible items.

The Classification of Notes.—The Notes Receivable account should carry only the short-time notes of customers, and thus be a truly current asset. Long-time notes and those secured by mortgage should be booked under separate account titles. For a similar reason, the notes receivable given by officers, employees, or stockholders of the corporation should have separate booking, as these notes are given for the purpose of making formal record and acknowledgment of indebtedness, usually without regard to time of payment. Such notes do not constitute easily convertible assets, and therefore should not be recorded under the same account with short-time customers' notes.

Notes Receivable Out as Collateral.—Notes receivable are sometimes given as collateral security for a loan. When they are so used, no bookkeeping problem is involved—though a memorandum to show their use as such should appear in the note account, and in case a balance sheet is drawn up, a cross-reference or a footnote should indicate the liability secured by the notes. However, the sale of the notes to satisfy the loan constitutes a regular business transaction, which should be recorded in the proper manner.

Note Renewals and Partial Payments.—The renewal of notes and partial payments are other features met in the accounting for notes. The renewal of a note is rather a question of business policy than of accounting procedure. When a note is renewed, it is usually better to deliver up the old note and secure a new one in its stead. The accounts should reflect the transaction by showing cancellation of the old and receipt of the new note. If the old note is extended, a memorandum of that fact should be entered in the ledger account.

From the financial standpoint, if neither note is interest-bearing, the amount of the renewal note should be larger than that of the old note, to cover the cost of deferring payment to a future date. For example, if the old note amounts to $1,000 and is renewed two months later, the amount of the new note should be fixed at $1,000 plus 1% interest, or $1,010.

In accounting for partial payments, no new accounting principle is involved. When such payments are numerous, additional space in the note journal and in the ledger should be provided for the purpose of facilitating the actual work of making the book record.

CHAPTER XLIV
DISCOUNTS

Definition and Kinds.—A discount is a deduction from a listed or named figure. The manufacturer or wholesaler in making up his catalogue for the trade usually enters his products at certain prices—called "list prices"—which are not selling prices but only nominal amounts on which the actual sale prices are based. For reasons to be explained later, he offers buyers a deduction from list prices which is called "trade discount." The usual quotation of sale prices is at so many per cent below the list prices.

Among practically all merchants it is a very common practice to bill goods to customers with settlement allowed on an optional basis. The goods may be billed "net," i.e., the full amount shown in the invoice must be paid. Since there is a relationship between the time allowed for payment and the amount to be paid, most concerns have an established credit term, at the end of which they expect full settlement of the account, but, as an inducement for earlier payment, they offer a reduction in the amount to be paid. This is stated usually at so much per cent below the billed price, and is generally called "cash discount." The practice had its origin in conditions prevailing at the close of the Civil War when business failures were numerous and the risk on open accounts even for short credit terms was very great.

Bankers when making loans usually deduct from the face of the loan the interest charge for the use of the money. This deduction is called "bank discount."

Merchants usually allow a deduction for the prepayment of a customer's note, and this is called "commercial discount," to distinguish it from bank discount, although the two kinds of discount are essentially identical; the only difference being that in the one case a bank buys a merchant's note, while in the other case it is a transaction between two commercial houses, the one buying back its own note before it is legally due.

Trade discounts are very seldom recorded on the books, the actual selling price and not the list price being entered. Cash discounts are invariably recorded. If the merchant knew at the time of the sale which optional basis of settlement the buyer would choose, he could record the transaction at a net figure on that basis without entering the discount portion. This would, of course, result in a varying figure at which sales were booked. Accordingly, the almost invariable practice is to record sales at the gross amount and show by means of the Sales Discount account the acceptance of any lesser sum in settlement in accordance with the sales contract. Bank discount has to be booked in order to show the cost of the loan which is the difference between the asset received, cash, and the asset parted with, notes. The matter of bank discount has been treated in some detail in Chapter XLII.

The Method and Purpose of Trade Discount.—Trade discounts are so universally met with in business that an extended discussion of them will be of value to the student. As has been stated, a trade discount is a deduction from the list price and it serves two purposes. It is apparent that the prices listed in the catalogue cannot be changed until a new catalogue is printed and that it would not be practicable to print a new catalogue to make a change in selling prices. Therefore, instead of reprinting the catalogue whenever market prices fluctuate and a change in the list prices must be made, sheets containing the discounts allowed from list prices are published, the expense of which is much less than that of a new catalogue.

The other purpose served by the trade discount is in partly concealing the real quotation. Without the rate of discount allowed from that list, the catalogue tells nothing of the real price. In this way a concern in publishing its catalogue does not lay itself open to the risk of being underbid by competitors publishing later catalogues.

Prices may be quoted at a single discount or by means of a series of discounts, each taking as its base the net amount left after deducting the next preceding discount. Examples will illustrate:

1. Goods listed at $250 are quoted at 20% off.
The sale price here is $200.

2. Goods listed at $500 are quoted at 50% and 20% off.
50% off $500 leaves $250.
20% " $250 " $200—the same real sale price as in No. 1.

3. Goods listed at $750 are priced at 50%, 33⅓%, and 20% off.
50% off $750 leaves $375.
33⅓% " $375 " $250.
20% " $250 " $200—the same as in Nos. 1 and 2.

It is apparent that the *list* prices without the trade discounts tell nothing as to the *real* prices.

Methods of Calculation.—Short methods for calculating trade discounts when given in a series are often employed. For a series of only two discounts, a single rate equivalent to the two may be found by subtracting their product from their sum—always treating them as decimals. Thus a series of 20 and 20 is equivalent to a single rate of 36,

$$(.20 + .20 = .40; .20 \times .20 = .04; .40 - .04 = .36).$$

Another method of calculating trade discounts, and one applicable to a series of any number of discounts, is to treat the discount off as equivalent to one-minus-the-discount on. Thus a discount of 15% is equivalent to 85% of the list. An additional discount of 10% is equivalent to 90% of the new base, or 90% of 85% of the original list, or 76.5%. Thus a continued multiplication of the "percentages on" gives the single sale price multiplier to be applied to the list price. If the single discount rate is desired, it is secured by subtracting the multiplier from 1, or 100%. Take the series 60, 20, 10, and 10 off. This is equivalent to 40, 80, 90, and 90 on, or 25.92% on

$$(.40 \times .80 \times .90 \times .90 = .2592).$$

The single discount rate equivalent to the series is, therefore, 74.08% (100%-25.92% = 74.08%).

The *order* in which the discounts of a series are used is immaterial, as the order of the factors does not affect the product.

The method just illustrated develops the reason for the first special rule given above for a series of two discounts. Let the discounts be "a"% and "b"%. The "percentages on" are, therefore, $(1-a)$% and $(1-b)$% whose product, algebraically, is $1- [(a + b)-ab]$, which is the single "percentage on"; from which it is readily seen that the single rate discount is $a + b-ab$, i.e., the sum of the two rates minus their product. Similar rules can be developed for longer series, but they are too complicated for easy application.

There is now available a "discolog" table, an ingenious reference table, which is operated somewhat like a logarithmic table. It gives quickly and easily the single discount rate equivalent to any series of discounts.

The chief value of the single rate equivalent to the discount series is in its use for comparative purposes, as it indicates which of two discount series is the more favorable. When a large number of selling prices must be computed, all having the same discount series, the single rate method of calculation also has a great advantage over the long method, which makes use of the series. This is true especially when the work is done with the use of a calculating machine.

The Nature of Cash Discount—Its Basic Elements.—Where goods are sold on credit with a cash discount offering, four main factors of cost, not incurred when goods are sold for cash, must be provided for. These are:

- 1. Credit investigation and collection expense.
- 2. Bookkeeping and billing expense.
- 3. Loss from uncollectible accounts.
- 4. Interest for the use of the money—credit.

The cash discount is offered to free the vendor especially from costs (3) and (4), which are the heaviest of the four.

There is a direct relation between the credit period and the loss from bad debts. Thus, if a credit period of 30 days results in a given volume of such losses an extension of the credit term to 60 days would undoubtedly result in increased losses, assuming that all factors, such as investigation of the risk, credit supervision, collection effort, etc., remain the same. Inasmuch as the sale price must be sufficiently high to provide for loss from bad debts, the credit term enters into the determination of the price.

The other of the two main factors of cost, the interest charge on the cash sale price, represents the cost of being deprived of the use of the capital tied up in outstanding accounts.

Thus, when a discount is offered for early settlement, under normal conditions the controlling factors are the risk or cost of insurance against loss from bad debts and the interest cost. Special circumstances, however, may make it expedient to offer more or less favorable terms of settlement. Normally, terms of 2% off if paid within 10 days, the billed price being on a 30-day credit period (2/10, n/30), measures two things: (1) the saving secured by receipt of the money 20 days earlier; and (2) the saving in the item of bad debts expense brought about by shortening the term for which credit is extended from 30 to 10 days. How much of the cash discount is for interest and how much for bad debts can be seen by comparing the current interest rate, say 6%, with the discount rate reduced to a yearly basis. A discount of 2% which effects the collection of a debt at the end of 10 days, when the net credit term is 30 days, secures the use of the money by the vendor 20 days earlier than the full credit term would effect. 2% for 20 days is equivalent to 36% on a yearly basis.

Showing Cash Discount in the Trading Section.—Opinions differ among accountants as to the proper treatment of cash discounts in the profit and loss summary at the close of a period. Some maintain that the discount is a trading or selling item, and show it, therefore, in the trading section of the statement. Their theory is that discounts on sales partake somewhat of the nature of trade discounts, that the real selling price is, after all, what is received for a particular bill of goods. According to this theory, if goods are billed at $1,000, and $980 is accepted as full settlement, the sale should be shown only at $980 on the books. At the time of offering an optional basis for settlement, however, the merchant does not know which basis the customer will accept, and he therefore enters the sale on his books at the highest offer. Later, if the customer settles on the more favorable option, the discount he takes is logically a deduction from sales.

On the other hand, if the discount is explained as a bait offered to secure customers, it should be treated as a selling cost. Consequently, on either of these two theories, cash discount would have to be shown in the trading section of the profit and loss statement, in the one case as a direct deduction from sales, in the other as a selling cost.

Correct Method of Showing Cash Discount.—Other accountants maintain that cash discount is a financial management item; that a manager, in order to secure ready funds with which to take advantage of the discounts offered him on his own purchases, extends to his customers sufficient inducement to secure the early and prompt payment of their bills. The difference between the saving on purchases payments and the cost of securing early payment on sales, is the measure of the efficiency of such financial policy.

While this explanation of cash discount on sales as a cost of securing funds may have some foundation, it does not give a fully satisfactory explanation of the practice. If cash discount has been correctly analyzed as being composed of the two factors, interest and bad debts expense, there can be no question as to the place of its showing. Both factors are financial items and they should therefore be placed in that section of the profit and loss statement. In this work cash discounts will be treated as a financial management item.

Account Titles for Cash Discounts.—In booking cash discounts, two accounts are used—one for the discounts on sales, and the other for the discounts on purchases. Self-descriptive titles are Sales Discount and Purchases Discount, which seem better than Discounts Allowed and Discounts Received and other similar titles sometimes met with.

Methods of Booking Cash Discount.—In booking cash discounts, any one of four methods may be used. In Chapter XIX, "The Cash Journals," two of these methods were shown and the explanations will not be repeated here. Explanations of the other two methods follow.

1. Entry is made only in the cash book through the use of a non-cash-discount column on the receipts side. This was also fully explained and illustrated in Chapter XIX. In the illustration given there, this discount column was not used in finding the cash balance, because net cash columns were employed, thus making unnecessary the use of any other column to find the cash balance.

2. Entry is made as in method 1 above, but the discount column is used in finding the cash balance. Where, as sometimes happens, the net cash column is omitted, the true receipts can be found only by *subtracting* the amount of the discount from the other column totals.

The closing summary for the columnar cash book, explained in Chapter XIX, shows one method of handling the discount column total. While all other summary entries for the cash receipts are *credits*, the discount summary is a *debit*. Because of this fact, the discount total is sometimes shown on the disbursements side of the cash book among the summary entries of the other columns, in which case the word "contra" is written after the words "Sales Discount," showing that the amount has come from the discount column on the opposite page. Similarly for the Purchases Discount.

The only advantage of this method is to bring all summary debit postings on one side of the cash book and all credits on the other. Where the cash book is operated according to method 2, the closing summaries are made as shown in Form 42, using columns on the debit side for Customers, Sales Discount, and Sundry; and on the credit side for Creditors, Purchases Discount, and Sundry. As there is no net cash column, the totals for Customers and Creditors are not all cash. To clear them of their non-cash elements, the discounts can be subtracted from their respective Customers' and Creditors' totals, and only the net brought over into the Sundry columns; or the subtraction can be effected by adding the discounts to the opposite side. The use of a Net Cash column simplifies the summarization of the cash book and should always be employed. Treatment 2 is shown only because it is sometimes met with in practice.

Securing Information as to Neglected Discounts.—Some accountants have pointed out the desirability of bringing before a manager or proprietor the cost of his failure to take advantage of discounts offered him. To show this cost the following method of entering a purchase has been suggested:

Purchases	100.00	
Purchases Discount	5.00	
Vendor		105.00

The *net* amount of the bill is thus charged to Purchases, the discount offered to Purchases Discount, and the Vendor is credited with the billed amount. When payment is made on any of the optional bases offered, entry is made as follows:

(1) Vendor	105.00	
Cash		105.00

or

(2) Vendor 105.00

    Cash 103.00

    Purchases Discount 2.00

Form 42. Discount Columns Used for Cash Balance
(Method No. 2)

In the case of entry (1), the net result of the whole purchase transaction is a loss or expense of the amount in Purchases Discount, because of failure to take the discount. In entry (2), if the best option is taken, viz., the entire 5%, Purchases Discount shows no balance; any less favorable option, say 2%, results in a debit balance in Purchases Discount of 3%, measuring the expense incurred through failure to take the best option. Unquestionably, the information given a manager by this Purchases Discount debit balance will claim his notice and immediate attention.

A sales transaction handled on a similar basis results in a Sales Discount credit balance representing the excess of the offering of discounts over the amount taken by customers and has to be treated as income additional to the booked sales income.

Inasmuch as the sale or purchase, under this method, must be booked on a cash option basis, this treatment seems to result in a departure from true cost or in the mistake of booking only *some* of the elements which enter into the cost of merchandise. The price at which a merchant can sell his product must include all direct and indirect costs and provide a margin for profit. The sales discount offered is simply one of these indirect costs. It cannot be more accurately estimated than can the salesman's salary which is a part of the sale price. It is inconsistent practice to separate the invoice price into two elements and term one *real* selling price and the other sales discount cost when the *real* selling price is still a composite item. Rather, the sale should be booked at its full invoiced price and actual costs recorded as they accrue, to be closed out against Sales Income at the end of the fiscal period.

After all, the sales policy of each concern enters largely into the determination of its normal selling price. A concern with a normal credit term of 30 days fixes its sale price on that basis; one with a 60-day credit term will, in determining its sale price, take into account the risk and interest costs of the longer credit period; and one doing a cash business will determine its sale price accordingly. However, as a means of furnishing the information necessary for guidance under a particular sales policy, sales should be recorded on the basis of the normal credit term.

To secure the information sought as to neglected discounts, it is suggested that memorandum accounts be opened for that purpose and entry be made of the expense only when incurred. Thus failure to take a purchase discount would be recorded under these or similar captions:

- Neglected Purchase Discounts
- Reserve for Neglected Purchase Discounts

At the time the books are closed these memorandum accounts would be closed against each other, having served their purpose of giving the desired information through their inclusion in the trial balance submitted to the manager or owner.

Trade Acceptances and Cash Discounts.—Brief mention should perhaps be made of some recent discussions of the probable effect of the extended use of trade acceptances on the practice of allowing cash discounts. Some sellers, to whom the cash discount practice is troublesome and unsatisfactory, welcome the use of trade acceptances as an avenue of escape from the practice. Others have gone so far as to say that the trade acceptance will eventually do away with cash discounts. It should be said that the use of trade acceptances, while attractive from the seller's standpoint, has not as yet made a strong appeal to buyers, largely because of the fact that it offers little that the open account method does not secure for them and it may, on the other hand, interfere somewhat with the taking of cash discounts.

CHAPTER XLV
BALANCE SHEET VALUATION

The Two Problems of the Balance Sheet.—There are two major problems connected with the balance sheet: (1) the problem of form, and (2) the problem of content. The form of the balance sheet, which was discussed rather fully in Chapter III, has to do with the arrangement of the items for the purpose of intelligent reading. It deals with the principles in accordance with which the asset, liability, and net worth items are to be marshaled and set up in groups and arranged within the group with a view to facilitating the comparisons between groups and the calculations made in judging the financial condition of the concern.

The second problem of the balance sheet, that of content, which was also mentioned in Chapter III, concerns itself mainly with the valuation of the items in the balance sheet, assuming of course that all the assets and liabilities are included in the statement. A balance sheet may be correct in form but, unless its content is reliable, it has little or no value when judged from the standpoint of its chief purpose, namely, that of showing the financial condition of the concern. The problem of the form of the balance sheet has to do with the technical or mechanical side of accounting, while the problem of its content or the valuation of its items has to do with the questions of the concern's financial administration, for the solution of which the accounting department must furnish in proper form the necessary information.

Kinds of Value.—It is first necessary to state the limitations within which the principles of valuation to be laid down are applicable to the commercial balance sheet. In business many different kinds of value are found and used. Thus we have the terms, sale or liquidation value, cost value, and replacement value. By the term "sale value," when applied to a going business, is meant the value which a willing buyer offers to a willing seller. "Liquidation value" means the value or price offered for a commodity or an entire business when the concern is winding up its affairs and going out of business. Liquidation is, therefore, forced value. There is thus a marked difference between sale value and liquidation value. The term "cost value" is understood to mean the price paid for a purchased article. From the discussion of the principles of debit and credit as applied to merchandise and to fixed assets, it has been shown that the price paid should include not alone the invoice cost but the other expenditures needed to put the article purchased in such a position that it can be used by the business in the customary way. Replacement value means the cost to replace an article. It differs from first cost mainly in that the price level may have changed between the date of the original purchase and the present time. Thus, because of the changes in prices, an article, costing $1,000 in 1914, might have had a replacement cost of $1,800 in 1917, and $1,400 in 1922.

Manifestly, before the principles to be followed in valuing balance sheet items can be laid down, there must be some understanding as to what kind of value is under discussion. The kind of value used in the ordinary commercial balance sheet is termed "going concern value." By this is meant the value which is applied to a going business—a business which expects to continue in operation, not one which expects to sell out to other owners nor one which expects to discontinue operations.

Source of Data as to Values.—In a going concern the information as to value is found chiefly in the books of account. The data in the accounting records are, of course, supported by the original documents evidencing the purchases and sales. It is a necessary corollary that if the books of account are to give reliable information as to values, a correct analysis must be made of all transactions previous to their entry. Mention was made in an earlier chapter of the necessity of a clear differentiation between capital and revenue charges and the effect of failure to make such differentiation. If at the time of an expenditure a correct classification of accounts has been made, particularly of the broad classes of assets, liabilities, and proprietorship, the accounts should reflect the true values as of the various dates of record. For purposes of detailed information it is equally necessary that a correct classification be made of the accounts affected by an entry within any of these main groups. It has been seen that because of practical difficulties no effort is made to have the accounts reflect day by day the correct value of the various items. It is considered sufficient to bring the book record into agreement with the facts in respect to value once each fiscal period, namely, at its close. The true financial condition and correct operating results are then determined.

It will thus be seen that a correct analysis of every transaction recorded in the accounts is an absolute prerequisite to the use of the accounts for determining correct values. It is very vital that a clear line of demarcation be maintained between capital and revenue expenditures—that great care be exercised that no cost is charged into the asset group of accounts unless such cost really enhances the worth of an asset. A cost incurred for the purpose of maintaining the value of the asset is an expense charge, and repairs and maintenance charges must be very carefully distinguished from replacements. *Maintenance* has to do with those costs which maintain an asset in good operating condition; *repairs* have to do with those costs necessary to put an asset in operating condition after a condition of inefficiency has been reached which the maintenance costs have not been able to prevent; a *replacement* cost is incurred when it becomes necessary to replace some part or the whole of an asset, neither maintenance cost nor repair costs having been able to maintain the asset in efficient operating condition. Where only a part of an asset is to be replaced, it is often spoken of as a *renewal* of parts. When so used, the term "replacement" is limited to the renewal or the replacement of the whole asset.

When a renewal or replacement is made, it becomes necessary to determine whether the cost of the renewal or replacement is more than the cost of the part or the whole replaced. For example, if an asset costing originally $1,000 is replaced by one costing $1,200, there has manifestly been an addition of $200 to the value of the asset. The new asset may be an exact duplicate of the old but if prices have risen so that the new actually costs more than the old, the books must record the asset at its new cost value. The amount by which a new asset or part of an asset exceeds the cost of the old asset or old part is called a *betterment*. A betterment is always an asset.

The student will readily see that at times it must be difficult to draw the line between repairs and replacements. In practice the line is usually drawn only when the expenditure exceeds a certain amount. This amount is not uniform and is determined by each individual business. For example, when the cost of placing the asset in efficient condition for operation is less than, say, $100, it is charged as repair cost and therefore does not increase the book value of the asset. If the cost exceeds $100, an analysis is made to determine what portion of it, if any, increases the value of the asset. The amount of the betterment is of course a charge to the asset account, while the rest of it is a charge to some expense account.

Treatment of Special Items.—In the determination of the classification of charges, some kinds of items require special consideration:

ORGANIZATION EXPENSE. The group of expenditures explained in Chapter XXXVIII, as incident to the organization of a corporation, is recorded under the title "Organization Expenses" and is classified for purposes of the balance sheet as an asset. It is a kind of asset, however, which has no tangible value and most businesses desire to consider it more in the nature of a deferred charge to operations. It is recognized that frequently intangible assets add no strength to the business. While, therefore, in strict theory organization expenses are assets, in practice it is best to write them off against income during a period of from three to five years.

COST-CUTTING CHANGES. Another similar class of charges is met in costs incurred in making changes in the arrangement of building and other facilities which will tend to bring about a more economical handling of some phases of the business; for example, a rearrangement of a receiving and packing room in order to facilitate the receipt and delivery of goods. Where these costs are inconsiderable it is best to charge them against the income of the period in which they are incurred. Where, however, a big expenditure is necessary, it seems best to set the costs up under a suitable descriptive title and spread them over several periods. In other words, at the date of their incurrence the costs are treated as an asset whose value is to be written down at the end of successive fiscal periods until finally it has all been charged against the operations of the business.

INTEREST DURING CONSTRUCTION PERIOD. Where a business builds its own home, all costs incurred during the period of construction are proper charges to the costs of the construction. Thus, if a mortgage or bond issue is used as a means of partially financing construction of the building, the interest paid to the mortgagee or bondholders during the period of construction is a proper charge to the building account. Costs of this kind follow the general principle laid down previously, that all costs up to the point of placing the asset in condition ready for use are proper charges to the asset.

Basic Rules for Valuation of Balance Sheet Groups.—We may now consider the principles applicable to the valuation of the various groups on the balance sheet. In the standard form of balance sheet the assets are divided into the three groups: (1) Current, (2) Deferred Charges, and (3) Fixed.

It has been seen that the assets of the current group are used for purposes of settling debts, the payment of expenses, and the purchase of merchandise. In judging the sufficiency of these assets for this purpose, it is absolutely essential to know that the values at which they are carried will be realized when they are converted into cash. From the standpoint of conservative business management an understatement of realizable value may be made, but never an overstatement. Accordingly, the fundamental principle of valuation applicable to this group is that these assets are to be valued at cost or market, whichever is the lower. When so valued, the figures at which they are carried in the balance sheet will usually represent an amount slightly less than the amount which it is expected will be realized from their conversion into cash.

The function of the deferred charges group of assets is to secure an equitable distribution of expense charges between the current and the following period. It is only because certain expenditures have been made during the current period which will benefit the succeeding period, that it is necessary to set up this group of assets. Here the problem of valuation is, therefore, simply the problem of dividing the cost of the expenditures between the current and the next period on the basis of the benefits accruing to each. In some cases the basis of division is one of time, as where an insurance policy is purchased for a definite term. The portion of the policy which has expired during the current period is the portion of its cost to be charged to the current period, the balance being deferred to succeeding periods and therefore carried as an asset. In other cases a physical inventory is necessary to determine the distribution of the cost of expenditures, as when supplies of fuel have been purchased and not entirely consumed during the current period. The basis of the value carried over to the next period is of course a fair portion of the original cost. Market or replacement cost does not have any effect on the valuation of the deferred portion.

Fixed assets are acquired as more or less permanent equipment without which it is impossible to operate the business. The time during which an asset continues in use is the customary basis for a classification of its cost as between expenses and fixed assets. Thus, an asset acquired for purposes of business operation which, however, will be used up completely during the current period is charged immediately to some expense account, whereas an asset which will continue in use over several periods is charged to an asset account. Fixed asset purchases are never for purposes of resale. It is expected that they will continue in use until they are discarded because of failure to perform the service for which they were acquired. Neither the sale value nor the replacement cost value of such assets has, therefore, any influence on their value to the business. That value is the full cost adjusted periodically by an equitable distribution of that cost over the operations of the periods benefited by the services rendered by the asset. This principle of valuation is usually expressed by the formula, cost less depreciation.

Valuation of Assets

CASH. Cash as carried on the balance sheet is the asset which is used, without conversion, for payment of the liabilities of the business. There should, therefore, ordinarily be no problem of valuation. However, because of the practice of including checks, drafts and notes due and in course of collection, cash balances held abroad and therefore subject to the fluctuations of exchange, and other similar items in the account Cash, it is oftentimes necessary to examine all these items carefully and arrive at a figure which represents the amount expected to be realized from them.

NOTES AND ACCOUNTS RECEIVABLE. The claims against customers, both on note and open accounts, constitute an intermediate step in the conversion of merchandise into cash. At the time credit is extended to a customer it is expected that he will pay the amount due. The experience of every business man shows, however, that during each period there is a shrinkage in these claims due to some customers failing to pay the amounts they owe. In valuing these claims it is therefore necessary to take cognizance of the amount of the shrinkage. This amount is different in different businesses, depending on the length of the credit term, the policy as to investigation of credit risks, and on the rigor of the collections policy. On the basis of the experience within a given business, it is therefore necessary to make an estimate of the loss from uncollectible accounts.

The manner of making the record of estimated bad debts has already been explained. The reason for placing the amount by which the asset is estimated to shrink as a credit in the Reserve for Doubtful Accounts account rather than in the Accounts Receivable account has also been explained. The custom of estimating the amount of loss on the basis of the sales for the period rather than on the amount of claims outstanding at the close of the fiscal period has been referred to. Here it is desired to explain the manner of handling the reserve at the time claims are definitely determined uncollectible. Until a claim is determined uncollectible it is carried as a part of the assets, Notes or Accounts Receivable. The amount of the estimated shrinkage in these assets due to failure to collect claims is indicated by the Reserve for Doubtful Accounts account. This amount cannot be applied directly to particular notes and accounts until it is definitely known that such notes and accounts cannot be collected. When that is learned, it is necessary to transfer from the reserve account the amount needed to cancel from the books the uncollectible notes and accounts receivable. This is done by the following entry:

- Reserve for Doubtful Accounts
- Notes (and Accounts) Receivable

PROBLEM. Assume that the accounts receivable amount to $75,000, of which it is estimated that $5,000 will not be collectible. During the succeeding period a customer owing $500 becomes bankrupt and nothing is realized on his account.

The accounts will then appear as follows:

ACCOUNTS RECEIVABLE

Dec. 31 75,000.00   Feb. 28   500.00

RESERVE FOR DOUBTFUL ACCOUNTS

Feb. 28   500.00   Dec. 31 5,000.00

It will thus be seen that the decrease in value of the accounts receivable as estimated by the amount in the Reserve for Doubtful Accounts can never be applied to the asset until it is definitely determined what particular customer's account included in the Accounts Receivable account is bad and must therefore be written off the books. Inasmuch as the Bad Debts account set up at the close of each fiscal period to indicate the loss or expense due to uncollectible accounts, has been charged as an expense of operating for that period, it would manifestly be duplicating the expense charge if a debt that proved bad were charged to the Bad Debts account rather than to the Reserve for Doubtful Accounts. Only during the first period of operation of a business are debts, if determined bad during that period, charged to the Bad Debts account. Even here, if it is expected at the close of the first period to base the estimate of uncollectible accounts on the sales for the period rather than on the amount of outstanding accounts at the end of the period, it would be necessary to charge the debts becoming bad during the period against the Reserve for Doubtful Accounts account—even though at the time of the charge it contained no credit entries—and not to the Bad Debts account. The desirability of establishing a standard routine for the handling of all items should be kept in mind. Best practice, therefore, demands that all debts shall be charged against the Reserve for Doubtful Accounts whenever they are determined to be bad, regardless of the amount held in reserve in that account. If such practice creates a debit balance in the Reserve for Doubtful Accounts, it is an indication that the estimate of uncollectible accounts made in previous periods has not, as a matter of fact, been sufficient and a larger estimate must be made for future periods.

MERCHANDISE. Merchandise is purchased for the purpose of resale at a profit. Sale price is dependent, in a free market, on the force of demand and supply and not at any given time on cost. Until the goods are sold no profit, as a matter of fact, has been secured. Conservatism, therefore, demands that sale price should not ordinarily be used as the basis for the inventory valuation. Unless there has been a decided change in prices, it is the confident expectation of the management that at least the cost price of the merchandise will be realized when the goods are sold. Ordinarily, therefore, merchandise will be priced in the balance sheet at cost. When, however, there has been a change in price levels, particularly when the indication is that there is a generally declining market and not simply a temporary fluctuation in prices, it is the part of conservatism to value the merchandise at its replacement cost, or even at a lower figure, if stocks are large and market conditions are such that customers are withholding their purchases until price levels have dropped still further. The basic principle for valuing all current assets requires that they be valued as nearly as possible at the realization figure. Therefore, the amount expected to be realized governs or influences the valuation basis. The valuation formula or rule-of-thumb method, in accordance with which merchandise inventory is usually valued, is expressed as cost or market, whichever is the lower. As indicated above, there are times when exception is taken to this basis.

INVESTMENTS. Stocks and bonds representing the investment of temporary surpluses of cash are valued on a realization basis. Inasmuch as the tying up of cash in these securities is only temporary and it is expected that they will be converted again into cash as needed, the amount which can be realized from their sale on the date of the balance sheet is the amount to be considered when judging the financial condition on that date. A large amount of discretion must be used in valuing these securities, because of the violent fluctuations to which quotations on the various stock exchanges are subject. Here also conservatism does not usually authorize value at the market if the market is higher than the cost. Accordingly, the valuation formula is cost or market, whichever is the lower.

ACCRUED INCOME. The income accrued on the date of the balance sheet is determined on the basis of a fair distribution between the periods during which the income accrues. Thus, the income from money loaned during the current period but not due until a succeeding period must be distributed over two or more periods. Where the income is dependent on time, the portion applicable to the current period is determined on a time basis. Where the income is dependent on some other basis, such as sales or units of work done, the portion applicable to the current period is determined by the ratio of the whole to the amount completed during the present period. Thus, in the case of a contract entered into to sell goods on a commission basis, the commission income accrued during the current period will usually be based on the amount of sales made during that period.

DEFERRED CHARGES. The valuation principle for deferred charges has been stated above in connection with the principles of valuation to be applied to the various groups of accounts on the balance sheet.

FIXED ASSETS. Fixed assets may usually be divided into two classes: (1) assets not subject to depreciation, and (2) assets subject to depreciation. The usual example of assets not subject to depreciation is the land on which a building stands. Land used for growing crops may easily be subject to depreciation. Land subject to the exploitation of the natural resources under its surface is similarly subject to depreciation. To distinguish the decrease in value of such natural resources because of the fact that they enter into and become a part of the commodity dealt in, the term "depletion" is used. Thus, a coal mine or oil well decreases in value with every unit of product taken therefrom. It is not purposed hero to discuss the principles of valuation applicable in such cases, the assets under discussion being limited in meaning to those of a mercantile business. (See Volume II, page 312, for a discussion of depletion.)

The valuation formula for assets not subject to depreciation is cost. Increase in value due to changed market conditions is not usually to be taken account of.

The second group of assets, those subject to depreciation, are to be valued on the basis of original cost less the amount of depreciation accrued to the date of the balance sheet. The valuation of such assets, therefore, requires the determination of the amount of depreciation.

Depreciation arises from several causes, the chief of which are:

1. Wear and tear, due to use.

2. Decrepitude or age, due to lapse of time.

3. Obsolescence, due to a changed demand for the article or to an advance in the arts which makes the continued use of the asset uneconomical.

4. Inadequacy, brought about by several causes, one of which may be the change in the market which renders the asset inadequate for furnishing the product or service in the amount required.

Obsolescence and inadequacy, because of their very nature, are usually difficult of determination and frequently cannot therefore be considered in determining the amount of depreciation accrued at a given time. Where measurable they should, of course, be taken into account. Depreciation due to lapse of time is calculable on a time basis. Depreciation due to wear and tear is calculable on the basis of the use to which the asset has been subjected. It is in practice difficult to separate these two types of depreciation. The estimate for depreciation is in the majority of cases made on a time basis. In manufacturing establishments, oftentimes a use or output basis proves more satisfactory. These more difficult problems met in the determination of depreciation are discussed in Volume II. Here only the most usual method of depreciation estimate on a time basis, known as the straight-line method, will be explained.

For determining the periodic amount of depreciation of any asset it is necessary to know: (1) the original cost of the asset; (2) its scrap value, that is, the estimated value as scrap on the day it is junked; and (3) the estimated life of the asset in years or fiscal periods. The following symbols will be used in working out the formula:

V_1 = Original value.

V_n = Scrap value at the end of n years, its estimated life.

n = The estimated number of years in the life of the asset.

D = The amount of depreciation during a period.

r = The rate to be applied to V_1 in order to determine D.

It is apparent that V_1-V_n is the amount to be depreciated over the life of the asset. The amount to be charged off periodically as depreciation is, therefore:

$$\frac{V_1 - V_n}{n}$$

Accordingly

$$D = \frac{V_1 - V_n}{n} \quad (1)$$

The amount to be written off each year is thus seen to be constant. The percentage to be applied to the original cost in order to determine the periodic depreciation D is, therefore, found by dividing D by V_1. Hence the formula:

$$r = \frac{D}{V_1} \quad (2)$$

Having determined by careful estimate the method of calculating the periodic amount of depreciation, the problem of valuation of the asset at any given time during its life is ordinarily simple. In the case of renewal of any parts, the question of betterment comes in and requires careful handling. In unusual cases it may often be necessary to revise the rate of depreciation in order to write off the betterment during the remaining life of the asset. Depreciation is at the best but an estimate and unless there are major betterment items it is not usually necessary because of them to revise the estimate of depreciation. When a renewal takes place it is theoretically necessary to determine the value of the replaced part at the time of its replacement. The excess of the cost of the new part over this value is the amount of the betterment, when only the values of the old and new parts are considered. In such cases, however, the new part will not usually have value apart from the asset to which it is attached. In practice, therefore, the amount of the betterment recorded is the difference between original—not present—value of the old part and the cost of the new part. An example will illustrate the problems involved and the accounting treatment.

PROBLEM. Assume that an asset—office equipment—costing $1,000 has an estimated life of ten years and no scrap value. After six years of this life it becomes necessary to replace a part of the asset, estimated to have cost originally $100, the cost of the new part being $150. At the time of the replacement the depreciation reserve carries an amount of $600.

The first step in booking the transaction is to transfer from the reserve account to the asset account the original cost of the part replaced. Just as in the case of bad debts, now that a part of the asset has been discarded and the amount of the decrease in value of the asset is definitely known, this amount held in suspense until the present time in the reserve account must be applied as a definite reduction in the carrying value of the asset. The entry to effect the transfer is:

Depreciation Reserve, Office Appliances 100.00

    Office Appliances   100.00

The next step is to set up the cost of the new part which replaces that discarded. This follows the usual entry at the time of purchase of any equipment. The entry needed is:

Office Appliances 150.00

    Cash   150.00

The student will note that the office appliances account now carries a value of $1,050, of which the $50 represents the value of the betterment.

It might appear that since the renewal occurs at the end of six years there has been accumulated in the reserve by that time only $60 covering this specific part, and that therefore only $60 should be transferred from the reserve account, the other $40 being charged to a proprietorship account to represent the additional expense or loss not yet provided for by the depreciation charges during the past six years. That is not the situation, however, for if the periodic depreciation has been correctly estimated, the entire amount, $100, has already been charged off and is therefore included in the reserve. When the asset was originally installed and the length of its life estimated for the purpose of determining the periodic depreciation charge, the policy as to repairs and renewal of parts was taken into consideration. Such estimates cannot, of course, be absolutely accurate. However, until such time as a definite basis is given on which to check the amount of the over-or under-estimate, it is the standard practice to charge against the reserve the original value of the renewed part. Always at the time of discard of the entire asset—and sometimes sooner—such a definite basis is given and adjustment must be made in accordance with the facts then ascertained. A problem will illustrate the considerations involved.

Continuing the foregoing example, assume that the office appliance, now valued at $1,050 with a reserve of $500, is discarded after ten and a half years' service.

At the end of the tenth year the annual depreciation charge of $105 will have brought the reserve account to a total of $920. Six months later, at the time of discard of the asset, there will be accrued depreciation, not yet booked, amounting to $52.50. It is, accordingly, necessary to book this amount by means of the following entry:

Depreciation   52.50
    Depreciation Reserve Office Appliances   52.50

This entry charges the current period with its share of the consumed value of the asset. The next step is to transfer the reserve account to the asset account, to show in that account the amount of the inaccuracy in the depreciation estimate—the amount by which the actual depreciation differs from the estimate. The entry is:

Depreciation Reserve Office Appliances   972.50
    Office Appliances   972.50

The office appliance account now shows a debit balance of $77.50, which indicates the value or amount of the asset which has been consumed but which has not been charged against the income of the periods during which the asset was used. It is manifestly inequitable to charge this amount against the income of the six months of the current period, and it is impossible to go back and spread it over the previous periods because their records have been closed. The charge must therefore be made direct to the Surplus account in the case of a corporation, or to a final section for extraordinary profits and losses of the regular Profit and Loss account in other cases. It may be handled by this latter method also in the case of a corporation. The entry needed is, therefore:

Surplus   77.50
    Office Appliances   77.50

In case the reserve is more than the value of the asset at the time of discard, it means that more than the cost of the asset has been charged as expense. Accordingly, the excess represents real profit and must be transferred to surplus. The necessary entry is:

- Office Appliances
- Surplus

GOOD-WILL. Good-will is an intangible asset depending for its value upon the ability of a business to make more than normal profits. It is not usual for a business to show an asset of good-will unless it has purchased another business and has paid for the latter's good-will. In other words, good-will is not brought on to the books until a purchase determines its market value. Where good-will is purchased, it is customary to carry it at its cost value. Depreciation is not taken into account. Because of the intangible nature of good-will and its more or less speculative value, some businesses prefer not to show it. In such cases it may be written off against surplus at any time and in any amount until it has all disappeared from the books. While, therefore, good-will is not subject to depreciation, it is subject to this writing off process, which usually bears little or no relationship to time. It should not be charged against the profit of any period or several periods, but when written off should be charged direct against surplus.

Liabilities.—The problem of valuation of liabilities is simple. From the standpoint of a going concern, its liabilities decrease only when they are paid off, and increase only because of services or assets purchased and not paid for. The main problem in connection with balance sheet liabilities is the determination of the fact that all liabilities are shown on the balance sheet. This oftentimes involves the consideration of contingent liabilities. The amount of a liability may sometimes be in dispute, in which case a careful and conservative estimate of the probable amount must be made and shown.

Proprietorship.—Since proprietorship is always the difference between assets and liabilities, the problems of valuation of proprietorship are solved almost automatically if the valuation of assets and liabilities have been handled properly. There may sometimes be problems in connection with the various items in the proprietorship group. These concern surplus, undivided profits, and various reserves. The problems here are largely those of determining whether a company has lived up to its contract or other agreements in the maintenance of the proper values in the various proprietorship accounts.

Conclusion.—The problems of valuation are vital to any business and intimately concern its financial integrity. In order to maintain at least the original capital investment in a business, it is necessary to make provision for the decrease in asset values due to different causes. The financial management of the business must watch this feature closely, else capital will be dissipated and the business rendered incapable of performing the functions for which it was organized.

CHAPTER XLVI
BUYING AND STOCK CONTROL

Importance of Buying.—Buying as a major function in a mercantile concern is intimately related to, and dependent on, the other functions of the business. Buying must always have regard to the sales activities. To buy without reference to the ability to sell is suicidal. Both overbuying—buying more than can be disposed of at a profit—and underbuying—buying less than is needed to meet the sales demand—are conditions to be avoided. Underbuying means a loss of sales. Unless their needs are met promptly in accordance with their orders, customers will go elsewhere. Overbuying means the unnecessary tying up of capital in a stock of goods which increases the possibilities of loss resulting from changes in fashions and the level of prices. The relation of the rate of turnover to profits in merchandising was discussed in Chapter VII. Manifestly the ideal situation, so far as the amount of stock carried is concerned, is one in which the least amount of capital is used to provide an adequate stock for meeting the requirements of customers and in which the loss from unsalable stock is reduced to the lowest level.

Many business houses fail to realize the wastes resulting from slow turnovers. The Chamber of Commerce of the United States has called attention to these losses and has analyzed them under the following heads:

1. The unnecessary use of capital in merchandise that could be more profitably employed in other productive sources.

2. The increased cost of borrowed capital, the carrying of larger stocks and their slow turnover, necessitating the borrowing of larger amounts of capital for longer periods.

3. The marking down of the sale price due to the fact that the goods will not move at the higher sale price.

4. An increase in overhead expenses due to the larger storage and display equipment needed for goods and to the costs incident to handling the larger stock, and re-marking the stock when it is necessary to lower sale prices.

5. The loss of prestige and reputation from carrying unstylish and shopworn goods.

Relation between Buying and Finance.—From what has already been said, it is evident that there is a very necessary relation between the buying policy of a business and its ability to finance purchases. Even though it may be possible to increase sales, unless the business is in a position to finance not only the additional credits extended to customers but also the additional purchases needed to take care of the increased sales, it will not be feasible to pursue a policy of sales expansion and therefore of increased buying. Hence, buying cannot be considered as a business activity by itself, but as one dependent upon the sales activities and the financial resources of the business.

Organization for Buying.—In large merchandising businesses the duties and authority of the buying department are not uniform. In some, this department is organized entirely distinct from the selling department; in others (and this is particularly true of the large department stores), the buyer is head merchandise man with control over the selling activities of the business. It is also quite usual for the buyer to be in charge of a given department and his success or failure to be judged by the profits he makes in that department. A profit quota is sometimes assigned to each department, for which the buyer is responsible. In other words, in the management of the buying and selling activities and therefore in the control of his merchandise stock the buyer is supreme, subject to the general limitations placed by the financial resources at his disposal. Under the control of the buyer, therefore, will be stock clerks, the clerks which mark and re-mark the merchandise, and the sales force. Above and in control of all the departmental buyers is usually an executive or high official of the company whose chief function is to correlate the activities of the buyers with the concern's general buying, selling, and financial policy.

Characteristics of the Buyer.—To perform his functions properly, the buyer must be a man of broad experience, with a keen sense of values and the marketing possibilities of merchandise. On the buying side he must have complete information as to the available sources of the merchandise he desires to secure, both in staple and in novelty lines. On the selling side he must know the demands of his customers and the possibility of creating new demands. The best index of the buying power of his customers is the volume of sales made in previous years. Past performance, considered in connection with general trade conditions and plans for the further development of the business, is the only basis for judging the sales possibilities of the future. He must know the quality of merchandise and the reliability of the people from whom he buys. He must be a keen judge of prices. He must know the financial resources of his own store and strive to secure the best possible credit and discount terms.

Buying Procedure.—In Chapter XXII, where the goods invoice was discussed, a typical purchasing procedure was set forth. Here only the chief points in that procedure will be mentioned. In a large establishment the buying requisition should be the basis of all purchase orders. This is particularly true when the buyer does the buying for several departments. The requisition should be made out in triplicate by the department head, two copies going to the buyer and one being retained in the department. Upon the issuance of the buying order, the second copy of the requisition is returned to the department as evidence that the goods have been ordered.

The purchase orders are made in manifold, the original going to the vendor, one copy to the treasurer to notify him of the future need for funds, one to the controller or accounting department, and one being retained by the buyer as a basis for follow-up. Upon receipt of the invoice, which usually precedes the goods, the buyer compares it with the order and if it is found correct, he passes it to the accounting department, where it is held until the receiving slip, showing the receipt of goods, is received from the receiving room. If the three documents now in possession of the accounting department, namely, the copy of the original order, the invoice, and the receiving slip, agree, the invoice is passed for entry on the books and is filed for payment in accordance with the financial policy of the business. After payment, the invoice with its supporting documents is filed. Great care must be exercised to make sure that an invoice is not put through more than once for payment and that every invoice represents goods properly ordered and actually received.

Requirements of Successful Buying.—Successful buying rests on a knowledge of two things: (1) when to buy, and (2) what to buy. The timeliness of buying has regard rather to the sales requirements than the market possibilities. Goods are bought for the purpose of satisfying needs of customers. A knowledge of the trend of the market is necessary but buying wholly in accordance with market trends too often leads to speculation in merchandise, due weight not being given to the sales requirements. A knowledge of the specific commodities needed to satisfy the requirements of customers is equally important. The regular use of the "want slips" of customers calling for goods not in stock is one source of information. The records of the paid "shoppers" as to the commodities and prices of competitors is also some indication.

In answering both these questions, when to buy and what to buy, the records of the business itself should furnish the fundamental information needed to secure a proper control of the movement of merchandise. Some system of perpetual inventory is almost indispensable. In a small business where the buyer, usually the owner, is in intimate contact with all departments, a fairly satisfactory control of merchandise can be secured without a perpetual inventory. In a business of some size, however, the perpetual inventory is an almost absolute essential if movement of stock is to be kept under control.

Control of Merchandise Movement.—The beginning of merchandise control is the fixing of the sales quota, that is, the making of an estimate of sales for the next period. Without a definite goal to be aimed at control is impossible. Buying and finance are dependent on it. A knowledge of the stock on hand at any time is needed to determine the buying requirements. Even in a small business the inventory can at least be estimated on the basis of past performance as to percentage of gross profit and therefore the percentage of cost of goods sold. The application of this figure of percentage of cost of goods sold to the sales for the period gives the cost of goods sold, which, subtracted from the opening inventory plus goods purchased, gives an estimate of the goods in stock. A perpetual inventory kept by quantities rather than by values serves the purpose in many establishments. What is known as the "retail system," by means of which the value of the stock on hand can be estimated at any time, is used in many large retail establishments. In addition to, and in conjunction with such a system, the use of commodity control cards, as illustrated in Form 43, gives a sure index of the condition of stock and the movement of merchandise at any time.

The Retail Method of Inventory.—The retail system of inventory is based on the carrying of all goods purchased at a retail sale price as well as at cost price. In the financial records purchases are, of course, always booked at cost. A stock record is kept, however, which carries purchases at retail sale price as well as at cost price. The principle of the perpetual inventory under this method is shown by the fundamental formula:

$$\text{Opening Inventory} + \text{Purchases} - \text{Cost of Goods Sold} = \text{Final Inventory}$$

It is apparent that if all the values on the left side of the equation are retail sale values, the right side of the equation represents the final inventory valued at the retail sale price. Thus, if the opening inventory for use in the stock record is set up at the marked sale price, and purchases are similarly set up, the subtraction of the sales to date from the sum of the opening inventory and purchases gives the amount of stock on hand valued at the sale price.

In order to reduce an inventory, valued at retail sale price, to a cost basis, the per cent of mark-on of the cost price to give the original sale price must be applied. This per cent is based on the sale price and not the cost price, being determined by dividing the difference between sale and cost price (that is, the gross profit figure) by the sale price. Thus, a commodity, costing $60 and marked to sell at $100, will, if sold, yield a gross profit of $40, which, given in terms of the sale price, is a 40% gross profit. This 40% is spoken of as the "mark-on per cent." The cost is, therefore, the difference between 100% and the per cent of mark-on, in this case 60%. That is, 60% of the sale price gives the cost price.

Accordingly, to reduce the inventory value at selling price to a cost price basis, it must be multiplied by 100% minus the per cent of mark-on.

The use of the retail method is thus seen to require a stock record from which the goods on hand as valued at selling price can be determined almost instantly and from which the per cent of mark-on can also be determined. In principle the method is simple. In practice it must be operated very carefully, else unreliable results will be secured. It seldom happens that merchandise will always move at the marked sale price. Adjustments are necessary. On an upward market, perhaps, a higher price can be secured than the marked price. On a downward market or in order to move certain colors and styles, it is necessary to mark down from the original sale price. The fluctuations arising from mark-ups and mark-downs are treated in Chapter XI of Volume III and will not be discussed here. Some applications of the retail method will be explained, however.

Some Buying Records and Their Use.—The chief purpose of the main records kept in business is the securing of control over the activities of the business. The control over merchandise must always be based on records. The first step in securing the necessary control is a proper departmentization of stock. Analysis of purchases and sales by departments is fundamental. In addition, a knowledge of what others in the same line are doing serves as a criterion by which to judge one's own results. Trade associations and research bureaus are giving invaluable information by furnishing standards for judging results.

Three major problems from the buyer's standpoint are always met. They are not independent problems but, as indicated above, are intimately related to selling and financial policies. These problems are: (1) the determination of the average stock to be carried; (2) the determination of the buying quota for a given period; and (3) the determination of the "open-to-buy" amount at a given time. Too often these matters are decided in a haphazard fashion. Only by means of a careful analysis of all the factors and the results obtained in the various departments as compared with average or standard results can a sound basis of stock control be secured.

Average Stock to be Carried.—Stock control rests, in the first place, on estimated requirements for the future. Estimates for the future must always be based on past performance, as modified by present market conditions and contemplated changes in basic merchandising policies. In estimating the amount of stock to be carried, the volume of expected sales must be taken into account. The other factor is the rate at which the merchandise should turn during the period. Thus, if estimates are made for a period of six months, the estimated sales for the period divided by the number of times the stock is expected to turn during the six months will give the average amount of stock to be kept on hand. Seasonal fluctuations must be taken cognizance of in determining the changes from average stocks to be carried at particular times during the period. Thus, if the estimated sales in a given department are $50,000 for the next six months and the merchandise turns twice during that time, manifestly a stock of $25,000, as priced at retail, must be carried. If the mark-on is 40%, the cost of the average stock will be 60% of $25,000, or $15,000, representing the average capital to be tied up in stock for that department.

The Buying Quota.—The determination of a buying quota for a given period must take cognizance of the stock on hand at the beginning of the period, the stock which it is planned to have on hand at the end of the period, and the estimated sales for the period. If, from the sum of the stock planned to be on hand at the end of the period and the sales estimate for the period is subtracted the stock on hand at the beginning of the period, the buying quota for the period is determined. This buying quota is, of course, at retail price and must be reduced by use of the mark-on percentage to a cost basis. An illustration will show the method:

Stock planned to be on hand at end of period	$25,000
Estimated sales for period	50,000
	$75,000
Stock on hand at beginning of period	23,000
Buying quota at retail price	$52,000

Mark-on is 40%, i.e., cost is 60% of selling price.

    Therefore $31,200 = buying quota at cost

The "Open-to-Buy" Estimate.—The buying quota is estimated at the beginning of the period. At various times throughout the period, if stock is to be properly controlled, it is necessary to know how much of the buying quota is available. Furthermore, because estimates made at the beginning of the period never quite coincide with the facts of actual performance, it is necessary to take cognizance of these data of performance in determining the amount of stock to be bought at a given time. The difference between the estimated sales for the period and the actual sales to date is the estimated sales to be made during the remainder of the period. If from the stock on hand at a given date is subtracted the estimated sales for the rest of the period, the difference will be the estimated stock remaining on hand at the end of the period, providing no more purchases are made. If this amount is less than the amount of stock planned to be on hand at the end of the period, the department is "open-to-buy" to the amount of the difference. If the estimated amount on hand at the end of the period is more than the planned inventory for the end of the period, no additional stock should be purchased, except of course to replenish certain stocks which have become depleted and which it is necessary to have on hand to meet the needs of customers. In calculating the stock on hand at a given time, cognizance must be taken of stock in the warehouse, in transit, and on order. A typical open-to-buy calculation is shown below:

Stock on hand today	$ 40,000.00	
Stock in warehouse	15,000.00	
Stock in transit	10,000.00	
Stock ordered		
(to be received before end of period)	25,000.00	
Total available stock		$90,000.00
Sales planned for period	$175,000.00	
Sales made to date	105,000.00	
Estimated sales for balance of the period		70,000.00
Estimated stock at end of the period		$20,000.00
Planned stock at end of the period		30,000.00
Open-to-buy amount		$10,000.00

This open-to-buy figure should be amended in the light of experience with regard to the way in which actual sales are running as compared with the estimated sales. If it is apparent that the sales are running ahead of the estimate, the sales quota should be enlarged accordingly, which will in turn increase the open-to-buy balance. A similar adjustment should be made in the event that actual sales are not keeping pace with the estimated quota.

The Stock Control Card.—The problem of stock control is not solved solely by a maintenance of buying quotas and limits. The movement of individual commodities must be watched very closely. The tying up of funds in large stocks of slow moving commodities may soon use up the buying quota needed for faster moving commodities. To maintain control over the movement of individual commodities, a record called the "stock control card," which is similar to the stock book, is of great value in some lines. To other lines it will not be found adaptable. It is not the purpose of this chapter to attempt to lay down specific methods adaptable to all situations but only to discuss basic principles and to illustrate them by methods found applicable to certain situations. The control card illustrated in Form 43 is one used in a retail shoe store.

On the form shown as Form 43, Style, Bought From, Description, and Material, are self-explanatory. On the line below, cost is shown in the first column, size in the next, and the month with days along the rest of the line follows. Horizontally are entered on the dates shown the quantities of stock received (Rec'd), on hand (O. H.), sold (Sold), and on order (O. O.).

According to the form, on August 1 there were on hand 19 pairs of shoes, size 9, and 11 pairs of size 9½. During that week, on consecutive days, 3, 4, 3, 6, 2 pairs of size 9 shoes were sold, of which 2 pairs (circled) were returned on the 4th and 5th; and 2, 2, 1, 3, 4 pairs of size 9½ shoes were sold, of which 1 pair was returned but again sold on the 5th.

On the first day of the following week 24 pairs of each size which had been ordered on the 2d of August were received. Upon their receipt the O. O. (on order) figures were inclosed in circles. On that day also the O. H. (on hand) figure was placed in its proper place in the size 9 group. All of size 9½ had been sold during the first week of August and there was of course no figure to be entered there.

The record is continued by daily postings of sales and by a weekly posting or entering of the stock on hand. Orders are entered on the day they are placed.

Form 43. Stock Control Card

Taken from Bulletin issued by the
United States Chamber of Commerce

With such a stock record a perpetual inventory is maintained and control over the movement of merchandise is secured.

Problems Connected with the Merchandise Inventory.—Proper accounting for merchandise at the time of inventory-taking and the close of the fiscal period requires a consideration of the following points:

GOODS IN TRANSIT. It may happen that certain goods have been ordered during the period, and that the invoice has been received but that the goods themselves are still in transit. The question whether or not such goods shall be included in the inventory may be viewed from different angles, as follows:

1. If the goods have been paid for in advance, they have undoubtedly been entered on the books as a charge to Purchases. If this is the case, the goods in transit must of course be included in the inventory as if actually received.

2. If the goods are still in transit but have not been paid for, it is customary not to charge them to Purchases until they arrive. If not charged to Purchases, or other similar account, they must not be included in the inventory. However, theoretically, this method is incorrect. The fact that the goods have been ordered and are now in transit makes the business liable for their purchase price, and although not actually received, in reality they form a part of the asset merchandise. It is true that until the goods are received, inspected, and accepted, the purchaser has the privilege of refusing them if they are not as ordered, but this privilege is exercised only in exceptional cases. Generally speaking, therefore, it is better to consider such goods as a completed purchase, include them in the inventory and credit the vendor for the amount of his invoice. Instead of being charged to Purchases account, such goods may be charged to Purchase Commitments which will better indicate their status.

GOODS RECEIVED BUT NOT YET BOOKED. In concerns where a separate shipping and receiving department is maintained, it may happen that the goods received by this department are not immediately transferred to stock or storage, in which case they may not have been taken up on the books. At the end of the period it is important to see that all such goods are properly recorded as purchased and are included in the inventory.

GOODS IN OR OUT ON CONSIGNMENT. Still another problem in connection with the inventory has to do with goods which do not belong to the business because they have been consigned to it for sale on account of their owner. Inward consigned goods must not be included in the inventory, if taken into stock, it is very important that they be so marked as easily to distinguish them from the regular stock.

Similarly, if goods are out on consignment to another market, they still belong to the business and must not be overlooked at inventory time. If the proper record is made at the time the goods are shipped, as will be explained in Chapter XLVIII, the memorandum accounts on the ledger will call attention to them. In some concerns all such goods are entered as sales at the time of shipment. If at the end of the period part of these consigned goods are still unsold and in the hands of agents, they should be deducted from the sales for the period and included in the inventory at full cost.

GOODS FOR FUTURE DELIVERY. Goods sold for future delivery are best handled at inventory time in the manner suggested in Chapter XLVII, even if they are set aside ready for delivery.

GOODS READY FOR CURRENT DELIVERY. Finally, goods sold for current shipment but delayed in delivery on account of congestion in the service or for some other cause are best treated as sales and excluded from the inventory.

CHAPTER XLVII
SALES

Importance of the Sales Department.—Of the major departments into which business activities are commonly classified, the selling department ranks first in point of relative importance. Regardless of the efficiency secured in the other branches, regardless of the economy in buying and the excellence of administration, the life of a business largely depends upon the results obtained by the selling division. Since the sales department plays such an important part in the development of the business, it is evident that the accounting and financial problems connected with sales should be given careful attention and should be handled by the most scientific and up-to-date methods.

As before stated, one of the most important principles of modern accounting is that the system by which the records are to be kept must be planned in advance. The modern accountant must first know the kind of information that is desired and he then can classify the accounts so that the information may be obtained from the ledger or other records at any time, with the least possible effort.

Basis for Sales Classification.—The majority of enterprises at the present time deal in a number of commodities, the kind, quality, and grades of which are of such variety that careful classification is imperative. Formerly all goods sold were classed together under a single title "Merchandise," with the result that no detailed information concerning the sale of particular goods, qualities, and grades was available and the manager or proprietor was unable to study the movement of specific classes of commodities.

Applying the principle of classification to sales, the basis for classification depends on the character of the business and the nature of the goods sold. Where the commodities dealt in are of such variety that it is impracticable to have a separate account for each kind, a more general grouping by classes may be necessary. Where the concern manufactures some of its commodities and buys the remainder in the open market, an analysis of sales on the basis of "own" product and "other" product may be wanted. Sales may be classified also on the basis of the sales contract, as cash, credit, instalment, sales to branches, consignment sales, approval sales, etc. Accounting problems in connection with these various types of classification will be treated in the present chapter.

Principles Governing Analysis in Books of Original Entry.—It is evident that the kind of classification shown in the ledger determines the journal analysis. That is to say, the analysis in books of original entry, and therefore their columnar ruling, always depends upon the way in which the accounts are classified and grouped in the ledger.

The various types of analyses, both in journals and in ledgers, make use of either (or both) horizontal or vertical distribution. In most forms or records, except in banking and allied institutions, the generally accepted practice is to reserve vertical distribution for showing chronological sequence, and horizontal distribution for any other kind of classification. The reason for this lies in the fact that the time basis requires practically unlimited space and the requirement can be met only by vertical distribution, consecutive pages being considered as the continuation of preceding pages. Horizontal distribution, on the other hand, is limited to the width of the page.

By reference to Chapter XLI, "Handling the Cash," it will be noted that for the purpose of horizontal classification the sheet contains a number of money columns, each headed by an individual class title, and that each item is first entered in the general column and then extended to one of the subsidiary columns. This serves as a check against error, since it is evident that the total of the general column must be equal to the sum of the totals of the other columns, thus furnishing a fair though not complete proof that the extensions have been made correctly. All books where analytical processes are involved should provide some kind of internal check. The student should refer to Chapters XVIII, XIX and XX, where form of analytic journals and explanation of them were given.

Use of the Sales Ticket in Analysis.—Since the sales invoice or ticket is the basis for entry and analysis in the sales journal, it must give on its face the information necessary for making the analysis. In accordance with the basis of classification used, it should show the department number, the kind of goods sold, whether for cash or credit, etc. The use of invoices with printed department numbers and of different colors for cash, charge, and C.O.D. sales, aid in making the record effective.

In a business of any size, the entry on the main sales journal only shows the total for the day's sales. The sales tickets lend themselves easily to grouping, and therefore a day's sales may be analyzed by sorting and grouping the sales tickets. Under any method of this sort, of course, each ticket must be used for the record of only one class of goods. Thus the totals of each of these sorted groups may be entered in the sales journal at the end of the day. Besides furnishing the totals for each group of sales, the individual tickets are used also for the purpose of posting the sales to the accounts of the particular customers.

After use in these various ways the tickets are filed away in binders for reference. Thus, the main books are freed of a mass of comparatively unimportant detail, to which it is necessary to refer only in rare cases.

Analyzing Sales Returns.—Attention should be called to the necessity of analyzing returned sales, allowances, and rebates, on the same basis as sales. Provision should also be made for a separate sales returns journal since the ordinary journal does not lend itself economically to an analyzed record of that kind.

Purchases and Returned Purchases.—It has been pointed out that the basis of classification of sales in the ledger determines the analysis in the sales journal. The same classification should also be applied to purchases, returned purchases, and inventories, because only in this way is it possible to determine the profit from the different classes of merchandise.

Similarly, all inward costs, such as duty, freight, insurance, handling, etc., which enter into the cost of goods sold must be analyzed on the same basis and apportioned to each group on some equitable basis. Because of practical difficulties, however, this analysis or apportionment usually is not made upon the first entry of these items on the records, but a distribution on a more or less arbitrary basis is made at the close of the period. In a large concern where very detailed information as to results is desired, an analysis of many other expenses and costs applicable to each sales group is made. Such a distribution of expense, however, leads into the field of cost accounting which is beyond the scope of the present discussion.

The Handling of Cash Sales.—Where an analysis by kind of commodity is unnecessary, a simple method of booking cash sales is by entry in a "Sales" column provided in the cash book, the total of which is posted to the credit of "Sales" in the ledger. Under this method, cash sales need not be entered in the sales journal. In previous chapters where the functions of the subsidiary journals were discussed, the practice of entering a cash sale in both cash book and sales journal was advised, so that the summaries of each may show true totals for those groups of business activities. However, this principle is often departed from and the method just described for booking cash sales is followed. Where an analysis of the sales is desired, the practical difficulty of providing analysis columns in the cash book for the cash sales in addition to analysis columns in the sales journal for the sales on account gives added weight to the principle stated.

It is sometimes desirable to distinguish between cash and charge sales, thus requiring two accounts, the "Sales on Account" and the "Cash Sales," to show the total sales for the period. This is easily accomplished by the use in the sales journal of the "On Account" and "Cash" columns whose totals furnish the amounts for posting to the two ledger accounts. Even were it desired to have two sales accounts, the cash and charge, for each department, the necessary information can be secured by providing in the sales journal two columns, a cash and a charge for each department and posting their totals to the two sales accounts carried for each.

A more complicated problem arises when it is desired to keep an account to show the total cash sales of *all* departments and at the same time to keep one sales account for each department, in which will be recorded both cash and charge sales. The information can be placed on the ledger, but not without destroying the usual meaning of the Cash Sales account. The purpose is accomplished by providing the sales journal with two total or general columns—in addition to the departmental columns—one for charge and one for cash sales, and by carrying a Cash Sales column in the cash book. The items in the Cash Sales column in the sales journal are distributed to the proper analytic columns for classification. At the end of the period the totals of these analytic columns (which include both cash and charge sales items) are posted to the credit of the proper departmental accounts in the ledger. The total of the Cash Sales column in the sales journal, however, is posted to the *debit* of Cash Sales in the ledger, which will be offset by a corresponding credit item from the Cash Sales column in the cash book. These two totals should agree provided the books are completely posted.

Sales to Branches.—Sales to branches are made on different bases in different concerns. Sometimes such sales are charged to the branch office at cost, sometimes at full selling price, and sometimes at a fictitious figure. The first method is theoretically the best, but is not always desirable because head offices frequently prefer to keep their branches ignorant of cost prices. For this reason such sales are frequently charged to the branch office at the regular selling price. By this method, however, the books of the head office record the goods as if actually sold, while in reality they have been merely transferred to a branch office. Consequently, the books show a profit which is not yet earned. In order to correct this, it is necessary at the end of the period to make an adjustment entry covering all goods still in the possession of the branch office unsold at that time. By billing the goods at a fictitious figure the branch is also kept in ignorance as to real profits, but proper adjustment should be made at the close of the period for the reason explained just above.

Whichever method is followed, sales to branches should always be kept separate from the regular sales accounts. Where shipments of goods to branches are frequent and a matter of regular routine, a branch shipments journal similar to the sales journal should be provided; otherwise a special column in the sales journal will suffice. The total of such sales should be credited to a Branch Shipments, Branch Consignments, or some similar account, so as not to confuse these transactions with regular sales. The subject of accounting for both domestic and foreign branches is treated in Volume II.

Consignment Sales.—Consignment sales—which in some respects resemble branch sales—should also be recorded separately from regular sales. This is so because the title to goods out on consignment is still vested in the consignor and no element of profit appears in the transaction until an actual sale is made. However, in the case of an *occasional* consignee as distinguished from a factor who deals regularly in consigned goods, it has usually been held that the title has passed to the consignee so far as the consignee's dealings with all except the consignor are concerned. Only in this way can the interests of innocent third parties be adequately protected.

The accounting for consignments is treated in Chapter XLVIII.

Instalment Sales.—The instalment sale should be treated in a different manner from regular sales because of certain special features connected with it. The chief characteristic of the instalment sale is the probability of the goods coming back into the seller's possession through forfeiture because of non-payment of instalments, the profit on the transaction of course being affected thereby.

The sale of goods with the privilege of payment in instalments is a well-recognized custom in certain lines, particularly in the furniture, piano, book subscription, and similar businesses. To protect the seller, the sale contract almost invariably contains a clause to the effect that title to the goods shall remain in the seller until final payment has been made, that failure to pay any instalment when due shall result in the cancellation of the contract, and that in such case the goods shall be returned to the seller. Experience with this class of sales shows that a large number of contracts are forfeited with or without return of the goods. Where the goods are returned, there is frequently a large loss through depreciation, the returned goods having to be treated as second-hand. In some instances, to enforce return of the goods might entail greater expense than loss of the goods themselves. These are, of course, questions of business policy rather than of accounting, although the results shown by the accounting department enter into their settlement.

Accounting for Instalment Sales.—The accounting for sales under the instalment plan is not different from accounting for other sales. They are, in their first record, charged to the customer and credited to Sales or various departmental sales accounts. If the goods are forfeited and returned, the record is to Returned Sales for the debit and the customer is credited for the unpaid instalment. Whatever profit or loss there may be on the transaction will be shown in the Profit and Loss account when the inventory is taken and the returned goods are appraised. If the customer fails to pay his instalments but does not return the goods, the loss is one from bad debts.

Separation of Instalment from Regular Sales Records.—Where both instalment and regular sales are made, as is usually the case since few concerns limit their activities entirely to the instalment method, it is best to keep a separate instalment ledger with a controlling account, called "Instalment Accounts Receivable" or "Instalment Contracts." The two classes of customers should be kept separate because of the greater liability to loss in the one class than in the other. Before profits for the period can be correctly determined, it is necessary to estimate the probable loss on contracts closed during the period. In the balance sheet separate showing should be made of the reserve for this class of accounts receivable and the reserve for the other class. The estimated loss on the instalment accounts is of course a figure based upon experience, but a conservative policy requires that the amount should be fairly liberal.

Delinquency Records.—Forfeiture of contracts is not usually enforced upon first failure to pay an instalment, but such delinquencies should be brought to the attention of the management and particularly of the credit and collection department. Delinquency may even be recorded in the books by transfer from the Instalment Accounts Receivable to a "Delinquent Instalment" account. This makes an up-to-date analysis of the Instalment Receivable account and so furnishes a better basis for estimating losses from bad debts than where no separation is made.

Chief Considerations in Handling Instalment Sales.—From the accounting standpoint, the chief question is that of making the estimate for loss from uncollectible accounts. From the standpoint of financial management, instalment sales present the problems of passing on credits before taking the risks and afterwards of pushing collections so as to prevent, whenever possible, forfeiture and consequent loss. It is not purposed to treat of these phases here, for which the student is referred to standard works on credits and collections.

Sales for Future Delivery.—From a legal point of view, the receipt of a purchase order gives rise to certain rights and obligations enforceable at law between buyer and seller. While the seller may not be able to enforce specific performance of the contract, yet he is entitled to the damage incurred through nonperformance. Every merchant knows, however, that the cost of securing the remedy is usually higher than the resulting gain and, furthermore, an action against the customer frequently causes the loss of his trade.

Sales for future delivery do not always materialize, since either the buyer or the seller may wish to cancel the contract. A conservative policy therefore demands that the sale be not booked until delivery is made. The order, however, may be received in one fiscal period and the sale be credited to the period in which the goods are delivered, while the major part of the expenses in connection with the sale may have been incurred during the period in which the order was received. The current period then is charged with the expenses but does not receive the credit to which it seems entitled. Therefore, the portion of the selling expense incurred during the period in which the order was secured should be deferred to the period which receives the credit for the sale.

This policy should be followed even when the goods covered by the future sale are set aside specifically for future delivery and the sale should not be booked until delivery is made. At inventory time such goods should be included at cost, with the deferred expense charge as above. Occasionally an unscrupulous merchant in need of cash will bill such goods and discount the invoice; but for the reason given above such goods should not be charged to the customer until delivery is made.

Department Store Sales.—As indicated above, in a department store sales are usually classified by departments. The two classes of sales tickets, cash and credit, are sorted by departments and the totals are entered daily either in the sales journal or on the loose sales sheets which, when filed in a binder, make up the sales journal. At the end of the month the journal is posted to the various department sales accounts. Each day the entries on the sales journal are checked against the cashier's record of cash received from sales and the bookkeeper's record of charges posted to customers.

C. O. D. Sales.—For this class of sales the credit is booked in the usual way but the debit is made to a C.O.D. account. The packages are charged on the shipping department's memorandum records to the various delivery men who are credited with the collections turned in. These collections form the basis for the credit to the C.O.D. account on the ledger. Any balance in the C.O.D. account shows the amount of the undelivered goods still on hand in the shipping department or on the wagons and therefore charged against the various drivers.

Approval Sales.—In many lines of business approval sales are common. Merchandising concerns frequently send goods to customers for trial and inspection, with the privilege of return if the goods prove unsatisfactory. Publishing houses often send out books—both single volumes and whole sets—with a few days' examination privilege. This class of business is often handled in a rather unsystematic fashion. Usually it is impossible to discriminate among prospective customers, since offers of this kind must be made to all alike. Consequently the privilege is often abused by the unscrupulous.

Accounting for Approval Sales.—This abuse creates the problem of a correct method of handling approval sales. The difficulty is rather one of organization and administration than of accounting procedure; the record-keeping presents no new difficulties and under certain conditions may be likened to the methods of recording outward consigned goods. In no sense are such transactions to be regarded as sales and handled in the regular sales records, thereby showing a profit not yet earned. The correct method, both from an accounting and a legal viewpoint, is to keep a memorandum record of approval sales similar to that made for consignments.

Unlike consignments, however, the price shown in the invoice is the actual selling price of the goods, and the sale if consummated is treated as a regular sale, no effort being made to keep the profit or loss on approval sales separate from the profit on regular sale transactions.

In the retail trade the prevailing practice in handling approval sales is to enter the charge to the customer's account when the goods are sent out and to credit the account for all returns. In this way the books keep record of all goods out on approval and provide an adequate check against lost or misplaced goods.

When transactions of this kind are large in number, subsidiary books devoted exclusively to their record may be kept.

Tickler File Method of Handling Approval Sales.—Approval sales transactions must usually be completed within a comparatively short space of time, either by acceptance or by return of the goods, and in such cases a shorter method of recording them is followed. The sales tickets or invoices covering approval sales are made with some kind of a distinctive mark—color of paper, title, etc.—to allow their easy separation from the regular sales tickets. These tickets are kept in a temporary tickler file in the order of the expiration dates of the approval period. If the sale is consummated, the ticket bearing a stamp to that effect is sent through for record as a regular cash or credit sale. If the goods are returned, the ticket may be filed as a part of that particular customer's record; in this way a cumulative record is secured which would in some cases give an interesting commentary on human nature. If the customer is one who makes it his or her practice to buy on approval to secure the free use of nice wares for an evening or for some social function, the record would show it. A rigorous and unrelenting collection and follow-up system, supplemented by a full credit and information record, is the only safeguard against unscrupulous customers and oftentimes even this proves inadequate.

At inventory time all goods out on approval as shown by the approval sales file must be included in the inventory at inventory price, for the goods are still owned by the firm. As stated above, they must never be treated as sales.

The Bill and Charge System.—By this name is known the method of writing up the customer's bill and using it as the basis for the charge to his account. The system is operated somewhat as follows: The duplicate sales tickets go to the auditing department, where they are first sorted by departments to secure the departmental analysis of the sales, and then re-sorted according to customers. Thus, if a customer has made purchases in more than one department, the tickets covering all his purchases are brought together. Each customer's monthly bill or statement of account is started at the beginning of the month on a folded billhead perforated at the fold, the duplicate or under portion usually being somewhat wider, with loose-leaf binder punchings. On these bill and duplicate blanks the charges for the day are entered from the sorted sales tickets. This work is usually done on a billing machine with carbon roll or with carbon paper insertion.

At the end of the day the total amount of the charges entered on all monthly statements is either found by means of an adding machine or is indicated by the "tally strip" of the billing machine. This total must of course be equal to the aggregate amount of all sales tickets for that day, thereby proving the work of the billing clerks.

Customers' bills after entry each day may either be passed on to the bookkeepers who charge each customer's account with the day's total purchases as shown by the bill, or the bills are returned to the file until used again for subsequent purchases. In such case the bookkeeper enters the total monthly charge to the customer's account, only once a month.

Returned goods and allowances are also entered on these customers' bills, but in a separate column or on another portion of the sheet.

The total charges entered on these statements must check against the total credit sales for the month, thus proving the additions of the bills.

At the end of the month the bill is torn from its duplicate and is passed to the bookkeepers. They enter the previous month's balance, if there is one, and the current payments on account, and extend the amount now due. After the bills or statements have been mailed to the customers, the duplicate bills are filed away, being virtually the detail of the ledger account, for use in case of dispute.

This method of handling credit sales provides a ready means of getting the bills out on time, of assuring agreement between the ledger accounts and the bills, of freeing the ledger accounts of unnecessary detail, and of checking the total billings against the total sales tickets.

Salesmen's Commissions and Efficiency Records.—Salesmen are often paid a commission in addition to salaries. Where the commission is based on the amount of sales, the sales ticket is made use of as the source of information for computing the commissions earned. To this end the tickets are sorted according to salesmen, and a record sheet, either separate or as an adjunct to the sales journal sheets, is filled in with each salesman's total sales for the day. These totals should prove against the salesman's record in the back of his book of sales tickets. At the end of the month his total sales are shown by his record sheet and his commission is determined therefrom. Of course, the total for all salesmen as shown by these sheets must equal the total sales for the period.

If the commission, often known as "spifs" or "P. M.'s," is allowed only on certain classes of sales in order to encourage the movement of old stock, each sales ticket should indicate the amount of premium or commission due, so that a record can be made without the necessity of depending on the records of the individual salesmen.

Salesmen's records besides being used for the particular purpose of computing commission, or bonuses due them, serve a wider object in that they contain fairly complete and reliable data in regard to the value and efficiency of individual salesmen. For this reason such records should be kept at all times, no matter whether a commission or bonus system is operated or not. Whenever an increase in a salesman's salary is considered or when the sales force is to be decreased in number, these efficiency records are a valuable aid in making the right decision.

CHAPTER XLVIII
CONSIGNMENTS

Definition.—When goods are shipped to another party to be sold by him for account of the shipper, the transaction is called a "consignment." In its original sense, to "consign" means to seal, sign, mark, or label in a formal way. In commerce this term has come to signify goods sent for sale through another party. Usually such goods are marked or labeled to distinguish them from those belonging to the consignee. The owner or sender is designated "the consignor"; the selling or receiving party "the consignee." Sometimes the word "shipment" is used by the consignor to designate the goods sent away for sale, and the word "consignment" to indicate the goods received by the consignee. Differentiation on this basis is convenient, but the terms "consignments-out" and "consignments-in" are more descriptive and will be used here.

Legal Status.—Before treating the accounts required to record consignment transactions, it is well to understand the legal relations between the consignor and consignee. The general law of bailments and of agency applies in a restricted sense to consignments. A bailment is defined as, "A delivery of goods for the execution of a special object, beneficial to the bailor, the bailee or both, upon a contract expressed or implied, to carry out this object, and dispose of the property in conformity with the purpose of the trust." Agency is the term used to indicate the legal relation between a principal and the agent who represents him. A person appointing another to act for him in his dealings with third parties is called the principal. The one appointed to represent the principal is the agent. A bailment is therefore a special class of agency transactions with particular rules governing the safekeeping of the goods of the principal in the possession of the agent. In the case of a consignment, the consignor is the principal and the consignee the agent. The relation of the consignee to the consignor as regards the care to be exercised in handling the consignor's goods is a bailment relationship.

The Broker.—A broker, although he acts as agent, usually is not a consignee. He acts "as a middleman, bringing people together to trade, or trading for them in the private purchase or sale of any kind of property, which property, ordinarily, is not in his possession." The charge for his service is usually in the form of a commission, sometimes called brokerage. There are several classes of brokers, named according to the kind of commodity they deal in; for instance, there is the exchange broker, the note broker, the insurance broker, the stock broker, the real estate broker, the merchandise broker, etc.

The Factor.—Other types of middlemen are the manufacturer's agent, who is a broker or sales agent, effecting sales usually by means of samples; and the factor or commission merchant who actually handles and sells the goods of his principal. The chief distinction between the broker and the factor is that the broker sells goods in the name and for the account of his principal, but the goods are delivered directly to the purchaser by the principal, who also collects the account; whereas the factor has the goods of his principal in his possession and sells them either in his own name or in the name of his principal.

The factor may operate under a specific contract with his principal, covering a single consignment, or under a general contract governing all consignment transactions between the two parties. Again, there may be no formal contract between them, in which case the law sets up a contract relationship based on trade usage and customs in any particular line. Where the factor operates under a specific or general contract, certain points may arise which are not provided for in such contract, and on these points trade custom governs.

Duties of the Factor.—Barring specific instructions, the factor may conduct the consignment transactions for his principal on the same basis and in the same general way as he would conduct them were the goods his own. In other words, he is expected to exercise the same care in the handling of consignment goods as he employs in handling his own property. In selling goods consigned to him he may extend credit to the buyer if it is the custom in that particular line to do so, and he must exercise due care as to the rating of the customer. He must push his collections with ordinary diligence. He may warrant the goods sold if that is customary. He can give good title to goods sold, and this title may even be better than the one possessed by the owner of the goods. A bona fide purchaser who does not know the principal is protected in a sale made by a factor even if the factor exceeded his authority.

Factor Must Protect Goods.—So long as any part of the principal's goods are unsold and in the possession of the factor, he must protect and safeguard them. He is not liable, however, for damage from forces or conditions over which he has no control. The degree of diligence required of him largely depends on the nature of the goods. What would be considered due diligence in one case, might be construed as gross neglect in the case of more valuable or perishable goods.

Consignments to be Kept Separate.—It is a fundamental requirement and of the very essence of the factor relationship, that the principal's goods must be kept distinct from all other goods in the factor's possession. This applies not only to the consigned goods as such, but also to the assets received by the factor upon the sale of such goods—as cash, accounts and notes receivable, etc. To satisfy this latter requirement it is usually held that actual separation is not necessary, but that it is sufficient to record these properties in such a manner that they can always be separated if the need arises. The principal's properties are held in trust for him by the factor but are subject to the legitimate claims of the factor.

Expenses Charged against Consignment.—Barring specific instructions to the contrary, the factor may incur certain expenses necessary to safeguard the interest of his principal and to effect the sale of his goods. These include such items as freight, insurance, duty, handling charges, allowances and rebates to customers for unsatisfactory goods, etc. All these are proper charges against the consignment, i.e., against the principal.

Factor's Lien on Consigned Goods.—For any legitimate expenses incurred and for any payments made the principal in advance of the settlement date, the factor has a lien on the consigned goods. It has been held in some cases that the factor has the right to sell the goods in satisfaction of the lien, and if the proceeds of the sale are not sufficient to satisfy the factor's claims against the principal, the latter is liable for the amount of the deficiency. The factor's commission from the principal is also protected by this lien and, if necessary, the factor may apply part or all the proceeds of the sale toward the payment of his commission. A lien, of course, is binding only so long as the goods are in the factor's possession.

Account Sales.—Upon completion of his service the factor must make a strict accounting of his transactions to the principal. In case of dispute he can be required to open to the inspection of the principal his records covering the consignment dealings. The usual method of settlement is by means of an "account sales" rendered by the factor to his principal. The account sales is a summarized statement of all transactions connected with a particular consignment. It constitutes the formal accounting for the consignment transaction. It must show the amount or quantity of goods received, the sales made, and the expenses incurred, the balance being the amount due the principal. This amount may be either remitted or credited to the principal's account, according to the contract between them. The usual form of account sales is shown in Form 44.

Goods may be billed to the factor at cost, at the current market price, or at some fictitious figure. This billing price does not enter into the accounting of the factor at all. It is the selling price of the factor which is the basis of income against which expenses are charged. The principal may indicate a selling price for his goods but this serves merely as a guide to the factor as to the price desired. If, however, the principal gives specific instruction as to sale price, the agent must govern himself accordingly.

ACCOUNT SALES
of fruit received via Seaboard Air Line, from
H. C. CLONEY, BRADENTOWN, FLA.,
to be sold for his account and risk

RENDERED BY GAYNOR & GAYNOR, 21 WHITEHALL ST.,
NEW YORK, MARCH 5, 19—

19—						
Feb. 2	Received:					
	250 bxs. oranges	@	$3.75	$937.50		
	100 " lemons	@	4.25	425.00	$1,362.50	
	SALES					
Feb. 3	100 bxs. oranges	@	$4.50	$450.00		
	75 " lemons	@	4.40	330.00		
5	150 " oranges	@	4.75	712.50		
	25 " lemons	@	5.00	125.00	$1,617.50	
	CHARGES					
	Freight & Cartage			$ 50.00		
	Commission 5%			80.88	130.88	
	Net proceeds by check enclosed				$1,486.62	
	E. & O. E.					

Form 44. Account Sales

Compensation of Factor.—The factor usually receives his compensation on a commission basis—so many per cent of the sales he makes. When the contract makes specific provision for it, he may sell the goods at a higher price than that fixed by the principal and retain part or all of the excess as compensation.

"Del Credere" Agency.—Where a factor sells on credit, the accounts belong to the principal and any loss through uncollectible accounts is borne by the latter. Sometimes the factor guarantees the collection of all accounts; in this case he is known as a "del credere" agent and receives additional compensation for assuming this risk. Such a guarantee really amounts to a sale of the accounts to the factor.

Advantages of Consignments.—While the practice of consignment trading is not so prevalent now as it was formerly, it still prevails in some lines and under certain conditions. Shippers to the produce market frequently consign their goods to city brokers whom they instruct to take advantage of the prices prevailing in the open market, and in this way they may realize higher prices than when they sell outright to the wholesaler. The consignment shipment has another advantage to the shipper, in that the title to the goods remains vested in him; hence a consignment is safer than a sale on credit to a consignee unless his rating is satisfactory. The practice of consignment trading is of sufficient importance to require a discussion of the accounting principles involved. These will be given first from the viewpoint of the consignor, and then from that of the consignee.

The Consignor's Entries.—The chief interest of the consignor lies in the net outcome of each sale in order to determine the advantage, if any, of the consignment policy over a straight sale policy. To accomplish this, he must keep a separate account with each consignment, either on the general ledger or on a subsidiary ledger with a total summary account on the general ledger. When the consignor sends the goods, whether they be invoiced at cost, sale, or some other price, entry should not be made direct to his Sales account, for no sale has been made as yet. He has merely placed some of his stock in another market, being still the owner of the goods.

Two Methods of Entering Sales on Consignor's Books.—There are two ways of recording correctly a consignment on the consignor's books at the time the goods are sent. According to one method, the goods are transferred from Purchases to another merchandise account, having for its title the word "Consignment," followed usually by the name of the consignee and the number of the particular consignment made to him, as "Consignment No. 4, J. B. Arscott." To this account are charged not only the goods at cost price but also all expenses of the transfer, as freight, duty, insurance, etc., the corresponding credits being to Cash or to Purchases as the case may require. This is the only record made, until the account sales is received from the factor. Upon the receipt of the account sales, the Consignment account may either be credited with the net proceeds or be charged with the expenses and credited with the gross sales, as shown in the account sales. If the money is remitted by the factor the Cash account is debited; otherwise the factor's account is debited for the net proceeds.

The Consignment account is now a true proprietorship account, showing income on the one side and cost of that income on the other side. The difference is either a profit or a loss according as the balance is a credit or a debit. In order readily to distinguish complete consignment transactions from those only partially completed, it is best to close the completed accounts by a transfer of the balance to a "Consignments Profit and Loss" account where it is held until the close of a fiscal period, at which time it is carried to the general profit and loss.

The second method of recording the transaction at the time of sending the consignment is to set up two memorandum accounts, Consignment and Consignment-Out (or Consignment Sales), debiting and crediting these respectively with the invoiced value of the consigned goods. In this case there is no credit to the Purchases account as under the first method given above. Any expenses incurred are charged to the regular expense accounts instead of to the Consignment account. For handling the consignment shipments no special books are required, original entry being in the general journal. If there are many such transactions, however, a special column in the sales journal or a special consignments-out journal is desirable.

Upon receipt of the account sales, the regular sales account is credited either with the net or with the gross proceeds; and the other accounts—as cash, the consignee, and expenses—are debited according to the manner of booking as explained in connection with the first method.

The two memorandum accounts, having served their purpose of calling attention to the fact that some goods have been sent to other markets for sale, should now be canceled by a reversing entry, since the goods have been sold and the record of their sale has been made in the regular sales account. The effect of this second method is to merge consignment and regular sales transactions into one record, making impossible a separate showing of the profit or loss on consignments. The particular method to be used, therefore, will depend upon the information desired.

Consignor's Inventory.—If the consignor's fiscal period closes before an account sales in full settlement is received, and if accounting treatment is by the first method, the goods shown in the Consignment account are included in the inventory of goods on hand and so represented in the balance sheet. If the second method is used, the Consignment and Consignment-Out accounts are both omitted from the balance sheet, being merely canceling memorandum entries, and the unsold portion of the consigned goods are included in the inventory. In determining the value of consigned goods, the expenses incurred in sending the goods to the new market may properly be included as a part of the cost.

The Consignee's Entries—First Method.—Two methods of making entries on the consignee's books at the time of receipt of goods are used. In the first method, two memorandum accounts, Consignments and Consignments-In, are set up, Consignments being debited for the billed value of the goods received, and Consignments-In being credited for the same item. The purpose of these accounts is merely to set up on the general books a reminder of the transaction.

A third account, John Doe, Principal, is used for current record. This account is charged with the expenses incurred in connection with the consignment and is credited with the sales made therefrom; it is charged also with the consignee's commission. The balance of the account is, at the completion of the sale, the amount due the consignor, Doe. When this is paid, the account is closed by a debit to John Doe, Principal, and a credit to Cash or Notes

Payable. So long as the balance is unpaid, the account, John Doe, Principal, shows the factor's liability to his principal. This is a special kind of liability, that of a trustee, which is indicated by the inclusion of the word "Principal" in the account title; in case of insolvency a portion of the assets equal to the balance of John Doe, Principal's account belongs to John Doe and, unless merged beyond possibility of separation, must be so treated. When the sale has been completed, the memorandum accounts, Consignments and Consignments-In, are canceled against each other, having served their purpose.

The Consignee's Entries—Second Method.—Under the second method, instead of an entry on the general books, the receipt of the goods is recorded in a blotter or memorandum book of consignments received, in which are entered all essential data, covering the name of consignor, quantity, price, legend or distinguishing marks, etc. Expenses incurred are charged to John Doe, Consignment account on the general books, and sales are credited to the same account. Settlement is made as with John Doe, Principal, as explained above, except that when the balance is not paid it frequently is transferred to a simple John Doe personal account, where so far as account title is concerned it loses its character as a trust account and is merged with all other creditors.

Consignments Must Have Distinguishing Marks.—In making his sales from the various consignments, the factor must be careful to record them in a way to distinguish the goods taken from different consignments. This is particularly true of sales on account, for if the accounts prove uncollectible it is important to know to which lot the loss must be charged. This is accomplished by recording the consignment legend or mark with the sale.

Factor's Books at Close of Fiscal Period.—When the factor's books are closed, the commissions earned to date on consignment sales, whether the entire consignment transaction is fully or only partially completed, should be taken into account. Commissions earned on completed consignments should already be on the books as debits to the various principals' accounts and credits to "Commissions Earned." The commissions on incomplete consignments are brought on the books by entry of the accrued income in the Commissions Earned account, the amount being based on the sales made from the incompleted consignments during the period. The accounts with these incomplete consignments may show either debit or credit balances. If a debit balance is shown, the account is an asset representing the consignee's claim against his principal for expenses incurred in excess of sales made. If a credit balance is shown, the account represents a trust liability as above. At a closing time the memorandum accounts of incomplete transactions should be adjusted to their present inventory values.

Consignee's Inventory.—Just as the consignor must be careful to include in his inventory all goods out on consignment, so the consignee must be equally careful to exclude from his inventory all goods of his principal's still unsold and in his possession.

Illustrative Entries on Consignor's and Consignee's Books.—An illustration of a simple consignment transaction from the viewpoint of both consignor and consignee is given below. It is assumed that a consignment transaction takes place between J. J. Querles and I. M. Factor as follows:

PROBLEM. Querles sends to Factor to be sold on his account goods amounting at cost to $1,250. He pays cartage $15, and insurance $25; while Factor pays freight, duty, and cartage amounting to $52.50. Factor makes sales of $1,600 and renders an account sales showing also allowances to customers of $27.30, a 5% commission charge and 1% for guaranteeing collection of all accounts, and the net proceeds credited.

1. Querles' books at the time of sending the goods to Factor:

Consignment, I. M. Factor, No. 1	1,250.00	
Purchases		1,250.00
Consignment, I. M. Factor, No. 1	40.00	
Cash		40.00
Cartage $15, insurance $25.		

2. Factor's books at the time of receipt of Querles' goods:

Consignment	1,250.00	
Consignments-In		1,250.00
To set up memo accounts of the receipt of Querles' goods.		
J. J. Querles, Principal	52.50	
Cash		52.50
Freight, duty, and cartage on Querles' goods.		

3. Factor's books during the course of consignment transactions:

Customers	1,600.00	
J. J. Querles, Principal		1,600.00

    To credit Querles with the sales.

J. J. Querles, Principal	123.30	
Customers		27.30
Commissions		80.00
Collections Guarantee		16.00

    To charge Querles with all expenses.

Consignments-In	1,250.00	
Consignment		1,250.00

    To reverse.

4. Querles' books upon receipt of the account sales:

Consignment, I. M. Factor, No. 1	175.80	
I. M. Factor	1,424.20	
Consignment, I. M. Factor, No. 1		1,600.00

    To credit the consignment with its sales and charge it with its expenses, including commission and to charge Factor with the balance due.

Consignment, I. M. Factor, No. 1	134.20	
Consignments Profit and Loss		134.20

    To transfer the profit on this consignment.

5. When Factor finally remits the balance of $1,424.20, his entry is:

J. J. Querles, Principal	1,424.20	
Cash		1,424.20

thus canceling his liability to Querles.

6. Querles' books will show:

Cash	1,424.20	
I. M. Factor		1,424.20

canceling his claim against Factor.

If the second method (see page 455) of making the consignor's record is used, the entries under No. 1 will appear as follows:

Consignment, I. M. Factor, No. 1	1,250.00	
Consignments-Out		1,250.00
Cartage	15.00	
Insurance	25.00	
Cash		40.00

and No. 4 would be:

Freight	52.50	
Sales Allowances	27.30	
Commissions	96.00	
I. M. Factor	1,424.20	
Sales		1,600.00
Consignments-Out	1,250.00	
Consignment, I. M. Factor, No. 1		1,250.00
To reverse.		

In these last entries made under the second method, consignment sales are included in the regular Sales account, and the profit or loss is merged with that from regular sales.

Decision as to which of the two accounting methods should be used must be made according to the information desired by the principal. Where consignment transactions are a side line, the record is usually kept by the first method which shows the profit or the loss on each transaction and thus furnishes valuable information for executives. This is sometimes called the occasional consignment theory or method. Where the consignment transaction is the usual method of effecting sales, the second method illustrated above is generally to be followed, because by this method all consignment transactions are properly included in the regular sales and expense records.

CHAPTER XLIX
ADVENTURE SALES

Adventure Transactions.—Before the day of easy transportation and communication between markets, adventure or venture undertakings were quite common. The inherent willingness of men to take a chance, and the desire to speculate, often led to the fitting out of cargoes of merchandise for sale in distant ports and the equipping of trading expeditions into unknown regions. Many dangers had to be met, the hazards and risks being great. Success attended many adventurers, and many also met with failure. Even today this method of seeking a market has its allurements.

Single and Joint Ventures.—Adventures are of two kinds, single and joint. The single adventure is merely an outward consignment by a single proprietor and is treated in accounting as such, i.e., it is charged with all its costs and credited with its returns, the balance being either a profit or a loss. The joint venture is accounted for on the same principle, although the procedure may be much more complicated. A joint venture account may be defined as the record of "commercial transactions of a particular kind, usually of a temporary nature, entered into jointly by several parties who combine together for the purpose, contribute the capital and the services, as may be arranged, and agree to share the losses or profits in certain proportions." Speculation in stocks, the chartering of a ship for a particular purpose, a particular voyage, or a fixed period of time—these are some lines of present-day joint venture endeavor.

Relations between Parties.—From the legal point of view, the combination under a joint venture is a special partnership, i.e., one entered into for the accomplishment of a special purpose, the several parties to it having control, as in a partnership, and sharing profits and losses either according to contract or, in its absence, equally. Usually, in a joint venture one of the parties or an outside agent is entrusted with the entire enterprise.

Accounting for the Joint Venture.—Accounting for the joint transactions is comparatively easy. If the undertaking is simple, one account for each such joint undertaking, viz., "Joint Venture," will suffice. This account will be carried on the records of the regular business of each party to the venture. The account is debited with the costs of the venture and credited with the returns from it.

If the enterprise is more complicated, it may be required to set up a number of separate accounts, or even a separate set of records, but the summary or clearing account for these will still exhibit costs set over against returns. If the partners are all in the same city and have access to the records, one set of accounts is all that is necessary. Where the partners are in different places, each should keep a record of all transactions as reported by the manager of the venture. Since the manager reports all transactions to each of the parties, the "Joint Venture" accounts as kept by the different partners will all be the same.

The other accounts affected by the joint transactions will either be the same or reciprocal. Upon the inception of the venture, some of the partners having contributed cash, others merchandise, still other facilities, services, etc., the Joint Venture account is charged with all contributions and each partner is credited. If the venture is managed by one of the partners, instead of a credit to his own personal account, his cash or merchandise account will receive the credit for his contribution. If the managing partner desires to separate his investment in the joint venture from his investment in his regular business, he will set up a Joint Venture Investment account to which the amount of his contribution to the joint venture will be transferred from his regular capital account. Expenses incurred are charged to the joint account and credited to the partner paying them. All sales made and collected are credited to the joint account and charged to the partner retaining the money.

Interest Allowances and Charges.—Because some partners may have made larger contributions than others, the agreement may provide that interest be credited the partners on their contributions. On the other hand it frequently happens that one or some of the partners have the use of the moneys received from joint sales until date of settlement of the venture, and the agreement may provide that interest shall be charged to those retaining the collected funds. This can be accomplished by charging the joint account and crediting the partners with interest from the dates of their contributions to the date of settlement, and by charging the partners retaining joint funds and crediting the joint account from the date when the funds come into their possession until the settlement date. A salary or a commission may be allowed the managing partner or partners. This also is a charge to the joint account and a credit to the partner.

Distribution of Profits.—After all transactions have been completed and all charges and credits made, the joint account for each venture will show by its balance the net profit or loss. This is distributed among the partners in agreed ratio, or in equal ratio in the absence of agreement. After this is done, only the partners' accounts remain, some with debit and others with credit balances. The managing partner should collect the debit balances and remit to those with credit balances, thus making a complete settlement of the joint undertaking.

Should the fiscal period of any of the partners close during the term of the venture, conservatism would generally require that his own accounts do not show a profit on the sales made to date, on the theory that losses on the incomplete portion may wipe out any profits on the completed portion. This is because the joint undertaking is considered as a whole and inseparable transaction and not as composed of numerous separate sales. The element of risk is always an important factor in undertakings of this sort. However, there might be circumstances under which the taking of at least a partial profit could be justified. Assuming that no profit is taken, the joint account becomes a balance sheet account at closing, asset or liability according as costs have been more or less than the sales as on the date of closing.

Joint Venture Accounts Illustrated.—An illustration will bring out the salient points in the above discussion:

PROBLEM. A, B, and C enter a joint venture to Mexico, with C as manager. A and C contribute merchandise valued at $5,000 and $8,000 respectively, and B $11,000 cash for the purchase of additional merchandise. C is to receive 3% commission on sales. C pays freight, duty, and insurance of $890 from his own cash, and buys merchandise with B's contribution. He makes sales, according to reports sent by him to A and B, aggregating $30,000, and holds the amount in his possession one month till settlement. The investment period is six months. Interest at 6% is to be credited to partners on their original investments and is to be charged to C on the $30,000 held by him for one month.[7] A, B, and C share profits in the ratio of their original contributions. Settlement is made by C in cash.

The following entries show the record of the above transactions on B's and C's books.

1. At the beginning of the venture the record will be:

On B's books:

Joint Venture, A and C, to Mexico	24,000.00	
A		5,000.00
Cash		11,000.00
C		8,000.00

To set up the venture transaction.

B, Capital	11,000.00	
Joint Venture, A and C, Investment		11,000.00

To show capital invested in joint venture.

Joint Venture, A and C, to Mexico	890.00	

C		890.00	
Freight, duty, etc., paid by C.			

On C's books:

Joint Venture, A and B, to Mexico	24,000.00	
A		5,000.00
B		11,000.00
Purchases		8,000.00
(As above.)		
C, Capital	8,000.00	
Joint Venture, A and B, Investment		8,000.00
(As above.)		
Joint Venture, A and B, to Mexico	890.00	
Cash		890.00
(As above.)		
C, Capital	890.00	
Joint Venture, A and B, Investment		890.00
Freight, duty, etc., paid by C.		

2. On B's books at the time of settlement:

Joint Venture, A and C, to Mexico	1,620.00	
A		150.00
Interest Income, Joint Venture, A and C		330.00
C		1,140.00
6% interest on original contributions of each partner for six months; 3% commission to C on sales.		

C	30,150.00	
Joint Venture, A and C to Mexico		30,150.00

    6% interest charged C on $30,000 for one month; C charged with his collections from sales $30,000.

On C's books:

Joint Venture, A and B, to Mexico	1,620.00	
A		150.00
B		330.00
Interest Income, Joint Venture, A and B		240.00
Commission Earned, Joint Venture, A and B		900.00
Cash	30,000.00	
Interest Cost	150.00	
Joint Venture, A and B, to Mexico		30,150.00

3. On the records of all the partners the Joint Venture account shows a credit balance, i.e., a profit of $3,640, the distribution of which will be as follows:

On B's books:

Joint Venture, A and C, to Mexico	3,640.00	
A		758.33
Profit and Loss, on Joint Venture, A and C		1,668.34
C		1,213.33

    To distribute profits on the venture in the agreed ratio 5:11:8.

On C's books:

Joint Venture, A and B, to Mexico	3,640.00	

A	758.33
B	1,668.34
Profit and Loss on Joint Venture, A and B	1,213.33

B's accounts now show a balance due A of $5,908.33; a claim against C for $18,906.67; his own share therefore being the difference, or $12,998.34. That this is the correct amount is seen by comparing it with the amount of B's Joint Venture, A and C, Investment account showing $11,000, his Interest Income Joint Venture, A and C, showing $330, and his Profit and Loss on Joint Venture, A and C, showing $1,668.34.

4. C now makes settlement in cash with his copartners for the respective amounts due them. The settlement transactions will appear as follows:

On B's books:

Cash	12,998.34	
C		12,998.34

    Cash from C in settlement of Joint Venture.

A	5,908.33	
C		5,908.33

    C reports settlement with A.

On C's books:

A	5,908.33	
B	12,998.34	
Cash		18,906.67

    Settlement with A and B on Joint Venture.

After these entries have been made on B's books, the joint venture with A and C will be shown completed. His books show a full net profit on the venture of $1,998.54, reflected in the excess of cash received from C over cash given him for investment. At the end of B's regular fiscal period, the profit on the venture will ordinarily be shown separately on the statement of profit and loss after the item, Net Profit from Operations. It will be set up as follows:

Joint Venture, A and C, to Mexico (Schedule B-5)		$1,998.34
Gross Returns in cash from C, Managing Partner	$12,998.34	
Original Investment	11,000.00	
Net Profit, as above	$ 1,998.34	

Schedule B-5 should give a complete report of the venture, somewhat as follows:

JOINT VENTURE, WITH A AND C, TO MEXICO

Gross Returns as reported by C, Managing Partner		$30,000.00
Costs:		
Merchandise Purchases	$24,000.00	
Expenses	890.00	24,890.00
Gross Profit		$ 5,110.00
Commission to C		900.00
		$ 4,210.00

Add:

Interest paid by C for use of funds after completion of venture		150.00
Net Profit to be distributed:		$ 4,360.00
A, Interest on Capital	$ 150.00	
Profit and loss share, $5/24$ of $3,640$	758.33	$ 908.33
C, Interest on Capital	$ 240.00	
Profit and loss share, $8/24$ of $3,640$	1,213.33	1,453.33

B, Interest on Capital	$330.00		
Profit and loss share, $^{11}/_{24}$ of $3,640	1,668.34	1,998.34	$4,360.00

At the close of the period the account, Joint Venture, A and C, Investment, having served its purpose, is transferred back to B's regular capital account.

C's accounts show a balance due A of $5,908.33; due B, $12,998.34; the remainder of the joint income, $11,243.33 {$30,150 - ($5,908.33 + $12,998.34) = $11,243.33}, being his own share.

After the same manner as B, C will make, at the close of his regular fiscal period, a summary of the joint venture, showing it in his statement of profit and loss somewhat as follows:

Joint Venture, A and B, to Mexico:

Commission as Managing Partner	$ 900.00	
Share of Profit (see Schedule B-5)	1,453.33	$2,353.33
Gross Returns in cash	$11,243.33	
Original Investment	8,890.00	
Profit, as above,	$ 2,353.33	

The student will note that the $150 interest paid by C for the $30,000 joint funds used by him for one month is not recorded as an interest cost of the venture, but is charged to C's regular Interest Cost account because the funds must have been used for the conduct of his regular business.

The accounts on each partner's books with his copartners are not ordinary asset and liability accounts but are more of the nature of capital accounts and might be entitled "A, Contribution," "B, Contribution," etc. The records of the joint venture comprise a group of accounts which constitute a unit within themselves, showing the partnership relation existing among the several parties from the inception of the partnership to its liquidation.

CHAPTER L
ACCOUNTS CURRENT

Definition.—An account current in its broadest sense is an account of current transactions. In a technical sense, it is an open personal account, one with an outstanding balance. Frequently accounts are allowed to run on between two persons, recording transaction after transaction with partial or full settlement at times but with no intention of closing the account. A principal may have constant dealings with his agent or representative, making periodical payments on account or making remittances to be used as needed by the agent. The agent may make purchases for the account of his principal, paying the bill out of his own funds. He may use in his own transactions any surplus funds of the principal in his possession. An account showing transactions of these various kinds is an account current. The customers' accounts in brokerage houses and the accounts between banks—banks and their correspondents—are other examples of accounts current.

Interest on Balances.—In handling accounts current between banks and in brokerage houses, it is the practice to charge the account with interest on the debit balances and to credit it with interest on the credit balances. It was formerly the practice in some lines of trade to charge interest on all overdue customers' accounts. Frequently today invoices carry a statement to that effect, although the policy is not often enforced through fear of loss of patronage.

Joint Venture Accounts.—In the case of joint ventures discussed in Chapter XLIX, a condition analogous to this was mentioned where the joint account was charged and the contributing partners' accounts were credited with interest, while the managing partner was charged and the joint account credited with interest on all joint funds retained in his possession.

Partners' Accounts and the Account Current.—Occasionally, also, in partnership adjustments at the close of a fiscal period, the agreement may require the business, i.e., the partnership, to allow each partner credit for interest on his investments and charge him with interest on his withdrawals. Each partner's account is treated very much as an account current of the business when such adjustments are prescribed.

Illustration of Account Current.—Thus, while the old account current as formerly understood and applied to the ordinary customer and creditor relationship is now very seldom encountered, the principle of it is met with frequently enough to demand explanation and illustration. No special form is necessary for the stating of an account current; the interest calculations on the various balances can be made outside the account and only the net result be embodied in the account. A form of account is shown in Form 45, however, which exhibits all necessary data on its face. Take the following account on which 5% interest is to be charged and allowed:

B. I. PERKINS, CURRENT ACCOUNT

19—			19—		
July 4	Cash	1,250.00	June 4	Balance	600.00
Aug. 11	Note 60 da., no int.	1,500.00	July 4	Mdse. n/30	1,400.00
Nov. 11	Cash	1,000.00	Aug. 3	Mdse. n/30	1,000.00
Dec. 7	Cash	400.00	Oct. 2	Mdse.	2,100.00
	10 Rtd. Goods of Dec. 4	50.00	Dec. 4	Mdse.	800.00

Form 45. Form of Adjusted Account Current

Adjusting the Account Current.—Adjustment of such accounts is usually made periodically. Referring to the illustration shown in Form 45, the interest calculation is made counting the exact number of days from each "date of value" to and including December 31. Interest is figured, for the sake of ease of calculation, on a 360-day basis. A 365-day basis would be more accurate and this is often done on current accounts between banks. The "date of value" is the date from which interest may be equitably charged or allowed. For example, in the above account, the credit for merchandise purchased on July 4, but with a credit allowance of 30 days, may not equitably be allowed till 30 days thereafter, or August 3. On the debit side, the note for $1,500 dated August 11, at 60 days with no interest, cannot be equitably counted until it comes due, i.e., on October 10. Similarly, the "date of value" on

December 10, for the goods returned of the transaction of December 4, must be reckoned as of the same date as the original transaction, for only a portion of the full credit set up is allowed to remain.

In the above problem, the credit interest exceeds the debit by $35.80. This amount is therefore brought as an additional credit into the account. The account as now adjusted will be sent to B. I. Perkins for his verification. When formally approved, or if no objection is made to it after a reasonable length of time, the account is balanced and it becomes now what is termed an adjusted account. This periodic adjustment makes possible the localization of disagreements and their settlement while the facts are still fresh in mind. Its effect, however, is to produce a slight compounding of interest unless the balance is immediately settled.

Another method of making the interest calculation is on the basis of the balance of the account after each transaction and the length of time it remains unchanged, i.e., until the next transaction changes the balance. This method follows somewhat the method illustrated in [Chapter XXXIII](#) for division of partners' profits on the basis of the amount of the investment and the length of time invested; but under this method it is not possible to make so condensed and apparent a statement of account as by the method illustrated in full above.

It sometimes happens that the "date of value" may fall beyond the settlement date, as where the term of credit throws the time of payment far enough ahead that payment cannot be demanded till after a periodic settlement time. The effect of such a condition is to reverse the interest charge for the period beyond the settlement date to an interest credit, or vice versa. The method of averaging accounts or equation of payments, as it is sometimes called, may be used to advantage here. Explanation and illustration of this method are given in [Chapter LII](#).

The Bank Account an Account Current.—The bank's account with a depositor is a good example of the account current. Except by special agreement, the allowance of interest is not customary. Periodically, the depositor's pass-book is balanced or a statement of his account is rendered by the bank. When the balanced pass-book, with canceled checks, is returned to the depositor, or when the statement of account is rendered by the bank, the record kept by the depositor—as shown by his check book stubs or by the bank column in his cash book—will not usually show the same balance as that indicated by the bank's statement, and adjustment or reconciliation is necessary to check the accuracy of the statement. In [Chapter XLI](#), regarding the handling of cash, the policy was recommended of depositing all receipts and paying only by check. A cash book kept under that plan, making use of a net cash column on both sides, does not need an additional column for the bank record because everything shown in the net cash columns has either been deposited in the bank or paid out by check. The cash book balance, therefore, should be the same as the bank's balance. If the record of the bank account is kept only on the check book stubs or interleaves, this balance should be the same as the bank's. But however kept, there will almost invariably be a few outstanding checks which the depositor's cash book or check book shows as having been issued, but which have not been presented to the bank for payment at the time the statement of account is rendered and which therefore are not included in the statement. This brings about a difference which must be reconciled.

Reconciliation of Bank Balance.—Two methods of reconciliation are used. The one brings the bank's balance into agreement with that of the depositor; the other starts with the depositor's balance and brings it into agreement with that of the bank. The first step in the reconciliation is to discover which of the checks issued by the depositor have not been paid by the bank. This is done by arranging the returned checks in numerical sequence and comparing these with the depositor's record of checks issued. Usually the total of these few unpaid checks will be equal to the discrepancy between the two records, and so will reconcile them.

The following problem is given to illustrate the above discussion:

PROBLEM. On March 20, at the close of the day, the bank's statement showed a balance of $1,525.14. The depositor's record on the same date showed $604.19. The following checks were outstanding: No. 529B, $214.50; 542B, $379.60; 557B, $119.40; 581B, $75.20; and 992A, $132.25.

Reconciliation statement, as on March 20, 19—:

Bank balance as per bank's statement $1,525.14

Outstanding checks:

No. 992A	$132.25	
529B	214.50	
542B	379.60	
557B	119.40	
581B	75.20	920.95

True balance as per cash (or check) book $ 604.19

Other method:

True balance as per cash book		$ 604.19
Outstanding checks:		
No. 992A	$132.25	
529B	214.50	
542B	379.60	
557B	119.40	
581B	75.20	920.95
Bank balance as per bank's statement		$1,525.14

Other Reconciliation Factors.—Oftentimes other items than those shown must be taken into consideration when reconciliation is made. Where several bank accounts are kept and a check register—in addition to the cash book—is used to keep record of the accounts with the various banks, it may happen that checks drawn on one bank are wrongly charged to another; that checks drawn, or deposits made one day, are not credited until the next; that certain drafts deposited with the bank for collection are not credited to the depositor's account until collection is made, whereas the depositor debited the bank at the time of the deposit; again it may be that the item of bank's charges for collection has not yet been recorded; or that interest on deposit balances has not been credited, etc. All such items must be considered when reconciliation is made. Where there are many of these adjustment items to be taken account of, it may be necessary to list them in formal schedules under such heads as:

- 1. Bank charges, we do not credit.
- 2. Bank credits, we do not charge.
- 3. We charge, bank does not credit.
- 4. We credit, bank does not charge.

Examples of transactions bringing about the above debits and credits are:

1. Protest fees charged against the depositor's account, of which he has not been notified.

2. Interest on bank balance credited by bank before the depositor is notified.

3. Deposits made and charged to bank but not yet credited by bank or credited in error to some other depositor's account.

4. Checks drawn but not yet presented to the bank for payment.

When the first method of reconciliation is used, items (1) and (3) must be added to the bank's balance and items (2) and (4) must be subtracted from it in order to arrive at the cash book balance. The following problem will illustrate this:

PROBLEM. In the bank's statement of July 1, 19—, with a balance of $675, are included protest fees in connection with the collection of checks amounting to $7.50, and interest allowed on our average bank balance of $16.67. Our deposits for June 30, 19—, totaling $250 in the morning and $100 in the afternoon, have not been credited by the bank. Outstanding checks amount to $180. Our cash book balance on July 1, 19— was $835.83.

Bank reconciliation statement as of July 1, 19—:

Bank balance as per bank's statement		$ 675.00
Add:		
Deposit not included in above balance	$350.00	
Bank charge not included in our balance—protest fees	7.50	357.50
		$1,032.50
Deduct:		
Outstanding checks	$180.00	
Bank interest, not included in our balance	16.67	196.67
Balance as per cash book		$ 835.83

It will be seen that neither the cash book balance nor the bank balance is a correct statement of the cash available for checking. The depositor, in order to find this amount, will have to take account of the figures given by the bank for items he has not known about. His checking balance in the above problem is ascertained as follows:

Cash book balance	$835.83
Less—Bank charges (expenses to the depositor)	7.50

	$828.33
Plus—Bank credits (income to the depositor)	16.67
True balance available for checking	$845.00

There is not usually so much difficulty in reconciling the bank account; but where several bank accounts are maintained, it is easy to misplace debits and credits and a formal statement of reconciliation should always be made and kept as a part of the record. This reconciliation should be made every time a statement is received from the bank. The frequency of asking for a statement of account from the bank depends somewhat upon the volume of transactions handled through the bank, but it should be secured at least every month and particularly whenever formal statements of profit and loss and balance sheet of the depositor are made up.

Reconciliation Statement a Permanent Record.—The reconciliation statement should be made as a permanent record. A customary place of record is on the check stub of the same date. Where a check register is used, it should be made a part of the record there. Occasionally it is incorporated in the cash book. Wherever made it should be easily available for proof at a subsequent period. When reconciliation is to be made as of a past date, i.e., at a time subsequent to the date on which reconciliation is desired, the bank's cancellation date on the returned checks must be used to determine what checks were outstanding on that date.

Reconciling Other Accounts.—Occasionally the dealings between two firms located at a distance from each other may be such that items are in transit one or both ways at the time when statement of account is rendered. If this is the case, the methods of reconciliation applied above to the bank account may have to be used before agreement or comparison of the two records can be effected.

CHAPTER LI
BALANCING METHODS

The "Fool-Proof" Trial Balance.—Double-entry bookkeeping is never satisfied with anything short of absolute proof of the mathematical accuracy of the work. Often such proof is very difficult to secure. There has not yet been devised—and in the nature of things, never will be—any so-called royal road to the trial balance. Yet one often sees claims put forth that there is no longer any need for trial balance troubles. The use of certain methods, which are disclosed only upon payment of fees in proportion to the advantages claimed for them, makes it possible, according to their devisers, to take a trial balance within an incredibly short time or to do away with trial balances altogether. As a matter of fact, satisfactory results can be obtained only by habits of accuracy and by proving the work done wherever possible. Some methods found useful in searching stubborn errors will be explained in this chapter.

Ledger Analysis.—By ledger analysis is meant an analysis of postings classified according to the books of original entry, i.e., on the basis of all journals whose record is transferred to the ledger. The process of making such an analysis is somewhat as follows: The ledger must be gone through carefully and for each account the last debit and credit figures which entered into the last *correct* trial balance must be marked distinctly so as not to be included in the analysis. If the analysis is for an interim period, the first debit and credit items belonging to the next period should be marked in a similar way, as shown in the illustration (Form 46). This must be done very carefully as the "date" is not always a safe guide. The use of subsidiary journals with one summary posting to offset many detailed contra postings and inaccurate dating of the summary posting, often make the "date" an uncertain guide. Care should therefore be exercised so that the points marked include a complete, i.e., a debit and credit, posting of every journal.

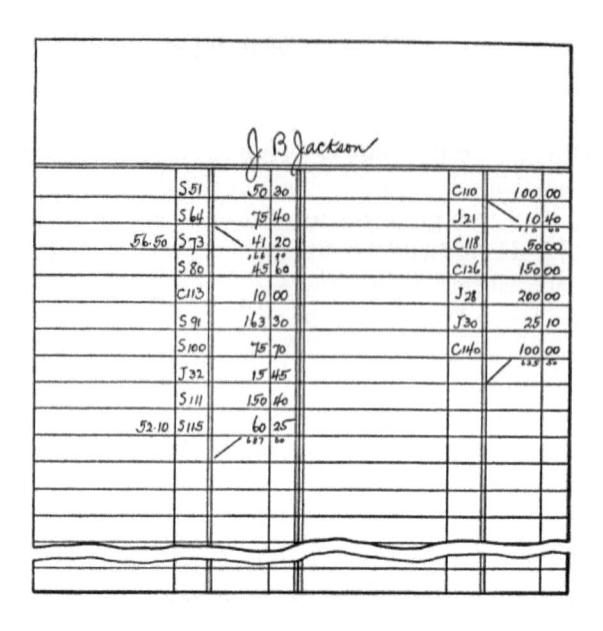

Form 46. Account Marked for Analysis

Procedure of Analysis.—The content of each account between the marked points is now analyzed according to the journals from which the postings have been made. Analysis paper, with debit and credit columns headed for each journal, may be used for this purpose. All debits in the account posted from the journal are entered in the debit journal column of the analysis sheet, all cash debits in the debit cash column, all sales journal debits in the debit sales journal column, etc. Similarly, the credit postings in the account are entered in the proper credit columns of the analysis sheet. Each item in the account should be checked or otherwise marked when transferred to the analysis sheet. Illustration of the analysis sheet is given in Form 47.

When the various accounts have thus been analyzed, there should remain no unchecked items in the period analyzed, unless there have been transfers between accounts made directly on the face of the ledger. If this has been the practice, an additional heading with debit and credit columns, entitled "Ledger Transfers," should be set up on the analysis sheet. *Every* account in the ledger is analyzed in the same way.

The Analysis Sheet.—It will be noticed in Form 46 that only the period between the two diagonal marks \ and / is under analysis. Accounts which have been closed but are within the period under analysis must, of course, be included. When all accounts have been analyzed, the columns of the analysis sheet are footed. For each journal the footings of the debit and credit columns should be equal. A difference will indicate that there is an error in the postings from that particular journal. In this way the error is localized and only these postings need to be checked individually.

The cash book columns in the analysis sheet (Form 47) may need some explanation. If no Cash account is kept on the ledger, the balance of the cash book for the period will have to be entered on the analysis sheet before equality of the cash columns will be shown. With the exception of the items transferred to the analysis sheet from the Cash account—where a Cash account is carried in the ledger—all items in the cash debit column of the analysis sheet represent, in the cash book, credits to certain accounts, and those in its credit column represent debits to certain accounts. The entries to the cash analysis column from the ledger Cash account, showing on its debit cash receipts and on its credit cash disbursements, must bring about the equilibrium. The column total, however, will not represent cash receipts and cash disbursements respectively, but the total of each column will be the sum of both receipts and disbursements; whereas the totals of the other columns are equal to the totals of the corresponding journals for the period. This is brought about by the fact that the two cash columns on the analysis sheet really cover two independent journals, viz., the cash receipts and the cash disbursements journals.

Form 47. Ledger Analysis Sheet

Agreement between the debit and credit totals of corresponding columns is proof of equilibrium in the postings from that book; but unless these column totals also equal the total of the corresponding journal, there is evidence of the omission from the ledger, both on the debit and on the credit side, of items recorded in the journal. Thus the ledger analysis serves also as a check against omissions; but when used for that purpose, account must be taken of duplicate entries in the various journals, such as cash sales entered both in the cash and sales journals but posted only from one of them.

Use of Ledger Analysis.—All that is claimed for the ledger analysis is that it localizes the error, if it is an error in posting, and so makes the work of searching for it less haphazard and renders unnecessary a checking of all postings in the ledger. All the means previously explained should be exhausted before this method is used. If the previous trial balance, i.e., the one at the beginning of the analysis period, is correct and the ledger analysis shows no errors in posting, then certainly the trial balance for the end of the analysis period must balance. If not, the error is an error on the face of the ledger and its computations must be proved.

The Slip or Reverse Posting System.—As indicated before, it is better to post carefully and accurately in the first place than to hunt for errors afterwards. A method of proving daily postings known as the slip or reverse posting system is used with success in many places. Formal slips of any convenient width and length are provided, one for the debit and one for the credit of each book from which postings are made. The debit slips may be easily distinguished from the credit slips by the use of different colors. The debit slips are ruled only with money columns and each slip bears the title of its journal. Reverse posting is made on the slip from the items posted to the ledger. Thus, when posting the debits from the general journal, the general journal debit slip is carried conveniently on the right of the ledger and entry of each debit posting to the ledger is made *from the ledger* to the slip. When all journal debit postings have been made, the reverse posting slip is totaled and must agree with the total of the journal debit column for the items posted. Similarly, the journal credits are posted, reverse posted, and proved. The debit postings must equal the credit postings and thus proof is secured of the equilibrium of the ledger. Each journal is posted, reverse posted, and proved in a similar way. The bookkeeper is, in this way, sure of the correctness of his work day by day. Oftentimes monthly recapitulation of these reverse posting slips are made and preserved as part of the business records. It will be seen that this method is identical with the ledger analysis method explained above but applied at the time of making the posting instead of at the close of the period.

Check Figures in Posting.—The use of the check figures 9 and 11 in the verification of the arithmetic processes of addition, subtraction, multiplication, and division was referred to earlier. Other odd numbers, such as 13, 17, and 19, are less frequently employed. The number 11 gives perhaps the most satisfactory results from the standpoints of ease of application and accuracy of results. Its use in the verification of postings is somewhat as follows:

An additional column similar to the folio column should be provided in all the books for the check numbers. As an amount is posted to the ledger the bookkeeper should determine the check number from the item as it is written in the ledger—not from the journal item—and enter it in the check column in both ledger and journal. When postings from the journal are complete, the journal is totaled and the check figure for its sum found. If this agrees with the sum of the check figure column in the journal, posting is presumably correct. If the two items do not agree, the check number for each amount in the journal debit column should be proved. Inasmuch as the check number used was obtained from the ledger amount, a wrong check number for the journal amount would indicate a wrong posting which should now be turned to and corrected.

The check numbers in the ledger accounts are used only for verifying account totals and balances and may even be carried into the trial balance for proving it. Practice in the use of any check number soon develops accuracy and speed and makes the method easy of application and commendable wherever the work must be proved day by day as completed.

Errors in Columnar Books and Controlling Accounts.—These are frequent sources of trouble unless handled with care. In the chapter on columnar books, it was laid down as a basic principle that *all* items appearing in the general amount column should be entered in some analysis column, i.e., analysis columns should be provided for distribution of *all* items. This makes proof of distribution possible and establishes formal equilibrium of the book so that errors in posting are not so likely to occur.

Care must be exercised in posting the discount columns of the cash book to the proper sides of the respective accounts.

In the use of controlling accounts, where a special column is not provided, as for Accounts Receivable on the credit side of the cash book, posting of the item should be made both to the individual account and also to the controlling account.

Trial Balance Adjustment Account.—Where error creeps into the ledger and seems impossible of detection at a monthly trial balance period, the device of forcing a balance is sometimes used by setting up an account called "Trial Balance Adjustment," "Error in Trial Balance," or some other similar title. To this is charged or credited the amount of the difference in the trial balance. It is a temporary makeshift, a method of holding the item in suspense until the error is located. Needless to say, the inclusion of such an account does not improve the appearance of a trial balance, but may be countenanced as a temporary expedient.

CHAPTER LII
SOME APPLICATIONS OF INTEREST AND PROPORTION

The Nature of Interest.—Interest may be defined as the charge made for the use of money. Sprague defines it as the increase in principal due to the lapse of time. The ethics of the practice of charging interest was questioned by the ancient world and not fully conceded as right until modern times. Various economic theories have been evolved to explain the true character of interest. Whatever they may be, interest as a commercial phenomenon is thoroughly established and countenanced by the law, although in many states an exorbitant interest charge is declared to be usury.

Commercial Interest.—Commercial interest, so-called, usually contains an element in addition to the time-charge for the use of money. That element may be: (1) in the nature of a premium for insurance against the risk of losing the money loaned; or (2) where capital in some fixed form is loaned, in the nature of an allowance or additional charge to cover the shrinkage in the asset loaned due to wear and tear.

Simple and Compound Interest.—As to its method of calculation, interest may be simple or compound. Simple or single interest is figured on the single base known as the principal, the only other element being the length of time. Compound interest periodically adds the unpaid interest to the previous principal, and so secures interest not only on the original principal but on all unpaid interest as well.

In accounting both kinds of interest are recorded under the common title Interest. Some applications of the interest principle to certain special accounts will be discussed.

Equation of Payments.—The practice of averaging accounts is occasionally met with at the present time in American business. In proceedings in bankruptcy, all claims against the bankrupt on open or running account comprising several items, when filed with the trustee, must show the average due date of the items if interest is to be secured on the overdue amounts.

The problem involved may best be shown by an example. The following account appears on A's books, showing charges against B:

B

Jan. 5 Mdse. 2/10, n/30. 100.00

Feb. 1 Mdse. 2/10, n/60. 350.00

Apr. 10 Mdse. net 200.00

June 2 Mdse. 2/10, n/60. 2,000.00

If B does not settle the various amounts as they come due, A is deprived of the use of his money longer than contemplated in the sale contract. In justice to him, interest on the overdue amounts ought to be allowed. If B should pay any of the amounts earlier than the terms of sale require, he should be allowed a discount, i.e., a rebate equal to the interest for the time of prepayment. Further, shortly after the last purchase on June 2 at 60 days, amounting to $2,000, B may desire to settle his entire account, taking his discount for prepayment on the $2,000 and allowing A interest on the overdue amounts. If the date of settlement is fixed, the amount necessary for an equitable settlement may be determined by the method used for the account current in the previous chapter.

Average Due Date.—But B may want to know the date on which he can settle equitably by paying the exact amount of the account without either paying interest on the overdue items or taking discount on the $2,000. The problem involved is that of averaging or equating accounts. The equated date, due date, or average date of payment are the terms variously applied to the date of equitable settlement. If the account has only debits or only credits, the equation is called a simple or single equation or average; if it has both debits and credits, the equation is called a compound or double equation.

In order to determine the equated date, an arbitrary one, called the focal date, is taken for the purpose of computing the interest charges and credits, and from that date the days of interest are counted backwards or forwards according to the result arrived at through use of the arbitrary date. Interest is calculated at an arbitrary rate, usually 6% (100% per day is used by another method of calculation), and in the case of compound equation the same rate must be used on both debits and credits.

To illustrate the method of calculation for the simple equation and the interest principle involved, the account above cited will be equated. In order that the expired time between the focal date and each date of value may be easily computed, the last day of the previous year is taken as the focal date. Interest is at 6%.

Date of Entry	Date of Value	Expired Time	Amount	Int. on Total Amount for 1 Day	Int. on Each Amount for Expired Time
1/5	2/4	35 da.	$ 100		$ .58
2/1	4/2	92 "	350		5.37
4/10	4/10	100 "	200		3.33
6/2	8/1	213 "	2,000		71.00
			$2,650	.44⅙	)$80.28
					182 da.

This calculation shows that theoretically, had the various transactions been under contemplation on December 31, the focal date, payment of the total $2,650 could equitably have been made with a discount of $80.28. The interest (or discount) on $2,650 for 1 day is 44⅙ cents. A discount amounting to $80.28 can therefore be demanded on $2,650 only as the result of an offer to prepay 182 days (80.28 ÷ .44⅙ = 182) before the payments are equitably due. Hence, payment of $2,650 without discount would settle the account equitably 182 days after the focal date, or on July 1. That this is true can easily be proved by using July 1 as the settlement date and figuring as for a current account. It will be found that interest on the overdue items on that date amounts to $10.42, while the discount on the item not yet due amounts to $10.33; the difference .09 not being a large enough fraction (9 ÷ 44⅙) to justify payment one full day earlier.

The 100% Method.—A short method of calculation may be used, employing the 100% per day method. Any date may be taken as a focal date, and very frequently the date of the first or last transaction is used. In the illustration below, November 30 of the previous year is taken as the focal date so that the expired time on each item is immediately indicated by the *number* of the month and the day in the "date of value" column. The use of the 100% per day method makes the calculation of interest on each item a simple matter of multiplication by time and amount, i.e., it reduces each amount to a "day-dollars" figure, and on that basis one day's interest on the account total is equal to that total, and therefore the divisor in the division made to determine the focal date is the amount of the account. This greatly simplifies all the operations. Sometimes the expired time is calculated by calendar months and days, converting fractions of a month on a 30-day basis.

The method is used in the illustration below, where the problem shown above by the accurate interest method is solved by the 100% method.

The "month-dollars" column divided by the "amount" column gives 6, shown in the "equated date, months" column, with a remainder of 2,500. This is reduced, by multiplication by 30, to day-dollars and carried to that column, whose total, 80,100, is divided by 2,650, giving 30 as shown in the "equated date, days" column. The equated date is therefore June 30 (6/30). The one day's difference between this and the other method is accounted for because each calendar month is counted as 30 days.

Time					Equated Date	
Months	Days	Amount	Month-Dollars	Day-Dollars	Months	Days
2	4	$ 100	$ 200	$ 400		
4	2	350	1,400	700		
4	10	200	800	2,000		
8	1	2,000	16,000	2,000		
		$2,650)	$ 18,400	$ 5,100	6	30
			15,900			
			$ 2,500			
			30	75,000	6	30
			$80,100			
			79,500			
			$ 600			

Compound Equation.—Where the account has both debits and credits, the estimate is made similarly. Calculation of the month- and day-dollars is made for each side separately. At this point the totals on both sides are combined to find the balance of the account and the balance of the discounts, and these two balances are used to find the equated date. If the balance of the account is on the same side as the balance of the discount, the equated date is forward from the focal date because, if settlement were made on that date, the man who owes the balance is entitled to the theoretical discount also. If the balance of the account and the balance of interest are on different sides, the count is backward from the focal date. The following account and solution will illustrate:

S. L. DAVIS

19—			19—		
Mar. 8	Mdse. net	1,000.00	Apr. 30	Note, 30 da., 6%	500.00
June 20	" n/30	1,500.00	Aug. 30	Cash	1,500.00
Sept. 5	" n/60	2,000.00	Sept. 10	Note, 60 da., no interest	2,000.00

Debits:

Expired Time			Interest	
Months	**Days**	**Amount**	**Month-Dollars**	**Day-Dollars**
3	8	$1,000	$ 3,000	$ 8,000
7	20	1,500	10,500	30,000
11	4	2,000	22,000	8,000
	Totals	$4,500	$35,500	$46,000

Credits:

4	30	$ 500	$ 2,000	$15,000
8	30	1,500	12,000	45,000
11	9	2,000	22,000	18,000
	Totals	$4,000	$36,000	$78,000

Balances:

Amount	Dr. $500		
Interest		Cr. $500	Cr. $32,000

Dividing we get 1 month, 64 days, i.e., 3 months, 4 days. The balances being on opposite sides, the equated date is 3 months, 4 days, backward from November 30 (11/30), i.e., 11/30 - 3/4 = 8/26 or August 26. Equitable settlement could therefore be made by interest-bearing note for $500, dated August 26, or by cash payment of $500 plus interest on $500 from August 26 until date of actual settlement, as would be the case had the account been handled as an account current with adjustment as of August 26.

The Cash Balance.—When an account has been equated, to determine the cash sum which will be required for equitable settlement on a given date subsequent to the equated date, the balance of the account plus interest on that balance from the equated date to the date of settlement will be the correct amount. This amount is technically called the cash balance of the account. It is exactly the same as the adjusted balance of an account current, and may be determined by such adjustment of the account instead of by the method of equation of payments just described.

Interest on Partial Payments.—Under the heads of accounts current and equation of payments, the question of partial payments on open account has been treated. There remains to be discussed a statement of the practices governing partial payments on notes. Two methods of calculating are in use, the legal or United States method and the so-called merchants' method. The merchants' method is used for short-time notes and on any other kind by agreement. The method is exactly similar to that of adjustment of current accounts. Interest is charged on the face of the note from its date of issue till its due date, and allowed on each partial payment from its date of payment till the due date of the note. The difference between the sum of the face of the note plus its interest and the partial payments plus their interest accruals is, of course, the balance due.

United States Rule.—The United States Supreme Court has ordered the application of the partial payments somewhat differently. The first partial payment must first be applied to the payment of the accrued interest on the principal up to the date of the first payment. Any excess shall be applied to a reduction of the principal. Each succeeding payment is similarly applied first to cancellation of accrued interest on each new principal and then to a reduction of the principal. In case any payment is insufficient to meet the accrued interest, the payment is held in reserve, the principal remaining unchanged until a payment or payments are made which added to the previously reserved payment or payments are sufficient to cancel all interest accrued to that date. Any excess is used to retire the principal.

Interest on Daily and Savings Bank Balances.—In the handling of balances between banks, interest on daily balances is usually figured in the settlement. Calculation is on a 365-day basis in the larger banks. Banks frequently allow large depositors a low rate of interest on daily balances maintained above a certain fixed minimum. Take the following account:

X. Z. & CO.

Date	Dr.	Cr.	Balance	Interest Base	Interest
Jan. 2			1,500	500	

3	300	500	1,700	700	
4	800	100	1,000		
5	400	600	1,200	200	
6	500	400	1,100	100	
7	700	1,100	1,500	500	.11
				2,000	

In the above account interest is allowed on all amounts above $1,000 at the rate of 2%. If settlement is periodical, interest may be calculated on the total of the "interest base" column for one day. Usually, however, if a monthly settlement basis is used, the total minimum balance for the month is subtracted from the total of the "balance" column, and the remainder is the interest base. In savings banks no interest is allowed on amounts which have been withdrawn during the interest period, regardless of how long the sum may have been on deposit previous to date of withdrawal. There is no uniform practice as to when deposits shall begin to draw interest, in some banks at the beginning of the month after deposit, unless deposit is made on the first day of the current month; in others, not until the beginning of the next interest period. Great care must be exercised, therefore, in handling deposit and withdrawal dates.

Bank and True Discount.—Bank discount has been defined as the prepaid or collected interest on a discounted note, calculation being on the basis of the amount to be collected on the note at its maturity.

True discount is the difference between the face of a debt and its present worth, meaning by present worth that sum of money which placed at interest now will equal or be worth the face of the debt at maturity.

Proportion, Simple and Weighted.—Proportion is defined as an equality of ratios. Thus, if the ratio of a to b is the same as the ratio of c to d, this relation may be expressed as follows:

$$\frac{a}{b} = \frac{c}{d} \quad \text{or} \quad a:b = c:d$$

the fractional form being preferred. In accounting it is often required to divide amounts in certain ratios, as when profits must be apportioned among partners, when insurance, taxes, and other expense charges must be distributed over departments, etc. This is usually entitled "apportioning." It is not necessary to illustrate simple proportion, but a problem in "weighted proportion" will be given here.

Apportion an insurance charge of $1,000 over departments A, B, and C according to the property values in those departments, taking account of the fact that the rate on A is double that on B and C. The property values are: A $10,000; B $15,000; C $35,000.

The proper basis for distribution cannot be found, as in simple proportion, by an addition of the values in the departments. Before addition, the value in A must be weighted by 2, i.e., doubled. This gives a basis of $70,000 ($20,000 for A + $15,000 for B + $35,000 for C = $70,000). Of the $1,000 insurance cost, department A will have to bear $20/70$; B $15/70$; and C $35/70$. The charges will be therefore:

A, $20/70$ of $1,000 or $ 285.71

B, $15/70$ " 1,000 " 214.29

C, $35/70$ " 1,000 " 500.00

$1,000.00

Apportioning Freight Charges.—In-freight and cartage are treated as additions to the cost of goods bought; consequently, at inventory time it is necessary to add the correct amount of in-freight to the cost of goods on hand. However, it is seldom possible to apply the freight costs directly to each unit of product on hand and yet theoretically this should be done. Usually the ratio of freight costs to the total amount of purchases during a given period is taken as the basis for adding freight to the inventory. Thus, if that ratio has been 5% for the period, a commodity costing $100 would be valued at $105 for the inventory. Thus the freight expense is deferred.

This usually is deemed sufficiently accurate for most purposes. Where departmental records are kept, or where accurate factory costs are required, a closer apportioning is sometimes necessary. The freight classifications are such that the rates are not proportionate to the *values* of the goods; but other factors such as weight, kind of goods, method of crating, etc., all enter into the freight rate. Of these, the only factor which is easily obtainable is the weight. A distribution of freight on the basis of *value* and *weight* has been suggested—a weighted proportion method of apportionment. This, of course, requires an involved calculation which is usually "shied" at by bookkeepers and is not necessary except where very accurate and detailed costs are required.

CHAPTER LIII
SINGLE OR SIMPLE ENTRY

Different Systems of Bookkeeping.—Except in small enterprises, the only satisfactory system of bookkeeping is double entry. The system—or rather lack of system—known as single entry antedates double entry and is met today occasionally, particularly in small retail stores. It seems necessary, therefore, to give the student an explanation of its main features.

An early writer defines bookkeeping as "the art of recording mercantile transactions in a regular and systematic manner." In further elucidation he says: "A merchant's books should contain every particular which relates to the affairs of the owner. They should exhibit the state of all the branches of his business; the connection of the various parts; the amount and success of the whole. They should be so full and so well arranged as to afford a ready information in every point for which they may be consulted." Single entry hardly measures up to these requirements, but there are places and circumstances where it gives results satisfactory enough. Bookkeeping has had a development contemporaneous with industrial life. Only simple records are needed so long as industries are simple, but with the increasing complexity of industrial enterprise, previous methods become inadequate.

Single Entry.—Single entry may be defined as that method of keeping records which sorts out and classifies debits and credits only as they apply to persons, the proprietor included, and usually also to cash. To justify the strict application of the term, a *system* must needs keep record of *all* transactions. Methods—not systems—of single-entry account-keeping are sometimes met with which do not make full record. The point of view of single entry is personal. All features of the business not connected with persons are looked upon as being under the direct hand of the owner and subject to his control. But uncompleted transactions with persons, whether customers or creditors, are not capable of such oversight without the aid of individual, classified records. The necessity of safeguarding the cash and keeping its flow under review makes the classified cash record an almost universal feature of single entry. As a usual thing, therefore, single entry is characterized by: (1) a record of all transactions; (2) a debit and credit analysis applied only to persons and to cash; and (3) a classified and grouped record, i.e., ledger record, only as to persons and cash. It does not analyze every transaction in its relation to the business as a whole. It has a single point of view, i.e., it considers only persons and cash and makes entries accordingly. Hence, its name.

Books Required and Methods of Record—The Journal.—In a single-entry system three books of account are necessary—the journal, the cash book, and the ledger. The cash book records all cash transactions, receipts and payments, classified as to persons but otherwise in narrative form. The journal records all other transactions following the same method. The ledger makes secondary record only under the heads of customers, creditors, and proprietor. The journal is the standard two-column journal, the first column being used as an "items" column, and the second for totals. A three-column journal is advantageous, the first column being used for items and for all unposted amounts, the second for debit postings, and the third for credit postings. This aids in proving the ledger postings, as will later be seen. Transactions affecting persons are recorded under those persons' names followed by "Dr." or "Cr.," according to the analysis of the transaction. This is necessary since position does not show it, the method of left and right position for debit and credit not being used in the single-entry journal. All other transactions are recorded in narrative form, merely a memorandum being made of them.

Cash Book.—The cash book is the same as for double entry, receipts on the left and disbursements on the right-hand page or column, according as a double- or single-page cash book is used. Where the double page is used, one of the two columns on either side is sometimes used for the exclusive extension of the amounts to be posted to personal accounts. This facilitates posting, since these are the only amounts which are to be transferred to the ledger.

Ledger.—The single-entry ledger is the same as the double-entry and uses the debit and credit principle of double entry. As stated above, accounts are kept only with persons, including the proprietor. It is seen, therefore, that single-entry books make a record of *all* transactions but fail to analyze all those transactions in their relations to one another and in their effects upon the business.

Single Entry as Adapted to Modern Needs.—Recognizing the value of the analysis secured by double entry but overestimating the work required to make the record, some concerns have developed single-entry systems through use of subsidiary records and columnar books, from which they derive very full information for management purposes. A sales journal gives volume of sales, a purchase journal shows the amount of goods purchased, and analytic columns in the cash book show the main sources of receipts and their amounts, and the main classes of expenditures and their amounts. A bill book is used for recording notes receivable and payable, and inventory books for scheduling all kinds of property, assets and liabilities. All of these make a system approaching the double entry in completeness of detailed information, but one which lacks the fundamental principle on which the double entry rests, viz., an equality of debits and credits brought about by a classified analysis of every transaction into its debit and credit elements at the time of first entry on the books. It does not tie together the whole into a mathematically provable system.

Since the advent of double entry there have always been strong adherents to the single-entry method. An early writer, William Perry, presented in 1777 a treatise on bookkeeping by either method. Most small enterprises, even if they keep their records by the single-entry method in the beginning, usually adopt the double-entry system as their business increases, realizing that the latter furnishes better accounting control than is obtainable under simple entry.

Debits and Credits.—To one who knows the double-entry method, single-entry bookkeeping presents few difficulties. Debit and credit as applied to personal accounts are usually of easy determination and are exactly the same as in double entry. The debits and credits for cash are based on the same principles in both systems. The method of writing them in the books of original entry was sufficiently indicated where those books were explained. Posting is done just as in double entry. With regard to all work upon single-entry books, there is always a temptation to do slovenly, inaccurate work because the system does not provide internal proof as the double-entry system does. Thus, where rebates have been allowed, only the net amount received may be shown in the cash book with explanation that the payment is in full of account. After this amount is posted to the customer's account, the item does not fully offset the original debit and it is necessary to make a note in the ledger to the effect that the item is fully settled. The same thing holds true for creditors' accounts. Of course, this is not good bookkeeping whether practiced in single or double entry.

The Proprietor's Account.—The handling of the proprietor's account under single entry is very similar to that under double entry. The proprietor's capital account shows the original investment on the credit side; his personal account, if kept separately, is debited with his withdrawals, whether in merchandise or cash. Inasmuch as the single-entry ledger does not show the profit or loss, the manner of handling the proprietor's account at closing is somewhat different. The profit, as determined by the method shown a little later, may be brought directly and without journal entry from the statement of profit and loss into the proprietor's capital account so that this account will show the true net worth of the business as at that time. The personal account is simply ruled off after its figures have been used in determining profit.

Proof of Posting.—The only proof of work possible under single entry is a checking of the secondary record against the original. A trial balance of the ledger cannot be taken. A schedule or list of account balances may be prepared and debit and credit totals of the list made. This compared with a similar list prepared at the close of the last period will show the changes that have taken place during the current period. A list of the debits and credits to personal accounts in books of original entry for this period must check against the net change shown by the above comparison. Virtually this amounts to a second posting of the items, and if the two postings agree, the presumption is that the ledger is correct. The use of the "personal" posting column for the cash book as explained above, and of similar columns in sales and purchase journals, makes possible a much easier debit and credit summary of the books of original entry if some proof of posting is desired.

Profit and Loss.—Inasmuch as many of the factors affecting the net worth have not been analyzed in making the original entry, no detailed showing of profit and loss, as understood under double entry, can be made. It is, of course, possible to go back over the books and make such an analysis, but this would result practically in rewriting the books on a double-entry basis. Single entry, therefore, has recourse to another method which is characterized by a complete inventory-taking and appraisal. It is sometimes called the "asset and liability method" as explained in the following sections.

Inventory and Appraisal.—A physical inventory or count of all assets, fixed, current, and deferred, is made. The books furnish only the accounts receivable and the cash. All other assets are usually made up by physical count and reappraisal. It is consequently very easy to lose sight of some assets, particularly in the case of additions and betterments to existing assets. For the deferred items, the inventory of supplies on hand supplemented by the proprietor's memory is the customary source.

Liabilities.—Liabilities are more difficult of correct determination. The accounts payable are shown on the ledger, the notes payable should be shown in the bill book or by stubs in the bound blank book of notes. Any unpaid bills may be found in the current file of unpaid invoices if one is maintained. For all other liabilities, including deferred income, the memory must serve. The haphazard manner in which this statement must be made up is therefore apparent.

Accrued and Deferred Items.—There is usually little or no notice taken of accruals and deferred items on account of the difficulty in securing trustworthy and full information. The theory of averages, viz., that these items at one period will offset, in the long run, those at another, is the theory by which the failure to include accruals and deferred data is excused. A comparison of this method with the double-entry method for handling similar items throws into strong relief the inaccuracies of the single-entry method.

The Balance Sheet and the Determination of Profit.—The balance sheet, listing all assets and all liabilities, makes a determination of proprietorship or net worth possible. Under the inventory and appraisal method it must be taken periodically. A comparison of the net worths as shown by successive statements develops the gain or loss for the period, provided no other elements affecting net worth have become involved. The additional element to be taken into consideration is the relation of the proprietor to the funds of the business. He may have withdrawn some of the assets or he may have made additional investments, so that the condition of the assets as shown at the end of the period is not entirely the result of business activities and transactions.

Profits determination by this method, therefore, must take cognizance of the two factors: (1) comparative net worths, and (2) proprietor's interim drawings and investments. A withdrawal of cash during the period equal in amount to the profits for that period would result in the same net worth at the close as at the opening of the period. Drawings in excess of profits would cause a net worth less at the end than at the beginning; and withdrawals less than profits would cause an increased net worth. But under none of the three cases stated would a comparison of the two net worths show the actual profits.

Similarly, additional investments have an opposite effect, bringing about an increase in closing net worth in the exact amount of the additional investment and so obscuring the true amount of profit or loss for the period. Accordingly, the increase or decrease of net worth as shown by the comparative statements of financial condition must be adjusted in accordance with the proprietor's withdrawals and additional investments to make a correct determination of profits. To determine the profits for the year, to the change in net worth—treated algebraically, i.e., positive if an increase and negative if a decrease—must be added the withdrawals, and from this sum the additional investments must be subtracted.

Single and Double Entry Compared.—From the foregoing discussion and from the illustrations in the next chapter it will be seen that single entry can be worked through to a conclusion as to profit and loss. It tells nothing, however, of the sources of that profit or loss, nor does it give any control over expenses. It is true that a comparative statement of assets and liabilities as shown in Chapter IV, presenting increases and decreases of the various assets and liabilities, will give additional information, but even that does not show the reasons for the change and so affords no basis for control. For such purposes the statistical totals of the sales and purchase records, and of the cash book, where analytical columns are used, furnish the only information available under single entry. Its only advantage, then, is brevity, the saving of labor in making the record. No difficult analysis is met with in the original record and posting is a less heavy task than in double entry. But brevity and labor-saving are secured at the expense of the very information which the business man needs.

The advantages of double entry may be summarized as follows:

1. The ledger shows a classified record of every transaction.

2. Expenditures for capital purposes, i.e., for new assets or additions and betterments to existing assets, are recorded as such, so that there is no danger of losing sight of them.

3. A gross profit figure is obtainable and percentages of profits and expenses, making possible an *estimate* of merchandise inventory at any time. This is particularly valuable in case of fire loss.

4. The double-entry method provides a proof of the mathematical accuracy of the ledger.

5. A full statement of sources of profits and causes of expenses can be obtained in double entry.

Where the above advantages and information are not desired nor necessary, as in a very simple business under the immediate supervision of the proprietor, or in simple executorship transactions, etc., single entry may suffice.

Change from Single to Double Entry.—If it is desired to change from single to double entry, all that is necessary is a complete inventory and appraisal, to be used as the basis for an opening journal entry, debit and credit, as for any opening entry. If the former single-entry ledger is to be used, only the items not already posted, i.e., the impersonal items, will be posted from this opening entry. The proprietor's account should first be adjusted to its correct figure by a determination of profits by the single-entry method. If this is done, no posting to his account is needed from the opening entry for the double-entry books. This opening entry posted will bring the ledger into equilibrium, which will be maintained under the double-entry method. If a new ledger is to be used, the opening entry above referred to will be posted completely—personal and impersonal items—which will of course bring about the equilibrium desired. Thereafter all transactions will be analyzed and entered according to the double-entry system.

CHAPTER LIV
ILLUSTRATION OF SINGLE ENTRY

Opening Entries.—In opening a set of single-entry books, as complete a record should be made as under double entry. If the proprietor begins business with an investment of cash only and without any obligations, an entry in the cash book of the amount invested as a credit to the proprietor's capital account is all that is necessary. If the investment consists of a variety of properties and liabilities to creditors, and obligations on leases, salaries, etc., are assumed, a very careful and complete record should be made in the journal, showing the kinds and values of the properties invested, and the kinds and amounts of the liabilities assumed. This is best arranged in schedule or statement form, with extension into the posting money columns only of those personal items for which accounts are to be opened in the ledger. Illustration will be given of a simple set of single-entry books, the journal, cash book, sales and purchase records, and the ledger. In order that the entries may be traced, a separate statement or diary of the transactions will be given, covering in summarized form a six months' period.

PROBLEM. June 30, 19—, A. B. Cornell purchased a store and business, paying $7,750.

He took over the following assets and liabilities at the values shown:

- Store building and lot $3,000.
- Furniture and fixtures $500.
- Horse and wagon $250.
- Accounts receivable:
- B. C. Davis $50;
- C. D. Elliot $75;
- D. E. Foley $100;
- E. F. Gaynor $25;
- F. G. Harvey $125.
- Stock of merchandise $5,250.
- Mortgage on real estate $500.

- Accounts payable:
- G. H. Jackson & Co. $250;

- H. J. Kelsey $375;
- J. K. Landon Co. $500.

He deposited $500 as an additional investment.

During the six months the following transactions took place:

- Cash sales $10,000.
- Sales on account:
- Davis $300;
- Elliot $400;
- Foley $500;
- Gaynor $600;
- Harvey $700.
- Purchases were:
- Cash $3,500;
- Jackson & Co. $500;
- Kelsey $450;
- Landon $750;
- Morey & Co. $1,000.

Cornell returned goods to Morey & Co. $50, and received an allowance from Kelsey $20.

He made Harvey a rebate of $25.

- He received cash on account from Davis $250;
- Elliot $300;
- Foley $400;
- and notes from Gaynor $250 and Harvey $500.
- He paid on account cash to Morey & Co. $500;
- Jackson & Co. $600;
- Kelsey $675.
- He gave his note for $1,000 to Landon.
- He paid off the mortgage with interest $530.

- Expenses paid were:
- Clerks $750;
- cashier, stenographer, etc., $250;
- N. Y. C. Ry. for freight $250;
- horse feed and expense of driver $125;
- newspaper and street-car advertising $300.

Cornell drew $2,000, and made an additional investment of a safe valued at $250.

At the close of the year inventories and appraisals of data not on the ledger were as follows:

- Store building and lot $2,970.
- Furniture and fixtures $725.
- Horse and wagon $235.
- Merchandise $3,000.
- Notes receivable $750, with accrued interest $2.50.
- Notes payable $1,000, with accrued interest $15.
- Accrued salaries and expenses $25.

It was decided to value the accounts receivable at face value less 2%.

JOURNAL

19—		L.F.	Items	Dr.	Cr.
June 30	A. B. Cornell commenced business, purchasing the store and stock of the .... Company, taking over all its assets and assuming all its liabilities and obligations. He deposited $500 as a working fund for the business. The following shows his investment assets and obligations:				

Assets

Store Bldg. and Lot	3,000.00		
Furniture and Fixtures	500.00		
Horse and Wagon	250.00		
Merchandise	5,250.00		
Accounts Receivable:			
B.C. Davis Dr. 50.00		5	50.00
C.D. Elliot Dr. 75.00		5	75.00
D.E. Foley Dr. 100.00		5	100.00
E.F. Gaynor Dr. 25.00		5	25.00
F.G. Harvey Dr. <u>125.00</u>	375.00	5	125.00
Cash	<u>500.00</u>		
Total Assets		9,875.00	

Liabilities

Mortgage on Real Estate	500.00		
Accounts Payable:			
G. H. Jackson & Co. Cr. 250.00		5	250.00
H.J. Kelsey Cr. 375.00		5	375.00
J. K. Landon Co. Cr. <u>500.00</u>	1,125.00	5	500.00
Total Liabilities		1,625.00	

	A. B. Cornell, Capital	Cr.	6	8,250.00	8,250.00
Dec. 31	Morey & Co.	Dr.	5	50.00	
	Returned goods as unsatisfactory.				
	H. J. Kelsey	Dr.	5	20.00	
	Allowance a/c inferior goods.				
	F. G. Harvey	Cr.	5		25.00
	Rebate a/c dissatisfaction.				
	E. F. Gaynor	Cr.	5		250.00
	Note at 3 mo. 6% on a/c.				
	F. G. Harvey	Cr.	5		500.00
	Note at 60 da., no interest on a/c.				
	J. K. Landon Co.	Dr.	5	1,000.00	
	Note at 6 mo. 6% on a/c.				
	A. B. Cornell, Capital	Cr.	6		250.00
	Made additional investment of office safe.				
				1,445.00	10,400.00

JOURNAL

19—		L.F.	Items	Dr.	Cr.
Dec. 31	FINANCIAL STATEMENT				

Assets

Store Bldg. and Lot	2,970.00
Furniture and Fixtures	725.00
Horse and Wagon	235.00
Merchandise	3,000.00

Accounts Receivable:

B.C. Davis	100.00	
C.D. Elliot	175.00	
D.E. Foley	200.00	
E.F. Gaynor	375.00	
F.G. Harvey	300.00	1,150.00
Less—Bad Debts est.	23.00	1,127.00
Notes Receivable		750.00
Accrued Interest on above		2.50
Cash		1,970.00
Total Assets		10,779.50

Liabilities

Notes Payable		1,000.00
Accrued Interest on above		15.00

Accounts Payable:

G. H. Jackson & Co.	150.00
H. J. Kelsey	130.00
J. K. Landon Co.	250.00

Morey & Co.	450.00	980.00		
Accrued Salaries and Expenses		25.00		
Total Liabilities			2,020.00	
Net Worth			8,759.50	

A.B. Cornell, Capital, 6/30	8,250.00			
Additional Investment	250.00			
	8,500.00			
Drawings	2,000.00			
	6,500.00			
Net profit this period	2,259.50		8,759.50	
A.B. Cornell, Personal	Cr.	6		2,259.50

To carry the net profit to Cornell's Personal account.

A.B. Cornell, Personal	Dr.	6	259.50	
A.B. Cornell, Capital	Cr.	6		259.50

To transfer the balance of profit left in the business to Cornell's Capital account.

Totals			259.50	2,519.00

Dr. CASH			CASH Cr.		
19—			19—		
June 30	A. B. Cornell ✓	500.00	Dec. 31	Purchases	3,500.00

- 416 -

Dec. 31	Sales		10,000.00	Morey & Co. on a/c	5	500.00	500.00
	B.C. Davis on a/c	5	250.00 250.00	Jackson & Co. "	5	600.00	600.00
	C.D. Elliot "	5	300.00 300.00	H.J. Kelsey Co. "	5	675.00	675.00
	D.E. Foley "	5	400.00 400.00	Mortgage and Interest			530.00
				Clerks			750.00
				Cashier Stenographer,			250.00
				N.Y.C. Ry. Freight			250.00
				Horse Feed and Driver Expense			125.00
				Newspaper Advertising			300.00
				A.B. Cornell	6	2,000.00	2,000.00
				Balance			1,970.00
			950.00 11,450.00			3,775.00	11,450.00

19—

Jan. 2   Balance   1,970.00

Sales Journal

19—				
Dec. 31	Cash			10,000.00
	B. C. Davis	5	300.00	
	C. D. Elliot	5	400.00	
	D. E. Foley	5	500.00	
	E. F. Gaynor	5	600.00	
	F. G. Harvey	5	700.00	
	Sales on Account		2,500.00	
	Sales for Cash		10,000.00	10,000.00
	Total Sales		12,500.00	

Purchase Journal

19—				
Dec. 31	Cash			3,500.00
	G. H. Jackson & Co.	5	500.00	
	H. J. Kelsey	5	450.00	
	J. K. Landon Co.	5	750.00	
	Morey & Co.	5	1,000.00	
	Purchases on Account		2,700.00	
	Purchases for Cash		3,500.00	3,500.00
	Total Purchases		6,200.00	

B. C. Davis

19—				19—		
June 30		J2	50.00	Dec. 31	C4	250.00

| Dec. 31 | | S4 | 300.00 | | | |

C. D. Elliot

19—				19—		
June 30		J2	75.00	Dec. 31	C4	300.00
Dec. 31		S4	400.00			

D. E. Foley

19—				19—		
June 30		J2	100.00	Dec. 31	C4	400.00
Dec. 31		S4	500.00			

E. F. Gaynor

19—				19—		
June 30		J2	25.00	Dec. 31	J2	250.00
Dec. 31		S4	600.00			

F. G. Harvey

19—				19—		
June 30		J2	125.00	Dec. 31	J2	25.00
Dec. 31		S4	700.00	”	”	”	500.00

G. H. Jackson & Co.

19—				19—		
Dec. 31		C4	600.00	June 30	J2	250.00
				Dec. 31	P4	500.00

H. J. Kelsey

19—			19—		
Dec. 31	J2	20.00	June 30	J2	375.00
" "	C4	675.00	Dec. 31	P4	450.00

J. K. Landon Co.

19—			19—		
Dec. 31	J3	1,000.00	June 30	J3	500.00
			Dec. 31	P4	750.00

Morey & Co.

19—			19—		
Dec. 31	J2	50.00	Dec. 31	P4	1,000.00
" "	C4	500.00			

A. B. Cornell, Personal

19—			19—		
Dec. 31	C4	2,000.00	Dec. 31	J3	2,259.50
" "	J3	259.50			

A. B. Cornell, Capital

			19—		
Net Worth (down)		8,759.50	June 30	J2	8,250.00
			Dec. 31	J3	250.00
			" "	J3	259.50
		8,759.50			8,759.50
			19—		

Jan. 1   8,759.50

LEDGER LIST (BEFORE CLOSING)

B. C. Davis	$ 100.00	
C. D. Elliot	175.00	
D. E. Foley	200.00	
E. F. Gaynor	375.00	
F. G. Harvey	300.00	
G. H. Jackson & Co.		$ 150.00
H. J. Kelsey		130.00
J. K. Landon Co.		250.00
Morey & Co.		450.00
A. B. Cornell, Personal	2,000.00	
A. B. Cornell, Capital		8,500.00
	$3,150.00	$ 9,480.00
		3,150.00
Excess of credits		$ 6,330.00

PROOF

Total postings from			Journal	$1,445.00	$10,400.00
,,	,,	,,	Sales Journal	2,500.00	
,,	,,	,,	Purchase Journal		2,700.00
,,	,,	,,	Cash Book	3,775.00	950.00

	$7,720.00	$14,050.00
		7,720.00
Excess of credits as above		$ 6,330.00

Net Profits.—Inasmuch as the change in proprietorship is determined only by a comparison of the two financial statements, at least the result of the comparison should be incorporated into a journal entry and so be brought into the ledger account. Sometimes the statement itself and the calculation of change in net worth are made on the face of the journal, thus making permanent record of them. This is worth while since they are an essential part of the system. A permanent statement book will accomplish the same result. In the illustration the statement is entered in the journal. The net profit of $2,259.50 may be set up in the proprietor's personal account, and the balance of that account, being the amount of profits retained in the business, transferred to the capital account; or the net amount left in the business may be transferred directly to the capital account and the personal account ruled off without balancing as suggested in Chapter LIII. The same result is accomplished, but the ability to prove postings against the books of original entry is lost. Hence the first method which is the one shown in the illustration is the better.

APPENDIX A
PRACTICE WORK FOR STUDENT—
FIRST HALF-YEAR

Accounting principles cannot be mastered without adequate practice work. Practice work cannot be properly done unless the principles on which it is based have been developed and explained. Practice work should, so far as possible, follow closely after the explanation of new principles. This applies particularly to the introductory work of the first half-year. Later work is cumulative in its effect and may use all principles previously developed as well as the new principles just developed.

The practice work for the first half-year consists largely of disconnected problems. However, a few longer problems running through several assignments are included. Effort has been made to keep to a minimum the purely mechanical work of computation. While emphasis should be placed always on the principles involved, the need for accuracy should not be lost sight of; in its practice in business, accountancy requires accurate and, where possible, proven results.

Of the budget of stationery provided for this work, the loose-leaf supplies—statement, journal, and ledger paper—are for the first half-year's work. The three-column paper is to be used for balance sheet and profit and loss statements, unless other directions are given for particular assignments. The use of journal and ledger paper is indicated where necessary. Observance of directions given and of forms to be followed, together with careful and accurate work in drafting solutions, will save much time in the location and correction of errors.

Sufficient practice work is furnished to accompany 30 hours of lecture or classroom work, opportunity being provided for two review periods, one at mid-term and one at the close of the semester. Where the lecture period is two hours in length—the class usually meeting but once a week—two of these assignments should be given to accompany each such lecture period. The student should make his solutions as a part of his home-work and these should be taken up for discussion at the next class session and correct solutions should be presented there so that always the student may have a criterion with which to compare his own work. Where more practice work is desired than is provided in this appendix, a collection of miscellaneous problems is given in Appendix C.

I

1. On January 1, 19—, H. L. Lewis has the following property:

- Bank deposit $1,893.74.

- Merchandise $14,987.42.
- Office equipment: safe, desk, counters, cash register, $850.
- Delivery equipment $836.
- Securities held as investments $6,950.
- Accounts due him from customers as follows:
- John Morris $ 90.87.
- Peter Conley $135.
- Chas. Grant $742.93.
- Frank Hewitt $157.48.
- L. M. Moore $790.72.
- N. T. Taylor $48.95.
- A. S. Keene $75.

For merchandise bought there remains unpaid:

- To Jones Bros. $1,350.45.
- " T. J. Langdon $890.
- " Stewart & Co. $965.
- " T. M. Lawes & Co. $4,862.97.
- And a note for $125.

Draw up a statement to show H. L. Lewis' capital as of the above date.

2. From the following information determine the total amount of the liabilities:

- Cash in bank $840.
- Goods on hand $2,500.
- Accounts receivable $1,600.
- Supplies on hand $320.
- The year's rent $600, was paid in advance and the
- premises have now been occupied for six months.
- The capital is $2,500.

3. From the following items in a balance sheet, which is complete except as to the asset cash, determine the amount of cash:

- Capital $2,500.
- Supplies $87.50.
- Real estate $2,500.
- Ford delivery truck $575.
- Accounts receivable $2,280.
- Accounts payable $1,800.
- Notes receivable $300.
- Notes payable $500.
- Salaries due but unpaid $50.
- Mortgage on real estate $1,000.

4. The following data, complete excepting for the amount of a certain mortgage and interest accrued thereon, are taken from the records of Benjamin Goodwin for the year ending June 30, 19—. Determine the face amount of the mortgage payable, and the amount of the interest accrued thereon at 6% for one year.

- Cash on hand $75, and subject to check $1,200.
- Factory $6,100.
- Land $2,000.
- Office furniture $185.
- A three-year insurance premium was bought one year ago for $300.
- Accounts receivable $4,500.
- Goods on hand $2,800.
- Goods in process of manufacture $1,450.
- Raw materials inventory $2,250.
- Supplies $295.
- Accounts payable $9,150.
- Notes payable $4,650.

- Accrued wages $135.
- Mortgage payable and interest.
- Capital $5,000.

5. The following was taken from the books of the treasurer of the Yorktown Lodge:

- Balance in Fifth National Bank, January 1, 19—, $689.22.
- The receipts during the year were:
- Proposition fees $515.
- Initiation fees $2,510.
- Lodge dues $4,904.60.
- Interest on Liberty bonds $332.14.
- Summary disbursements for the year were:
- Grand lodge dues $554.
- Printing and postage $818.25.
- Entertainment $2,199.86.
- Sundries $216.20.
- Returned proposition fees $80.
- Rent for lodge room $750.
- Salaries $387.50.
- Charity $1,211.84.
- Supplies $38.80.
- Testimonial dinner $846.48.
- There is also cash $4,498.67, on deposit in the Irving Savings Bank
- December 31, 19—, on which interest at the rate of 4% per annum
- is now due for one-quarter.
- The treasurer holds $10,000 in Liberty bonds.

Submit statement showing the available balance of cash for the new year.

II

1. Make up three problems, using your own data, to illustrate the three types of business organization.

2. On January 2, 19—, Allen B. Dawes has in his business the following assets and liabilities which you are to classify for balance sheet purposes according to the definitions which have been given, changing the descriptions here used to standard titles:

Alongside of a railroad spur, on a plot 100 by 75 feet, costing $2,500, Dawes has erected a plant for $12,000, for a part of which he is still indebted to the Mutual Savings Bank, which debt is secured by a claim for $5,000 against the property.

In the plant Dawes has installed stationary operating apparatus amounting to $19,750, and loose operating parts and supplementary devices amounting to $250.

The value of the models and patterns which he uses amounts to $1,215.

His stock, totaling $12,215, is in three distinct phases or conditions:

- Raw materials $4,305.
- Partly finished or in process goods $4,020.
- Completed stock $3,890.

In the plant Dawes has $725 worth of furniture.

In the bank he has a balance of $940 and $83.50 in the safe.

Some of his customers owe him for goods bought, the total being $5,397.50 on open account and $875 on signed promises to pay.

Dawes owes creditors on account $4,857.50.

He has formally acknowledged and accepted drafts amounting to $543.50.

He is liable for a pay-roll of $150, earned but not yet due.

Draw up a statement showing assets, liabilities, and net worth, using standard titles.

3. Dawes has reached a point where it is not only profitable but really necessary to expand his business if he is to retain the good-will of his old customers and secure new ones. He has therefore persuaded Edward A. Robbins, a capitalist, to put cash into the business equal to Dawes' net interest and so become a partner with him.

The partnership uses $3,100 of this new capital to purchase additional raw material, and $2,500 for some partly finished stock (bought at a sacrifice sale). They spend $1,600 for new machinery, $250 for tools, and $100 for new patterns. With an eye toward future building facilities they acquire another and adjoining strip of property with a building on it. The latter costs them $5,470 and the land $2,500.

To facilitate securing and delivering goods, the partners invest $1,800 in a small truck. They add shop furniture amounting to $80.

These various deals were consummated by the early afternoon of January 2, 19—. The partners ask you for a new balance sheet to show the condition of the business and the respective interests of each.

4. At the end of the year's operation, Dawes & Robbins ask you to draw up a statement of assets, liabilities, and net worth, the following figures being submitted:

- Balance of cash in the bank $28,000.
- Accounts owing the partnership $12,000; notes $6,000.
- The inventory is again split up into:
- Raw materials $9,000.
- Partly finished goods $5,000.
- Finished stock $500.
- Still on hand unused:
- Advertising material $640.
- Oil, waste, and supplies $500.
- Packing supplies $750.
- Other assets:
- Models and patterns $500.
- Loose tools $75.
- Shop furniture is to be shown at the last balance sheet figure
- less an estimated depreciation in value of $161.
- Machinery in the same manner less depreciation of $2,669.
- Delivery equipment less depreciation of $360.
- Factory less depreciation of $3,498.

- Land as it was on the last balance sheet.
- Liabilities are as follows:
- Accounts owing to creditors $1,000.
- Notes $250.
- Accrued pay-roll $200.
- The mortgage had been reduced to $2,000.

5. Robbins is anxious to withdraw from active participation in the partnership. To facilitate this and to secure additional funds with which to buy new models and other things needed for the growing business, it had been decided some time ago to incorporate and to dispose of some of the stock to outsiders. The necessary steps had already been taken. In accordance therewith the corporation takes over the business at the values shown in the balance sheet of Problem 4, with the exception of $14,252 cash which Robbins retains. For the good-will of the business the corporation gives the partners $15,000 of its capital stock. $25,000 of the capital stock is sold to outsiders for $25,000 cash. The rest of the capital stock is used in purchasing the partnership.

Set up the balance sheet of the corporation.

III

1. A. K. Sutton is proprietor of hardware store. On June 30, 19—, he has the following assets and liabilities:

- Bank deposits $1,980.47.
- Notes receivable $450.
- Accounts due from customers:
- L. M. Taylor $190.
- L. K. Jones $275.
- G. Sanford $18.73.
- F. Daly $87.54.
- C. Baker $103.13.
- Merchandise inventory $4,745.
- Office equipment $135.
- Delivery equipment $575.

- He owes:
- First National Bank $565.
- Chas. Goodwin $487.97.
- L. Birch $150.
- H. Tuttle $92.50.
- James Bros. $325.

Sutton's 60-day promissory note for $200 with interest at 6% is due today, but payment is deferred, with consent of the creditor, to tomorrow morning.

On the above date Sutton buys out the automobile accessory business of his neighbor, A. M. Lawrence, and combines it with his own. The deal was completed on the basis of the balance sheet submitted below, except that Lawrence is to retain the cash. Sutton pays Lawrence in cash from his hardware business. Lawrence's balance sheet contains the following items:

- Cash $347.90.
- Accounts receivable:
- Taxi Service, Inc. $49.50.
- The Market Shops $18.50.
- Whitney's Delivery Service $80.
- Merchandise inventory $1,597.
- Delivery equipment $475.
- Office equipment $90.
- Accounts payable $850.

Draw up a balance sheet to show Sutton's condition after his purchase of Lawrence's business.

Why is Sutton's net worth the same as before buying Lawrence's business?

Instructions

Show accounts receivable and accounts payable as totals, with a supplementary schedule listing each separately.

2. From the following particulars prepare a balance sheet of the Mountel Manufacturing Company as of December 31, 19—:

- Premises $2,500.

- Machinery $11,500.
- Buildings $5,300.
- Capital stock $30,000.
- Stock-in-trade: finished goods $12,500;
- goods in process of manufacture $8,670;
- and raw materials $4,980.
- Loose tools $490.
- Models and patterns $650.
- Patents $1,000.
- Good-will $3,000.
- Trade creditors $15,540.
- Cash $50.
- Motor truck $1,580.
- Bank deposits $1,740.
- Outstanding claims against customers on open account $8,975.
- A 60-day note payable for $1,000 had been discounted
- at the bank at 6% and is due in 30 days.
- Office equipment $250.
- Supplies $500.
- Notes receivable $4,970.
- First National Bank stock and other investments $4,000.
- Unexpired insurance premium $150.
- Accrued wages $75.
- Other notes payable outstanding amount to $8,960.
- Purchase money mortgage on machinery $5,500, due in 18 months.
- Mortgage on buildings $2,000, due in six months.
- Unpaid motor truck expense $85.

It is estimated that during the year machinery has depreciated 10% and buildings 5% from the values shown above.

Investigation shows that the present market value of finished goods is 75% of that carried on the books, goods in process 90%, and raw materials 100%.

It is decided to reduce the values of stock-in-trade to present price levels.

A reserve of 5% is to be created for bad debts, 50% for models and patterns, and 20% for the delivery truck.

Loose tools are valued at $245.

3. The Cordovan Tanning Company has issued $3,000,000 of capital stock. It suffered heavy losses due to the drop in prices during the year. The following balance sheet submitted to the stockholders as of December 31, 19—, showed:

- Cash on hand $1,805; on deposit $378,090.
- Customers' acceptances unmatured $249,754.
- U. S. Liberty bonds $47,500.
- General investments $82,950.
- Loans receivable $15,280.
- Income accrued on investments $3,450.
- Accounts receivable $2,948,582.
- Reserve for doubtful accounts $56,125.
- Notes receivable $82,000.
- Prepaid insurance $14,950.
- Finished goods $750,000.
- Goods in process $697,974.
- Raw materials $460,900.
- Plant and equipment, $4,980,760.
- Depreciation reserve for plant and equipment was $460,640.
- Accounts payable $1,980,760.
- Notes payable $350,000.
- Dividends payable January 15 of the next year, and constituting
- a present liability of the company $230,000.

From the following information and the balance sheet as of December 31, 19—, prepare the balance sheet as of December 31 one year later.

- 432 -

- Cash on hand December 31 was $1,790; on deposit $162,875.
- Customers' acceptances unmatured $449,500.
- The market value of the Liberty bonds was $46,000,
- and general investments $50,000.
- Loans receivable $16,000.
- Income accrued on investments $1,800.
- Accounts receivable $2,310,000.
- Reserve for doubtful accounts $60,000.
- Notes receivable $150,000.
- Prepaid rent $2,400.
- During the year $380,000 worth of goods was added to
- finished stock, and $420,000 at cost price was sold.
- It is decided that the balance must be marked down
- 50% to conform to market replacement costs.
- Goods now in process are valued at $315,890.
- Raw materials carried on the books at $670,000 are to be
- written down 30% to market value.
- 5% of the cost of plant and equipment is to be added to
- the reserve for depreciation.
- Accounts payable $3,670,980.
- Notes payable $1,475,000.
- A dividend of 5% had been declared and was payable
- January 15 of the next year.

4. By comparing the two December 31 balance sheets of the Cordovan Tanning Company, what can you tell as to the progress of the company during the year? Did it make a profit or suffer a loss?

IV

1. Draw up a comparative balance sheet as of December 31, 19— of the Interurban Railway Company, from the balance sheets of December 31, 19— and December 31 of the previous year.

- Balance sheet of 19— showed:
- Cash $40,909.18.
- Accounts receivable $33,097.49.
- Securities deposited with Workmen's Compensation Commission $4,893.75.
- Materials and supplies $27,112.28.
- Prepaid insurance $5,732.16.
- Work in progress $7,509.81.
- Road and equipment $696,622.49.
- Accounts payable $17,058.81.
- Notes payable $70,000.
- Accrued interest on first mortgage bonds $3,645.84.
- Accrued taxes $6,450.65.
- Depreciation reserve for road and equipment $19,995.96.
- Surplus $223,725.90.
- Capital stock $300,000.
- First mortgage 5% bonds $175,000.
-
- Balance sheet of the year previous showed:
- Cash $34,313.78.
- Accounts receivable $57,779.47.
- Securities deposited with Workmen's Compensation Commission $4,893.75.
- Materials and supplies $29,308.56.
- Insurance prepaid $3,639.19.
- Work in progress $98.64.
- Road and equipment $694,216.73.
- Depreciation reserve for road and equipment $15,813.46.
- Capital stock $300,000.

- Accounts payable $25,973.61.
- Notes payable $100,000.
- Accrued interest on bonds $3,645.84.
- Accrued taxes $8,872.31.
- First mortgage bonds $175,000.
- Surplus $194,944.90.

2. Can you tell definitely and in detail how the increase in surplus in Problem 1 was effected?

3. The annual report of the Northeastern Power Company for year ending December 31, 19—, gave the following balance sheet as of December 31, 19—:

- Investments in subsidiary companies $4,244,855.57.
- Cash $1,927,898.84.
- Accounts receivable $1,514,605.11.
- U. S. Government Liberty Loan 4¼% bonds $915,102.
- Canadian Victory Loan 5½% bonds $497,769.88.
- Securities deposited with State Workmen's Compensation Commission $8,893.75
- Other securities $241,001.
- Mortgages owned $13,500.
- Materials and supplies $364,410.81.
- Work in progress $12,931.10.
- Prepaid insurance $231,350.66.
- Prepaid taxes $624,744.28.
- Real estate, plant and transmission systems $48,230,896.04.
- Mortgage on real estate $15,000.
- Accounts payable $867,763.35.
- Accrued taxes $707,870.94.
- Interest payable $213,896.68.
- Dividends payable $201,519.50.

- First mortgage 5% bonds $10,000,000.
- 6% refunding mortgage bonds $8,226,000.
- 6% debentures $10,200,000.
- Depreciation reserve $2,254,476.13.
- Surplus $138,932.44.
- Capital stock outstanding $26,002,500.

The report for the following year gives the following particulars as to the balance sheet of that year:

- Cash $1,677,663.43.
- Accounts receivable $1,286,731.23.
- U. S. Liberty bonds 4¼% $1,106,452.
- Canadian Victory Loan 5½% bonds $747,769.88.
- Securities deposited with State Workmen's Compensation Commission $8,893.75.
- Other securities $170,501.
- Mortgages owned $15,500.
- Materials and supplies $391,645.
- Prepaid insurance $355,302.71.
- Investments in subsidiary companies $1,406,325.67.
- Prepaid taxes $607,575.33.
- Real estate, plant, and transmission systems $53,470,089.04.
- There were no changes in the various bond issues nor in the
- capital stock during the year.
- Mortgages on real estate $20,000.
- Accounts payable $875,214.37.
- Notes payable $1,650,000.
- Accrued taxes $484,806.02.
- Interest payable $215,509.58.
- Dividends payable $201,519.50.

- Reserves for depreciation $2,532,715.94.

Draw up a comparative balance sheet and determine the profit for the year.

4. Make an analytical statement showing the effect on the various assets and liabilities of the profits made during the year.

5. Discuss these changes and so far as possible show how they were brought about.

V

1. On December 31, 19—, James Good's books revealed the following facts:

- Cash $25,000.
- Due from customers $130,000.
- Plant and equipment $100,000.
- Other assets $15,000.
- Due creditors for merchandise $55,000.
- Accrued expenses $7,980.
- Mortgage on plant $50,000.
- Other liabilities $49,500.
- Merchandise now on hand $67,800.
- Capital at beginning of year $150,000.
- Drawings during the year $10,000.
- Sales $300,000.
- Initial inventory $75,000.
- Purchases $200,000.
- Selling expenses $30,000.
- General administrative expenses $27,480.

Draw up a balance sheet with the net worth section expanded to show the operations for the year.

2. On January 2, 19—, the value of the goods on A. R. Knight's shelves amounted to $85,980, and he bought $275,600 worth during the year. On December 31 of the same year the inventory was $106,720. What was the amount of gross sales, if gross profits were $96,000 and returned sales $17,500?

3. Expenses for conducting Knight's business for the year were as follows:
- Salesmen's salaries $18,750.
- Advertising $2,750.
- Expenses of shipments $4,580.
- Office help $12,800.
- Rent $18,000.
- Insurance $2,500.
- Supplies $5,400.
- Depreciation on buildings $6,500.
- Interest $5,250.
- Taxes $3,920.

What was the net profit?

4. During the year 19—, the Morton Trading Company's books showed:
- Net sales amounting to $265,000.
- Purchases were $148,000, of which $7,540 worth of goods
- were returned.
- The cost of goods sold was 60% of the net sales and the
- final inventory was $84,900.
- Sales salaries $29,760.
- Advertising $30,000.
- Shipping expenses $4,680.
- Office salaries $10,260.
- Rent $4,800.
- Insurance $1,500.
- Depreciation of plant $6,890.
- Supplies $1,230.
- Taxes $4,430.

Prepare a statement of profit and loss for the year.

VI

1. The books of Alfred Gristede show the following record at the close of business September 30, 19—:

- Inventory September 1, 19—, $500,000.
- Purchases $2,500,000.
- Purchases returns $50,000.
- Sales $3,250,000.
- Sales returns $100,000.

If the gross profit is $850,000, what is the final inventory?

2. The profit and loss records of A. C. Dye for the year 19— show the following figures:

- Merchandise January 1, 19—, $235,960.
- Sales $875,900.
- Sales returns $6,900.
- Purchases net $586,900.
- Advertising $16,000.
- Office salaries $22,500.
- Sales salaries $34,800.
- Insurance $6,300.
- Taxes $21,700.
- Depreciation on buildings $4,630; on motor fleet $1,875.
- Accounts written off as uncollectible $36,875.
- Interest on notes and accounts receivable $6,790.
- Interest on notes payable $3,275.

At the end of the year the merchandise amounted to $216,735. Draw up the statement of profit and loss for the year.

3. Prepare a formal profit and loss statement of the Lincoln Leather Company for the year ending December 31, 19—, from the data below taken from the company's books:

- Sales $1,559,087.

- Sales returns $13,456.
- Merchandise on hand January 1, 19—, $487,693.

Leather bought during the year $876,019, of which there were returns because of defects amounting to $8,716.

Inventory on December 31, 19— disclosed $513,860 worth of goods on hand.

- Expenses of operation were:
- Advertising $247,920.
- Sales salaries $143,560.
- Sales commissions $88,723.
- Sales traveling expenses $6,423.
- Freight-out $1,976.
- Delivery expenses $38,976.
- Rent $38,500.
- Taxes $12,890.
- Insurance $7,680.
- Light $4,320.
- Heat $15,648.
- Interest paid $3,216.
- Interest received $4,872.
- Office salaries $27,875.
- Sundry expenses $9,213.

4. The Interurban Railway Company whose comparative balance sheet was the basis of work in Assignment IV, Problem 1, had the following particulars for its statement of profit and loss for the year ending December 31, 19—:

- Operating revenue, i.e., income received from sale
- of service to community, $152,228.11.
- Other income $1,191.83.
- Operating expenses $100,582.96.
- Deductions from income were:

- Interest on 5% first mortgage bonds $8,750.
- Interest on notes payable $4,727.41.
- Taxes $10,578.57.

What was the amount of the net profits for the year?

Compare this with the surplus change as developed by the comparative balance sheet in <u>Assignment IV, Problem 1</u>.

5. Draw up a comparative profit and loss statement of the Interurban Railway Company for the years ended December 31, 19— and December 31 of the previous year from the information submitted in Problem 4 and the following data for the year ended December 31 of the previous year:

- Operating revenues $181,016.11.
- Other income $526.52.
- Operating expenses $122,143.23.
- Deductions from income:
- Interest on the first mortgage bonds $8,750.
- Interest on notes payable $6,030.
- Taxes $13,634.59.

VII

1. The financial condition of the Subway Seller at the beginning of the year is shown by the following balance sheet:

THE SUBWAY SELLER
BALANCE SHEET
January 1, 19—

Assets

CURRENT ASSETS:

Cash	$100,000.00	
Notes Receivable	15,000.00	
Accounts Receivable	225,000.00	
Merchandise Inventory	450,000.00	
Liberty Bonds	50,000.00	$840,000.00

DEFERRED CHARGES:

    Prepaid Insurance $ 25,000.00

    Supplies Inventory   20,000.00   45,000.00

FIXED ASSETS:

    Furniture and Fixtures $ 30,000.00

    Delivery Equipment   18,000.00

    Buildings   350,000.00

    Land   200,000.00   598,000.00 $1,483,000.00

Liabilities

CURRENT LIABILITIES:

    Notes Payable $300,000.00

    Accounts Payable   20,000.00

    Accrued Expenses:

        Salaries   12,000.00

        Taxes   25,000.00

        Interest on Mortgage   10,500.00 $367,500.00

FIXED LIABILITIES:

    Mortgage on Land and Bldg   350,000.00   717,500.00

Net Worth

REPRESENTED BY:

    Capital Stock $500,000.00

    Surplus   265,500.00 $ 765,500.00

At the end of the year the following facts are taken from the books of account:

- The profit and loss records show:
- Sales $2,125,000.
- Sales returns and allowances $15,000.
- Purchases for the year $1,200,000.
- In-freight $15,000.
- Purchase returns and allowances $8,000.
- Advertising $125,000.
- Sales salaries $190,000.
- Delivery expense $50,000.
- Depreciation on furniture and fixtures $3,000,
- and on delivery equipment $2,250.
- Superintendence $50,000.
- Clerical salaries $75,000.
- Repairs and maintenance $20,000.
- Supplies $30,000.
- Insurance $60,000.
- Telephone and telegraph $10,000.
- Bad debts $10,625.
- Depreciation on building $14,000.
- Taxes $30,000.
- Interest on notes payable $15,000.
- Interest on the mortgage $21,000.
- Sales discounts $15,000.
- Interest received on Liberty bonds $2,000.
- Purchase discounts $24,000.
-
- The balance sheet records show:

- Cash $141,000.
- Notes receivable $15,000.
- Accounts receivable $335,000.
- A reserve for doubtful accounts of $10,625.
- Merchandise inventory $350,000.
- Prepaid insurance $15,000.
- Supplies inventory $30,000.
- Furniture and fixtures $27,000.
- Delivery equipment $15,750.
- Building $336,000.
- Notes payable $300,000.
- Accounts payable $25,000.
- Accrued sales salaries $15,000.
- Accrued taxes $30,000.
- Accrued interest on mortgage $10,500.
- Mortgage on land and building $250,000.

Other figures on the balance sheet of January 1, 19— have remained unchanged excepting surplus, the amount of which you are required to determine.

- From the above information:
- (a) Prepare a comparative balance sheet.
- (b) Prepare a statement of profit and loss.
- (c) Determine the following ratios:
- 1. Current assets to current liabilities
- 2. Working capital turnover
- 3. Merchandise turnover
- 4. Accounts receivable to sales
- (Assume a normal credit period of 60 days)
- 5. Net profit to net worth

- 6. Gross profit to net sales
- 7. Selling expenses to net sales
- 8. Net operating expenses to net sales
- 9. Net profit to net sales

2. From the following particulars taken from the books of the United Steel Company, prepare a pro forma balance sheet, and a statement of profit and loss:

- Stocks of goods on hand from preceding year $4,964,792.
- Purchases $12,945,983.
- Sales $14,987,653.
- Sales salaries $52,500.
- Sales traveling expenses $8,613.
- Sales commissions $1,780.
- Cash $1,420,909.
- Executive salaries $32,500.
- Interest on notes payable $18,604.
- Rentals $17,000.
- Capital stock outstanding $38,669,600.
- Interest income including the accrued, $29,911.
- Real estate, plant, and equipment $34,469,867.
- Trade debtors $7,082,026.
- Notes receivable $302,638.
- Customers' acceptances unmatured $4,446,000.
- Trade creditors $1,609,101.
- Notes payable $250,000.
- Repairs to plant $8,790.
- Investments in subsidiary companies $3,358,933.
- Advertising cost to date $35,680, exclusive of
- the amount prepaid.

- Telegraph $2,514.
- Telephone $8,716.
- Freight-out $4,978.
- Demurrage $1,972.
- Taxes expense $39,447, of which $17,017 is unpaid.
- Surplus without taking account of the current year's profit is $13,678,362.
- Goods now on hand $7,004,339.
- Interest accrued on notes receivable $5,510.
- Prepaid advertising $11,892.
-
- Note: Show Interest Income Accrued as a current asset.

3. The warehouse of the Eastern Distributing Company is destroyed by fire. The records at the main offices showed that there were $785,960 worth of merchandise in the building on January 1, 19—.

The fire occurred on October 3, 19—, and to that date purchases had been made amounting to $2,486,475, of which $18,920 were not yet delivered. Included in the cost of purchases is $22,500 for freight paid.

Sales had amounted to $2,930,760. Statistical records for the ten years previous to the loss, showed a gross profit on sales of 51.42%.

The loss is complete except as to a small amount of goods salvaged, the realizable value of which is estimated at $125,000.

It is necessary, according to the terms of the fire insurance policy, to file an immediate claim for goods destroyed. Prepare such a claim, having due regard to a form suitable for showing the loss.

VIII

1. Draw up from your own data the balance sheet of a corporation, with at least twelve assets and at least five liabilities and a total asset figure of over $250,000.

2. Making your own assumptions set up a balance sheet for the succeeding year and a comparative balance sheet for the two years.

3. Determine the ratios of fixed assets to capital stock, of working capital to net worth, and of current assets to current liabilities.

4. Write a brief statement of about 150 words giving your opinion of the financial condition of the concern.

IX

1. Enter in ledger "T" accounts the information for the "end of the year" given in Assignment VII, Problem 1, page 525.

2. Using the account titles in the ledger of Problem 1, draw up a chart of accounts similar to Form 2, page 75.

3. Show and explain how the ledger of Problem 1 is the proprietorship equation.

4. Draw up a profit and loss statement to account for the change in proprietorship shown by Assignment VIII, Problem 2, making your own assumptions as to items in the various sections of the statement.

5. State the probable business transactions occurring to bring about these changes in proprietorship (Problem 4), i.e., show the interaction of the profit and loss elements with the asset and liability elements in causing the changes in financial condition.

Instructions

Problem 1. A ledger "T" account is a skeleton account ruled only with the horizontal "title" line and the vertical line separating the left section from the right, date and amount columns being left without formal ruling.

Problem 3. The illustration on page 41 gives the form to follow in solving this problem.

Problems 4 and 5. Make your assumptions reasonable as to the turnover and the ratios of expenses and profit to sales. Assume a merchandise turnover of 5, and a gross profit of 40% of sales. From these determine roughly the cost of goods sold, the purchases, and the sales figures. Make reasonable provision for bad debts, depreciation, interest, etc., in accordance with the balance sheet requirements. Make the other expense items whatever amounts are necessary to produce the same net profits as is shown by the comparative balance sheet.

Follow closely the illustration in Chapter VII for the form of solution to be used for Problem 5.

X

1. Using the schedule shown on page 82, write out three examples of each class and show their effects in each of the three opposite classes (27 examples).

2. Set up ledger "T" accounts for each of the illustrations on pages 82-84, entering therein the proper amounts, debit and credit.

XI

1. (a) Analyze the following transactions from the seller's viewpoint and name the debit and credit elements of each to show:

1. The increase or decrease of assets, liabilities, and proprietorship.

2. The account titles under each of the general groups.

The Dairymen's League on August 1, 19— owed the Union Car Line Company $19,780 for transportation services rendered, and paid $9,780 cash on account, and gave a 60-day note (6%) for $5,000.

Services to the League for the week ending August 7 totaled $2,920.

A claim of $720 was allowed the League on the 12th for goods lost in transit.

The bill of August 7 was paid in full August 14, less 5% for prompt payment.

On the 15th the note for $5,000 was discounted at the bank at 6%.

(b) Set up the Dairymen's League account on the books of the Union Car Line Company.

2. (a) Analyze the following transactions of Samuel Lawson and name the debit and credit elements of each to show:

1. The increase or decrease of assets, liabilities, and proprietorship.

2. The account titles under each of the general groups.

On September 5, 19—, Lawson entered a claim for $1,000 against the Mohawk and Westchester Railroad Company for goods bought but lost in transit on August 12.

September 16 one of Lawson's trucks was destroyed by fire and a claim was entered against the Shippers Fire Insurance Company for $5,800. The truck was new and cost $7,500.

September 20 a bill for $23,400 for services was received from the Union Transport Company.

Payment of $16,900 was made September 23 to the Transport Company.

September 30 the claim of September 5 was paid in cash by the M. and W. R. R. Company to Lawson, and he paid by check the balance due the Transport Company.

(b) Set up the Union Transport Company account on the books of Samuel Lawson.

3. (a) From the data of Problem 1, set up the Union Car Line Company account on the books of the Dairymen's League.

(b) From the data of Problem 2, set up the Samuel Lawson account on the Union Transport Company books.

4. (a) Analyze the following transactions from the viewpoint of the business and name the debit and credit elements of each to show:

1. The increase or decrease of assets, liabilities, and proprietorship.

2. The account titles under each of the general groups.

- Balance of cash on hand July 1, 19—, $8,940.
- July 2, received from cash sales over the counter $760.
- July 3, received from customers in payment of notes $575.
- July 5, paid for salaries $175, motor repairs $85,
- advertising $325, postage $22.
- July 6, discounted $1,000 6% 30-day note at the bank.
- July 7:
- Paid for new Ford truck $925, f.o.b. Detroit, and
- freight-in on truck, $38.75; insurance $75.
- Paid creditors $4,290.
- Made a promissory note in favor of a creditor for $500 for
- three months at 6%.
- Paid note for $2,000 due on the 8th of July with interest at
- 6% for three months.
- Bought a Liberty bond for $887.50 with accrued interest of $16.50.

(b) Set up the Cash account.

(c) Show the account properly ruled and balanced.

5. Name the debits and credits for each of the following transactions and set up the Notes Payable account:

- On October 1, 19—, discounted 30-day 6% note for $2,500 at the bank.
- Paid six months' promissory note at 6% for $1,000 on the

- 10th and gave to a trade creditor our note for $3,750
- due in 30 days without interest for balance of open account.
- Discounted trade customer's three months' 6% note for
- $5,000 at bank on the 15th, the discount period being 60 days.
- Paid note for $2,500 at the bank on the 31st.

6. The Willow Spring Dairy Farm purchased a new Cleveland Tractor April 1 for $1,850, f.o.b. Cleveland. Freight charges were $32.90; insurance in transit $15; hauling the accessories from the station to the farm $12; attachments cost $435; and assembling the parts cost $35. After being used for six months the machine with accessories was sold for $2,000.

Set up the Farm Implements account and determine the profit or loss. Disregard depreciation.

7. On January 15 a tract of land was purchased for $32,000, which amount included the cost of searching title $800, and unpaid taxes at time of purchase $350. The cash paid included all but the taxes.

- On March 1 a new road was completed through the tract at a cost of $1,250.
- April 1 the unpaid taxes of $350 were paid.
- August 1 assessments were levied for the state highway amounting to $3,280.
- Half of the land was sold, December 10, for $18,500.
- Name the debits and credits of each of these transactions and set up the Land account.

Instructions

Problems 1, 2, and 4. Set up each item somewhat in the following manner:

- Paid $9,780 cash on account
- (Dairymen's League paid to Union Car Line Company).
- Debit:
- Increase of Assets (Cash, $9,780).
- Credit: Decrease of Assets
- (Accounts Receivable, Dairymen's League $9,780).

XII

1. (a) Analyze the following transactions and name the debit and credit elements of each to show:

1. The increase or decrease of assets, liabilities, and proprietorship.

2. The account titles under each of the general groups. [Refer to (b) for account titles to be used for this.]

- Paid, March 1, repairs on auto truck $62.50; by check, rent $100.
- March 4, $18 for office supplies; advertising circulars $128;
- postage $25; telephone $18.50.
- March 8, interest on borrowed money $12; new sign on door $22.
- March 15, received interest on Liberty bonds $21.25.
- March 18, typewriter repairs cost $8; gasoline and oil $57;
- wrapping paper and general supplies $20.
- March 25, advertising $75; electric light $17; insurance $15.
- March 31, salaries of manager $125; office force $100;
- telegrams $12.80; discount on borrowed money $5; coal $50;
- sales salaries $75; traveling expenses $14.

(b) Prepare accounts with:

- 1. Delivery Expense
- 2. Advertising
- 3. Interest Cost
- 4. Interest Income
- 5. General Office Expense
- 6. Postage, Telephone, and Telegraph
- 7. Selling Expense
- 8. Cash

and set up the debits and credits of the transactions therein. All transactionsare for cash.

Be careful always to maintain the debit and credit equilibrium.

2. Prepare accounts with Delivery Expense, Delivery Supplies, Delivery Wages, and Cash, and set up therein the debits and credits of the following transactions, all of which are for cash:

- November 1, paid $5.40 for gasoline and $1.20 for oil.
- November 6, bought a new inner tube for $3.50, and the following day a new shoe for $42.50.
- November 10:
- Paid $4.50 for gasoline, and $1.20 for oil.
- Paid the driver $35 for wages and $22.50 to the helper.
- Removing carbon cost $2 and patching a tire $.50.
- November 15, the car was repaired for $75.
- November 18:
- A short-term insurance policy for $25 was taken.
- Paid the driver $35 for wages, and $22.50 to the helper.
- The driver was arrested and fined $10 for passing a
- trolley car while it was discharging passengers.
- November 19, the car was wrecked by going down a
- washed-out embankment and the helper hurt. Hospital
- expenses were $50, which the
- Casualty Insurance Company paid on the 25th. It cost $60
- to take the car to a garage and repairs cost $275.
- Suit was entered against the township for costs.

3. (a) Analyze the following transactions and name the debit and credit elements of each to show:

- 1. The increase or decrease of assets, liabilities, and proprietorship.
- 2. The account titles under each of the general groups.
-
- R. C. Rockwell goes into the wholesale grocery business and
- invests $20,000 in capital.

- Due to a need for cash to take advantage of a favorable
- purchase of securities for personal use, he withdraws $5,000 cash.
- He sells some of his personal securities for $500 to buy
- merchandise for the store.
- He pays out of business funds household expenses of $400,
- and a personal note due on his touring car for $500.
- By selling two acres of land for $500 he returns the $500 he
- paid on the car.
- At the end of the month he transfers to his capital account
- $1,000, being the debit balance in his personal account.

(b) Set up the proprietor's capital account as carried on the books of the grocery business.

4. (a) Analyze the following transactions and name the debit and credit elements of each to show:

- 1. The increase or decrease of assets, liabilities, and proprietorship.
- 2. The account titles under each of the general groups.
-
- There is a credit balance in Profit and Loss of $4,000.
- A debit balance in George B. Kelly, Personal, of $1,500.
- A credit balance in George B. Kelly, Capital, of $35,000.
- A debit balance in Cash of $5,000.
- Mr. Kelly paid bills for the business out of personal funds:
- Heat and electric light $75.60.
- Water rent $25.
- Store rent $400.
- Gas bill $26.50.
- R. G. Dun rating dues $10.
- Trade association dues $15.
-

- He received personally and retained the following amounts due the business:
- Interest on notes receivable $375.
- Cash in settlement of last month's disputed electric light bill $15.
- Rent of desk room $150.
- Mr. Kelly withdrew $400 cash for personal use.
- He paid for telegrams for the business $15.
- He had his touring car repaired and took $75 store cash to pay for it.

(b) Prepare accounts with:
- 1. Profit and Loss
- 2. George B. Kelly, Personal
- 3. George B. Kelly, Capital
- 4. Cash

and set up the debits and credits therein.

Transfer the net balance of Profit and Loss account to Kelly, Personal; and transfer the net balance of the latter account to Kelly, Capital.

XIII

1. Analyze the following transactions and name the debit and credit elements of each to show:

1. The increase or decrease of assets, liabilities, and proprietorship.

2. The account titles under each of the general groups.

- Credit sales to customers $389,650.
- Sales returns $9,480.
- Inventory at beginning of year $62,780.
- Credit purchases $206,240.
- Purchase returns $4,760.
- Cash received from customers $250,000.
- Sales discounts allowed $1,280.

- Purchase discounts taken $3,560.
- Cash paid creditors $175,000.
- Freight-in $2,670, and freight-out $3,935, were paid in cash.

2. Bought a motor truck for $2,250, on which the freight charges were $40 in addition. Accessories cost $150 and of these the speedometer was later sold for $50, its cost price. Set up the Delivery Truck account and show it properly adjusted at the close of the period to take account of 10% depreciation.

3. An old building cost $10,000.
- Renovation with betterments $1,200.
- Assessments for paving the street were $750.
- An extension not joined to the main building cost $2,000.
- The extension was sold for $2,500 cash early
- in the second year.
- Loss by fire at the end of the third year amounted
- to $3,000, which the insurance company made good
- by repairing the damage.
- Depreciation at 5% per annum is calculated on the
- balance of the Building account at the end of each year.

Show the Building account and its depreciation reserve at the end of the fifth year.

4. The Office Supplies account shows $450, of which $400 is still on hand at the end of the period. Show the account properly adjusted and closed.

5. From the data of Problem 1, prepare a single Merchandise account. Assume a final inventory of $75,000, and show the account adjusted and closed.

6. Analyze the following transactions relating to a business plant, and name the debit and credit elements of each to show:
- 1. The increase or decrease of assets, liabilities, and proprietorship.
- 2. The account titles under each of the general groups.
-
- Purchased a building for $100,000 from James Jackson & Co.

- Paid James Jackson & Co. $40,000 cash and executed a mortgage
- for the balance.
- Installed a new heating plant at a cost of $15,000 cash,
- $1,000 cash being received from sale of old plant.
- A new roof, at a cost of $5,000 cash, was put on.
- The old roof had no value as scrap.
- One year later the entire heating plant was covered with
- asbestos to conserve fuel. The cost was $500 cash.
- The roof was repainted at a cost of $100 cash.
- Glass broken by a hail storm was replaced at a cost of $50 cash.
- Two new skylights costing $750 cash were built.
- Gutters and down-spouts were replaced at a cost of $150.

XIV

1. Allowing five lines for each account and for the necessary depreciation reserve accounts which should follow immediately their particular assets, set up the following accounts on the ledger in proper form and under correct titles, and take a trial balance as of December 31, 19—.

- C. M. Loomis, capital investment $50,000.
- Withdrawals $3,000.
- Initial inventory of merchandise $19,740.
- Purchases $63,800; returns $1,524.50.
- Sales $99,360; returns $1,480.
- Cash in bank $2,750.
- Office equipment $800.
- Delivery trucks $5,000.
- Accounts receivable $40,950.
- Notes receivable $5,000.
- Liberty bonds $5,000.
- Notes payable $1,700.

- Interest and discount $90, Dr.
- Supplies $600.
- Salesmen's salaries $3,500.
- Advertising $1,200.
- Delivery expenses $569.50.
- Office salaries $4,655.
- Legal advice $50.
- Light and heat $150.
- Insurance $75.
- Building $22,910.
- Taxes $245.
- Land $2,500.
- Mortgage $10,000.
- Accounts payable $18,980.
- Depreciation incurred during previous years on
- buildings $2,000; on delivery equipment $500.

2. Loomis' final merchandise inventory is $20,680. He estimates depreciation on buildings at 5%, and on delivery equipment at 10%. 5% of the outstanding accounts and notes are deemed uncollectible. Office equipment is to be written down $300. Unexpired insurance is $25; accrued mortgage interest $300; accrued taxes $250; accrued sales salaries $350; and supplies on hand $200.

Prepare a statement of profit and loss and a balance sheet.

XV

1. Give three examples each of deferred expense and income, and accrued expense and income (12 examples). Show these in account form after the account has been adjusted.

2. From the following particulars, take a trial balance of the ledger of the Builders' Supply Co. on June 30, 19—.

Warehouse	$ 22,500.00
Land	7,800.00

Capital Stock	300,000.00
Surplus	50,193.00
Stock-in-Trade	245,680.00
Furniture and Fixtures	2,500.00
Good-Will	25,000.00
Trade Debtors	362,400.00
Cash	38,490.00
Trade Creditors	176,700.00
Notes Payable	15,700.00
Notes Receivable	18,900.00
Sales	589,760.00
Purchases	356,420.00
Salaries	38,900.00
Coal	4,200.00
Repairs	2,800.00
General Expenses	17,900.00
Depreciation Reserve Warehouse	5,000.00
Mortgage Payable	10,000.00
Interest Expense	475.00
Interest Income	662.00
Lighting	700.00
Telephone	600.00
Insurance	1,860.00
Taxes	890.00

Draw up a balance sheet and profit and loss statement for the year, taking consideration of these additional data:

- The merchandise on hand is $256,920.

- Coal on hand $500.
- Accrued mortgage interest $600.
- The warehouse has depreciated 5%, and furnitures and fixtures 10%.
- 3% of the Trade Debtors balance is deemed uncollectible.

Note: Do not classify expenses in the profit and loss statement. List them under the two titles, Operating Expenses and Non-Operating Expenses.

3. (a) Using the trial balance data of Problem 2, set up the ledger of the Builders' Supply Co.

(b) Close the ledger in accordance with the data given.

(c) Take a trial balance of the ledger after it is closed.

XVI

1. The following transactions are to be set up, debit and credit, on the ledger. Use the transaction number as the date of the month of June. Set upon your ledger the following account titles, in the order given, allotting to each the number of lines indicated by the numeral following the title:

Cash	35
Notes Receivable	10
C. H. Scovil	10
M. K. Dorns	10
A. B. Sutton	10
J. P. Nevin	10
B. T. Stanton	10
C. J. Moger	10
R. B. Karell	10
Reserve for Doubtful Accounts	10
Merchandise Inventory	10
Furniture and Fixtures	10
Depreciation Reserve Furniture and Fixtures	10
Notes Payable	10

Crew Brothers & Co.	10
Morris, Lee & Co.	10
Bondell & Co.	10
R. Kennedy	10
C. H. Wyss, Capital	10
C. H. Wyss, Personal	10
Profit and Loss	15
Sales	25
Sales Returns and Allowances	10
Purchases	15
Purchase Returns and Allowances	10
Freight-In	10
Salaries	10
General Expense	15
Depreciation	10
Bad Debts	10
Expense Supplies	10
Interest Income	10
Interest Expense	10
Purchase Discount	10

- June
- 1. C. H. Wyss invested $10,000 cash.
- He paid $5,000 cash for merchandise; and $200
- for one month's rent of a storeroom.
- Bought for cash, furniture and fixtures $1,000.
- 2. Bought merchandise, $2,750 of Crew Brothers & Co. on account.
- Sold merchandise for cash $675.

- 3. Sold merchandise for cash $1,345.
- Paid for office supplies $35.75.
- 4. Sold C. H. Scovil $500 of merchandise, receiving $200 cash.
- 5. Bought office safe for $150; and typewriter for $65.
- 6. Bought merchandise of Morris, Lee & Co. $957.80, paying $257.80 cash.
- Gave Crew Brothers & Co. our 6% 30-day note for $1,000.
- Wyss took merchandise for his own use, $50.
- 8. Cash sales were $1,585.
- Advertising cost $275.
- 9. Paid salesman $22; and office clerk $18; and $24 for coal.
- 10. Bought merchandise for cash $480.
- 11. Sold R. B. Karell merchandise for $90, and took his check in payment.
- 12. Paid $25 for Merchant Association dues; postage and stationery $15.
- 13. Sold bill of merchandise $358.90 to M. K. Dorns,
- receiving $158.90 in cash and accepting from Dorns,
- at its face value, R. C. Home's note,
- non-interest-bearing, for $50, due in 10 days.
- 14. Gave Crew Brothers & Co. a 10-day 6% note for balance due.
- Dorns returned as unsatisfactory $10 worth of merchandise
- sold to him on the 13th.

XVII

1. The following transactions of C. H. Wyss are to be set up on the ledger in the same manner as those given in the practice data of Assignment XVI.

- June
- 16. Cash sales were $875.55.
- Paid salesman $22; and office clerk $18.
- 17. Paid freightbill of $35; and express $5.80.

- 18. Wyss drew for personal use $400 cash.
- Paid electric light bill of $18.90.
- 19. Bought on account 2/10, net 20, merchandise
- from Bondell & Co. for $5,600.
- 20. Cash sales were $925.50.
- Sales on account to A. B. Sutton $1,275;
- J. P. Nevin, $150; C. J. Moger $99.70;
- and R. B. Karell $285.90.
- 22. Returned merchandise $400 to Bondell as unsatisfactory.
- 23. Paid salesman $22; and office clerk $18.
- 24. Received payment of R. C. Home's note for $50.
- Was allowed by Bondell & Co. $50 on claim.
- 25. Paid Crew Brothers & Co. note in their favor,
- with interest at 6%.
- C. H. Scovil paid $100 on account.
- 26. Paid freight $38.50.
- Wyss took goods for his own use $45.
- Sold B. T. Stanton $175 merchandise, receiving $50
- cash and James Harvey's note for $100 at 6% for
- 60 days, accepted at face value.
- 27. Paid telephone bill $13.90; advertising $52;
- and circulars $10.
- Allowed C. J. Moger's claim for $10 for spoiled goods.
- Paid Bondell & Co. amount due.
- 29. Cash sales were $470.
- Wyss drew for private needs $200.
- Collections were: A. B. Sutton $275;
- J. P. Nevin $150; C. J. Moger $59.70;

- and R. B. Karell $185.90.
- 30. Paid Morris, Lee & Co. $500 on account.
- Paid salesman $22; office clerk $18.
- Cash sales were $950.
- Purchased from R. Kennedy a desk for store use
- valued at $75, Kennedy taking merchandise to
- the value of $50 in part payment and the balance
- being credited.

Instructions

Note that the Bondell & Co. bill was paid within the discount period. (2/10, net 20, means that 2% can be deducted from the amount due if it is paid within 10 days and that the face amount of the bill is due in 20 days from date of rendering.)

XVIII

1. Take a trial balance of C. H. Wyss' ledger completed in Assignment XVII and record it on a piece of journal paper.

Draw up a balance sheet and profit and loss statement for the end of the month, taking account of the following adjustments:

- Interest accrued on notes receivable $.67.
- $49.53 worth of accounts and notes receivable will probably
- prove to be bad. Set up a reserve on the balance sheet.
- Inventories on hand: merchandise $7,218.20; expense supplies $25.75.
- Depreciation of $11.45 on furniture and fixtures for the month.
- Interest accrued on notes payable $4.
- Salaries accrued $5.71

2. The following transactions are to be entered in a purchase journal. Make daily postings to vendor accounts and a summary posting at the end of the month to Purchases account.

April

2. Bought from Endicott-Johnson Company, 61 Hudson St., N.Y.C.:

    20 pairs men's bluchers, black @ $ 4.75

    36 pairs ladies' single strap pumps, patent leather @ 3.50

    10 pairs men's white buckskin @ 2.50

10. Bought from Lounsbury-Soule Company, 47 Duane St., N.Y.C.:

    25 pairs men's Scotch brogues @ $ 6.00

    8 pairs men's kangaroo bluchers @ 4.50

15. Bought from Lexington Shoe Company, 141 Duane St., N.Y.C.:

    20 pairs men's sport oxfords @ $ 4.00

    15 pairs women's sport oxfords @ 3.75

20. Bought from Charles A. Eaton, 127 Duane St., N.Y.C.:

    12 pairs women's two strap oxfords, black @ $ 2.50

    6 pairs women's pumps, black kid @ 1.75

    8 pairs women's two strap sandals, white @ 2.65

26. Bought from I. Miller, 560 Fifth Avenue, N.Y.C.:

    5 pairs Russian boots @ $10.00

    12 pairs riding boots @ 12.00

    16 pairs single strap suede pumps @ 6.00

3. Enter the following transactions in a purchase journal ruled for two departments—Prescription and General. Make daily postings to vendor accounts. Summarize and post at end of month.

May

  1. Bought from Park Davis & Co., Detroit, Mich.:

	For Prescription Dept.	Invoice #10	2/20, n/60	$650.00
	For General Dept.	Invoice #11	2/20, n/60	425.00

3. Bought from Lehn & Fink, Inc., 635 Greenwich St., N. Y. C.:

For Prescription	Invoice #61	1/20, n/30	$150.00
For General	Invoice #62	1/20, n/30	87.50

7. Bought from Eastman Kodak Co., Rochester, N.Y.:

General	Invoice #675	1/30, n/60	$126.50

13. Bought from Park & Tilford, New York City:

General	Invoice #256	1/10, n/30	$ 22.50

From McKesson & Robbins, 91 Fulton St., N.Y.C.:

Prescription	Invoice #27	2/20, n/60	$ 75.00

17. Bought from Hospital Specialty Co., New York City:

General	Invoice #27	1/30, n/60	$ 76.00
Prescription	Invoice #28	1/30, n/60	98.00

23. Bought from Crescent Drug Sundry Co., Philadelphia, Pa.:

General	Invoice #75	1/30, n/60	$ 135.00

29. Bought from Marcus & Smith, New York City:

General	Invoice #861	1/10, n/30	$ 65.00

From J. M. Dalton, New York City:

General	Invoice #10,680	n/30	$ 16.00

31. Bought from Denver Pharmaceutical Co., Denver, Colo.:

    Prescription   Invoice #16   1/20, n/60 $165.00

    From United Drug Exchange, New York City:

    Prescription   Invoice #205   1/30, n/60 $267.00

Instructions

Problem 1. Do not close the accounts in the ledger. Make up the statements from the trial balance figures and the adjustment data given.

Problem 2. Use two-column journal paper—the inner column for detail and the outer column for totals. Follow Form 7 shown on page 142.

Use plain paper with "T" accounts for the ledger.

Problem 3. Use three-column journal paper. Rule in additional lines to make it conform with Form 9 on page 144. Follow carefully the illustration on that page in making the entries.

Use plain paper with "T" accounts for the ledger.

XIX

1. Close C. H. Wyss' ledger, taking account of the adjustments mentioned in Assignment XVIII. Use the profit and loss statement already drawn up to show the order in which the accounts should be closed.

Take a post-closing trial balance, recording it on a piece of journal paper, and compare it with the balance sheet.

2. The following transactions are to be entered in a sales journal. Make daily postings to customers' accounts and a summary posting at the end of the month to Sales account.

April

    3. Sold on account to Mrs. A. K. Foster: 3 waists @ $1.50;

        1 suit $45; and 6 pairs hosiery @ $1.10.

        Cash sales were $175.

7. Sold on account to Mrs. R. F. Burns: 1 evening dress $75; 1 evening cloak $125; 3 pairs hosiery @ $3.30.

    To Mrs. B. J. Scott: 1 riding habit $65; 1 pair riding boots $20; 1 riding crop $7.50; 1 riding hat $12.

    Cash sales were $225.

15. Sold to Miss Alice Hanna, on account: 1 pair 18-button gloves $7.50; 1 evening dress $45; 1 pair cut-steel buckles $25; 1 pair evening slippers $16.

    Cash sales $376.

21. Sold to Mrs. W. S. Jordan, on account: 1 evening dress $97.50; 1 afternoon dress $72.50; 1 business suit $45; 1 pair sandals $8.50; 1 pair evening slippers $16; four pair hosiery $20.

    Cash sales $413.

28. Sold to Mrs. Franklin Perry, on account: 1 bathing suit $13.50; 1 pair hose $1.50; 1 pair bathing shoes $2.50; 1 rubber cap $1.75.

    Cash sales, $365.

3. The following transactions are to be entered in a sales journal ruled for two departments—Prescription and General. Make daily postings to customers' accounts. Summarize and post at end of month.

May

2. Sold to Alhambra Pharmacy, Invoice #325, 1/30, n/60: Prescription, $325; General $215.

    To Alpha Drug Co., Invoice #326, 1/30, n/60: General $165.

    Cash sales: Prescription $614; General $528.90.

6. Sold to Ambassador Pharmacy, Invoice #350, 1/20, n/30:

Prescription, $235; General $129.

To Anglo-American Drug Co., Invoice #352, 1/10, n/30:

Prescription $12; General $137.25.

Cash sales: Prescription $562; General $489.

10. Sold to Arcade Drug Store, Invoice #375, 1/20, n/30:

Prescription $27; General $439.

Cash sales: Prescription $281; General $314.

18. Sold to Boston Pharmacy, Invoice #401, 1/30, n/60:

Prescription $426; General $237.

To Boyer-Gordon Drug Co., Invoice #402, 1/30, n/60:

Prescription $374; General $472.

Cash sales: Prescription $489; General $654.

24. Sold to Bronx Pharmacy, Invoice #431, 1/30, n/60:

Prescription $256; General $416.

Cash sales: Prescription $617; General $529.

28. Sold to Terminal Drug Co., Invoice #465, 1/20, n/30:

Prescription $10; General $438.

Cash sales: Prescription $675; General $981.

Instructions

Problem 2. Use two-column journal paper—the inner column for detail and the outer column for totals. Follow Form 7 shown on page 142.

Use plain paper with "T" accounts for the ledger.

Problem 3. Use three-column journal paper. Rule in additional lines to make it conform with Figure 9 on page 144. Follow carefully the illustration on that page in making the entries.

Use plain paper with "T" accounts for the ledger.

XX

1. The following transactions are to be entered in a cash receipts journal and posted, where necessary, to ledger accounts. At the end of the week summarize and post to a Cash account. Follow the <u>illustration on page 148</u>.

May

1. A. K. Foster, on account $56.10; S. C. Kramer $66.25.

    Cash sales $316.

2. Miss Alice Hanna, on account $93.50; W. S. Jordan $259.50.

    Cash sales $425.

3. Cash sales $543.

5. C. A. De Forest paid his note for $1,000, due today, with interest $15.

    Mrs. Irene Brush paid on account $235.

    Cash sales were $276.

6. Mrs. Lena Dupont paid on account $67.25.

    E. F. Gibbs paid on account $100.

    Cash sales were $347.75.

7. James W. Law, on account of his non-interest-bearing note $126.75.

    Mrs. Molly Lee, on account $257.25.

    E. D. Wynne, for commission on goods sold for him, $25.

    Cash sales $482.

2. Enter the following transactions in a cash disbursements journal and post daily to "T" ledger accounts set up on plain paper. Follow the form of journal <u>shown on page 149</u>. Post total disbursements for the week to the ledger Cash account used in Problem 1.

May

1. Paid Acme Cloak & Suit Co., on account $235;

    American Cloak Co. $165.

    Bought postage stamps and stamped envelopes $50.

2. Paid Green & Greenberger on account $175.

   Bought office stationery $51.75.

   Paid Ideal Cord & Trimming Co. on account $45.

3. Paid Lakeview Garment Co. on account $127.50;

   Lang Trimming Co. on account $25.

   Paid salesmen's salaries $225.

5. Paid Empire Dress & Suit Co. on account $137.

   Paid telephone bill for April $30.14.

   Paid Elmer Cloak & Suit Co. $75.

   Our note #25 for $1,000 came due and was paid with interest $10.

6. Paid electric light bill for April $27.50.

   Paid rent May 15 to June 15, $263.

   Paid Standard Novelty Works on account $115.

7. Paid Magic Cloak & Suit Co. on account $67.50;

   Textile Trimming. Works on account $75.

   Paid office salaries $100.

3. The following transactions are to be entered in a cash book, cash receipts and cash disbursements bound together. Post daily to "T" ledger accounts set up on plain paper. Follow Forms 10 and 11 shown on pages 148-149. Post total receipts and total disbursements for the week to the ledger Cash account used in Problem 1.

May

8. Balance from previous week's transactions, $1,691.96.

   Paid Green & Greenberger on account $135;

   American Cloak Co. $45.

   Received on account from Miss Frances Clyne $102;

   and Miss Lula Fields $178.

   Cash purchases were $340.25.

9. Paid Acme Cloak & Suit Co. $165;

　　Lakeview Garment Co. $135.

　Received on account from Miss Louise Fox $215;

　　and Miss Alice Gaynor $176.

　Cash sales were $189.

10. Paid salesmen's salaries $230; for delivery service $150.

　Received on account from Miss Katherine Kennedy $216;

　　and Mrs. Johanna Lambert $75.

　Received rent from portion of store $50.

12. Paid Empire Dress & Suit Co. on account $150;

　　Elmer Cloak & Suit Co. $125.

　Paid freight on purchases $41.37.

　Received on account from Miss Pauline Marks $167.50.

　Cash sales $576.

13. Paid telephone bill, $27; advertising bill for

　　newspaper insertions $75.

　Received on account from Mrs. D. J. McCormack $167.

　Received payment of note of J. I. Ardsley $500, and interest $7.50.

14. Paid Daisy Cloak & Suit Co. $150 on account.

　Paid office salaries $100.

　Received from Miss Sue Robertson $125.

　Proprietor, M. D. James, drew for personal use $50.

　Cash was short $4.87.

4. The following data have been taken from the ledger of the Port Bedford Terminal Company, on December 31, 19—.

Real Estate, Wharves, and Warehouses	$30,932,394
Terminal Railway	807,052

Marine Equipment	298,994
Machinery and Electric Plant	177,588
Depreciation Reserve, Real Estate, Wharves, and Warehouses	4,187,074
Terminal Railway Depreciation Reserve	45,817
Marine Equipment Depreciation Reserve	23,942
Machinery and Plant Depreciation Reserve	16,894
Cash in Bank	192,806
Accounts Receivable	451,406
Materials and Supplies Purchases	128,894
Investments in U. S. Liberty Bonds	1,809,000
Capital Stock	15,000,000
First Mortgage 4% Gold Bonds, due August 1, 1951	12,000,000
Accounts Payable	652,644
Notes Payable	247,000
Surplus	1,231,540
Warehouse Income	2,681,694
Income from Piers	2,140,562
Sundry Income	436,353
Maintenance of Property	1,160,453
Selling and Service Costs	1,081,526
General Expenses	462,386
Taxes	681,021
Bond Interest	480,000

(a) Set these items up in the ledger.

(b) Take a trial balance.

Instructions

Problem 1. Use plain paper with "T" accounts for the ledger.

Problem 3. Use a double sheet of two-column journal paper for the cash book. On the receipts side enter the balance brought forward in the outer column. For current and summary entry follow carefully the forms shown on pages 148-149.

At the end of the week summarize the cash book and post the totals to the ledger Cash account. Balance and rule the cash book, being careful to carry forward the balance to the next week.

XXI

1. The following transactions should be entered in a general journal, debit and credit, with full explanation.

On November 15, 19—, John Henry and James Raymond form a partnership to carry on a retail grocery business. Losses and gains are to be shared equally. Each partner is to be allowed a salary of $150 per month.

Henry invests the following assets from a business of which he has been sole owner:

Cash $150; notes receivable $570; accounts receivable $7,320; merchandise $24,360; furniture and fixtures $4,230.

The partnership also assumes the following liabilities for Henry: Notes payable $3,000; accounts payable $8,815.

Raymond invests these assets: Cash $5,500; furniture and fixtures $2,500; building $17,000.

2. At various times the following transactions of the partnership occur. Record them in the journal with full explanation.

Nov.

20. Returned goods to Austin Nichols & Co. $215;

to Bronx Sugar Co. $65;

to Continental Food Products Co. $87.50.

22. Received 30-day 6% note of J. D. Jordan for $75.

Accepted draft of Armour & Co., 60 days from sight,

in favor of the American Live Stock Co., $127.50.

24. Goods sold during previous week were returned by Franklin K. Adams $25; Eugene Alread $35; Preston Freeman $16.50.

26. The partners gave their 90-day 6% note to Swift & Company, payable at the store, for $725.

28. Investigation upon a complaint from James Ortner, a customer, showed that a sale of $150 to George Ortner had been charged to the former in error.

Dec.

8. Made Joseph Horowitz, a customer, an allowance of $25 on account of dissatisfaction with a recent purchase.

10. Sold bill of goods $425.50, to Ben. B. Brady, receiving cash $125.50, and J. S. Gordon's 60-day acceptance for the balance.

20. Purchased a plot of ground for $4,000 from the Bond & Mortgage Co., paying $1,000 cash and executing a mortgage for the balance.

3. The following particulars relating to Problem 4, Assignment XX, must be taken into account to show the true condition of the Port Bedford Terminal Co. as on December 31, 19—:

- Materials and supplies on hand $68,894.
- Depreciation for the period:
- On real estate, wharves, and warehouses $308,401.
- On terminal railway $22,581.
- On marine equipment $16,714.
- On machinery and electric plant $4,978.
- Estimate of uncollectible accounts $10,000.

- Interest accrued on Liberty bonds $21,488.
- Accrued maintenance of property $25,980.
- Accrued selling and service costs $16,460.
- Accrued rents on warehouses $50,000.
- Accrued rents on piers $30,000.
- Taxes payable $50,000.
- Warehouse rents prepaid $20,000.

- (a) Draw up a balance sheet for December 31, 19—.
- (b) Draw up a statement of profit and loss for the
- twelve months' period ending December 31, 19—.

Instructions

Problem 3. The net worth section of the balance sheet should be set up as follows:

Capital Stock $

Surplus:

   At beginning of period $

   Net profit for period

   At end of period $

- Classify the items of the profit and loss statement
- on the basis of:
- 1. Operating income
- 2. Operating expenses
- 3. Non-operating income
- 4. Non-operating expenses

XXII

1. Albert Johnson and Harold Taylor enter into a copartnership agreement for the purpose of buying and selling Christmas novelties. Each contributes cash, no other resources of use to this undertaking being available. Taylor, because of wide acquaintance among manufacturers, is to handle the buying end, and Johnson is to have charge of the details of store management and selling. They are to share profits and losses equally.

On November 15, 19—, operations begin. They keep a full record of all transactions, using a cash book, purchase journal, sales journal, general journal, and ledger. The following accounts are kept:

- Cash
- Notes Receivable
- M. K. Lord
- C. H. Marks
- K. P. Temple
- L. K. Lewis
- F. M. Wood
- T. C. Bailey
- Merchandise Inventory
- Furniture and Fixtures
- Notes Payable
- Imbrie & Co.
- Bonbright & Co.
- Halsey, Stewart & Co.
- B. W. Chapman & Co.
- Albert Johnson, Capital
- Albert Johnson, Personal
- Harold Taylor, Capital
- Harold Taylor, Personal
- Profit and Loss
- Sales

- Sales Returns and Allowances
- Purchases
- Purchases Returns and Allowances
- Freight-In
- Salaries
- General Expense
- Expense Supplies
- Bad Debts
- Interest Expense
- Interest Income
- Purchase Discount

Enter the following transactions in their respective journals:

Nov.

15. Each partner deposits $7,500 in the firm name of Johnson & Taylor at the Park National Bank.

    Paid $1,000 for furniture and fixtures.

    Paid rent $250 and advertising $100.

    Bought merchandise from Imbrie & Co. $2,000, paying $500 cash, giving a note for $1,000, due in 30 days at 6%, and the balance remaining on account.

    Johnson withdrew $200 in funds for personal use.

16. Cash sales $430.80: on account to F. M. Wood $569.20; K. P. Temple $500.

17. Bought for cash, paper and twine $29.50; miscellaneous supplies $10.

18. Sold merchandise to M. K. Lord for $1,000, accepting his 10-day 6% note for $500 and $300 in cash.

Cash sales amounted to $450.

19. Bought a cash register for $150.

    Cash sales $400.

20. Bought merchandise from Bonbright & Co. for $500, 2/10, n/30.

    Paid Imbrie & Co. on account $450.

    Taylor took merchandise $25, for his own use.

    Cash sales were $800.

22. Cash sales were $300.

    Sold on account to Lewis $950; and to Marks $350.

23. Paid Bonbright & Co. the bill of the 20th.

    Paid salaries $40.

24. Sold T. C. Bailey, on account, $450 of merchandise.

    Johnson took $100 cash for current needs.

    The firm bought $1,400 merchandise from Halsey, Stewart & Co.

26. Bought of B. W. Chapman & Co., merchandise $250.

    Cash sales were $450.

27. The firm is notified that C. H. Marks has failed.

29. Sold bill of merchandise of $200 to T. C. Bailey, receiving $100 in cash, and a 6% note for the balance, due in 10 days.

    Cash sales were $300.

30. Returned $50 merchandise to B. W. Chapman & Co.

    Paid freight $35; insurance $15.

    Lord paid note of $500 and interest.

    Paid $40 in wages and gave Halsey, Stewart & Co. a 10-day 6% note for amount due.

2. Using the adjustment data of Assignment XXI, Problem 3, close the ledger of the Port Bedford Terminal Co. and take a trial balance after closing.

Instructions

Problem 1. The purpose of this assignment is to give practice in the operation of the five journals in a going concern. The ledger will not be used.

Use a double sheet of two-column journal paper for the cash book. A single sheet of two-column paper will be sufficient for each journal.

Make full opening entry on November 15.

Do not summarize the journals until directions are given.

Note that the firm takes advantage of the Bonbright discount offer.

Make no entry as to the Marks' failure until further instructions.

Problem 2. Transfer the balance of the ledger Profit and Loss account to the Surplus account.

XXIII

1. Continue the following as in Problem 1, Assignment XXII.

Dec.

1. Johnson took $100 for personal use.

    The firm paid $50 for freight bills.

    T. C. Bailey returned merchandise $50.

2. Bought supplies for $18.50 cash.

    Electric light bill $18, and telephone bill $12, were paid.

3. Cash sales were $240.

    They received $400 on account from Bailey.

4. Lewis paid $850 on account.

    Bought from Imbrie & Co. $200 of merchandise.

6. Taylor sold for $650 cash merchandise, for which the firm had paid $1,000.

    Sold on account to K. P. Temple $450; and to F. M. Wood $235.

7. Paid $40 for salaries; and $15 for supplies.

8. Paid $72 on insurance.

   Bailey paid his note of $100 and interest.

9. Cash sales were $275.

   The firm bought from Imbrie & Co. $675; Bonbright & Co. $800.

10. Paid Halsey note with $2.33 interest.

11. Received on account from Lord $100; and from cash sales $150.

13. Temple gave a non-interest-bearing note due in 30 days for $500.

14. Paid freight-in bill $32; and coal bill $17.

    Salaries of $40 were paid.

15. Paid note to Imbrie & Co. with interest.

    The receivers of C. H. Marks paid $164, the balance of

    the claim being valueless.

Summarize all journals (referring to Problem 1, Assignment XXII, and the above) and balance the cash book.

2. The following information has been taken from the books of the Valhalla Company after the ledger was adjusted:

- Sales $2,896,745.
- Sales returns $22,840.
- Sales allowances $12,615.
- Inventories January 1, 19—, $3,096,720.
- Purchases were $1,216,000.
- Purchase returns $5,675; and allowances $4,200.
- Inventories on December 31, 19—, were $3,514,900.
- Rent expense $54,000.
- Bad debts $45,000.
- Depreciation $89,700.
- Advertising $50,000.
- Sales salaries $686,000.

- Traveling expenses $64,892.
- Freight-in $17,990.
- Freight-out $8,960.
- Delivery expense $22,600.
- Office supplies $13,400.
- Lighting $4,825.
- Office salaries $54,000.
- Telephone $2,190.
- Insurance $8,900.
- Taxes $22,940.
- Interest expense $7,890.
- Mortgage interest $60,000.
- Interest income $10,890.
- Income from securities $2,400.
- Sundry expenses $2,890.
- Repairs $14,890.

Draw up the statement of profit and loss.

3. Draft the journal entries necessary to close the ledger of the Valhalla Company.

4. Draw up the Profit and Loss account as it would appear in the ledger of the Valhalla Company.

5. Anthony B. Mans is the proprietor of a drug business owning assets and subject to liabilities as follows:

- Cash $5,150.
- Accounts receivable $795.
- Stock of merchandise $25,340.
- Store furnishings $3,420.
- Soda fountain $1,250.
- Notes payable $4,500.

- Accounts payable $9,305.

He sells the business as above, excepting the cash which he retains, to James R. Hart for $20,000 cash, which includes a bonus of $3,000 for his good-will. Mans withdraws all cash and deposits it in his personal bank account.

Make the necessary entries in Mans' journal and cash book to record the sale transaction and the withdrawal of cash.

XXIV

As bookkeeper for Wm. C. Baldwin, dealer in coal and coke, you will use a general journal, a sales journal, a purchase journal, a cash book, and a ledger. Four *double* pages of journal paper and three *double* pages of ledger paper will suffice. At the top of the first page write "Journal of Wm. C. Baldwin." Allow 130-150 lines for your Journal. The next blank *double* page will be used for a cash book, marked on the left at the top, "Dr." and near the middle, "Cash." Similarly the right page, "Cash"; and at the top, right-hand margin, "Cr." Allow 80-100 lines for each side of the cash book. The next blank page mark "Sales Journal," allowing 70-90 lines. The next blank page mark "Purchase Journal," allowing 1 page. The last 3 pages, reserve for trial balances and statements. Number consecutively all pages in journal and ledger.

In the cash book use the first column on either side for items and the second column for totals and balances. *Balance and rule the cash book at the end of each week*, extending the "items" total before balancing and marking it for posting purposes "Cash, Dr." or "Cash, Cr." as the case may be. Enter the balance on the "Dr." side in the "Total" column, and so keep each week's receipts segregated. At the bottom of the page, unless it happens to coincide with the end of the week, carry "totals" of each side forward, not the balance.

In the sales and purchase journals mark the first column "On Account" and the second "Cash," and make entries in them according as sale or purchase is "on account" or "cash." If "cash," entry must be made in the cash book also, in which case check the item in the ledger folio column in both journals, as total cash, sales, and purchases are to be posted from their respective journals. In making summary entries for the sales journal at the end of the month, rule and total each column, and bring the cash column total over on the next line into the "On Account" column, marking it "Cash Sales, Total." Add these two and rule off, marking them "Sales, Cr." The purchase journal will be handled similarly.

Open the following accounts in your ledger, beginning on the first page in the order given and allowing the number of lines to each account indicated by the numeral following each:

Cash	10
Notes Receivable	5
M. R. Hamilton	10
F. S. Kent	10
H. T. Avery	10
G. C. Furnald	10
C. P. Pell	10
S. T. Hartley	10
A. D. Livingston	10
Reserve for Doubtful Accounts	5
Coal Inventory	5
Furniture and Fixtures	10
Depreciation Reserve Furniture and Fixtures	5
Building	5
Depreciation Reserve Building	5
Land	5
Notes Payable	10
M. H. Hanna & Co.	10
American Coke & Chemical Co.	10
Peabody & Co.	10
Seabord By-Product Coke Co.	10
Midtown Realty Co.	8
Wm. C. Baldwin, Capital	10
Wm. C. Baldwin, Personal	10
Profit and Loss	20
Sales	15
Purchases	10

Purchases Returns and Allowances	8
Freight & Delivery Inward	10
Salesmen's Salaries	10
Advertising	10
Delivery Expense	10
Expense Supplies	15
Rent	5
Insurance	8
Office Salaries	10
Sundry Expense	8
Cash Short and Over	7
Interest Expense	8
Depreciation	5
Bad Debts	5
Interest Income	8

Before recording any transactions, study carefully the accounts, particularly the expense accounts, which you will keep. Make your classification strictly according to them. Keep no additional accounts.

May 2, 19—, Wm. C. Baldwin, long interested in the coke business, bought out the Newark Coke Company on the basis of the values shown below.

The assets taken over were:

- Stocks of coal and coke $18,902.10.
- Accounts receivable:
- M. R. Hamilton $6,950.
- F. S. Kent $7,920.
- G. C. Furnald $2,450.
- C. P. Pell $7,125.
- S. T. Hartley $9,840.
- A. D. Livingston $2,890.

- Furniture and fixtures $1,200.
- A note made by G. C. Furnald for $7,800, due May 11,
- after which it was to bear 9% interest. This note
- was taken over at its face value.

The liabilities assumed were:
- Accounts payable:
- M. H. Hanna & Co. $8,942.50.
- American Coke & Chemical Co. $12,437.18.
- Peabody & Co. $5,647.92.
- A note dated February 20, 19—, for three months at 6%,
- in favor of the Seaboard By-Product Coke Co., for
- $5,485.50, the accrued interest assumed being $65.83.
- In addition to the above investment Baldwin opened an
- account with the National City Bank for $15,000 as
- working capital.

May

3. Bought for cash, account books $10; stationery $18;
    stamps $25; paid rent to June 2, $500.
   Sales were: on account, M. R. Hamilton $1,293.75;
    for cash $890.40.
4. Bought coal and coke from M. H. Hanna & Co.
    on account $6,497.95.
   Paid freight-in $169.72.
   Bought insurance policy for one year $360.
   Sales were: on account, F. S. Kent $3,497.82; cash $614.80.
5. Paid Peabody & Co. balance due.
   Sales on account: H. T. Avery $1,876.49;

G. C. Furnald $5,973.80; cash $617.90.

6. Bought from Seabord By-Product Co. on account $5,890.40.

    Allowed by M. H. Hanna & Co. $400 on account of impurities in coke.

    Paid freight-in $126.72.

    Sales were: on account, S. T. Hartley $3,487.60;

    M. R. Hamilton $2,947.30; F. S. Kent $2,476.30; cash $457.80.

7. Received cash on account from M. R. Hamilton $1,000;

    F. S. Kent $2,750; H. T. Avery $975; G. C. Furnald $5,250.

    Paid bookkeeper $30; stenographer $25; clerks $40.

    Sales for cash were $1,075.

    Baldwin drew $100 in cash and $80 in coal for his home.

    Paid delivery expenses $200; and sales salaries $300.

> Balance, summarize, and post the cash book. The summary entry, "Cash, Dr.," must, for this first week only, be set up opposite the total of the cash receipts journal, so as to include the cash capital invested. In all subsequent summary entries, the "Cash, Dr." must include only the current week's receipts—not the "Balance."

9. Paid the American Coke & Chemical Co. on account $7,500; cash for supplies $62.50; and advertising $1,000.

    Sales on account: H. T. Avery $2,146.70;

    G. C. Furnald $1,786.42; C. P. Pell $792.50;

    A. D. Livingston $863.47.

10. Bought from the American Coke & Chemical Co. $5,746.80 on account.

Paid by check $350 for safe; and $125 for typewriter.

Received payments from C. P. Pell $2,500;

and S. T. Hartley $2,150.

11. Paid M. H. Hanna & Co. $8,942.50; paid freight-in $248.50.

Canceled $250 of order of the 10th from

American Coke & Chemical Co.

12. Sales on account: A. D. Livingston $2,387.50; H. T. Avery $1,820.

Paid demurrage charges $290.75 by check.

Instructions

May 2. To determine Baldwin's net investment and to serve as a guide for the order of entry of the various items in the journal, make a rough draft of balance sheet. Enter the "cash" investment in the Journal as a part of the compound opening entry, and also in the "Total" column of the cash receipts journal. Check (✓) the "cash" item in the general journal and also check the capital investment entry in the cash receipts journal.

May 12. Charge demurrage costs to the Freight and Delivery Inward account.

XXV

May

13. Bought from Peabody & Co. on account $4,910.

Paid freight-in $144.70; paid to M. H. Hanna & Co.,

the balance due.

Sales on account were: S. T. Hartley $1,875.20.

14. Paid bookkeeper $30; stenographer $25; clerks $40.

Cash sales for the week were $3,679.80.

Baldwin drew $200 in cash, and gave on his personal account

5 tons of coal worth $60 to the Community Association.

Delivery expense was $220; and sales salaries were $300.

Balance, summarize, and post the cash book.

16. Bought from M. H. Hanna & Co. on account $4,895.70.

    Paid freight-in $82.93; Merchants' Association dues $50; stationery $55.25.

    Received cash on account: G. C. Furnald $1,275; C. P. Pell $1,350.

17. Bought a multigraph for cash $75, and paid freight on it of $10.22.

    Paid $96.17 for supplies.

    Returned $800 worth of coke to M. H. Hanna & Co.

    Cash was short $5.48.

    Paid on account: A. D. Livingston $1,375; M. R. Hamilton $3,500; F. S. Kent $4,035.

    Sold on account: H. T. Avery $1,275; G. C. Furnald $862.70; and C. P. Pell $1,872.60.

18. Received a 30-day 6% note from S. T. Hartley for $5,000, to apply on account; and a note dated May 16 at 6%, due July 16, for $3,000, from A. D. Livingston.

19. Paid $38.90 for repairs to office steps, which were broken by accident, not chargeable to the landlord.

    Canceled a $100 lot from Peabody & Co. on the last order.

    Bought from the American Coke & Chemical Co. on account $7,580.

    Paid $103.72 in-freight.

20. Paid Seaboard By-Product Coke Co. note $5,485.50,

and interest.

Purchases for cash were $1,270.

21. Baldwin discounted his own note at the bank for $1,000, for 30 days at 6%.

    Paid bookkeeper $30; stenographer $25; clerks $40.

    Cash sales for the week were $3,195.60.

    Baldwin withdrew $400 in cash.

    Paid sales salaries $300; delivery expense $235; and American Coke & Chemical Co. $5,000 on account.

    Balance, summarize, and post the cash book.

23. Sold on account: A. D. Livingston $975.70; and M. R. Hamilton $1,392.65.

    Paid Patrol Protection Service $50; and $175 to repair heater and boiler, the latter item being allowed as applicable to future rent.

24. Sold refuse for cash $15.80.

    Bought from Peabody & Co. $2,120 on account, and paid freight $174.37.

25. Cash was short $1.04.

    Paid lighting bill of $31.75.

26. Received cash on account: F. S. Kent $1,500; H. T. Avery $1,875; G. C. Furnald $1,000.

    Sold on account: C. P. Pell $1,587; F. S. Kent $1,623.80; A. D. Livingston $1,217.80.

27. Purchased from Peabody & Co. on account, shipment of

Pocahontas coal $900.

Bought $50 worth of stamps.

Cash was over $1.37.

28. Paid bookkeeper $30; stenographer $25; and clerks $40.

Cash sales for the week were $2,175.80.

Baldwin withdrew $250 for personal expenses.

Delivery expenses were $245; and sales salaries $300.

Paid the Seaboard By-Product Coke Co. bill of May 6.

Balance, summarize, and post the cash book.

31. Paid Peabody & Co. $1,000 on account.

Bought of M. H. Hanna & Co. on account $6,250.

Telephone bill was $52.45; and cash was over $.51 (51 cents).

Bought of Seaboard By-Product Coke Co. on account $2,890.70, paying $52.18 in-freight.

Gave the American Coke & Chemical Co. a 90-day note at 6% for $1,250.

A. D. Livingston paid $500 on account.

Cash sales were $480.90.

Received on account: M. R. Hamilton $3,000; F. S. Kent $2,000; C. P. Pell $2,500.

Bought from Midtown Realty Co. the lot in which the yards were located for $2,000, and the buildings with equipment for $8,575, giving $5,575 in cash and executing a 6% mortgage on private properties not carried on the books of the business for the balance.

Instructions

May 14. The coal given to charity is a personal expense of Baldwin's.

May 31. Record the purchase of lot and building as a credit for the entire amount to the vendor. Cancel the liability to the vendor by entry in the cash book for the cash portion, and in the general journal for the mortgage.

XXVI

Balance the cash book, total, and make summary entries for the sales and purchase journals.

Post completely the sales and purchase journals, then the general journal and cash book. Be sure to post the weekly totals of cash receipts and cash disbursements as well as the totals for the end of the month.

Take a trial balance of account balances and record it on page 13 of your journals, labeling it

"Trial Balance, May 31, 19—, Wm. C. Baldwin."

Instructions

Refer to pages 142, 148, 149, for the form of the various journal summaries and to 547-548, practice data, for the method of summarizing.

Be very careful always to cross-index every posted item in both ledger and journals just as soon as the posting of that item is completed. The ledger folio columns in the journals are thus an indication as to how far the work of posting has proceeded, in case the bookkeeper is interrupted before completing the postings.

XXVII

Draw up a balance sheet and statement of profit and loss for Wm. C. Baldwin, taking into account the following adjustments and inventories:

- Interest prepaid on note at bank $3.33.
- Interest accrued on following notes:
- G. C. Furnald $39.00
- S. T. Hartley   10.83
- A. D. Livingston   7.50
- ———
- Total $57.33
- Expense supplies inventory $14.50.
- Insurance unexpired $330.
- Merchants' Association dues prepaid $47.92.

- Delivery expenses accrued $75.
- Salesmen's salaries accrued $100.
- Advertising accrued $50.
- Advertising prepaid $200.
- Office salaries accrued $31.67.
- Prepaid rent $207.26.
- Furniture and fixtures are to be depreciated at the rate of 1% per month.
- Uncollectible accounts are estimated as ½% on sales for the month.
- Coal inventory $19,352.30.

Instructions

Use the method of the work sheet in doing this assignment. Follow closely the illustration in the text. After the work sheet has proved the accuracy of the work, draw up the formal statements.

XXVIII

1. Adjust and close Wm. C. Baldwin's ledger, taking account of the adjustment data given in Assignment XXVII.

2. Take a post-closing trial balance.

APPENDIX B
PRACTICE WORK FOR STUDENT—
SECOND HALF-YEAR

The practice work for the second semester is designed to give facility in the use of accounting records, and accuracy and confidence in the handling of a volume of transactions. Accordingly, this work consists largely of two somewhat extended problems to be recorded in blank books. The first is a problem in partnership, involving particularly the adjustment of partners' accounts at the close of the fiscal period. Many points met in the operation of records using controlling accounts are included. The second is concerned with a trading corporation. Here some of the problems peculiar to the corporation are met, as well as those connected with the operation of a departmental business.

The stationery furnished provides two sets of blank books, as indicated above, the one for the partnership, the other for the corporation. Specific directions for their use are given with each problem. Upon completion of the problem these blanks are to be turned in for inspection and may be retained by the school if deemed best. A few miscellaneous problems are also provided. The loose-leaf supplies will usually be found suitable for their solution.

Here, also, sufficient practice work is furnished to accompany 30 hours of lecture or classroom work. If desired, this may be supplemented by the use of material in Appendix C. If an adequate understanding of the use and operation of accounting records is to be secured, disconnected problem work should not be substituted for the practice work provided in this Appendix B.

In handling this semester's work, the student must not allow himself to fall behind in the preparation of the assigned work There is quite a volume of work to be done and the material of the various assignments is so interrelated that unless the practice work is kept up to date, most of its value is lost through the student's not being ready to carry out instructions given covering the current work. Careful work and the proving of its accuracy will prevent much waste of time in making corrections.

I

This set comprises a general journal; a sales journal, a purchase journal, and the cash journals, for convenience bound together in one book; and a general ledger, purchase ledger, and sales ledger, also bound together in one book. Of the general journal, pages 1-15 inclusive will be used for transactions which cannot be recorded in the special journals, the rest of the blank being used as a place of record of the monthly trial balances. Of the special journal blank, pages 1-4 inclusive will be used for sales; pages 5-7 inclusive for purchases; page 8 and following for the cash book. For the purpose of securing a better comprehension of some features of the operation of controlling accounts the general journal is not provided with the customary analysis columns. The student is thus compelled to consider the effect of each entry on the controlling account as well as on the subsidiary account.

The sales journal provides for the analysis of sales into cash, credit, and partners' withdrawals, the first column being the total or general column in which all items are to be entered; the others, "On Account," "Cash," and "Partners' Withdrawals." The same provisions, with the exception of the Partners' Withdrawals column, are to be made in the purchase journal.

The cash book columns will be, on the debit side, General, Accounts Receivable, Sales Discount, and Net Cash; and on the credit, General, Accounts Payable, Purchase Discount, and Net Cash. All items affecting the controlling accounts, "Accounts Receivable" and "Accounts Payable," are to be entered gross in their respective columns, the totals of which are posted to the controlling accounts when the cash book is summarized. The discount columns on both sides of the cash book are to be used for the recording of sales and purchase discounts, and all items to be posted to general ledger accounts other than the controlling accounts should be entered gross in the "General" columns. All amounts will be extended net into the "Net Cash" columns, and the difference between these two columns will represent the cash balance.

The general ledger will include pages 1-27 inclusive, the sales ledger pages 28-34 inclusive, and the purchase ledger 35-40 inclusive. The first four pages preceding ledger ruling are to be used for index purposes.

All transactions affecting individual customers', creditors', and partners' accounts are to be posted daily to those accounts. The postings to the controlling accounts will follow the explanations in the text or special instructions.

This set affords the student facility in handling a partnership set of books operated under a controlling account system. The operation of this set will require great care in posting to controlling and subsidiary accounts in order to keep them in agreement.

To secure the maximum of practice with a minimum of detail work, the transactions for each month are summarized and are to be dated as of the last day of the month. The dates of issuance or maturity of the notes, however, are given so that this can be recorded.

The student should become familiar with the following ledger accounts to which he should strictly adhere in the classification of all transactions. These accounts are to be opened in the ledger at the places indicated. The first numeral following the account title indicates the page, the second the line on that page. "Line 1" refers to the very first line at the top of the page.

LEDGER ACCOUNTS (40 pages)
General ledger, pages 1-27
Sales ledger, " 28-34
Purchase ledger, " 35-40

	Page	Line
Cash	1	1
Investments	1	12
Notes Receivable	1	18
Accounts Receivable	1	30
Reserve for Doubtful Accounts	2	28
Merchandise Inventory	2	34
Notes Receivable, Special	3	1
Deposit with Westchester Lighting Co.	3	11
Delivery Equipment	3	21
Depreciation Reserve Delivery Equipment	3	31
Store Furniture and Fixtures	4	1
Depreciation Reserve Store Furniture and Fixtures	4	11
Office Furniture and Fixtures	4	22
Depreciation Reserve Office Furniture and Fixtures	4	31
Building	5	1
Depreciation Reserve Buildings	5	11
Notes Payable	5	22
Accounts Payable	6	1
Mortgage Payable	6	30
C. Allen Cotten, Profits Loan Account	7	1
Scott Wooster, Profits Loan Account	7	12

Landsdowne Woolsey, Profits Loan Account	7	26
C. Allen Cottenm Capital	8	1
C. Allen Cotten, Personal	8	13
Scott Wooster, Capital	9	1
Scott Wooster, Personal	9	13
Landsdowne Woolsey, Capital	10	1
Landsdowne Woolsey, Personal	10	13
Profit and Loss	11	1
Sales	12	1
Sales Returns and Allowances	12	19
Purchases	13	1
Purchases Returns and Allowances	13	19
In-Freight and Cartage	14	1
Salesmen's Salaries	14	13
Salesmen's Traveling Expenses	14	26
Advertising	15	1
Delivery Expense	15	13
Shipping Supplies	15	26
Out-Freight	16	1
Office Salaries	16	13
Office Supplies	16	26
Office Expense	17	1
General Expense	17	13
Cash Short and Over	17	29
Charity Donations	18	1
Association Dues	18	13
Light and Heat	18	26

Rent	19	1
Insurance	19	13
Taxes	19	26
Depreciation	20	1
Sales Discount	20	13
Bad Debts	20	26
Interest Cost	21	1
Purchase Discount	21	13
Interest Income	21	26
Miscellaneous Sales	22	1

On pages 28-34 inclusive, enter the following customers' accounts, four to the page:

- Arnold Sheriff & Co.
- Atlas Dry Goods Co.
- Baird Dry Goods Co.
- Bostonian Dry Goods Co.
- Burrows Dry Goods Co.
- Century Dress Goods Co.
- Childs & Son
- Daniel & Co.
- Eagle Dress Goods Co.
- Emporium Dry Goods Co.
- Falk & Taylor
- Hudson Dry Goods Co.
- Macmillian & Co.
- Marquis Dress Goods Co.
- Melrose Dry Goods Co.

- Metropolitan Dry Goods Co.
- Henry Miller
- T. H. Miller
- National Dress Co.
- New York Silk Co.
- Public Bargain Store
- Rogers & Son
- Silk & Dress Goods Exchange
- Southern Dry Goods Co.
- Thompson Hudson Co.
- Wilson Williams Co.
- Young, Smith, Field Co.

Beginning on page 35, enter these creditors' accounts, four to a page.

- American Dry Goods Co.
- Associated Dry Goods Co.
- Bentley, Gray & Co.
- Claflins, Inc.
- Carter Dry Goods Co.
- Marshall Field & Co.
- Miller & Rhoades, Inc.
- Newcomb Endicott Co.
- Wm. Taylor, Son & Co.
- U.S. Dry Goods Co.
- Wico Mills, Inc.

II

C. Allen Cotten, who has long been in the wholesale merchandising business, anticipating a revival of commercial activity in the early part of 19—, decided to enlarge his business. Accordingly, on January 2, 19—, he enters into a partnership agreement with Scott Wooster, a former executive of the United

Dry Goods Co., of Philadelphia, and Landsdowne Woolsey, a retired real estate and insurance broker of New York.

According to the terms of the partnership agreement, Cotten's investment was his business, based upon the following balance sheet which represented the book value of the items:

C. ALLEN COTTEN

BALANCE SHEET, December 31, 19—

Assets

CURRENT ASSETS:

Cash		$ 3,065.00
Notes Receivable (See Schedule 1)		2,500.00
Accounts Receivable (See Schedule 2)	$25,150.00	
Less—Reserve for Bad Debts	600.00	24,550.00
U. S. Liberty Bonds		3,000.00
Accrued Interest		90.00
Merchandise		21,780.00

DEFERRED CHARGES TO OPERATION:

Prepaid Insurance	$ 100.00	
Office Supplies	150.00	
Garage Rent	75.00	325.00

FIXED ASSETS:

Delivery Trucks	$ 5,000.00	
Less—Depreciation Reserve	500.00	4,500.00
Total Assets		$59,810.00

Liabilities

CURRENT LIABILITIES:

Notes Payable (See Schedule 3)	$ 4,000.00	
Accounts Payable (See Schedule 4)	25,600.00	
Accrued Interest on Notes	20.00	
Accrued Taxes	190.00	
Total Liabilities		29,810.00

Net Worth

Represented by:

C. Allen Cotten, Capital	$30,000.00

Schedules appended to the balance sheet of C. Allen Cotten:

Schedule 1. NOTES RECEIVABLE:

Baird Dry Goods Co.	$ 1,500.00
60-day 6% note due February 1.	
Childs & Son	1,000.00
Non-interest-bearing note, due February 15.	
	$ 2,500.00

Schedule 2. ACCOUNTS RECEIVABLE:

Atlas Dry Goods Co.	$ 2,283.00
Burrows Dry Goods Co.	2,000.00
Century Dress Goods Co.	4,800.00
Falk & Taylor	3,400.00
Marquis Dress Goods Co.	2,795.00
T. H. Miller	1,425.00
National Dress Co.	2,892.00

Rogers & Son	3,650.00
Wilson Williams Co.	1,905.00
	$25,150.00

Schedule 3.   NOTES PAYABLE:

Marshall Field & Co. $ 2,000.00
  90-day 6% note due March 1, 19—.
American Dry Goods Co.   2,000.00
  90-day 6% note due March 15, 19—.
                          $ 4,000.00

Schedule 4.   ACCOUNTS PAYABLE:

Associated Dry Goods Co.	$ 3,950.00
Claflins, Inc.	6,290.00
Wico Mills, Inc.	2,780.00
Miller & Rhoades, Inc.	5,672.00
Newcomb Endicott Co.	3,678.00
Marshall Field & Co.	3,230.00
	$25,600.00

Cotten guaranteed the collection of all notes and accounts outstanding, and the partnership agreement provided that in case any of the accounts should be judged uncollectible by agreement among the partners or otherwise, such amount is to be charged to Cotten's personal account on the date such items are found uncollectible.

Wooster's investment was $20,000 cash, his services and experience; and Woolsey was admitted as a special partner investing $50,000 in cash.

The partnership agreement further provided that Cotten was to be allowed an annual salary of $4,800, Wooster $6,000, but Woolsey was to receive no salary; and that interest at the rate of 6% per annum was to be charged on the drawings in excess of the salary allowed for the fiscal period from the date such drawings exceeded salary until the date of closing the books. The drawings of Woolsey were also to be charged at 6% per annum from the date of draft to the date of closing the books. Interest at 6% per annum was to be allowed on capital, and in all cases was to be figured on the basis of 360 days to the year, 30 days to the month. Profits and losses were to be shared as follows: Woolsey 20%, Cotten 36%, and Wooster 44%. The fiscal period was to consist of six months, ending on June 30 and December 31, respectively.

The partnership agreement also provided that the capital accounts of the partners were to remain intact and that any credit balances remaining in the partners' personal accounts at the close of the fiscal period were to be transferred to their loan accounts which were to be treated as current accounts bearing 6% interest and subject to adjustment of interest at the close of each fiscal period.

Make the necessary entries in general journal and cash book to record the respective investment transactions, and post.

Instructions

Make a *full* but *concise* statement of the partnership agreement, following the form of opening entry illustrated on page 166. This opening statement is the first record in the general journal and should provide all of the information needed by the bookkeeper for the proper handling of the partners' accounts at the close of the fiscal period.

Immediately following this narrative will be the formal investment entries. On the line just preceding the formal investment entry for each of the partners, use the following—or similar—phraseology: "C. Allen Cotten made the following investment." A separate investment entry is made for each partner.

These entries are to be made complete in the general journal and posted immediately, except the several cash items, which, included in the totals of the cash book, will be posted at the end of the month. These cash items will therefore be checked both in the journal and in the cash book, where they must be entered in the "General Ledger" and "Net Cash" columns.

III

Summarized transactions for the month of January were as follows. Enter these in their respective journals. Posting of these entries will comprise the next assignment.

- Purchases:
- American Dry Goods Co., 2/10, n/60, $10,817.50.
- Bentley, Gray & Co., 2/10, n/60, $5,694.
- Claflins, Inc., 2/10, 1/30, n/60, $12,639.
- Carter Dry Goods Co., 2/10, 1/30, n/60, $18,709.48.
- U. S. Dry Goods Co., 3/10, 2/15, n/60, $12,104.90.
- Miller & Rhoades, Inc., 2/10, 1/30, n/60, $2,689.40.
- Wm. Taylor, Son & Co., 3/5, 2/10, n/30, $1,897.42.
- Marshall Field & Co., 3/10, 2/15, n/60, $11,744.60.
- Cash purchases were $2,564.73.
-
- Sales:
- Arnold Sheriff & Co., 2/10, 1/15, n/30, $5,264.80.
- Baird Dry Goods Co., 2/10, 1/15, n/30, $4,872.35.
- Bostonian Dry Goods Co., 2/10, 1/15, n/30, $3,843.68.
- Century Dress Goods Co., 2/10, n/30, $5,492.72.
- Childs & Son, 2/10, 1/15, n/30, $4,794.12.
- Daniel & Co., 2/10, n/30, $4,683.38.
- Eagle Dress Goods Co., 2/10, n/30, $5,978.35.
- Emporium Dry Goods Co., 2/10, n/30, $2,461.93.
- Falk & Taylor, 2/10, 1/15, n/30, $5,947.60.
- Hudson Dry Goods Co., 2/10, 1/15, n/30, $3,678.90.
- Macmillian & Co., 2/10, n/30, $4,642.50.
- Marquis Dress Goods Co., 2/10, n/30, $4,267.50.
- Metropolitan Dry Goods Co., 2/10, n/30, $4,180.
- Silk & Dress Goods Exchange, 2/10, n/30, $3,780.40.
- Cash sales were $847.56.
- Cotten took woolens on January 15, $50.

- Journal:
- Goods for $500 were returned by Falk & Taylor as unsatisfactory.
- Macmillian & Co. was credited with $435 because of goods lost in
- transit, for which a claim was filed against the
- Central Hudson Railway Co.
- Damaged goods were returned to Carter Dry Goods Co., $897.80.
- Received 6% 60-day note, due March 28, from Century Dress Co.
- for January bill $5,492.72 less a special discount of 5%.

- Cash Receipts (excluding those listed above):
- Arnold Sheriff & Co., January bill $5,264.80 less 2%.
- Bostonian Dry Goods Co., January bill $3,843.68 less 1%.
- Falk & Taylor, balance of January bill $5,447.60 less 2%.
- Hudson Dry Goods Co., January bill $3,678.90 less 1%.
- Atlas Dry Goods Co., December bill $2,283 net.
- Century Dress Goods Co., December bill $4,800 net.
- Falk & Taylor, December bill $3,400 less 2%.
- Rogers & Son, December bill $3,650 less 2%.

- Cash Disbursements (excluding those listed above):
- Shelving, partitions, counters, etc., for store $3,800.
- Desks, tables, mimeograph, and typewriters for office $1,250.
- A new Pierce motor truck $5,000.
- Deposit with the Westchester Lighting Co. $50.
- Salesmen's salaries $2,000.
- Salesmen's traveling expenses $997.84.

- Wages of chauffeurs and shipping clerks $500.
- Garage rent $125.
- Repairs to cars $50.
- Licenses for trucks $50.
- Oil and gasoline $50.
- Boxes, crates, nails, paint, etc., for shipping $297.13.
- Advertising according to contract with
- Baten Advertising Co. $5,000
- Freight and haulage $312.49.
- Insurance on stock $250.
- Lighting and heating service cost $502.60.
- Office salaries $990.
- Stationery, pads, pencils, envelopes, etc., $193.97.
- Telephone and telegraph $422.
- Postage and special messenger service $237.84.
- Wages of cleaners, watchman, repairs to elevator $594.70.
- Check to American Red Cross $100.
- Semiannual dues to the Merchants' Association $50.
- Rent for January $1,250.
- Cotten drew $400; Wooster $500.
- Associated Dry Goods Co., December bill $3,950 less 2%.
- Claflins, Inc., December bill $6,290 less 2%.
- Wico Mills, Inc., December bill $2,780 net.
- Newcomb Endicott Co., December bill $3,678 less 2%.
- Marshall Field & Co., December bill $3,230 less 2%;
- and January bill $11,744.60 less 2%.
- Carter Dry Goods Co., balance of January bill $17,811.68 less 2%.
- U. S. Dry Goods Co., January bill $12,104.90 less 3%.

- American Dry Goods Co., January bill $10,817.50 less 2%.
- Cash was short $3.16.
- Rent for February $1,250.

Instructions

All cash transactions are to be entered in the cash book whether listed under "Cash" above or not. In recording a cash sale or cash purchase in the cash book, extend the amount into the "General Ledger" and "Net Cash" columns only.

Be sure to classify and post all items correctly, inasmuch as a wrong classification or posting may necessitate many correction entries.

The claim against the railroad company will be charged to Sales Returns and Allowances until a settlement is effected. Such items are often charged to a Freight Claims account, with suitable adjustment to Sales Returns and Allowances when settlement is made for less than the amount claimed.

The word "balance," as in the phrase, "Falk & Taylor, balance of January bill $5,447.60 less 2%," calls attention to an adjustment of some sort—returns or allowance—which has been or is to be considered in determining the amount still due.

Charge the freight and haulage to In-Freight and Cartage.

Great care must be exercised in the general journal entries affecting individual customers' and creditors' accounts, since these also affect their respective controlling accounts. Inasmuch as the general journal does not provide the customary analytic columns, it will be necessary, when making every such entry, to indicate the controlling account affected and, when posting, to post the item both to the individual account and to the control account. The following illustrations should be followed in making entries of this kind:

(1) Sales Returns and Allowances   12   500.00

       Falk & Taylor (Accounts Receivable)   26/1   500.00

(2) Carter Dry Goods Co. (Accounts Payable)   33/6   897.80

       Purchases Returns and Allowances   18   897.80

(3) Notes Receivable   1   5,218.08

     Sales Discount   20   274.64

| Century Dress Co. (Accounts Receivable) | | 25/1 | 5,492.72 |

Note particularly the way in which the ledger folios are shown for both accounts.

IV

Summarize the sales, purchase, and cash journals; balance the cash book.

In summarizing the sales journal, first total each column and draw a horizontal line under these amounts. On the next line record the summary entry, entering the amounts to be debited in the first money column and those to be credited in the second. The total of the partners' withdrawals should not be posted, for they have already been transferred to the general ledger accounts at the time they occurred. The amount will therefore be checked in the summary entry. The total cash sales will also be checked, inasmuch as these have already been recorded in the cash book. The summary entry for the sales journal will appear as follows:

Accounts Receivable, Dr.		....
Partners' Personal, Dr.	✓	....
Cash, Dr.	✓	....
Sales, Cr.		....

The purchase journal should be summarized somewhat similarly but the total purchases are to be debited to "Purchases," the purchases on account credited to "Accounts Payable," and the cash purchases are to be checked. The summary entry of this journal will be:

Purchases, Dr.		
Accounts Payable, Cr.		....
Cash, Cr.	✓	....

In summarizing the cash journals, pencil-foot all columns of both journals. Then formally foot the columns on both sides, using the same line on both sides, i.e., the totals must appear on one line extending across both pages of the book. This may leave blank lines on either side according as one has had more entries than the other. Underline the totals. Make summary entries somewhat as follows:

In the receipts journal:

Cash

Sales Discount

    Accounts Receivable

    General   ✓

In the disbursements journal:

General   ✓

Accounts Payable

    Purchase Discount   ....

    Cash   ....

Use the first two money columns on either side for the entry of the amounts. Underline these entries through the four money columns. When posting these summary entries, the items "General" on either side will be checked as the details composing them have already been posted.

On the next line write in the Explanation columns on either side, "Net Cash as above," and extend the total amounts of cash receipts and cash disbursements into the Net Cash columns on their respective sides. Balance the cash book by entering "Balance" on the disbursements journal and extending the amount in the Net Cash column. Show totals at the same level on both sides and draw double lines through all columns on both sides except the Explanation columns. Bring the cash balance down in the receipts journal.

Post completely all books of original entry. When posting the general journal, be very careful to post to the indicated controlling accounts. See Assignment III, Instructions, for the method to be followed.

Take a trial balance of your general ledger and record it under date of January 31, beginning on page 16 of the journal blank. Write "Trial Balances, 19—" at the top of the page and in the small space over the money columns "January 31." From the general ledger, copy the names of all accounts, whether or not there are as yet any entries in them, in the order there shown.

Do not include the individual customers' and creditors' accounts in the above list, for these are taken care of by the inclusion of their controlling accounts. Be careful to write the account name at the extreme left of the explanation space, close to the date column. Leave one line at the bottom of page 16 and at the top of page of 22 for "Totals" and "Totals Forward."

Since one page is not sufficient to complete the record, continue it on page 22, there recording the rest of the accounts and heading the page and columns as on page 16. The intervening pages will be used as shown in Assignment VI.

Prove the controlling accounts against their subsidiary accounts. To make this proof, at the top of page 30 of the general journal, write "Balances of Accounts Receivable, 19—" and list the names of all customers' accounts, writing the account name to the extreme left of the explanation space, close to the "Date" column. Place the words "January 31" in the small space over the first money column, in which the balances of accounts receivable for January will be recorded. Do not use the second money column on this page; this will be used for February balances.

Beginning on page 34, make a similar list of creditors' accounts. The instructions covering the listing of accounts receivable apply here also, with the exception that the words "Accounts Payable" are to be substituted for "Accounts Receivable."

List the individual account balances of customers' and creditors' accounts for each month, as described above, and record the total of each list in their respective columns. These totals must agree with the balances shown in the corresponding controlling accounts, i.e., the total of customers' accounts outstanding for January must be equal to the balance of the controlling account, "Accounts Receivable," shown in the general ledger. A discrepancy between a controlling account and its subsidiary accounts must always be located and corrected.

V

Summarized transactions for February were:

- Purchases:
- American Dry Goods Co., 2/10, 1/30, n/60, $13,487.92.
- Associated Dry Goods Co., 2/10, n/60, $13,562.70.
- Claflins, Inc., 2/10, 1/30, n/60, $10,897.80.
- U. S. Dry Goods Co., 3/10, 2/15, n/60, $12,247.80.
- Marshall Field & Co., 3/10, 2/15, n/60, $17,792.90.

- Cash purchases $2,987.50.
-
- Sales:
- Arnold Sheriff & Co., 2/10, 1/15, n/30, $5,287.45.
- Atlas Dry Goods Co., 2/10, n/30, $5,794.32.
- Baird Dry Goods Co., 2/10, 1/15, n/30, $4,618.73.
- Burrows Dry Goods Co., 2/10, n/30, $3,289.49.
- Bostonian Dry Goods Co., 2/10, 1/15, n/30, $6,642.
- Century Dress Goods Co., 2/10, n/30, $4,497.35.
- Eagle Dress Goods Co., 2/10, n/30, $4,127.49.
- Emporium Dry Goods Co., 2/10, n/30, $4,793.80.
- Henry Miller, 2/10, n/30, $5,008.34.
- Melrose Dry Goods Co., 2/10, 1/15, n/30, $4,278.18
- New York Silk Co., 2/10, 1/15, n/30, $3,874.70.
- Southern Dry Goods Co., 2/10, n/30, $5,087.92.
- Public Bargain Store, 2/10, n/30, $4,972.
- Cash sales $2,989.90.
- Cotten took woolens, February 28, $50.
-
- Journal:
- Goods were returned by Century Dress Goods Co. $340, and
- Southern Dry Goods Co. $845, as unsatisfactory.
- Made Public Bargain Store an allowance of $85.
- Analysis of the January freight bill showed that $147.60
- was paid for freight on sales.
-
- Returns to American Dry Goods Co. $978.
-

- Cash Receipts:
- Baird Dry Goods Co., January bill $4,872.35 less 2%.
- Burrows Dry Goods Co., December bill $1,000 on account.
- Childs & Son January bill $4,794.12 less 1%.
- Daniel & Co., January bill $4,683.38 net.
- Eagle Dress Goods Co., January bill $5,978.35 net.
- Emporium Dry Goods Co., $1,000 on account.
- Arnold Sheriff & Co., February bill $5,287.45 less 2%.
- Atlas Dry Goods Co., February bill $5,794.32 less 2%.
- Bostonian Dry Goods Co., February bill $6,642 less 2%.
- Century Dress Goods Co., balance February bill $4,157.35 less 2%.
- Henry Miller, February bill $5,008.34 less 2%.
- Public Bargain Store, balance February bill $4,887 net.
- Cash was over $1.21.
- The note of Baird Dry Goods Co. for $1,500 was paid February 1
- with interest, amounting to $15.
- The note of Childs & Son was paid, $1,000.
- Sold miscellaneous ends, $48.50.
-
- Cash Disbursements:
- Bentley, Gray & Co., January bill $5,694 less 2%.
- Claflins, Inc., January bill $12,639 less 2%.
- Miller & Rhoades, Inc., December bill $5,672 net.
- Wm. Taylor, Son & Co., January bill $1,897.42 less 2%.
- Salesmen's salaries $2,000.
- Salesmen's railroad fares, hotel bills, etc., $1,013.48.
- Chauffeurs' wages $240.
- Garage rent $125.

- Shipping clerks $210.
- Gasoline and oil $75.60.
- Fine for stopping car in front of hydrant $10.
- Paper, wrapping supplies, crates, $308.30.
- Wooster withdrew $500 February 15.
- Advertising as per schedule $3,000.
- Freight and haulage bills $257.80.
- Rent for March $1,250.
- Lighting and heating bills $497.58.
- Office manager's and clerks' salaries $998.
- Stationery, mimeograph supplies, etc., $214.40.
- Wages of cleaners, watchman, repairs to windows
- and new steps at door, $874.50.
- Telephone and telegraph $175.80.
- Messengers $128.
- Bought five $1,000 U. S. Liberty bonds at 95½, with
- accrued interest of $59.88.
- Cotten drew $400; Wooster $500.
- U. S. Dry Goods Co., February bill $12,247.80 less 3%.

Notice has been received that a receiver has been appointed for Wilson Williams Co.

Instructions

In making general journal entries affecting customers' or creditors' accounts, be sure to indicate the posting to the corresponding controlling accounts.

At the time the freight bills are paid, the total amount is charged to In-Freight and Cartage. They are analyzed later into freight paid on sales and in-freight, and the amount paid on sales is transferred to the proper account by means of a journal entry.

Record the sale of miscellaneous ends and the like in the cash receipts journal and post to Miscellaneous Sales.

Charge the $10 fine to Delivery Expense.

Be careful to charge the accrued interest on Liberty bonds to the proper account.

VI

Summarize the special journals. In summarizing the cash receipts journal for February and the following months, do not underline the totals of the General and Net Cash columns, as instructed in Assignment IV. Deduct the balance as of the first of the month from the totals shown in both columns, indicating, in the explanation column, the nature of this amount. (See page 282 for illustration.) Underline these amounts and write the summary entry for the cash receipts journal as previously explained, taking care that the Cash account is debited only with the receipts of the current month.

Post completely, being particularly careful in handling items affecting controlling accounts, especially when posting the general journal.

Take a trial balance of the general ledger as of February 28. In making record of this and succeeding trial balances, to obviate the necessity of rewriting account titles, fold back the two money columns on page 17 so that they "face up" on page 18, thus providing four money columns. This shortened leaf may now be used for recording trial balances for February and March. Similarly with succeeding leaves.

Do not fail to record the balances of customers' and creditors' accounts in the proper places, and prove the totals against their respective controlling accounts.

VII

Summarized transactions for March were:

- Purchases:
- Wm. Taylor, Son & Co., 3/5, 2/10, n/30, $8,942.50.
- Newcomb Endicott Co., 2/15, n/60, $7,414.
- U. S. Dry Goods Co., 3/10, 2/15, n/60, $7,609.40.
- Wico Mills, Inc., 2/10, 1/30, n/60, $8,337.80.
- Carter Dry Goods Co., 2/10, 1/30, n/60, $8,790.
- Bentley, Gray & Co., 2/10, n/60, $10,890.45.
- Marshall Field & Co., 3/10, 2/15, n/60, $10,219.
- Cash purchases $3,390.
-

- Sales:
- Young, Smith, Field Co., 2/10, n/30, $6,874.32.
- Thompson Hudson Co., 2/10, n/30, $4,732.46.
- Rogers & Son, 2/10, n/30, $3,146.34.
- Public Bargain Store, 2/10, n/30, $3,590.70.
-
- National Dress Co., 2/10, n/30, $4,346.90.
- New York Silk Co., 2/10, 1/15, n/30, $6,784.50.
- Melrose Dry Goods Co., 2/10, 1/15, n/30, $7,894.80.
- T. H. Miller, 2/10, n/30, $6,237.40.
- Macmillian & Co., 2/10, n/30, $2,476.50.
- Hudson Dry Goods Co., 2/10, 1/15, n/30, $4,475.
- Falk & Taylor, 2/10, 1/15, n/30, $4,790.
- Eagle Dress Goods Co., 2/10, n/30, $3,105.
- Daniel & Co., 2/10, n/30, $3,490.70.
- Childs & Son, 2/10, 1/15, n/30, $4,789.40.
- Arnold Sheriff & Co., 2/10, 1/15, n/30, $3,980.40.
- Cash sales $2,462.75.
- Wooster drew merchandise $100.
-
- Journal:
- Gave Marshall Field & Co. our 60-day 6% note due May 15,
- for their bill of February, $17,792.90 less 3%.
- Received merchandise returned by Melrose Dry Goods Co. $1,487.90.
- Returned goods to Associated Dry Goods Co. $416.90.
- Received a credit memo for $162.40 from Claflins, Inc.
- for spoiled goods.
- Macmillian & Co. gave us their 60-day 6% note, due May 25,

- for balance of January bill $4,207.50.
- Marquis Dress Goods Co. was allowed $485 for delay in transit.
- Out-freight for February was $139.86.
- Metropolitan Dry Goods Co. issued their 30-day 6% note,
- due April 15, for January bill $4,180.
-
- Cash Receipts:
- Century Dress Goods Co. paid their note due March 28 with interest.
- Baird Dry Goods Co., February bill $4,618.73 less 2%.
- Burrows Dry Goods Co., February bill $3,289.49 net.
- Eagle Dress Goods Co., February bill $4,127.49 less 2%.
- Emporium Dry Goods Co., January bill $1,461.93 net.
- Marquis Dress Goods Co., December bill $2,795 net.
- Melrose Dry Goods Co., February bill $4,278.18 less 1%.
- T. H. Miller, December bill, $1,000 on account.
- National Dress Co., December bill, $1,000 on account.
- Southern Dry Goods Co., balance of February bill, $4,242.92 less 2%.
- Young, Smith, Field Co., March bill $6,874.32 less 2%.
- Thompson Hudson Co., March bill $4,732.46 less 2%.
- New York Silk Co., March bill $6,784.50 less 1%.
- Hudson Dry Goods Co., March bill $4,475 less 2%.
- Daniel & Co., March bill $3,490.70 less 2%.
- Childs & Son, March bill $4,789.40 less 2%.
- Arnold Sheriff & Co., March bill $3,980.40 less 2%.
- Rogers & Son, March bill $3,146.34 net.
- The receivers for Wilson Williams Co. declared March 15 an
- initial liquidating dividend of 35%, which was received.

- Cash Disbursements:
- Salesmen's salaries $2,000.
- Salesmen's traveling expenses $1,896.42.
- Chauffeurs' and shipping clerks' wages $435.
- Garage rent $125.
- Gasoline, oil, and minor parts, $116.84.
- Crates, boxes, and packing materials, $412.80.
-
- Advertising as per schedule $3,000.
- Rent for April $1,250.
- Insurance policies, elevator, fire, plate glass, burglary, $550.
- Lighting and heating $512.90.
- Office salaries $1,872.
- Books, stationery, $226.40.
- Telephone and telegraph, postage, $896.40.
- Changing partitions $280.
- Wages of cleaners and watchman $490.
- Painting of partitions $28.
- New bell on elevator $18.75.
- Contribution to Salvation Army Drive $100.
- Cotten drew $400; Wooster $500.
- Cash was short $12.92.
- Freight bill $262.90.
- American Dry Goods Co., balance of February bill $12,509.92 less 2%.
- Associated Dry Goods Co., balance of February bill $13,145.80 less 2%.
- Claflins, Inc., balance of February bill $10,735.40 less 2%.
- Miller & Rhoades, January bill $2,689.40 net.

- Marshall Field & Co., March bill $10,219 less 2%.
- Paid Marshall Field & Co. and American Dry Goods Co.
- December notes with interest.
- Lent $5,000 to Woolsey, in return for which he issued to the
- order of the firm his six months' 6% note for a similar amount.

Instructions

Record the interest received on notes receivable in the General Ledger column of the cash receipts journal.

Enter the Woolsey note in the proper account.

A liquidating dividend represents the amounts disbursed by a receiver to the creditors of the bankrupt.

VIII

Summarize the subsidiary journals.

Post completely.

Take a trial balance of the general ledger as of March 31.

Prove the totals of the subsidiary accounts against the totals of their respective controlling accounts.

IX

Summarized transactions for April were:

- Purchases:
- American Dry Goods Co., 2/10, n/60, $8,292.50.
- Associated Dry Goods Co., 2/10, n/60, $7,784.90.
- Claflins, Inc., 2/10, 1/30, n/60, $10,467.70.
- Miller & Rhoades, Inc., 2/10, 1/30, n/60, $6,742.80.
- U. S. Dry Goods Co., 3/10, 2/15, n/60, $8,276.40.
- Marshall Field & Co., 3/10, 2/15, n/60, $28,450.
- Wico Mills, Inc., 2/10, 1/30, n/60, $4,970.80.
- Cash purchases $1,988.75.
-
-

- Sales:
- Arnold Sheriff & Co., 2/10, 1/15, n/30, $7,145.90.
- Atlas Dry Goods Co., 2/10, n/30, $6,890.70.
- Baird Dry Goods Co., 2/10, 1/15, n/30, $7,294.60.
- Bostonian Dry Goods Co., 2/10, 1/15, n/30, $9,874.50.
- Century Dress Goods Co., 2/10, n/30, $4,927.90.
- Daniel & Co., 2/10, n/30, $7,847.40.
- Hudson Dry Goods Co., 2/10, 1/15, n/30, $8,475.90.
- Henry Miller, 2/10, n/30, $5,982.90.
- Rogers & Son, 2/10, n/30, $7,826.90.
- Southern Dry Goods Co., 2/10, n/30, $7,495.80.
- Thompson Hudson Co., 2/10, n/30, $6,475.80.
- Young, Smith, Field Co., 2/10, n/30, $5,162.70.
- Cash sales $1,920.80.
-
- Journal:
- Returned to Marshall Field & Co., $1,250 worth of merchandise
- of the February purchase, cash adjustment effective as of
- April 15 to be made at time of paying note.
- Returned goods to Miller & Rhoades, Inc., $650.
- Transferred a desk costing $125 from the office to the sales
- department of store.
- Received returned goods from Bostonian Dry Goods Co.,
- $1,090; and from Henry Miller $785.
- Received a 30-day 6% note from the Silk & Dress Goods Exchange
- for January bill $3,780.40, due May 23.
- Out-freight for March was $152.90.
- The failure to book a payment of $10 for repairs on an

- annunciator partly explained the cash shortage in March.
-
- Cash Receipts:
- Note of Metropolitan Dry Goods Co. for $4,180 was paid
- April 15, with interest.
- Burrows Dry Goods Co., balance of December bill, $1,000.
- Eagle Dress Goods Co., March bill $3,105 less 2%.
- Emporium Dry Goods Co., February bill $4,793.80 net.
- Falk & Taylor, March bill $4,790 less 2%.
- Macmillian & Co., March bill $2,476.50 less 2%.
- Marquis Dress Goods Co., balance of January bill $3,782.50 net.
- T. H. Miller, March bill $6,237.40 less 2%.
- Melrose Dry Goods Co., balance March bill $6,406.90 less 1%.
- New York Silk Co., February bill $3,874.70 net.
- National Dress Co., on account, December bill, $1,000.
- Arnold Sheriff & Co., April bill $7,145.90 less 2%.
- Baird Dry Goods Co., April bill $7,294.60 less 2%.
- Hudson Dry Goods Co., April bill, $8,475.90 less 2%.
- Southern Dry Goods Co., April bill $7,495.80 less 2%.
- Thompson Hudson Co., April bill $6,475.80 less 2%.
- Young, Smith, Field Co., April bill $5,162.70 less 2%.
- The firm discounted its 90-day 6% note, due July 15,
- at the Merchants National Bank for $5,000.
- The receivers for Wilson Williams Co. declared another
- liquidating dividend of 15%.
- Received from the railroad $25, an overcharge on demurrage.
-
-

- Cash Disbursements:
- Sales salaries $2,975.
- Salesmen's traveling expense $2,243.60.
- Delivery expense $763.87.
- Packing supplies $513.90.
- Advertising for April $3,000, and for May $3,000,
- less $250 as discount for prepayment.
- Freight bills $297.60.
- Light and heating $212.50.
- Office salaries $2,140.
- Office supplies $365.70.
- Office expense $988.95.
- General expense $897.12.
- Rent for May $1,250.
- Bentley, Gray & Co., March bill $10,890.45 less 2%.
- Wico Mills, Inc., March bill $8,337.80 less 2%.
- U. S. Dry Goods Co., March bill $7,609.40 less 2%.
- Wm. Taylor, Son & Co., March bill $8,942.50 less 2%.
- American Dry Goods Co., April bill $8,292.50 less 2%.
- Claflins, Inc., April bill $10,467.70 less 2%.
- Newcomb Endicott Co., March bill $7,414 less 2%.
- Miller & Rhoades, Inc., balance of April bill, $6,092.80 less 2%.
- Woolsey withdrew April 30 $500; Cotten, $400; and Wooster $500.
- New adding machine and desks for office $500.
- Paid taxes $190.

Instructions

Include the discount received on advertising with the purchase discounts. The charge to Advertising will, therefore, be gross.

Be sure to make the purchase discount adjustment necessitated by the returned goods transaction with Marshall Field & Co. Though this and the returned goods are to be taken into consideration when the note is paid, do not enter them now in the Notes Payable account, that adjustment being made at time of payment of note. Enter them in the Marshall Field & Co. account.

Disregard the depreciation adjustment on the desk transferred to the sales department.

Record the face of the discounted note in the General Ledger column, the amount of discount in the Sales Discount column with an (X) mark, and the net amount in the Net Cash column. In summarizing the cash book, this discount should be segregated from the total to be posted to Sales Discount, inasmuch as the former will be posted to Interest Cost.

Credit the overcharge on demurrage to In-Freight and Cartage.

X

Summarize the journals. In summarizing the debit side of the cash book previous to posting, remember that included in the Sales Discount column is an item of bank discount on the firm's $5,000 note, which must be shown separately and charged to Interest Cost. Be sure you show this in the summary entries, in addition to the Sales Discount summary. To accomplish this the total of the Sales Discount column is best shown in two portions, the Sales Discount total on the one line, and the Interest Cost item on the next line.

Post completely.

Take a trial balance of the general ledger as of April 30.

Prove the subsidiary accounts against their respective controlling accounts.

XI

1. Summarized transactions for May were:

- Purchases:
- Bentley, Gray & Co., 2/10, n/60, $9,764.90.
- Carter Dry Goods Co., 2/10, 1/30, n/60, $29,417.70.
- Newcomb Endicott Co., 2/15, n/60, $10,846.40.
- Wm. Taylor, Son & Co., 3/5, 2/10, n/30, $9,497.50.
- Marshall Field & Co., 3/10, 2/15, n/60, $11,145.80.
- Cash purchases $1,872.45.

- Sales:
- Arnold Sheriff & Co., 2/10, 1/15, n/30, $9,465.80.
- Baird Dry Goods Co., 2/10, 1/15, n/30, $8,467.90.
- Century Dress Goods Co., 2/10, n/30, $9,748.80.
- Daniel & Co., 2/10, n/30, $7,492.40.
- Hudson Dry Goods Co., 2/10, 1/15, n/30, $9,948.30.
- New York Silk Co., 2/10, 1/15, n/30, $9,742.50.
- Silk & Dress Goods Exchange, 2/10, n/30, $9,865.80.
- Southern Dry Goods Co., 2/10, n/30, $10,480.
- Thompson Hudson Co., 2/10, n/30, $8,942.75.
- Young, Smith, Field Co., 3/10, n/30, $16,290.
- Cash sales $1,694.90.

- Journal:
- Young, Smith, Field Co. returned $1,985 worth of merchandise;
- and Century Dress Goods Co., $625 worth.
- Out-freight for April was $147.42.
- Received from the National Dress Co., a 60-day acceptance drawn
- on the United Textile Co. in favor of the firm, due July 15,
- for $5,000.
- Returned to Newcomb Endicott Co. $2,200 of merchandise.
- Gave Associated Dry Goods Co. our 90-day note dated May 15,
- non-interest-bearing, but with 90 days' interest, $114.43,
- included in the face, for their bill of April $7,784.90
- less 2% cash discount.
- Marshall Field & Co. note adjusted.
- Final settlement of Wilson Williams Co. was effected May 15.

- (See "Cash Receipts.")
- Due to temporary embarrassment of the Silk & Dress Goods Exchange, their note was extended one month.
-
- Cash Receipts:
- Arnold Sheriff & Co., May bill $9,465.80 less 2%.
- Atlas Dry Goods Co., April bill, $3,000 on account.
- Baird Dry Goods Co., May bill $8,467.90 less 2%.
- Bostonian Dry Goods Co., balance of April bill,
- $8,784.50 less 2%.
- Century Dress Goods Co., April bill, $2,500 on account.
- Daniel & Co., April bill, $5,000 on account.
- Hudson Dry Goods Co., May bill $9,948.30 less 2%.
- New York Silk Co., May bill $9,742.50 less 2%.
- Public Bargain Store, March bill, $2,500 on account.
- Southern Dry Goods Co., May bill $10,480 less 2%.
- Young, Smith, Field Co., balance May bill, $14,305 less 2%.
-
- Interest on Liberty bonds due May 15, $119.75.
- Cash was over $42.65.
- For use of one of the motor trucks for the week,
- $100 was received.
- Sold packing materials, $80.75.
- Macmillian & Co., paid their note with interest May 25.
- Received $275 from the Central Hudson Railway Co. on our claim
- made in January.
- The receivers for Wilson Williams Co. paid a final liquidating
- dividend of 10%.

-
- Cash Disbursements:
- Salesmen's salaries $2,985.
- Salesmen's traveling expenses $2,213.72.
- Delivery expenses $886.94.
- Shipping and packing materials and supplies $516.70.
- Advertising for June $3,000 less $250 discount for prepayment.
- Rent for June $1,250.
- Freight and haulage $467.90.
- Lighting and heating $186.40.
- Office salaries $2,040.
- Office supplies $240.60.
- Office expense $1,167.70.
- General expense $912.67.
- A contribution of $250 was made to the State University fund.
- Paid Marshall Field & Co. note May 15 with interest
- and adjustment.
- Newcomb Endicott Co. balance of May bill, $8,646.40 less 2%.
- Cotten withdrew May 15, $400; Wooster $500; and Woolsey $1,000.
- Carter Dry Goods Co., March bill $8,790 net.
- Wico Mills, Inc., April bill $4,970.80 less 1%.
- U. S. Dry Goods Co., April bill $8,276.40 less 2%.
- Wm. Taylor, Son & Co., May bill $9,497.50 less 3%.
- Marshall Field & Co., May bill $11,145.80 less 2%.

2. The Acorn Manufacturing Company, a corporation, is organized with a capitalization of $250,000 of which $150,000 is common stock and the remainder preferred. The company buys the plant of Brown & Towne, whose balance sheet appears below, issuing therefor $75,000 of common

stock and $25,000 of preferred stock. The partners transfer all assets except cash and the vendee assumes the liabilities.

BALANCE SHEET OF BROWN & TOWNE
July 1, 19—

Assets		Liabilities	
Cash	$ 10,000.00	Notes Payable	$ 2,000.00
Notes Receivable	30,000.00	Accounts Payable	1,000.00
Accounts Receivable	20,000.00	Mortgage Payable	5,000.00
Inventory	30,000.00	Brown, Capital	46,000.00
Plant and Machinery	10,000.00	Towne, Capital	46,000.00
	$100,000.00		$100,000.00

July

5. The remainder of the preferred stock is subscribed for at 90 and paid in cash.

12. Subscriptions to common stock for $25,000 at 110 are received and paid in cash.

20. The remaining common stock is subscribed for at 90 to be paid for in four equal instalments at intervals of one month.

Dec.

1. All calls were met as due. Paid the organization tax and filing fees in cash $250.

Prepare journal entries for the above on the books of the Acorn Manufacturing Company.

3. The A B Corporation is formed with a capital stock of $100,000, consisting of 1,000 shares par value $100 each. A subscribes for 500 shares, B for 200, C for 200, and D for 100. B, C, and D pay cash for their subscriptions. A pays in full for his subscription by turning over a business he has been

conducting. The corporation acquires the assets and assumes the liabilities of A's business as follows:

A'S BALANCE SHEET

Assets		Liabilities	
Merchandise	$15,000.00	Accounts Payable	$ 6,000.00
Accounts Receivable	19,000.00	A, Capital	40,000.00
Notes Receivable	12,000.00		
	$46,000.00		$46,000.00

(a) Make the necessary entries to open the books of the corporation.

(b) Make the necessary entries to close the books of A.

Instructions

Transfer the net claim against Marshall Field & Co., appearing in their account, to Notes Payable through the general journal. The balance of the note remaining in the latter account will be offset by the debit to be posted from the cash disbursements journal. In calculating the interest to be paid on the above note, take cognizance of an interest adjustment dating from April 15.

Transfer a sufficient amount from the Wilson Williams Co. account to the Reserve for Doubtful Accounts so that the balance of the latter account will be wiped out. The balance in the Wilson Williams Co. account is to be charged in accordance with the partnership agreement.

Credit the amount received for the use of the delivery truck to Delivery Expense.

The payment made by the railroad company should be credited to Sales Returns and Allowances to offset the debit made previously.

Problems 2 and 3 are, of course, separate problems not to be recorded in the books of Cotten, Wooster & Co.

XII

1. (a) Summarize the subsidiary journals.
   (b) Post completely.
   (c) Take a trial balance of the general ledger as of May 31.

(d) Prove the subsidiary accounts against their respective controlling accounts.

2. At the end of the year net profits amount to $15,000, with a previous surplus balance of $50,000. Preferred stock amounts to $100,000, of which $20,000 is treasury stock; common amounts to $150,000, of which $50,000 has not been issued. The directors declare an 8% dividend on the preferred, and a 10% on the common, and appropriate $5,000 to a sinking fund reserve. Later the above dividends are paid. Make the entries needed to bring the above onto the books.

3. A corporation authorizes a $250,000 bond issue, of which $150,000 are traded for a plant, and $50,000 are sold on the open market at 102. The bonds bear 6% interest, payable semiannually. Show how you would handle the above transactions. Show your treatment at the time of the first interest payment, assuming the bonds to mature in 25 years.

Instructions

Problem 1 refers to the Cotten, Wooster & Co. problem.

Problems 2 and 3 do not relate to Cotten, Wooster & Co.

XIII

Summarized transactions for June were:

- Purchases:
- American Dry Goods Co., 2/10, n/60, $16,145.75.
- Associated Dry Goods Co., 2/10, n/60, $15,927.80.
- Claflins, Inc., 2/10, 1/30, n/60, $17,894.60.
- Wico Mills, Inc., 2/10, 1/30, n/60, $4,792.45.
- U. S. Dry Goods Co., 3/10, 2/15, n/60, $15,867.42.
- Miller & Rhoades, Inc., 2/10, 1/30, n/60, $16,279.80.
- Newcomb Endicott Co., 2/15, n/60, $15,318.40.
- Wm. Taylor, Son & Co., 3/5, 2/10, n/30, $5,728.
- Marshall Field & Co., 3/10, 2/15, n/60, $6,716.90.
- Cash purchases $1,813.40.
- Sales:
- Arnold Sheriff & Co., 2/10, 1/15, n/30, $8,465.90.

- Baird Dry Goods Co., 2/10, 1/15, n/30, $7,964.60.
- Burrows Dry Goods Co., 2/10, n/30, $6,279.45.
- Bostonian Dry Goods Co., 2/10, 1/15, n/30, $9,763.80.
- Childs & Son, 2/10, 1/15, n/30, $7,942.45.
- Eagle Dress Goods Co., 2/10, n/30, $8,246.70.
- Emporium Dry Goods Co., 2/10, n/30, $7,847.65.
- Falk & Taylor, 2/10, 1/15, n/30, $8,972.70.
- Hudson Dry Goods Co., 2/10, 1/15, n/30, $7,432.80.
- Macmillian & Co., 2/10, n/30, $6,972.50.
- Marquis Dress Goods Co., 2/10, n/30, $8,414.
- Metropolitan Dry Goods Co., 2/10, n/30, $3,985.
- Melrose Dry Goods Co., 2/10, 1/15, n/30, $8,945.
-
- New York Silk Co., 2/10, 1/15, n/30, $7,987.50.
- Southern Dry Goods Co., 2/10, n/30, $9,475.65.
- Cash sales $1,472.60.
- Journal:
- Out-freight for May was $157.90.
- Returned goods received from Daniel & Co., $1,875;
- and Thompson Hudson Co., $935.
- Received from Rogers & Son, Charles L. Sutton & Co.'s 90-day
- 6% note for $5,000, dated May 5, with 40 days' interest
- accrued, in payment of their April bill, the balance of
- the payment in cash.
- Returned $967.50 of merchandise to Miller & Rhoades, Inc.;
- and $614.75 to Wico Mills, Inc.
- Cash over of May was partly accounted for by failure to book
- sale of old crates and supplies for $35.

- The note of the Silk & Dress Goods Exchange, extended to and due June 23, was not paid, as the firm was still in difficulties.
- A mortgage for $25,000 was given to complete the purchase of the building. (See "Cash Disbursements.")
- Cash Receipts:
- Arnold Sheriff & Co., June bill $8,465.90 less 2%
- Atlas Dry Goods Co., balance of April bill $3,890.70.
- Century Dress Goods, balance of April bill $1,802.90.
- Daniel & Co., on account $5,000.
- Henry Miller, on account $2,500.
- National Dress Goods Co., balance March bill $238.90.
- Public Bargain Store, on account $500
- Rogers & Son, balance April bill $2,793.57.
- Thompson Hudson & Co., balance May bill $8,007.75 less 2%.
- Bostonian Dry Goods Co., June bill $9,763.80 less 2%.
- Southern Dry Goods Co., June bill $9,475.65 less 2%.
- Macmillian & Co., June bill $6,972.50 less 2%.
- Cash Disbursements:
- Salesmen's salaries $5,340.
- Salesmen's traveling expenses $2,917.94.
- Delivery expenses $978.42.
- Shipping supplies $523.80.
- Advertising for July $3,000, less $250 for prepayment.
- Freight and haulage $569.70.
- Rent for July $1,250.
- Insurance on auto trucks $250.
- Lighting and heating $92.70.
- Office salaries $2,465.

- Office supplies $369.74.
- Office expenses $1,254.60.
- General expenses $1,219.62.
- Cotten withdrew June 15 $400; Wooster $500.
- Bentley, Gray & Co., May bill $9,764.90 less 2%.
- Wm. Taylor, Son & Co., June bill $5,728 less 2%.
- Semiannual dues to the Merchants' Association $50.
- Purchased a lot and building for $35,000, paying
- $10,000 in cash and the balance remaining on mortgage.

Instructions

Charge the Silk & Dress Goods Exchange note to their account.

Additional data on the mortgage transaction are given under "Cash Disbursements." In the general journal entry make explanation of the entire transaction, including the cash portion, which will of course be entered formally only in the cash book. In the cash book entry, by way of explanation, give cross-reference to the general journal explanation.

XIV

Summarize the subsidiary journals.

Post completely.

Take a trial balance of the general ledger as of June 30.

Prove the totals of the subsidiary accounts against their respective controlling accounts.

XV

Prepare a work sheet, as of June 30, 19—, for the six months, taking account of the following adjustments and inventories. Follow carefully the form shown in Chapter XXVII.

- Accrued Expenses:
- Salesmen's salaries $485.
- Shipping clerks' and chauffeurs' wages $265.
- Unpaid garage bills $182.50.
- Freight bills $55.60.

- Office salaries $287.50.
- Lighting expense estimate $25.
- Watchman's and cleaners' wages $106.
- Taxes $300.
- Prepaid Expenses:
- Advertising $3,000.
- Rent $1,250.
- Insurance $790.
- Merchants' Association dues $50.
- Interest on note payable to the order of the
- Associated Dry Goods Co. $57.21.
- Interest on the note due the Merchants' National Bank $12.50.
- Accrued Income:
- Interest on Liberty bonds $47.50.
- Interest on the note of Charles L. Sutton & Co. $46.67.
- Word has been received from the attorneys that the note of
- the Silk & Dress Goods Exchange, which had been extended
- and not paid when presented, will be met in full with
- accrued interest of $42.84.
- Out-freight for June, $169.70.
- Charge depreciation as follows: 10% per annum on office and store
- furniture and fixtures; 20% per annum on delivery equipment.
- Create a reserve for bad debts equal to ½ % of gross sales.
- Inventories were: merchandise $102,560;
- office supplies $257.80; shipping supplies $387.60.
- Charge and credit the partners with interest as per the
- partnership agreement.

Instructions

Do not close the books of the firm nor draw up the formal statements.

Be content for this assignment with the making of the work sheet.

Close the work sheet as usual by the transfer of the net profit from the Profit and Loss columns to the credit column of the balance sheet.

Immediately following and on the same page with the work sheet, provide for showing the distribution of profits and interest and salary adjustments. The following illustration will indicate how this may be done.

ITEMS	PROFIT & LOSS	X PER 36%	Y PER 44%	Z PER 20%
Net Profit as above	$18,364			
Salary Allowances	$ 5,400	$2,400	$3,000	
Partners' Drawings		$3,000	$3,100	$1,500
Interest on Excess Drawings	36	18	3	15
Interest on Capitals	3,000	900	600	$1,500
Balance Distributed in Profit and Loss ratio	10,000	3,600	4,400	2,000
Balance of Personal accounts to Loan accounts		3,882	4,897	1,985
	$18,400 $18,400	$6,900 $6,900	$8,000 $8,000	$3,500 $3,500

The item "Net Profit as above" is taken from the work sheet. The Profit and Loss columns, in conjunction with the detailed distributions shown in the

- 532 -

"Partners' Personal" columns, contain all the data needed for the appropriation section of the profit and loss statement and also for distributing the net profit shown by the Profit and Loss account. By entering the drawings in the "Partners' Personal" columns, those columns are made to develop the amount of undrawn profits of each partner. They thus contain the same information which the respective personal accounts will contain after the ledger is closed. The work sheet, with this appended analysis of profits and partners' personal accounts, thus contains all of the information needed both for drawing up the formal statements and for adjusting and closing the books.

XVI

Draw up a pro forma balance sheet and a statement of profit and loss for the six months for Cotten, Wooster & Company. In drawing up the balance sheet, head it as follows:

Exhibit A

COTTEN, WOOSTER & COMPANY
BALANCE SHEET
June 30, 19—

Show the total of all customers' accounts as "Accounts Receivable (See Schedule A-1)." Attach to the balance sheet a list or schedule of all customers' accounts to support the title "Accounts Receivable (See Schedule A-1)," carried in the balance sheet. Give to it as a formal heading:

Schedule A-1

COTTEN, WOOSTER & COMPANY
LIST OF ACCOUNTS RECEIVABLE
June 30, 19—

The data for the schedule come from the customers ledger list or trial balance for June 30.

Attach schedules also for the other groups of items appearing in the balance sheet, viz.: Deferred Charges to Operation under which include in addition to the other items listed, the office supplies and packing materials still on hand; Accrued Income; Accounts Payable; and Accrued Expenses.

The use of schedules relieves the balance sheet of much detail and renders it more intelligible; it also makes the detail available if desired.

Set up the net worth section as follows:

Net Worth

Represented by:

  C. Allen Cotten:

    Capital $........

    Undrawn Profits (See Schedule A-6) .... $........

  Scott Wooster:

    Capital $........

    Undrawn Profits (See Schedule A-6) ....

  Etc.

Supporting Schedule A-6 will appear as follows:

Schedule A-6

COTTEN, WOOSTER & COMPANY

UNDRAWN PROFITS, June 30, 19—

DISTRIBUTIONS OF PROFITS	COTTEN 36%	WOOSTER 44%	WOOLSEY 20%
Salary for the half-year	$......	$......	
Interest on capital	....	....	$......
Share of Profit and Loss	....	....	....
Totals	$......	$......	$......
Deduct:			
Interest on overdrafts	$......	$......	$......

- 534 -

Drawings for the half-year	....	....	....
Totals	$......	$........	$........
Undrawn profits transferred to Loan Accounts	$......	$........	$........

The data for this schedule are secured from the "Profits Distribution" section of the work sheet.

In drawing up the profit and loss statement refer to the forms already shown. See Chapters XXVI and XXVII. The Miscellaneous Sales item should be added to the Net Sales short-extended and their total should be full-extended, from which should be deducted Cost of Goods Sold as usual.

After the item, "Net Profit for the period," set up the appropriation section, showing the shares of each of the partners, somewhat as follows:

Net Profit for the period $........

    Add:

Interest charged to partners on overdrafts:

    C. Allen Cotten $........

    Scott Wooster ....

    Landsdowne Woolsey ....

Amount to be distributed as: $........

Salary:

    C. Allen Cotten $........

    Scott Wooster .... $........

Interest on Capitals:

    C. Allen Cotten $........

    Scott Wooster ....

    Landsdowne Woolsey ....

In Profit and Loss Ratio:

    C. Allen Cotten, 36% $ . . . .

    Scott Wooster, 44%   . . . .

    Landsdowne Woolsey, 20%   . . . . $ . . . .

Excepting for the Accounts Receivable and Accounts Payable schedules, the detailed data for balance sheet and profit and loss statements come from the work sheet drawn up for Assignment XV. Set up the formal statements on letter size (8½ × 11) paper. Typewrite them if possible.

XVII

Using the "Adjustment" columns of the work sheet as a guide, make the adjusting entries in the general journal.

Using the profit and loss statement (including the appropriation section) as a guide, set up the closing entries in the general journal. Use the "Profits Distribution" section of the work sheet as the source of the transfer of the balances of the partners' personal accounts to the loan accounts.

Post the adjusting and closing entries.

Rule the ledger accounts.

Take a post-closing trial balance of the general ledger.

XVIII

This set comprises a general journal; a sales journal, a sales returns and allowances journal, a purchase journal, a purchase returns and allowances journal, and the cash journals, for convenience bound together in one book; a note journal to be used as a posting medium for notes receivable and notes payable; and a general ledger, a purchase ledger, and a sales ledger, bound together in one book. Of the subsidiary journal blank, page 1 is for the sales journal, page 2 the sales returns, page 3 the purchase journal, page 4 the purchase returns, and pages 6-9 the cash journals. Of the ledger blank, pages 1-15 comprise the general ledger, pages 16-19 the sales ledger, and pages 20-22 the purchase ledger. The general journal will be used as previously, i.e., for the record of all items not otherwise specially provided for. The sales journal provides for analysis of the sales, the first column being the total or general column; the others, Dept. A, Dept. B, and Out-Freight, respectively. The sales returns and allowances journal makes provision for the same analysis as the sales journal except that there is no Out-Freight column, that not being used; the purchase journal columns are respectively, Total, Dept. A, Dept. B, and In-Freight, with the same column headings for the purchase returns and allowances journal, except as to In-Freight. The cash book columns will be, on the debit, General, Accounts Receivable, Sales Discount, and Harding National Bank; and on the credit, General, Accounts Payable, Purchase Discount, and Harding National Bank. The note journal will be analyzed, summarized, and posted just as the other subsidiary journals.

The deposit account carried with the Coolidge National Bank is an inactive one. For this reason no extra column is provided for it in the cash book.

Daily posting of items affecting customers' and creditors' accounts should be made, carefully observing the terms of credit.

The general journal is provided with six money columns, three of which are to be devoted to charges and the other three to credits. The debit columns are to be headed, Accounts Payable, Accounts Receivable, and General, respectively. The credit columns will be headed similarly but in the reverse order, having the General column close to the ledger folio column. All amounts to be posted to accounts in the general ledger should be recorded in the General column, and those affecting a controlling account in its respective column. The latter amounts should be posted to the subsidiary account immediately, but will not be posted to the controlling account until the general journal is summarized at the end of the month. Record will be made of transactions for the last month of the fiscal year, the previous eleven months being summarized in the trial balance given to start with.

The Business Equipment Corporation was organized and incorporated under the laws of the state of New York. Its fiscal year closes on December 31. A trial balance from the general ledger on November 30, 19—, shows as follows:

1	Harding National Bank	$ 6,521.25	
1	Coolidge State Bank	5,000.00	
1	Consignment Accounts Receivable		
1	Petty Cash	200.00	
1	Notes Receivable	8,419.80	
2	Accounts Receivable	146,838.05	
2	Reserve for Doubtful Accounts		$ 2,574.85
2	Investments	12,750.00	
2	Notes Receivable Special		
3	Department A, Inventory	78,769.40	

3	Department B, Inventory	52,918.25	
3	Delivery Equipment	13,000.00	
3	Depreciation Reserve Delivery Equipment		8,000.00
4	Store and Warehouse Furniture and Fixtures	4,500.00	
4	Depreciation Reserve Store and Warehouse Furniture and Fixtures		2,000.00
4	Office Furniture and Fixtures	1,250.00	
4	Depreciation Reserve Office Furniture and Fixtures		500.00
5	Buildings	60,000.00	
5	Depreciation Reserve Buildings		15,000.00
5	Land	10,800.00	
5	Mortgage on Real Estate		35,000.00
6	Notes Payable		6,472.50
6	Accounts Payable		94,969.17
6	Dividends Payable Common		
6	Dividends Payable Preferred		
7	Capital Stock Common		100,000.00
7	Capital Stock Preferred		100,000.00
7	Surplus		34,792.80
8	Profit and Loss		
9	Department A, Purchases	478,860.00	
9	Department A, Purchases Returns and Allowances		15,678.90
9	Department B, Purchases	397,725.00	
9	Department B, Purchases Returns and Allowances		12,796.40

10	In-Freight and Cartage	9,642.57	
10	Department A, Sales		567,819.60
10	Department A, Sales Returns and Allowances	10,649.30	
10	Department B, Sales		471,932.40
11	Department B, Sales Returns and Allowances	7,427.80	
11	Salesmen's Salaries and Commissions	29,942.70	
11	Salesmen's Traveling Expenses	17,897.60	
11	Advertising	22,000.00	
12	Sales General Expense	23,649.30	
12	Out-Freight	472.73	
12	Insurance	7,562.40	
12	Office Expense	2,890.78	
13	Office Supplies	3,697.40	
13	General Expense	12,897.48	
13	General Salaries	32,894.72	
13	Interest and Bank Expense	2,344.52	586.13
14	Sales Discount	15,849.50	
14	Bad Debts		
14	Depreciation		
14	Purchase Discount		10,297.80
15	Taxes		
15	Mortgage Interest	1,050.00	
15	Consignment		
15	Consignment-Out		
		$1,478,420.55	$1,478,420.55

Instructions

Open all the above accounts in your general ledger, at the places indicated, and enter under date of December 1 the balances given in the trial balance. The number in front of the account title indicates the page on which to enter the accounts. Give each one-fourth of a page, except on page 2, where give Accounts Receivable two additional lines by shortening the space for Investments.

In the sales ledger (which is controlled by the Accounts Receivable account on the general ledger), beginning on page 16, open the following accounts, four to a page, and enter the balances as of December 1:

Alexander, Hill & Co.	$ 10,187.60
Automatic Pencil Sharpener Co.	1,279.00
Browne Morse Co.	4,279.85
Clark & Smith	6,798.94
General Fireproofing Co.	
Hall, Walter & Co.	2,967.09
Franklin Moffit Co.	22,897.42
Peerless Motor Co.	
John B. Scrivener	
Standard Truck Co.	217.90
Second Third National Bank	650.00
Willis, Dickson, Inc.	14,679.80
Yonkers Carpet Works	
Sundry Customers	82,880.45
	$146,838.05

In the purchase ledger (which is controlled by the Accounts Payable account on the general ledger), beginning with page 20, open the following accounts, four to a page, and enter the balances as of December 1:

American Banking Machine Co.	$ 7,894.20
American Duplicator Co.	2,985.75

American Kardex Co.	6,732.84
Automatic Pencil Sharpener Co.	480.00
Apex Office Supply Co.	2,797.90
Dictation Devices Co.	5,724.75
Filing Systems & Cabinet Co.	6,894.80
Library Bureau	7,894.90
Protectograph Co.	2,147.35
Yawman & Erbe Mfg. Co.	10,897.50
Sundry Creditors	40,519.18
	$ 94,969.17

The two accounts, "Sundry Customers" and "Sundry Creditors," are used to secure volume of transactions without involving too great detail. They should be treated in all respects as personal accounts.

In the notes receivable journal, enter the following notes:

No. 84, made by Clark & Smith in our favor, for merchandise, dated September 18, 19—, for three months at 6%, amount $1,987.50.

No. 87, made by Hall, Walter & Co., in our favor, for goods purchased, dated October 5, at 6% for two months, amount $2,500.

No. 88, draft drawn by the company on Willis, Dickson, Inc., dated October 28, at 60 days, amount $2,750.

No. 91, made by Franklin Moffit Co., in our favor, for merchandise, dated November 15, at 6% for 30 days, amount $1,182.30.

Total the "Amount" column and rule it off as this amount is already in your general ledger "Notes Receivable" account.

In the notes payable journal, enter the following notes:

No. 32, made by the company in favor of the Yawman & Erbe Mfg. Co., dated October 15, for two months for $1,472.50 at 6%.

No. 31, made by the company in favor of the Harding National Bank for discount, dated October 20, at 6% for 60 days, amount $5,000.

Enter these in the notes payable journal and treat as with notes receivable above.

Your books, general and subsidiary, will now show the condition as at the beginning of business December 1.

XIX

Make record in the various books of original entry of the following transactions for December, figures at left margin indicating day of month. Where needed, directions appear at the close of each assignment.

Dec.

1. Sold Browne Morse Co., 1/10, n/30, $1,538.40 (A), and $408.75 (B)

    on which the company prepaid freight and charged to them $58.85.

    Received on account from Willis, Dickson, Inc. $2,000.

    Paid cash on account to American Banking Machine Co., $2,000.

2. Bought of the Yawman & Erbe Mfg. Co., 2/5, n/20, $2,989.80 (A),

    and $3,347.65 (B).

    Sold Clark & Smith, 2/10, n/60, $3,276.40 (A), and $1,562.32 (B).

    Received cash on account from Alexander, Hill & Co., $3,500.

    Paid cash on account to Filing Systems & Cabinet Co. $2,000.

3. Sold General Fireproofing Co., 1/5, n/30, $2,190, (A).

    Received cash from Sundry Customers $5,547.80.

    Paid American Kardex Co. $3,500 on account.

5. Sold Hall, Walter & Co., 3/10, n/30, $1,279.60 (A), and $390.45 (B).

    Received payment on Hall, Walter & Co. note No. 84, with interest.

    Browne Morse Co. paid their bill of December 1, less 1%.

    Paid American Duplicator Co., November balance less 1%.

    Received $2,497.80 from Sundry Customers.

6. Bought of the Automatic Pencil Sharpener Co., 4/10, n/30, $679 (B).

    Bought from Apex Office Supply Co., 1/10, n/30, $1,497.80 (A), and $896.45 (B).

Sold Peerless Motor Co., 1/10, n/60, $2,679.40 (A), and $1,243.70 (B),

    with prepaid freight charged them $22.90.

Received $2,500 on account from Willis, Dickson, Inc.

Gave our 30-day note No. 33, at 6%, in favor of Library Bureau,

    to apply on account, $3,000.

Paid Sundry Creditors $8,191.75.

7. Sold Second Third National Bank, 1/5, n/60, $425 (B).

Paid Yawman & Erbe bill of December 2, less 2%.

Received from Sundry Customers $2,976.80 on account.

Sold Browne Morse Co., 1/10, n/30, $1,215.60 (A), and $671.15 (B).

Clark & Smith returned goods, invoice of December 2,

    $127.50 (A), and $16.18 (B).

General Fireproofing Co. paid their invoice of December 3 less 1%.

Second Third National Bank paid their November balance less 1%.

9. Bought of Dictation Devices Co., 1/10, n/30, $3,784.90 (A),

    and $1,781.19 (B).

Paid cash for insurance $275.

In making a deposit at the bank, a $20 note was found

to be counterfeit.

10. A note receivable for $2,500 was received from the president,

    due in six months at 6% in return for a loan made to him

    by the company.

Sold Automatic Pencil Sharpener Co. $896.40 (B), 1/5, n/30.

Received cash on account from Franklin Moffit Co. $7,500.

Browne Morse Co. paid $2,000 on account.

Paid Apex Office Supply Co., $2,500 on account.

12. Bought of the Protectograph Co., n/60, $2,976.80 (B).

    Sold Alexander Hill & Co., 2/5, n/30, $1,569.70 (A),

    and $972.80 (B).

    Hall, Walter & Co. returned goods, invoice of December 5,

    $92.78 (A), and $121.47 (B).

    Received balance from Clark & Smith, invoice of December 2, less 2%.

    Paid Yawman & Erbe Mfg. Co. $5,000 on account; and Dictation Devices Co. $2,500.

    The Second Third National Bank paid their invoice of December 7, less 1%.

13. John B. Scrivener, the secretary, withdrew for his home use

    $125.80 (A), and $48.90 (B).

    Sold Browne Morse, 1/10, n/30, $894.65 (A) and $1,292.45 (B).

    Returned to Automatic Pencil Sharpener Co. $207 (B) of the

    invoice of December 6.

    Paid $890 for changing the partitions in the warehouse.

    Took from stock a new sofa, $275 (A) for use in salesrooms.

14. Purchased from American Banking Machine Co., 3/10, n/30,

    $1,472.85 (A), and $4,561.40 (B).

    Sold Standard Truck Co., 1/10, n/30, $684.90 (A),

    and $516.75 (B), with prepaid freight charged them $62.81.

    Received $2,500 on account from Franklin Moffit Co.

    Paid Protectograph Co. $2,000 on account.

15. Sent a consignment of Department A goods, $1,200 to

    G. A. Roberts, to be sold on a 5% commission basis.

    Drew a 30-day sight draft on Alexander Hill & Co. to apply

    on account, $2,500, which was accepted.

Hall, Walter & Co. gave a 30-day 6% note for balance of their bill of December 5, less 3%.

The Franklin Moffit Co. note was paid with interest.

Received from Automatic Pencil Sharpener Co. in full settlement, the net balance due as shown by their two accounts, advantage being taken of the discounts both ways.

Paid Yawman & Erbe note due today with interest.

Instructions

December 5. Record the interest received from Notes Receivable in the Interest and Bank Expense account.

December 10. Be sure to enter the note received from the president to the correct account.

December 13. For stock withdrawn for use of business, make entry in the general journal.

December 15. Transfer through the general journal the claim of the Automatic Pencil Sharpener Co. to their account in the sales ledger, taking into consideration the sales discount to be allowed and the purchase discount to be taken. Remember to record these amounts in the proper columns. The balance of the latter account will be offset by the credit from the cash receipts journal.

XX

Dec.

16. Bought from American Kardex Co., 3/10, n/30, $629.50 (A), and $350.40 (B).

    Bought on account of the Yonkers Carpet Works, n/90, carpets and floor materials for showrooms. They charged $890 for the carpets, etc., and $125 for labor in laying them, with freight prepaid by them and charged to the company of $22.80.

    Returned to the Protectograph Co. $258 (B).

Gave Apex Office Supply Co. 30-day note at 6%,

    for bill of December 6, less 1%.

The Peerless Motor Co. paid their bill of December 6, less 1%.

17. Sold Franklin Moffit Co., 1/10, n/30, $987.40 (A),

    and $1,642.70 (B), with prepaid freight charged them $62.15.

Paid in-freight and cartage bills to date $569.47.

19. Bought of American Duplicator Co. $4,897 (A), n/60,

    with prepaid freight $297.69.

Sold Willis, Dickson, Inc., n/10, $892.50 (A), and $274.90 (B).

The Clark & Smith note was paid with interest.

Browne Morse Co. gave the company a 30-day 6% note

    for the bill of December 7, less 1%.

Drew from stock for completing showrooms, furnishings $2,790 (A), and $650 (B).

Hall, Walter & Co. paid the company $100 for the use

    of one of the motor trucks for the week.

Alexander, Hill & Co. paid their bill of December 12, less 2%.

Gave Dictation Devices Co. $2,500, 30-day note at 6%

    and the balance in cash, in settlement of invoice

    of December 9, less 1%.

Paid note due at bank today.

20. Sold Sundry Customers to date receiving full cash payments $2,447.50 (A), and $1,679.35 (B).

Sold Yonkers Carpet Works Co., 1/10, n/30, $889.70 (A), and $632.40 (B).

Paid American Banking Machine Co. $5,000 on account.

21. Returned to American Banking Machine Co. $289.50 (A),

and $186.70 (B), of invoice of December 14.

The company accepted the draft, to apply on account, drawn by the American Kardex Co., at 60 days from December 18, for $2,500.

Paid Filing Systems & Cabinet Co. $2,500 on account.

22. Bought from Filing Systems & Cabinet Co., 3/10, n/30, $3,695 (A), and $4,272 (B), with prepaid freight charges of $116.74.

    Sold Clark & Smith, 2/10, n/60, $1,462.80 (A), and $1,937.60 (B).

    Hall, Walter & Co. paid $1,000 on account.

    Browne Morse Co. returned goods $197.60 (A), and $59.70 (B).

23. Word was received that one of our Sundry Customers has gone into the hands of a receiver, owing $490, and settlement with creditors was made on the basis of 40% of all claims, cash being received for that amount.

    Bought of Library Bureau, 1/10, n/30, $2,897 (B).

    Sold Alexander, Hill & Co., 1/10, n/30, $1,785.90 (A), and $2,476.80 (B).

    Paid Library Bureau $3,000 on account.

    Browne Morse Co. paid balance of their bill of December 13, less 1%.

24. The company discounted its note at the Harding National Bank for 60 days at 6%, $5,000.

    Paid balance on American Banking Machine Co. bill of December 14, less 3%.

Bought of Yawman & Erbe Mfg. Co., 2/5, n/20, $4,567.90 (A), and $976.50 (B).

Received on cash sales $458.60 (A), and $1,124.70 (B).

Received a check from Willis, Dickson, Inc., for $5,000.

Paid Yawman & Erbe Mfg. Co. $5,000.

Standard Truck Co. gave a 30-day note at 6% for bill of December 14, less 1%.

27. We called to the attention of Willis, Dickson, Inc. an undercharge of $100 in the bill of December 19 in the Department B sale.

Returned merchandise to Sundry Creditors $1,910 (A), and $897.50 (B).

Sundry Customers returned goods $619 (A), and $1,490 (B).

Paid advertising $2,000.

Paid cash for purchases $4,209 (A), and $2,010.70 (B).

Franklin Moffit Co. paid $5,000 on account.

The Willis, Dickson, Inc. draft was given to the bank for collection.

28. The Willis, Dickson, Inc., draft was sent back because of insufficient funds. Protest fees paid by the bank and charged to the company were $2.50.

Sold Sundry Customers, n/30, $5,196.40 (A), and $8,927.30 (B).

Paid the American Kardex Co. bill of December 16, less 3%.

Received payment from Clark & Smith for bill of December 22 less 2%.

Paid the Filing System & Cabinet Co.'s bill of December 22, less 3%.

Instructions

December 16. Record the purchase made from the Yonkers Carpet Works in the proper column of the general journal. Charge Sales General Expense.

December 19. Credit the income received for the use of the motor truck to Sales General Expense.

December 23. Refer to page 411 of the text as to the handling of the balance of the firm's claim against the bankrupt customer.

December 24. Cash sales will be recorded in the sales journal and included in the debit to Accounts Receivable account at time of summary. To offset this inflated debit, at the time cash sales are recorded also in the cash book the amount will be entered there in the Accounts Receivable column—not the General Ledger—and will thus be included in the credit to the Accounts Receivable account.

December 27. Record the Willis, Dickson, Inc. undercharge in the sales journal.

The entry of cash purchases is similar to that of cash sales.

XXI

Dec.

29. Upon presentation at the office of Willis, Dickson, Inc., the draft due December 27 was paid with the protest charge.

    Bought from Library Bureau, 1/10, n/30, $3,297 (B),

    with in-freight $269.87.

    Made partial payment to Yonkers Carpet Works $300.

30. Bought of Sundry Creditors, n/30, $11,816.80 (A),

    and $16,519.70 (B).

    Sold Sundry Customers, n/30, $32,279.90 (A),

    and $26,819.40 (B).

    Yonkers Carpet Works paid their invoice of

    December 20 less 1%.

    Received cash from sale of old showroom fixtures

    $1,450. The fixtures cost $2,500 five years ago

    and have been depreciated at the rate of 10%

per annum since that time.

Received a check for $317.90 from Standard Truck Co.; and checks and cash from Sundry Customers $53,606.97, less $897.48; to one of whom we issued check for $25 due to inability to make change.

31. Reimbursed petty cash for cash vouchers $116.80, and distributed same: $62.40 to Sales General Expense; $23.10 to Office Expense; and the balance to General Expense.

Paid Sundry Creditors, invoices of $29,467.45, less $842.90 discount.

Paid sales salaries $4,200; salesmen's traveling expense $3,872.80; sales general expense $748.45; general salaries $3,764.90; advertising for January $2,000; general expense $1,714.92; office expense $482.70; interest and bank expense $86.80; office supplies $287.95.

The statement from the bank as of December 31 showed the following: Items not entered on the Business Equipment Corporation books:

- Interest credited, $24.79
- Collection charges, 2.36

Checks outstanding:

#1296,	$1,347.60
#1314,	75.80
#1315,	16.82
#1318,	192.47
#1329,	181.64
#1331,	296.70
#1342,	897.60

A check from a sundry customer for $100, deposited on December 30, was returned by the bank as uncollectible. The company had not yet been informed of this.

Balance by bank was $14,848.73.

Reconcile the bank statement with the cash book balance shown previous to the entry in the cash book of any items from the bank statement, and determine the true cash balance.

Summarize all books of original entry. Posting of these summary entries and any other unposted items will be deferred to the next assignment.

Instructions

December 30. Refer to <u>pages 416-418 of the text</u> as to the proper record to be made of the sale of the old showroom fixtures. Credit the gain on this sale to the Sales General Expense.

December 31. The amount of check for $25 is included in the amount received from sundry customers.

In summarizing the general journal, first foot all the columns and underline the totals. On the following lines write the summary entry which will appear as follows:

General			General
....	General Ledger	✓	
....	Accounts Receivable		
....	Accounts Payable		
	General Ledger		....
	Accounts Receivable		....
	Accounts Payable		....

Since the items making up the "General Ledger" totals have already been posted, these totals will be checked and will not be posted.

In summarizing the sales journal, the cash sales need not be segregated from the credit sales in the summary entry, inasmuch as the inclusion of such receipts in the total to be posted to Accounts Receivable from the cash receipts journal will eliminate the inflation of the claims against customers shown by the controlling account.

The purchase journal will be summarized in the same way as the sales journal.

The items shown on the bank statement but not yet entered in the cash book are to be entered there before summarizing the cash book. See page 562 for instructions as to its summary.

For summarizing the other journals follow the explanations given in Chapter XXXI.

XXII

Post completely.

Take a trial balance of the general ledger, recording it on a double sheet of journal paper. When posting customers' and creditors' accounts, make sure that the corresponding controlling accounts will receive, either in totals or in items, the same amounts.

Prove your sales and purchase ledgers and record the proof with the general ledger trial balance, i.e., make a list or schedule of the accounts and show the list totals as agreeing with their respective controlling account balances in the general ledger trial balance.

XXIII

Prepare a work sheet for the year ending December 31, 19—, taking the following adjustments into consideration:

- Accrued Expenses:
- Salesmen's salaries $385.
- General Salaries $416.90.
- Amount due on repairs to building $500.
- Mortgage interest $1,050.
- Interest on notes: Library Bureau note $12.50;
- Apex Office
- Supply Co. note $5.92;
- Dictation Devices Co. note $5.
- Accrued freight bills $824.34.
- Accrued taxes $378.
- Chauffeurs' wages $160.60.
- Garage bills $216 ($100 for gasoline and balance for repairs).

- Automobile tire $90.
- Prepaid Expenses:
- Interest on note discounted at the Harding National Bank $44.17.
- Advertising $2,000. Insurance $2,867.90.
- Prepaid dues to Merchants' Association $50.
- Accrued Income:
- Interest on following notes: notes receivable special $8.75;
- Hall, Walter & Co. $3.77;
- Browne Morse Co. $3.73;
- Standard Truck Co. $1.46.
- Bank interest on inactive deposit with Coolidge State Bank $24.36.
- Upon analysis, $387.86 of the freight bills was found to be
- out-freight.
- Take into account depreciation at the yearly rates of: 3%
- on buildings; 20% on delivery equipment; 10% on office
- furniture and fixtures.
- No depreciation is to be charged on the store and warehouse
- furniture and fixtures just installed.
- Create a reserve for doubtful accounts equal to 1/2% of net sales.
- Inventories showed the following on hand:
- Department A $79,897.80;
- Department B $51,764.32;
- office supplies $296.45.
- In-freight was apportioned between the departments on the
- basis of net purchases.
- Charge 90% of insurance expense to selling expenses.

In answer to our request, G. A. Roberts submitted the following information regarding his consignment:

Sales to customers $800.00

Expenses paid by him:

 Freight and drayage $58.22

 Insurance   12.54

A formal account sales will not be rendered till completion of sales of entire consignment. The quantities of unsold articles reported showed, upon pricing, a valuation of $600. Word was also received that a check for the amount due on sales as above would follow immediately after certification by the bank. It was decided to defer one-half of the above expenses reported by the consignee as applicable to the remainder of the consignment.

The Board of Directors declared the regular semiannual dividend of 4% on the preferred stock, payable January 25, and a 4% dividend on the common stock, also payable January 25.

Analysis, based on vouchers and invoices, showed the following content of the Sales General Expense account before adjustment:

Garage rent	$1,800.00
Chauffeurs' wages	8,969.34
Shipping clerks' wages	2,775.13
Gasoline and oil	2,491.68
Licenses, Trucks	96.00
Repairs	895.46
Stationery, supplies, and postage	1,237.29
Tires and tubes	714.78
Crates, boxes, and shipping supplies	1,374.30
Light and heat	3,775.37
Carpets and labor for showroom	1,037.80
Sundries	330.80
Profit on sale of old storage and warehouse furniture and fixtures	200.00

Renting of truck   100.00

Likewise, a similar analysis of the General Expense account before adjustment showed the following distribution:

Cleaners' and watchman's wages	$4,369.75
Repairs to buildings	2,174.65
Changes in partitions	1,215.79
Auditor's fees	1,500.00
Legal fees	2,500.00
Contributions	1,000.00
Light and heat	1,869.43
Merchants' Association dues	100.00
Sundries	824.08

Instructions

Refer to Chapter XLVIII of the text as to consignments. In this case make use of the Consignment Accounts Receivable account for recording the claim against the consignee, and be careful to charge the proper amount of expenses against the income to be taken into the earnings for this period. Handle the deferred expense items on the consignments in the Out-Freight account. Do not forget to adjust the memorandum accounts so that they will show the value of goods still out on consignment, and take the latter amount into consideration when setting up the final inventories on the books.

XXIV

Using the work sheet as a guide, draw up pro forma balance sheet and statement of profit and loss for the year ending December 31, 19—. Show the gross profit on the sales of each department. Support both the balance sheet and the profit and loss statement with properly set-up schedule.

Instructions

Balance Sheet. Where the number of accrued and deferred items is small, they may be shown on the face of the balance sheet or in attached schedules as preferred. See page 577 for form of schedules.

Profit and Loss Statement. Where the record of the period's business has been made by departments, it is desirable that the summary for the period show departmental results, at least so far as the gross profit stage. To get rid of the detail on the face of the statement, schedules may be appended showing such items as Cost of Goods Sold, the group of Selling Expenses, the group of General Administrative Expenses, etc. Such a statement of profit and loss, supported by schedules, is called a condensed profit and loss statement. Such a statement for a departmental business is shown by the following illustration. Only Schedule B-1 is given; the other schedules are merely lists with their totals shown.

Exhibit B

JACKSON EDWARDS COMPANY
STATEMENT OF PROFIT AND LOSS
For the Year Ending December 31, 19—

	Department A	Department B	Total
Sales	$100,000.00	$150,000.00	$250,000.00
Less—Returns and Allowances	5,000.00	6,000.00	11,000.00
Net Sales	$ 95,000.00	$144,000.00	$239,000.00
Cost of Goods Sold (Schedule B-1)	60,000.00	90,000.00	150,000.00
Gross Profit	$ 35,000.00	$ 54,000.00	$ 89,000.00
Selling Expenses (Schedule B-2)	$ 35,000.00		
General Administrative Expenses (Schedule B-3)	20,000.00		
Financial Management Expenses (Schedule B-4)	5,000.00	60,000.00	
Financial Management Income (Schedule B-5)		2,000.00	58,000.00
Net Profit			$ 31,000.00

Schedule B-1

JACKSON EDWARDS COMPANY
COST OF GOODS SOLD
For the Year Ending December 31, 19—

	Department A	Department B	Total
Inventory, January 1, 19—	$12,000.00	$ 18,000.00	$ 30,000.00
Purchases	60,000.00	87,500.00	147,500.00
In-Freight	3,500.00	5,000.00	8,500.00
	$75,500.00	$110,500.00	$186,000.00
Deduct:			
Purchase Returns	$ 2,000.00	$ 3,000.00	$ 5,000.00
Inventory, December 31, 19—	13,500.00	17,500.00	31,000.00
	$15,500.00	$20,500.00	$36,000.00
Cost of Goods Sold	$60,000.00	$90,000.00	$150,000.00

In preparing the schedules of expenses, refer to the previous assignment for the analysis of the Sales General Expenses and General Expense accounts.

Analyze the Interest and Bank Expense account into expense and income, and show these items separately in the statements.

XXV

Adjust and close the ledger through the general journal in accordance with the data given in Assignment XXIII.

XXVI

1. The sales of the Radcliffe Company last year January to June, amounted to $752,465. It is estimated that the price level for the current year will be 10% lower than a year ago. Due to plans for increased publicity and sales effort, it is expected that the *volume* of sales for the corresponding period this year will be 15% larger than last year's. The average rate of turnover is 3½ and the mark-on is 35%.

What will be the average amount of capital required to finance the merchandise stock?

2. In establishing a buying quota for a three-month period, the Gotham Novelty Company has available from its records the following data: present inventory at retail $79,800; sales corresponding period last year $316,000; estimated sales volume this year same as last but 15% less in value. It is thought that the rate of turnover can be increased. It is therefore decided to reduce the stock carried so that at the close of the period there will be on hand a stock 20% less in volume.

Assuming that the price level is 15% less at the end of the period and that the mark-on is 40%, determine the company's buying quota for the period.

3. The sales representative of the Natty Uniform Company is making his regular call on the Salem Dry Goods Co., whose buyer has just secured the following data from the accounting department:

- Salesroom stock on hand at beginning of period $32,000.
- Additions to salesroom stock to date $45,000.
- Sales to date $52,000.
- Stocks in transit and on present order $15,000
- There is no stock in the warehouse.
- Planned sales for the period are $75,000 but a revised estimate calls for a 10% increase.
- Stock planned to be on hand at the end of the period is $25,000.

Is the buyer open to buy and, if so, how much?

4. Your Notes Receivable account shows $25,000 of customers' notes on hand. Being in need of cash you discount $10,000 of these at the bank, receiving therefor a credit of $9,750 in your bank account. Fifteen days later the bank notifies you that $4,000 of these notes have been paid by their makers at maturity, but that a note for $1,000 signed by J. B. Grant has been charged back on account of non-payment.

Make all the entries, in journal form, to record the above.

5. On April 1, 19—, Jones of Trenton, N. J., ships an invoice of goods to Smith in New York. The goods are valued at $2,000, and the consignor pays freight amounting to $40, and insurance $30. The consignee pays cartage amounting to $50, and storage $40. On April 2, Jones draws a 30-day draft against Smith for $500, which is duly accepted on April 5. The goods are sold for $2,700. Smith's commission is 5%.

Set up the necessary accounts both on the books of the consignor and on those of the consignee properly to reflect the above transactions.

6. Prepare the closing entries for the following consignment sale. The consignment was received July 8, account of William Nevins & Co., showing an invoice value of $3,750. You paid freight and cartage $87.50, and insurance $18.75. Sales were made July 16, $1,000, and July 25, $1,525, on a

5% commission basis. On July 31, upon closing your books, you inventory the unsold balance of the consigned goods as $2,500.

7. From the following data, relating only to customers and creditors, prepare as of December 31, 19—, Accounts Receivable and Accounts Payable accounts. Indicate in folio column the book of original entry from which each item is obtained.

1.	Accounts receivable, balance January 1, 19—	$1,200.00
2.	Accounts payable, balance January 1, 19—	1,350.00
3.	Sales	4,000.00
4.	Purchases	2,500.00
5.	Return sales	200.00
6.	Return purchases	100.00
7.	Cash received from customers	3,200.00
8.	Discount allowed customers	100.00
9.	Cash paid creditors	1,800.00
10.	Discount allowed us	50.00
11.	Customers' notes indorsed to creditors	500.00
12.	Notes received from customers	600.00
13.	Freight paid by us for customers	40.00
14.	Cash received from creditor for overpayment	20.00
15.	Customer's check deposited returned by bank	300.00
16.	Customer's note indorsed to creditor (see item 11) dishonored and returned	250.00
17.	Protest fees on above	5.00
18.	Allowance for damages on goods purchased	30.00
19.	Cash returned to customer for overpayment	10.00
20.	In item 3 (Sales) included in total sales was one to creditor	100.00

XXVII

1. An investment company purchased for investment $100,000 of 6% 10-year municipal debentures at 96, and $200,000 of 5% industrial bonds, 15 years to run, at 104.

How would you treat the discount and the premium in the accounts? Give the journal entries.

2. The authorized capital stock of a corporation is $500,000, divided into 5,000 shares, par value $100. Of this amount $400,000 has been subscribed and paid for in full. The corporation purchases ten shares of a dissatisfied stockholder for $75 a share, and five other stockholders each donate five shares to the company. Five shares of the purchased stock and all of the donated stock are sold for $50 a share.

(a) Draft proper entries and show the ledger accounts and balances.

(b) How would the balances of the accounts in (a) appear in a balance sheet?

(c) Give the entries and show the ledger accounts and balances if the capital stock were of no specified par value, but 5,000 shares had been issued at $80 and the other conditions remain as stated in the first paragraph.

(d) How would the balances of the accounts in (c) appear in a balance sheet?

3. J. B. Brown and L. C. Smith are partners, and in order to raise more capital and to preserve the organization they decide to incorporate. A company was duly incorporated under the name of The Eclipse Company, with an authorized capital of $800,000 divided into 8,000 shares of the par value of $100 each.

The partners agreed to sell for the sum of $800,000, payable in capital stock of the corporation at par, all rights to and title in the net assets of the partnership, exclusive of the cash, which was divided between the partners in proportion to their several interests at the time of the sale of the property.

According to the articles of partnership, Brown and Smith were equally interested in the assets, but the profits and losses were on a basis of 60% and 40% respectively.

The partnership balance sheet at the time of the sale was:

Assets		Liabilities	
Land and Buildings	$200,000.00	Notes Payable	$100,000.00
Cash	10,000.00	Accounts Payable	40,000.00

Inventories	100,000.00	Brown's Capital	210,000.00
Accounts Receivable	150,000.00	Smith's Capital	210,000.00
Machinery and Equipment	100,000.00		
	$560,000.00		$560,000.00

For the purpose of providing working capital, the partnership donated $300,000 of the capital stock to the corporation, which was sold at $50 per share.

You are required to:

(a) Close the partnership books, showing ledger accounts of partners only.

(b) Open the corporation books.

(c) Prepare a balance sheet of the corporation before sale of donated stock.

(d) Prepare a balance sheet after sale of donated stock.

4. Before making the charges referred to below, the Profit and Loss account of a corporation for the year shows a credit balance of $60,000. The accounts receivable are $40,700, and the plant and machinery account is $55,000. The 6% preferred stock is $50,000, and the common stock $150,000. It is decided:

1. To provide out of the above-named profit and loss balance 7½% depreciation on plant and machinery.

2. To write off as uncollectible $1,500 of the accounts receivable, and to make a reserve of 2% of the remainder of the accounts receivable to provide for possible losses thereon.

3. To provide for the preferred stock dividend for the year.

4. To provide for a bonus of $7,500 to the employees.

5. To provide for a dividend on the common stock of 15% for the year.

6. To carry the balance then remaining on the Profit and Loss account to an Undivided Profits account.

Draft entries to comply with the above provisions.

5. A has $5,000 invested in a business. He sells B a half-interest for $3,000 and keeps the money. Make the entry.

6. Jones and Johnson form a copartnership, January 1, 19—, each investing $10,000. April 1, Jones pays in an additional $2,500, and Johnson draws out

$1,500. August 1, Johnson pays in $3,000, and Jones withdraws $1,000. The profits for the year ending December 31, 19— are $5,000.

Prepare statements showing each partner's investment and portion of profits, the profits being divided in proportion to capital invested and the time it is employed.

7. A, B, and C agree to start in business with a capital of $200,000, of which A is to furnish $100,000, and B and C $50,000 each. A is to have one half-interest in the business, and B and C each one-quarter. Interest at 5% is to be credited on excess, or charged on deficiency of capital. A contributes $100,000; B $45,000; and C $40,000.

How would the capital accounts stand on the books after adjusting the interest at the end of the year?

8. A and B are partners sharing losses and gains equally. A invested $3,000, and B invested $4,000. They are ready to wind up the business. The firm owes $5,000, of which $1,000 is due A and $500 is due B. They have $7,000 in cash.

Prepare the accounts showing the closing.

XXVIII

1. The cash book of the Chicago Grocery Company on December 31, 19—, shows a balance of $10,280.72 on deposit with the National City Bank of New York. The bank statement received by the firm as of the same date shows a credit balance of $9,707.15.

The firm finds that the following checks had not cleared:

Check	1264	$	4.00
	1329		52.80
	1499		1,080.70
	1510		108.07
	1511		2,500.00
	1512		3,281.70
	1513		2,223.77
	1514		100.80
	1515		150.17

The bank statement also shows the following items not entered in the company's cash book:

Charges:

Telegram	$ 1.80
Collection charges (5 items)	1.17
Check of Central Wholesale Grocery Co.	80.79

Credits:

Interest on daily balance for December	8.18

The company had mailed to the bank a note, due December 31, payable to the National City Bank of New York and had taken credit for it in the sum of $10,000. The bank had not yet credited the item.

Prepare a reconciliation statement.

2. John Doe commenced business with a cash capital of $15,000. At the close of the first fiscal period the ledger accounts (except Cash and Capital) were: Accounts Receivable $4,312.50; Merchandise, debit balance $5,062.50; Accounts Payable $5,375; Expense $900. Doe's net loss for the period was $2,775, and his sales were $50,000.

Prepare a statement of assets and liabilities and the profit or loss.

3. From the books of Messrs. Deas & Alexander, which are kept by single entry, the following balance sheet as at June 30, 19— was taken:

Assets			Liabilities		
Cash in Bank			Accounts Payable		$10,300.00
and on Hand	$10,800.00		Capital Accounts:		
Accounts Receivable	16,032.00		Deas	$3,263	
Inventories	29,980.00		Alexander	51,249	54,512.00
Buildings and Equipment	8,000.00				
	$64,812.00				$64,812.00

It was agreed that the partnership would be dissolved as at October 31 of the same year, but that Alexander would continue the business. It was further agreed that Deas would be paid the balance to his credit at June 30, 19—, together with a sum of $5,000 to cover his interest in the good-will of the business and his profit up to October 31, which latter was estimated at $1,200. From this amount, however, his drawings, amounting to $800, were to be deducted.

The following balances were shown on the books at June 30 of the next year: Cash in Bank and on Hand $8,310; Accounts Receivable $12,203; Inventories $29,143; Buildings and Equipment $8,103; Accounts Payable $8,706.

You ascertain that on April 30 of this year, merchandise valued in the books at $500 was destroyed by fire. As this loss was not covered by insurance, Mr. Alexander reduced the book value of his inventory to take care of the loss.

The additions to the buildings and equipment during the year cost $503, but the book value of these assets was reduced by the sum of $400 to take care of depreciation.

Alexanders personal drawings during the year amounted to $2,500.

You are instructed to prepare a balance sheet for Alexander as at June 30, 19—, a year after the balance sheet first given, together with statement showing profit or loss for the year and the distribution of same. You are also required to write up Alexander's capital account for the year to June 30, 19—.

No value is to be placed on the good-will.

4. A machine costing $12,000 was estimated to have a life of twelve years with a residual value of $1,500. At the close of each year a charge of $875 was made to depreciation, and a like amount credited to "reserve" for depreciation. Just prior to closing the books at the end of the twelfth year the machine was discarded and sold for $2,000 (cash) and a similar machine was bought, costing $16,000. Show the journal entries you would frame to make the proper record.

5. What is the equated time for the payment of the balance of the following account (30 days to the month and 6% per annum)?

Henry M. Doremus

19—			19—			
Mar. 16	Merchandise, 4 months	$444.57	July 1	Cash		$400.00

	30	Merchandise, 60 days	376.82		20	Cash	375.00
Apr.	20	Merchandise, 30 days	712.19	Aug.	16	Cash	700.00
May	17	Merchandise, 4 months	628.75		30	Cash	600.00
	28	Merchandise, 4 months	419.31				

Henry M. Doremus desires to settle the above account on September 13, 19—. What amount of money shall he pay?

APPENDIX C
MISCELLANEOUS PROBLEMS FOR SUPPLEMENTARY WORK

Controlling Accounts

1. From the following data prepare controlling accounts. Indicate beside each entry its source book. Balance and close the accounts.

- Sales $10,000.
- Purchases returns and allowances $200.
- Credit given customers for cash received $5,000.
- Purchases $16,000.
- Sales discount $180.
- Notes payable issued to creditors $8,000.
- Customers' notes dishonored $100.
- Credit received for cash paid to creditors $4,000.
- Notes received from customers $1,000.
- Purchase discount $80.
- Bad accounts charged off $100.
- Freight prepaid on sales $60.

2. Journalize the following transactions:

(a) In our accounts receivable ledger there appears a debit balance in the account of John Smith amounting to $200, and in our accounts payable ledger there is a credit balance to him of $500. We send him a check for the balance due him, taking into consideration the cash discount allowed by us of 2%, and that granted by him of 3%. (The general ledger contains controlling accounts for these two ledgers.)

(b) Henry White owes us on open account $1,000, which is subject to 5% cash discount. He settles his account by giving us a note, which has included in its face interest for six months at 6%.

3. Draw up rough forms of a general journal, sales journal, sales returns and allowances journal, purchase journal, purchase returns and allowances journal, cash book, and note journals, as used in a controlling account system, and make entries of the following transactions therein:

(a) John Norman dishonors a note for $700 which you left at the bank for collection. The bank charges $1.50 protest fees.

(b) Amos Clark returns $50 worth of goods and asks for an allowance of $30 on goods retained. You accept the returned goods and grant the allowance.

(c) C. Cohen is both a customer and a creditor but you desire to carry his account in the creditors ledger only. You sell him a bill of goods, $350.

(d) An error was made last month in crediting customers' remittances. James Jones was credited for $40 that should have been credited to John Jones. Correct the error.

(e) Settled your account of $800 with D. Flynn, a creditor, by returning goods $60, an allowance for defective goods $30, transferring a note you received from D. Morgan $570, and your check for the balance.

PARTNERSHIP—FORMATION

4. A has $5,000 invested in a business. He sells B a half-interest for $2,000, and places the money in the business. Make the entry.

5. X and Y bought merchandise to the amount of $12,000. X contributed $7,500; Y $4,500. They afterwards sold Z a one-third interest for $6,000. How much of this amount should X and Y receive respectively in order to make X, Y, and Z equal partners, assuming:

(a) Money paid into the business with no good-will.

(b) Money paid into the business with good-will.

(c) Money not paid into the business.

6. A and B carried on business in partnership and divided profits and losses in proportion to their capital, three-fifths and two-fifths, respectively. On January 1, 19—, A's capital was $52,500, and B's $35,000, as shown by a balance sheet of that date. They agreed to admit C as a partner from the same date on the following terms:

1. Assets and liabilities and capital to be taken as shown in the balance sheet.

2. $12,500 to be added to the assets for good-will.

3. The amount of good-will to be added to A's and B's capital in the proportion in which they divide profits.

4. C to pay to the partnership such a sum as will give him a one-fifth share in the business.

(a) State what amount of capital C has to bring in.

(b) Set out the capital accounts of each >partner in the new partnership.

(c) State in what proportions the profits will be divided in the future, A and B, as between themselves, sharing in the same proportion as before.

7. New, Knott, and Moore are partners, sharing profits in the proportion of their investments. On December 31, 1920, the balance sheet of the partnership is as follows:

Assets		Liabilities and Capital	
Cash	$18,000.00	Accounts Payable	$ 1,000.00
Other Current Assets	23,000.00	Moore, Capital	24,000.00
Fixed Assets	20,000.00	New, Capital	24,000.00
		Knott, Capital	12,000.00
	$61,000.00		$61,000.00

Moore decides to retire from active business and agrees to sell his interest to the other two partners for $26,400, taking $14,400 in cash and the balance in three equal instalments payable July 2, 1921, January 2, 1922, and July 2, 1922, evidenced by notes payable.

The business is very prosperous, but it becomes increasingly evident that more capital is required, especially in view of the approaching maturity of the first note given to Moore. New and Knott decide to admit John Less as partner as of date July 1, 1921, at which time the current assets have increased by $16,000, accounts payable by $10,000, and the partners' capital accounts by $6,000. They value the good-will at $12,000.

Less buys a one-third interest, but stipulates that all he pays must remain in the business and that the good-will shall not appear upon the books.

How much must he pay for the one-third interest? Present the balance sheet of the firm of New, Knott & Less as of July 1, 1921. (Ignore accrued interest on Moore notes.)

PARTNERSHIP—OPERATION

8. A, B, and C are partners. A is to receive a salary of $2,000 per annum, B $2,500, and C $3,000. The balance of profits, after payment of salaries, is to be divided as to the first $20,000, 2/3 to A, and 1/6 each to B and C; and profits above $20,000 are to be divided equally among the three. A retires from active business, and gives up his right to salary for 19—. The profits for the year, before charging salaries, amount to $35,000. To what extent are A, B, and C, respectively, affected by A's concession?

9. A and B, partners, finding themselves in want of further capital in their business, and both being possessed of real property, A deposited deed with

the bankers of the firm as security for a loan of $2,000 to the firm. B arranged on some of his own property a mortgage for $1,500 with a private friend and paid the proceeds into the firm's bank account. The bankers were eventually obliged to realize the security held by them which produced, after payment of all expenses, the sum of $2,850.

Prepare entries recording these transactions in the firm's books.

10. In making an audit of the books of the partnership of A and B, you find that the agreed division of profits was to be on the basis of the capitals and of the time that they were left in the business.

The books show as follows: A's account paid in January 1, $6,000; March 1, $2,000; June 1, $4,000; November 1, $1,000; withdrew April 1, $3,000; October 1, $2,000.

B's account, paid in January 1, $4,000; February 1, $1,000; August 1, $3,000; withdrew May 1, $2,000; December 1, $1,000.

Prepare a statement showing method of arriving at correct profit distribution.

11. Bull and Bear entered into partnership, Bull contributing $100,000, and Bear $75,000. Profits and losses were to be divided, Bull 60% and Bear 40%, and interest was to be allowed on capital at the rate of 6% per annum. The profits for the first two years (after charging interest on capital) were $19,600 for the first year, $22,400 for the second; and the drawings of the partners in excess of their salaries were, Bull $1,800 first year, $2,000 second year; Bear $2,000 first year, $2,400 second year.

At the end of the second year, Peak was admitted to partnership, and put into the business capital equal to Bull's capital at the time, on the same conditions as to interest. Profits were to be divided on the basis of capital.

The profits for the third year were $30,000, and the partners' drawings in excess of salaries were: Bull $2,000, Bear $2,500, and Peak $1,500.

Set up the capital accounts of the partners for each of these years, showing balance of each at the end of the third year.

PARTNERSHIP—DISSOLUTION

12. A, B, and C are in partnership. A invested $11,000; B invested $5,000 and C invested $1,200. Their agreement provides that profits or losses shall be divided as follows: A, $4/9$; B, $3/9$; and C, $2/9$.

The partnership has become insolvent and has therefore decided to dissolve. The cash value of assets is $10,000. The deficit is, therefore, $7,200. How should the assets be divided and how much money will each partner receive?

13. A, B, and C engage in business. A contributes $10,000 capital; B contributes $5,000; while C in lieu of any capital contribution agrees to undertake the active management at a salary of $3,000 a year, to be paid monthly.

After allowing 5% interest on capital, they are to divide the net result in the proportions of 5, 3, and 2 respectively.

At the end of eighteen months they ascertain the position to be unfavorable and decide to wind up. The assets realize $12,500; there are no liabilities except for capital and interest thereon and one month's salary, due to C.

Make up the partners' accounts showing the amount to be received by each.

14. Thompson and Murray are partners, sharing profits and losses equally. The partnership is dissolved December 31, 19—, at which time Thompson's capital investment is $20,000, and Murray's $7,000. Total liabilities are $55,000, included in which is $5,000 due Wilson on open account, and $7,000 due Murray on account. The whole of the assets had been disposed of for $60,000 cash by July 1 of the next year. Close the partnership books.

Corporation Books

15. On June 1, 19—, the Home Manufacturing Company is incorporated under the laws of the state of New York to acquire and conduct the business of the firm of R. O. Browning and H. E. Johnson. The authorized capital stock of the company is $250,000, par value $100 per share. The company has agreed to take over the net assets of the partnership at the following valuation, and to issue in payment 1,000 shares of stock to each of the two partners: real estate $120,000; tools and equipment $60,000; raw materials $20,000. A bill of sale is executed and the stock duly issued. E. O. Kitchell and R. K. Taylor subscribe for 100 shares each. On June 10 the stock subscribed for by Kitchell and Taylor is paid for and issued. On June 14 Browning and Johnson each donate 100 shares of stock to the company to be sold for the purpose of securing additional working capital.

From the foregoing data, make: (a) the entries on the books of the partnership for the sale of the assets; (b) the opening entry of the new corporation.

16. A corporation is organized with an authorized capitalization of 5,000 shares at a par value of $100 each. One-half of the stock is subscribed for at 90 and paid for in two instalments. R. K. Reymer, in return for 1,000 shares of stock, transfers to the corporation his shipyard valued at $80,000. A. R. Paine receives 100 shares of stock for his services in organizing the corporation.

Make the necessary opening entries on the books of the corporation for the above.

17. F. H. Cole and R. D. Harris have patented an improved electric meter and have borrowed $1,500 on their note with which to complete the invention. They organize a corporation with a capital of $50,000, shares $100 each. Cole and Harris each receive $20,000 worth of stock in return for the patent rights transferred to the corporation. The corporation also assumes the payment of the $1,500 note. A. G. Emery, an attorney, is given five shares to pay for services in fulfilling the incorporation requirements. Cole and Harris each donate to the company $10,000 worth of stock to be sold in order to provide working capital; 160 shares of the donated stock are sold for cash at 50% of the par value.

Make the entries on the corporation books for the transactions given above.

18. The Bristol Manufacturing Company issued and sold on the 1st of January, 19—, to A and B (50 to each at the same price), first mortgage bonds of $500 each, bearing interest at 4% per annum, and received $48,000 in cash.

What records of the transactions should be made and in what books?

19. A corporation has an authorized capital stock of $100,000, of which $75,000 is outstanding.

This year's profit and loss shows a profit of $4,125. The previous surplus balance is $20,150. They declare and pay an 8% dividend.

Show in journal form the entries covering the above.

20. A corporation's profits for the year ended December 31, 19—, amount to $451,000. The by-laws require a reserve equal to 10% of any dividend paid to common stockholders, and any surplus remaining after such dividend has been paid is also to be applied to the reserve, until such reserve account amounts to $250,000. The reserve at December 31, one year before, was $156,020. The capital is $2,000,000, one-half cumulative preferred 6%, and one-half common, all fully paid. On December 31, 19—, the date first mentioned, the preferred dividend is two and one-half years in arrears. On December 31, one year before, the Profit and Loss account was in debt $202,000.

Set out your treatment of the profit for the year between these dates.

21. On April 1, 19—, the Healey Manufacturing Company is incorporated with an authorized capital of $100,000 common stock, and $50,000 preferred stock. The preferred stock is subscribed for and paid in full. One-half of the common stock is subscribed for, less 10% discount, the subscribers paying one-half in cash, the balance to be paid in two months. On June 1, the

balance on the common stock subscribed for on April 1 is paid, and the remainder of the authorized common stock is sold for cash at 10% premium.

Make the entries required for the above transactions.

22. In auditing the accounts of a corporation for the current year, it was found that for the previous year the inventory had been undervalued $2,000; accrued wages $3,150, and rent receivable earned but not yet due $750, had not been taken into consideration. The surplus at that time, $25,000, is increased during the current period to $40,000. During the current year a piece of real estate owned by the corporation was sold at a profit of $5,000; a fire resulted in a loss of $10,000; accounts receivable that had been charged off as worthless were collected to the amount of $1,000. Dividends amounting to $15,000 were declared.

Bring the above transactions onto the books.

Cash and Petty Cash

23. On June 7, 19—, when balancing cash you found that you were over $153.75. Part of it was due to the following, which you corrected:

Duplicated an entry on the credit side for $12 paid for postage; an error of $10 in addition on the debit side, decreasing the total.

Not being able to locate any more errors, you make necessary entry to balance the cash book.

On June 15 you recalled a cash sale of merchandise $14.50 made on June 7 but not recorded.

On July 7 A. B. Potter returned your statement, saying he paid $75 on account June 7 which you had failed to credit him with.

Make the necessary adjusting entries.

24. (a) Show by journal entry the proper booking of the following transactions, indicating any items not to be posted:

- 1. Creation of a petty cash fund of $100.
- 2. Petty cash disbursements summarized:
- Office stationery and printing $35.
- Stamps and postage $30.
- Delivery expense $10.
- General expense $5.
- Repairs to furniture $15.

- 3. The petty cash fund is replenished.

(b) Set up the petty cash account in the ledger and show all postings to it.

25. The following balances are found on the books of a trading concern at the end of its first fiscal year:

Inventory Merchandise	$ 4,312.09
Salaries	4,622.89
Capital Stock	10,000.00
Real Estate, Buildings, and Fixtures	17,500.00
Sales	8,469.10
Notes Payable (Merchandise Creditors)	5,000.00
Mortgage Bonds Issued	15,000.00
Customers' Accounts	5,423.23
Accounts Payable (Merchandise Creditors)	2,436.28
Notes Payable, Bank	5,000.00

Total merchandise purchases as per invoices on file, less inventory, show the cost of merchandise sold to be 97% of sales. The cash at bank and in hand amounted to $1,302.14.

From the foregoing construct Cash account.

NOTES AND DRAFTS

26. Lang is in need of funds. Connelly, an associate of Lang, induces Moore to accommodate Lang. Accordingly, Connelly introduces Lang to Moore, for which Lang pays $500. Moore discounts for Lang a note for $15,000 due in three months and turns over to him $14,500.

Frame journal entries covering their interest.

27. X, a branch, buys from Y. Y draws on X for $2,000 at 60 days. The draft is accepted and is later discounted 40 days from maturity at 6% per annum. In addition to the above acceptances, Y holds a total of $15,000 acceptances from other customers; $12,000 of these are used as collateral for a loan of $10,000 at the bank.

State all necessary entries.

28. A corporation had discounted $25,000 of notes receivable that are not due until December 31, 19——. How should this be dealt with in preparing a

balance sheet at November 30, 19—? One of the above notes for $5,000 was not paid at maturity but was protested, the protest fee amounting to $15. The company drew its check for the amount to take up the note.

State the entries required to be made on the books to record the transactions.

29. Previous to examining the accounts of a corporation at the end of its first fiscal year, you find that notes receivable stand in the financial statement prepared for the banker at $5,500.

Upon investigation it is disclosed that $20,000 of notes from customers were received during the period, and that $10,000 of these notes were duly paid in full by the customers to the company at maturity, and $5,000 of the notes were discounted at the bank. Of the notes discounted, a note for $500 given by Brown & Company was not paid when due, and has been charged back to the Notes Receivable account. Notes to the amount of $1,500 are not yet due at the bank.

Partial payments have been made to the company to the extent of $500 on notes still due, and these payments have been credited to an account called "Partial Payments on Notes Receivable." This item is listed in the financial statement as a liability.

A customer's note of $1,000 is found to have been given as collateral for the payment of a note of the company discounted at the bank.

A 30-day note given by an officer of the company for $200 is treated as a cash item. The note is 60 days past due.

You are asked to give the journal entry or entries for obtaining the proper account or accounts to record the above facts.

DEPRECIATION

30. An engine installed in a factory December 31, 19—, at a cost of $1,000, is replaced four years later by one of larger capacity costing (second-hand) $2,800. The discarded machine was sold for $900. The cost of making the change was $200. It has been the practice of the company to charge off 10% depreciation annually (on the diminishing basis), carrying the credit to a Depreciation Reserve account.

Make the necessary journal entries.

31. A manufacturing concern has annually for the past six years made provision at the rate of 10% per annum for depreciation of its plant and machinery, crediting the amount of such depreciation to a suitable Reserve account. During the year an engine which cost originally $5,000, was replaced by an improved engine costing $6,800. The cost of the new engine was charged to Machinery account at time of purchase. $300 was realized from

the salvage of the old engine, this amount being credited to "Scrap Sales," when received, and later closed to Profit and Loss.

Draft the adjustment entries which you consider necessary and explain the principle upon which these entries are based.

MERCHANDISE INVENTORIES

32. The average gross profits on sales of the Blank Corporation for the past five years have been 50%. During 19—— the sales were $60,000. Purchases during the period were $50,000. In-freight and cartage was $3,000; returned purchases amounted to $2,500. At the beginning of the year the inventory was $20,000. It is estimated that current market prices are 10% above those at time of purchase.

What will be the cost of replacing the amount of stock on hand at the end of the year?

33. In examining a business for the two years ending December 31, 19——, it is found that an item amounting to $750 had been omitted from the initial inventory of the first year; that an error had been made in the footing of the final inventory of that same year, by which that inventory was overstated to the amount of $1,250; and that in pricing the final inventory of the second year, an error was made by which that inventory was understated to the amount of $1,500.

State fully the effect of these errors on the profit of each of the two years.

34. A certain trading corporation desires to prepare its financial statement as of September 30, 19——, but takes no inventory at that date. It has no perpetual inventory records, but the management states that the ratio of gross profit to net sales has remained substantially the same for many years, namely, 25%, and that the rate will remain the same for 19——.

The following information is given and you are asked to prepare a statement showing estimated inventory on hand September 30, 19——:

- Inventory January 1, 19——, $6,100.
- Purchases $28,450.
- Freight-in $985.
- Freight-out $1,200.
- Allowances on sales $2,360.
- Sales $44,500.
- Discounts on purchases $960.

- Buying expenses $2,500.
- Sales salaries $3,000.
- General office expenses $4,000.

35. The ledger accounts of Henry James on December 31, 19—, showed: Accounts Payable $16,125; Accounts Receivable $13,188; Expense $2,450; Debit Balance Merchandise account $15,187. He started in business January 1, 19—, investing $45,000 cash. His total loss for the year was $8,074.50.

Prepare a statement of assets and liabilities and the profit and loss.

CONSIGNMENTS AND JOINT VENTURE

36. Indicate by journal entries how the following transactions should be recorded upon (a) the books of the consignor, and (b) the books of the consignee:

1. Shipment of goods costing $12,000 which are expected to be sold for $16,000.

2. Sale of three-fourths of such goods to sundry customers for a total of $15,000, only $5,000 of which is received in cash.

3. Return by customers of $55 of goods sold as defective in quality.

4. Advance of $4,000 to consignor by consignee, and payment of $100 freight, and $150 warehouse expense by the latter.

5. Settlement of all customers' accounts except items totaling $200, which are written off as uncollectible.

6. Remittance to cover balance due consignor after consignee has deducted commission at the rate of 3% on the selling price of goods sold. (Account sales is rendered only when consignment is sold.)

37. On April 30, 1921, St. John & Company and Carpel Brothers enter into a joint venture agreement. They each contribute $4,000, with which they pay for goods that are shipped on May 1 to John Doe of San Francisco. St. John & Company advance $400 to defray freight and incidental expenses. John

Doe, the consignee, is allowed 10% on the cost of the goods and is to sell them at whatever price he can obtain for them.

On June 1, 1922, on the strength of a report sent by wire, Carpel Brothers draw at sight on John Doe for $4,000 to the order of Carl Peter of New York. On July 1, 1922, St. John & Company receive from the consignee a check for $11,200, all the goods being sold; on the same day St. John & Company settle with Carpel Brothers. Interest at 6% is allowed on all transactions affecting the partners in the venture.

Prepare all the ledger accounts brought about by the above on the books of St. John & Company, including a joint venture account. (Construct your ledger accounts in such a manner that they will explain fully what took place and make a cross-reference possible.)

Single Entry

38. The books of the Butter, Egg & Cheese Company, with an authorized and outstanding capital stock issue of $25,000, are kept by single entry.

It annually inventories all its assets and liabilities and from such inventory prepares a financial statement. At December 31, 19—, this inventory is as follows:

Office, Cash	$ 1,584
Balance, Bank A	10,824
Accounts Receivable	29,521
10 shares in competing company	1,000
Plant and Equipment	64,938
Merchandise Inventory	21,737
Prepaid Expenses	5,081
Overdraft, Bank B	5,003
Accounts Payable	19,747
Mortgage Payable	25,000
Notes Payable	20,000

From a comparison of the financial statements at the beginning and the end of the year, you find that the item of "Plant and Equipment" is stated in an amount less by $11,460 than it was at the beginning of the year, plus additions during the year.

The financial statement for the beginning of the year showed a surplus of $35,703.

From your analysis of the disbursements and unpaid accounts at the beginning and end of the year, you find total purchases amounting to $661,910, and expenses for salaries, wages, supplies, repairs, etc., amounting to $120,115.

The purchases, however, included $450 paid out for John Smith, an employee, for which he has not reimbursed the company; and the total expense of $120,115 included $250 in the hands of a buyer as a working fund.

The inventory of merchandise at the beginning of the year was $18,125 and of prepaid expense was $2,653.

There was canceled on the customers ledger during the year $3,206 of uncollectible accounts.

There was paid for interest and discount on notes payable $1,061, and for interest on mortgage $1,500.

A 10% dividend was declared but not paid.

From the foregoing prepare: (a) a balance sheet as at December 31, 19—; (b) a profit and loss statement exhibiting net sales, cost of sales, and gross and net profit for the year.

Interest, Discount, and Proportion

39. What single rate of discount is equivalent to the series 20%, 20%, and 15%? 50%, 25%, and 15%?

40. An invoice amounting to $1,000 reads: "Less 30%, 10%, and 5%. Terms 2/10, n/30." It is dated January 19, 19— and paid January 28, 19—.

Explain and distinguish between these reductions of the list price. Give the amount of the check sent in payment of the invoice.

41. Keene owed Sharpe $2,000. Sharpe offered a discount of 5% cash. Not having the ready money, Keene discounted his note at the bank for 60 days at the rate of 6%, the note producing the sum required to discount Sharpe's claim.

Calculate the amount of this note and make the necessary journal entries to take care of the entire transaction.

42. Equate the following account and find the cash balance due October 1, money being worth 7% per annum, 30 days to the month.

CHARLES L. BROWN

19—				19—			
Apr. 6	Mdse., 60 days		2,850.00	Apr. 14	Cash		800.00
15	"	90 days	1,475.00		Returned Mdse.		125.00
28	"	30 days	3,000.00	July 6	Cash		1,000.00
				17	Note, 30 days		1,000.00

43. A note for $2,500 dated September 15, 1920, bearing interest at 6%, had payments indorsed as follows: November 28, 1920, $750; May 6, 1921, $500; August 12, 1921, $300; January 18, 1922, $600.

Find the amount due May 8, 1922.

44. In a manufacturing concern the total value of property subject to insurance was $500,000, distributed as follows: assembling station $100,000; finished goods warehouse $200,000; raw materials warehouse $100,000; and the remainder on building. The annual insurance premium amounts to $18,890 per year.

Find the insurance burden chargeable to each department if the assembling room rate is 2½ times the raw materials warehouse rate; the finished goods warehouse, 80% of the rate of the assembling room and the manufacturing building rate, three times the assembling room rate.